THE IMPACT OF EUROPEAN INSTITUTIONS ON THE RULE OF LAW AND DEMOCRACY

Since 2010 the European Union has been plagued by crises of democracy and the rule of law, which have been spreading from Central and Eastern Europe (CEE), catching many by surprise. This book argues that the professed success of the 2004 big bang enlargement mirrored the Potemkin villages erected in the new Member States on their accession to Europe. Slovenia is a prime example. Since its independence and throughout the accession process, Slovenia has been portrayed as the poster child of the 'New Europe'. This book claims that the widely shared narrative of the Slovenian EU dream is a myth. In many ways, Slovenia has fared even worse than its contemporary, constitutionally-backsliding, CEE counterparts. The book's discussion of the depth and breadth of the democratic crises in Slovenia should contribute to a critical intellectual awakening and better comprehension of the real causes of the present crises across the other CEE Member States, which threaten the viability of the EU and Council of Europe projects. It is only on the basis of this improved understanding that the crises can be appropriately addressed at national, transnational and supranational levels.

Volume 5 in the series EU Law in the Member States

EU Law in the Member States

Located at the cross-section between EU law, comparative law and socio-legal studies, *EU Law in the Member States* explores the interaction of EU law and national legal systems by analysing comparative evidence of the impact landmark EU measures – from CJEU decisions and secondary legislation to soft-law – have had across different Member States. The nature and operation of EU law has traditionally been analysed in a highly 'centralised' way, through the lenses of Brussels and Luxembourg, and in terms of the Treaty and its interpretation by the Court of Justice. Beneath this orthodoxy, however, lies the complex world of the genuine life of EU law in the Member States. Judicial and administrative practices across the Union's 28 Member States considerably qualify and sometimes even challenge the long-standing assumption that doctrines such as the direct effect and supremacy of EU law ensure a uniform and effective application of its provisions.

Each volume brings together leading academics, national experts and practitioners in order to draw conclusions both for EU law generally and the specific area in question on the basis of Member State reports and broader horizontal papers, and will be of interest to generalist EU lawyers and specialists in each field across the Member States. Academic audiences will benefit from the tight integration of national case studies and doctrinal analysis, whilst practitioners and policy makers will find systematically presented comparative evidence and commentary.

Series Editors
Jeremias Prassl
Michal Bobek

Volume 1: *Viking, Laval* and Beyond
Edited by Mark Freedland and Jeremias Prassl

Volume 2: Central European Judges under the European Influence: The Transformative Power of the EU Revisited
Edited by Michal Bobek

Volume 3: Air Passenger Rights, Ten Years On
Edited by Jeremias Prassl and Michal Bobek

Volume 4: The Eurosceptic Challenge
Edited by Clara Rauchegger and Anna Wallerman

The Impact of European Institutions on the Rule of Law and Democracy

Slovenia and Beyond

Matej Avbelj
and
Jernej Letnar Černič
with a chapter by Gorazd Justinek

•HART•
OXFORD • LONDON • NEW YORK • NEW DELHI • SYDNEY

HART PUBLISHING

Bloomsbury Publishing Plc

Kemp House, Chawley Park, Cumnor Hill, Oxford, OX2 9PH, UK

1385 Broadway, New York, NY 10018, USA

HART PUBLISHING, the Hart/Stag logo, BLOOMSBURY and the Diana logo are trademarks of Bloomsbury Publishing Plc

First published in Great Britain 2020

A catalogue record for this book is available from the British Library.

Library of Congress Cataloging-in-Publication data

Names: Avbelj, Matej, author. | Černič, Jernej Letnar, author. | Justinek, Gorazd, author.

Title: The impact of European institutions on the rule of law and democracy : Slovenia and beyond/ Matej Avbelj and Jernej Letnar Černič with a chapter by Gorazd Justinek

Description: Oxford ; New York : Hart, 2020. | Series: EU law in the member states; 75 | Includes bibliographical references and index.

Identifiers: LCCN 2019050322 (print) | LCCN 2019050323 (ebook) | ISBN 9781509915057 (hardcover) | ISBN 9781509915064 (Epub)

Subjects: LCSH: Rule of law—Slovenia. | Constitutional law—Slovenia. | Law—Slovenia—European influences. | European Union—Slovenia. | Slovenia—Politics and government—1990-

Classification: LCC KKS6202 .A93 2020 (print) | LCC KKS6202 (ebook) | DDC 340/.11—dc23

LC record available at https://lccn.loc.gov/2019050322

LC ebook record available at https://lccn.loc.gov/2019050323

ISBN: HB: 978-1-50991-505-7
ePDF: 978-1-50991-504-0
ePub: 978-1-50991-506-4

Typeset by Compuscript Ltd, Shannon
Printed and bound in Great Britain by CPI Group (UK) Ltd, Croydon CR0 4YY

MIX
Paper from responsible sources
FSC® C013604
www.fsc.org

Acknowledgement of Funders

THIS BOOK HAS been written within the framework of a research project dedicated to the reform of the rule of law and democracy in Slovenia, which was financially supported by the Slovenian Research Agency[1] and New University.

NOVA UNIVERZA

SLOVENIAN RESEARCH AGENCY

[1] 'Reform of Democratic and Rule-of-Law State in Slovenia', Research Project J5-7359 (A) ARRS (1 January 2016–31 December 2018) Slovenian Research Agency, Nova Univerza, Fakulteta za Državne in Evropske Študije, www.fds.si/index.php/en/school/research-and-consulting/raziskovalna-skupina/research-projects/1232-reform-of-democratic-and-rule-of-law-state-in-slovenia (accessed 24 April 2019); 'Integral Theory of the Future of the European Union', Research Project J5-1791 (1 July 2019–30 June 2022) Slovenian Research Agency, Nova Univerza – Fakulteta za državne in evropske študije; 'Holistic approach to business and human rights: a normative reform of Slovenian and international legal order, Research Project J5-1790 (1 July 2019–30 June 2022) Slovenian Research Agency, Nova Univerza – Fakulteta za državne in evropske študije.

Contents

List of Authors

Matej Avbelj is Professor of European Law at New University, Slovenia.

Jernej Letnar Černič is Associate Professor of Human Rights and Constitutional Law at New University, Slovenia.

Gorazd Justinek is Assistant Professor of Economics at New University, Slovenia.

List of Abbreviations

CEE	Central and Eastern European
COE	Council of Europe
ECHR	European Convention on the Protection of Human Rights and Fundamental Freedoms
ECtHR	European Court of Human Rights
HDI	United Nations Human Development Index
FDI	foreign direct investment
NKBM	Nova Kreditna Banka Maribor
NGOs	non-governmental organisations
NLB	Nova Ljubljanska Bank
OECD	Organisation for Economic Cooperation and Development
SFRY	Socialist Federal Republic of Yugoslavia
V4	The Visegrad Group Countries

1

Constitutional Backsliding in Central and Eastern Europe in Lieu of Back to Europe

A specter is haunting Eastern Europe: the specter of what in the West is called 'dissent'. This specter has not appeared out of thin air.[1]

I. INTRODUCTION

1 May 2004 was a day of huge symbolic importance across Europe. The European dream of eight former Communist nations, left behind the Iron Curtain in the decades-long communist freeze of the Cold War, became a reality. Estonia, Latvia, Lithuania, Poland, the Czech Republic, Slovakia, Hungary and Slovenia returned to Europe. This was a historic moment to celebrate. Parties were held in all the big cities of the new Member States. Bands and crowds chanted farewell to Russia and the Balkans. Border controls were symbolically waived, and the leaders of the old and new Members States rejoiced, shook hands and raised glasses to toast the success of the big-bang enlargement. This time around, and not at the moment of the collapse of the Berlin Wall, history indeed came to an end[2] and the future was about to begin. At least for the peoples of the new Member States. Modernity, with its promise of individual and national emancipation, showing the capacity of humans to affect change and to use it for the better, following the idea(l) of progress,[3] in 2004 seemed to reach its climax in these Central and Eastern European (CEE) countries achieving EU membership.

In more down-to-earth, purely legal and economic terms, the moment of enlargement confirmed the successful conclusion of an almost decade-long

[1] Václav Havel, 'The Power of the Powerless', October 1978, https://s3.amazonaws.com/Random_Public_Files/powerless.pdf (accessed 24 April 2019), 1.

[2] Francis Fukuyama, *The End of History and the Last Man* (New York, Free Press, 1992).

[3] Matej Avbelj, 'Transnational Law Between Modernity and Post-modernity' (2016) 7(3) *Transnational Legal Theory* 406, 410.

process of accession to the EU. The purpose of this accession process was to ensure a legal, institutional, political and economic streamlining of the new Member States with the overall EU acquis. With the enlargement of the EU, the new Member States were considered on par with the old Member States. Having done their pre-accession homework, they were accepted as equal members of the club, subject to the same rights and duties stemming from the overall construction of the EU as the old Member States had been. If anything, there was no doubt that all Member States, but in particular the new ones, which had fought hard to escape years of communist tyranny, shared the same fundamental values. It was thus entirely impossible in 2004 to entertain even the slightest doubt as to *the fact* that 'the Union is founded on the values of respect for human dignity, freedom, democracy, equality, the rule of law and respect for human rights, including the rights of persons belonging to minorities'.[4] For these values were indeed 'common to the member states in a society in which pluralism, non-discrimination, tolerance, justice, solidarity and equality between women and men prevail'.[5] The elites in the old Member States did not anticipate any substantial hurdles in translating those values to the new Member States.[6]

The post-communist Member States set these values in their constitutional stone. They relied on them, in writing as well as in countless oral declarations, purposefully and explicitly to effectuate a discontinuity with their totalitarian past. The latter should be replaced by a new liberal constitutional identity, reflecting that of the Western EU Member States, from which the CEE countries were forcefully torn apart after World War II. All of this was best explicated and institutionalised in the Visegrad Group, pioneered by Vaclav Havel and established in 1991 by Poland, then Czechoslovakia and Hungary. As it follows from its founding declaration, the Group was destined to achieve five basic objectives: a full restitution of state independence, democracy and freedom; elimination of all existing social, economic and spiritual aspects of the totalitarian system; construction of a parliamentary democracy, a modern state of law, respect for human rights and freedoms; creation of a modern free market economy and full involvement in the European political and economic systems, as well as the system of security and legislation.[7] Full membership in the EU was a sign and confirmation of the achievement of these goals.[8] Or, so we believed. But we

[4] European Union, Treaty on European Union (Consolidated Version), Treaty of Maastricht, 7 February 1992, Art 2 [2002] OJ C325/5.

[5] ibid.

[6] Jernej Letnar Černič, 'Impact of the European Court of Human Rights on the Rule of Law in Central and Eastern Europe' (2008) 10(1) *Hague Journal on the Rule of Law* 111.

[7] Visegrad Declaration 1991; for a more in-depth discussion see Matej Avbelj, 'Central Europe as a Legal Phenomenon' (2015) 2(13) *European Perspectives – Slovenia's Role in Visegrad Group* 53.

[8] See Wojciech Sadurski, 'That Other Anniversary' (2017) 13(3) *European Constitutional Law Review* 417, 419, who has argued that: 'The accession by 10 Central Eastern European states was powerfully idealistic in nature, promoting romantic ideals of a "return to Europe" and pan-European solidarity. It was a timely reminder that the EU's identity is based on values, and not just a calculus.'

were fooled: in fact, 'the end of the end of history',[9] rather than the future, has just begun.

The Europhilia and European dream of the CEE countries has not lasted long. Just a decade later, the European Union was to witness a complete U-turn. It came from Central Europe, a region that Vaclav Havel in the early 1990s described not only as a historical and spiritual phenomenon, but as a special body that could make a genuine contribution to Western Europe.[10] It indeed has made a contribution, but one very different from that envisaged by Havel. Instead of enriching Western liberal constitutional values with their post-communist experience, these states have rather started a new populist movement in the form of constitutional backsliding whose final objective is the creation of an illiberal state.[11] As is well known, the main protagonist has been Viktor Orbán. He has, as one commentator succinctly put it, in only three years succeeded in transforming Hungary 'from one of the success stories of the transition from socialism to democracy to a semi-authoritarian regime based on the illiberal order systematically dismantling checks and balances and thereby undermining the rule of law'.[12] He could do so thanks to a landslide victory in the 2010 election in which the Hungarian people reacted to the complete fiasco of the preceding socialist government under whose rule the corruption and clientelism flourished as never before.[13]

Equipped with a constitutional majority, Orbán embarked on a systematic political overhaul, which has since been described as a constitutional capture of the state. It all started with the adoption of an unconstitutional constitution.[14] This has facilitated legislative hypertrophy by the Fidesz-run parliament which has dismantled the main checks and balances. The next goal was to populate the institutions of the state with ruling-party loyalists. The composition of the existing institutions has therefore been changed, but not infrequently new institutions have been created too, to make room for party loyalists and to ensure the gradual irrelevance of the old institutions without interfering with

[9] Kim Lane Scheppele, 'The End of the End of History', lecture, Berlin, 7 June 2017, www.rewi.hu-berlin.de/de/lf/oe/lsi/termine/prof-dr-kim-lane-scheppele-the-end-of-the-end-of-history (accessed 24 April 2019).

[10] Václav Havel, Speech in the Polish Parliament, 25 January 1990.

[11] Viktor Orban, Speech at the XXV-Bálványos Free Summer University and Youth Camp, quoted in Csaba Tóth, 'Full Text of Viktor Orbán's Speech at Băile Tuşnad (Tusnádfürdő) of 26 July 2014' *Budapest Beacon* (29 July 2014) https://budapestbeacon.com/full-text-of-viktor-orbans-speech-at-baile-tusnad-tusnadfurdo-of-26-july-2014/ (accessed 24 April 2019).

[12] Bojan Bugarič, 'Protecting Democracy and the Rule of Law in the European Union: The Hungarian Challenge', LSE 'Europe in Question' Discussion Paper Series No 79/2014; see also Jan-Werner Müller, 'The Hungarian Tragedy' [Spring 2011] *Dissent* 5.

[13] Jan-Werner Müller, 'Eastern Europe Goes South: Disappearing Democracy in the EU's Newest Member States' [March/April 2014] *Foreign Affairs*.

[14] Kim Lane Scheppele, 'The Unconstitutional Constitution' *New York Times* (2 January 2012) http://krugman.blogs.nytimes.com/2012/01/02/the-unconstitutional-constitution/ (accessed 24 April 2019).

them directly.[15] In particular, the judiciary came under attack. Under the pretext of lowering the special retirement age of judges to a general retirement age, several hundred judges were removed from their posts and replaced with those chosen by the Fidesz regime. The independence of the judiciary was thus directly assaulted. The country's Constitutional Court has not fared any better. Not only was its composition changed completely, its competences too were drastically restricted, reaching as far as voiding the pre-2012 jurisprudence of the Constitutional Court.[16] As a result, Hungary emerged as a politically distinctive case of authoritarianism,[17] but unfortunately not an exclusive one.

Due to a lukewarm, and essentially ineffective, reaction by the EU, to which we shall return below, the incipient illiberal democracy created in Hungary has been used as a role model by the new Polish government.[18] In 2015 the Law and Justice Party (PiS) took over the Polish parliament, but fell short of a constitutional majority which would enable it to constitutionally capture the state following the Hungarian example. Instead, the Kaczynski-influenced government decided to capture the country's Constitutional Court. Taking advantage of its political predecessor's attempt to fill the posts of the expiring judges' mandates prematurely, it appointed its own judicial loyalists, contrary to the clear and precise rules of appointment. Having done so, it additionally modified the organisational and procedural framework of the Constitutional Court to ensure that its forthcoming constitutional democracy transforming legislation enjoys at least a de facto constitutional immunity. In the next step, the target has moved to the ordinary judiciary. A set of laws has been proposed to enable the ruling coalition to replace more than 40 per cent of the Supreme Court justices and to control the selection of all others by effectively taking over the control of the National Council of Judiciary.[19] As Sadurski has convincingly argued, the Polish backsliding scenario is both milder and graver than the Hungarian one.[20] It is 'milder because the illiberal changes are not constitutionally entrenched, and graver because it involves a systematic set of actions that violate binding constitutional law'.[21] These, like in the Hungarian case, also stretch to the control of the public media and politicisation of the civil service.[22] In so doing, the existing

[15] Bugarič (n 12).

[16] Kim Lane Scheppele, '"Constitutional Revenge" in Hungary', *Eutopia Law*, 6 March 2013, https://eutopialaw.com/2013/03/06/constitutional-revenge-in-hungary/ (accessed 24 April 2019).

[17] See eg Erin K Jenne and Cas Mudde, 'Hungary's Illiberal Turn: Can Outsiders Help?' (2012) 23(3) *Journal of Democracy* 147.

[18] Arch Puddington, 'Breaking Down Democracy: Goals, Strategies, and Methods of Modern Authoritarians', Freedom House, June 2017, 38.

[19] Wojciech Sadurski, 'Judicial "Reform" in Poland: The President's Bills Are as Unconstitutional as the Ones he Vetoed', *Verfassungsblog*, 28 November 2017, http://verfassungsblog.de/judicial-reform-in-poland-the-presidents-bills-are-as-unconstitutional-as-the-ones-he-vetoed/ (accessed 24 April 2019).

[20] Sadurski (n 8) 419.

[21] ibid 424.

[22] For an overivew, see Gabor Halmai, 'Second-Grade Constitutionalism? The Case of Hungary and Poland', CSF-SSSUP Working Paper 1/2017, 9–12.

Polish Constitution, while formally untouched, has been de facto transformed.[23] All in all, constitutional standards have in many CEE countries slid backwards, to the surprise of many, even in some of those countries, in the last few years.[24] The European Commission monitors the state of the rule of law in Poland as it is compromised on a daily basis, similarly in Hungary.[25] More specifically, Uitz even argues that 'were the Hungarian government to succeed in its recent efforts, it may well seriously shatter whatever is left from the rule of law in Europe'.[26]

The described regression in the democratic rule of law and democracy itself, which took place abruptly and was conducted relatively swiftly, took everyone, academic and institutional stakeholders, somewhat by surprise. In particular, the response of the EU has been slow, mild, muted and, as a rule, ineffective and therefore frustrating. Theoretical, legal, political, democratic and geostrategic obstacles have stood in the EU's way of addressing the problem comprehensively and effectively. Theory has traditionally grappled with the rule of law as an essentially contested concept.[27] The elusiveness of the meaning, or rather meanings, of the rule of law in theory has also hindered its operationalisation in practice. The open-ended character of the rule of law has presented itself as a legal obstacle to the direct effect of Article 2 TEU, at least in the eyes of the Council's legal service. Politically, of course, this has provided more leeway to the rogue states in their de jure and de facto pursuit of a constitution-capturing agenda. Simultaneously, the consensus-seeking approach of the EU institutions has turned Article 7 TEU into a so-called nuclear option,[28] reducing the likelihood of launching a therein defined procedure and, even more so, of bringing the latter to its logical and meaningful conclusion while this was still at least theoretically possible. Even this possibility has, however, been lost as the Hungarian backsliding passed unaffected and the Polish imitators could now rely on Orbán's support in the European Council when its unanimity is necessary for launching a systemic infringement procedure, and vice versa. Furthermore, the European People's Party (EPP) has been very lenient toward Orbán in order not to estrange

[23] Wojciech Sadurski, 'What Is Going on in Poland Is an Attack against Democracy', *Verfassungsblog*, 15 July 2016, http://verfassungsblog.de/what-is-going-on-in-poland-is-an-attack-against-democracy/ (accessed 24 April 2019).

[24] Anne Sanders and Luc von Danwitz, 'The Polish Judiciary Reform: Problematic under European standards and a Challenge for Germany', *Verfassungsblog*, 28 March 2017, http://verfassungsblog.de/the-polish-judiciary-reform-problematic-under-european-standards-and-a-challenge-for-germany/ (accessed 24 April 2019).

[25] Agata Fijalkowski, *From Old Times to New Europe: The Polish Struggle for Democracy and Constitutionalism* (Aldershot, Ashgate, 2010).

[26] Renáta Uitz, 'The Return of the Sovereign: A Look at the Rule of Law in Hungary – and in Europe', *Verfassungsblog*, 5 April 2017, https://verfassungsblog.de/the-return-of-the-sovereign-a-look-at-the-rule-of-law-in-hungary-and-in-europe/ (accessed 24 April 2019).

[27] Jeremy Waldron, 'Is the Rule of Law an Essentially Contested Concept (in Florida?)' (2002) 21(2) *Law and Philosophy* 137.

[28] As the former Commission President Barroso referred to it in his 2012 State of the Union Speech, Strasbourg, 12 September 2012, http://europa.eu/rapid/press-release_SPEECH-12-596_en.htm (accessed 24 April 2019).

a member of the political family whose numbers in the European Parliament have been dwindling in recent years. These myopic, indeed hypocritical,[29] (in)actions of the European centre-right have further weakened the chances of any meaningful action being taken against Hungary. On the other hand, due to PiS being a member of the party of European Conservatives and Reformists, and not the EPP, the political approach to Poland has been more stringent than that to Hungary. This has again not acted in favour of the rule of law in the EU. It has permitted the Polish government to invoke grounds of discriminatory treatment and make a case for politically motivated charges.

On top of this, the EU lacks democratic legitimacy for interfering with the internal constitutional functioning of these Member States in order to turn them into well-ordered polities, observing the foundational values of the Union.[30] The half-built European constitutional structure, its competence handicap, legitimacy deficit and the democratic illusion in which citizens of Member States partake has allowed the backsliding Member States to get away with violations of even the most basic values of the Union.[31] Finally, the geostrategic situation, in particular the migration crisis has, unintendedly, provided an additional boost to the Orbán regime. By acting unilaterally, swiftly and determinedly he managed to portray himself as a saviour of (Christian) Europe and has thus won explicit, but even more so implicit, sympathies not just among his Eastern but also among his Western political counterparts who found that the Hungarian border-wall had relieved them of the refugee burden.

All the described factors hindered the European institutions from tackling the rule of law and democracy crisis in the new Member States effectively and while would still have been possible to reverse the course of these adverse political developments. This is now becoming increasingly unlikely. The single-market-based, judicially enforced violations against Hungary,[32] occasional (attempts at) judicial sanctioning of Poland,[33] the use of the informal rule-of-law framework, the formal initiation of the Article 7 procedure first against Poland[34] and eventually also against Hungary[35] are, even if they are ever brought to a successful

[29] Jan-Werner Müller, 'If You're not a Democracy, You're not European Anymore' [22 December 2017] *Foreign Policy*.

[30] Matej Avbelj, 'Pluralism and Systemic Defiance in the European Union' in András Jakab and Dimitry Kochenov (eds), *The Enforcement of EU Law and Values: Ensuring Member States' Compliance* (Oxford, Oxford University Press, 2017).

[31] Matej Avbelj, 'What Future for the European Union?', WZB Discussion Paper SP IV 2017-802.

[32] Judgment of the Court of Justice of the European Union (First Chamber), Case C-286/12, 6 November 2012.

[33] Judgment of the Court of Justice of the European Union (Grand Chamber), Case C-216/18 PPU, 25 July 2018.

[34] In December 2017 the Commission invoked the Art 7(1) procedure for the first time, by submitting a Reasoned Proposal for a Decision of the Council on the determination of a clear risk of a serious breach of the rule of law by Poland, http://europa.eu/rapid/press-release_IP-17-5367_en.htm (accessed 15 May 2019).

[35] In September 2018 the European Parliament invoked the Art 7(1) procedure also against Hungary: European Parliament, Press Realease, 'Rule of law in Hungary: Parliament Calls on the

conclusion resulting in the voting rights of the rogue states in the Council being suspended, simply insufficient. At best, they will just scratch the surface of the existing and still deepening rule-of-law and democracy crisis in this part of Europe. For this crisis is truly a systemic one and runs deep in the very mindset and comprehensive modus operandi of the post-communist societies in the CEE countries. To those who have been following the evolution of these transitional societies since the collapse of the communist regimes and to those who pride themselves with at least some basic knowledge of the history of this part of Europe, the political desire and the actual implementation of illiberal democracy, the systemic undermining of the rule of law and the authoritarian ambitions of political parties of any colour to use the state as an instrument of their political and indeed even more often for individual self-enrichment should come as no surprise. Unfortunately, it has come as such for many others.

Furthermore, the constitutional democracy and the rule of law in Slovenia and the majority of CEE countries, in contrast to Hungary and Poland, did not have anywhere to slide backwards to. The rule of law in those countries appears to have been, since the fall of the iron curtain, under attack from nouveau riche elites very much connected to the former totalitarian regimes. Old practices of corruption, nepotism, clientalism and 'dirty togetherness' have not only not been eradicated, but remain present in the centre of institutional and public space in certain CEE countries.[36] Most of those countries have not undertaken a fully fledged reform of the rule of law and have retained a post-socialist formal and authoritarian mentality. For instance, since democratisation, others, such as the countries of the former Yugoslavia, have faced serious difficulties of translating the values of the rule of law de jure into the rule of law de facto.[37] This trend has been underway for quite some time and from the number of pending applications before the Europan Court of Human Rights (ECtHR) at the end of 2018 it does not appear to be ceasing any time soon.[38] Similar developments can be seen in other CEE Countries.

Another facet of the rule-of-law crises concerns the influence of the Council of Europe institutions, particularly the ECtHR, on the constitutional democracy

EU to Act' (12 September 2018) www.europarl.europa.eu/news/en/press-room/20180906IPR12104/rule-of-law-in-hungary-parliament-calls-on-the-eu-to-act (accessed 24 April 2019).

[36] See eg Adam Czarnota, Martin Krygier and Wojciech Sadurski, 'Introduction' in Adam Czarnota, Martin Krygier and Wojciech Sadurski (eds), *Rethinking the Rule of Law after Communism* (Budapest, Central European University, 2005). See also Bojan Bugarič (2015) 'The Rule of Law Derailed: Lessons from the Post-Communist World' (2015) 7(2) *Hague Journal Rule Law* 175.

[37] Gentian Zyberi and Jernej Letnar Černič, 'Transitional Justice Processes and Reconciliation in the Former Yugoslavia: Challenges and Prospects' (2015) 33(2) *Nordic Journal of Human Rights* 132. See also Dragoljub Popović and Tanasije Marinković, 'The Emergence of the Human Rights Protection in Serbia under the European Convention on Human Rights: The Experience of the First Ten Years' in Iulia Motoc and Ineta Ziemele (eds), *The Impact of the ECHR on Democratic Change in Central and Eastern Europe: Judicial Perspectives* (Cambridge, Cambridge University Press, 2015) 373–400.

[38] The ECtHR in Fact & Figures 2018, https://www.echr.coe.int/Documents/Facts_Figures_2018_ENG.pdf, 4 (accessed 24 April 2019) 4.

and rule of law in Slovenia and elsewhere in Central and Eastern Europe. The impact of the ECtHR on the rule of law and human rights protection in Slovenia has been relatively positive, particularly in comparison with most of the other CEE states.[39] More specifically, it has had a three-fold dimension. First, it has introduced normative standards of the rule of law and human rights protections in the newly established Slovenian constitutional legal order. Second, the accession of Slovenia to the Council of Europe handed individuals the right to individual application in the case of alleged human right violations by the Slovenian authorities. Third, several areas of the exercise of the rule of law have been substantially improved following the ECtHR's judgments in all three pilot cases. On the other hand, Slovenia and several other countries have struggled to internalise the liberal values of the European Convention on Human Rights (ECHR) into the daily institutional life of all branches of the newly established states based on democracy and the rule of law. The judiciary, in particular, has shown resistance against the full internalisation of rights such basic as the right to a fair, independent and impartial tribunal. In other CEE states, including countries of former Yugoslavia,[40] most of those challenges have been tied to the old mentality and old ways of doing business, which are in short a complicated mixture of corruption, nepotism, clientelism, actual and perceived conflicts of interest, formalism and an authoritarian mentality. The ongoing presence of these characteristics has contributed to the liberal values of the ECHR not being fully internalised and as there has been strong resistance, and at times even organised opposition, to the internalisation and application of the rule of law and human rights standards.[41] For those observers familiar with the regulatory milieu of CEE countries, recent developments in the erosion of rule-of-law standards have been somehow expected. Those countries where democratic institutions have been demolished and captured after decades, not only in Central and Eastern Europe but beyond, have been easy prey for illiberal, authoritarian or even totalitarian forces to remerge or retain their old interests in newly dressed forms of democratic governance.[42] This book in the ensuing chapters therefore explains in detail the reception of EU and Council of Europe standards and reasons for rejection of their internalisation. The book also explores why deficiencies in the exercise of the rule of law and human rights protections have never been fully eliminated.[43] As a result, it outlines in chapter 12 sets of recommendations on how to reform the rule of law and democracy in Slovenia.

[39] Letnar Černič (n 6).

[40] Zyberi and Letnar Černič (n 37).

[41] Jernej Letnar Černič, 'The European Court of Human Rights in the States of the Former Yugoslavia' (2018) 1 *East European Yearbook on Human Rights* 32.

[42] See eg Luka Lisjak Gabrijelčič, Conversation with Timothy Snyder: 'Ljudje znamo dobro lagati in dobro znamo ubijati. Zelo težko pa priznamo, da smo ubijali zaradi laži' [Autumn 2016] *Razpotja* 46, 48. See also Timothy Snyder, *Black Earth: The Holocaust as History and Warning* (New York, Tim Duggan Books, 2015).

[43] Jernej Letnar Černič, *Slovenija na razpotju: Geneza varstva človekovih pravic v slovenski družbi* (Kranj, Nova Univerza–Fakulteta za Državne in Evropske Študije, 2018); Jernej Letnar Černič et al,

II. THE ARGUMENT OF THIS BOOK

This book argues that the surprise about the depth and breadth of the rule-of-law and democracy crisis in the EU provoked by CEE Member States derives from fundamental misunderstandings by old Member States and EU institutions about the sociopolitical nature of these countries and daily practices of not only their institutional and public spheres, but also of their ways of doing business in the private sphere. This misunderstanding has been born out of ignorance on the part of the Western stakeholders. It has been also caused, in part, by deception practiced by the CEE elites and the lack of internalisation of the values of modern liberal democracies in their domestic systems. Certainly, Western stakeholders have been aware of some of the challenges in the exercise of the rule of law in new Member States.[44] Finally, the current situation is in many ways the outcome of a deliberate, even if benign, neglect of the real sociopolitical state of affairs in these countries by the old Member States and the Brussels-based institutions out of a desire to make the EU big bang enlargement of 2004 a success story, or at least to portray it as such. To a certain extent the international- and supranational political as well as economic alliances played their role too. When these alliances have been undermined or even broken – largely under the duress of the financial and economic crisis that began in 2008 – the Potemkin village of CEE states irreversibly started collapsing too.

The country spearheading this Potemkin village scenario, and therefore the most suitable means for buttressing the enlargement success story, was the case of Slovenia. Since its independence and throughout the accession procedure, Slovenia was portrayed as the best disciple and as a poster-child for the New Europe. In less than 20 years after winning its independence from Yugoslavia, the country has become a full member of the EU, a member of the Schengen regime as well as of the eurozone. The Slovenian example has thus embodied the EU dream. It has proven the success of the enlargement and it has stood as a role model for all the countries east and south of the present EU borders that have been aspiring to full membership.

This book claims that the widely shared narrative of the Slovenian EU dream has, unfortunately, been just a myth. In many ways, Slovenia fares even worse than its contemporary constitutionally backsliding CEE counterparts. The understanding of the depth and breadth of the rule-of-law and democracy crisis in Slovenia, the authors of this book hope, will also contribute to critical intellectual awakening and better comprehension of the real causes of the present

Slovenija pred Evropskim Sodiščem za Človekove Pravice: 1994–2016 (Ljubljana, Fakulteta za Državne in Evropske Študije, 2017).

[44] See eg European commission, 'Cooperation and Verification Mechanism for Bulgaria and Romania', https://ec.europa.eu/info/policies/justice-and-fundamental-rights/effective-justice/rule-law/assistance-bulgaria-and-romania-under-cvm/cooperation-and-verification-mechanism-bulgaria-and-romania_en (accessed 24 April 2019).

crises across CEE Member States, which threaten the viability of the EU project as such. It is only on the basis of such better understanding that causes of the crisis can be more accurately identified and, consequently, also more appropriately addressed on the national, transnational and supranational levels. All in all, this book aims, first, to portray the various pathways of the backsliding of the rule of law and democracy in Slovenia, and secondly to draw parallels and lessons for the broader CEE region.

The existing international literature on constitutional democracy and the rule of law has been at best partial and at worse misinformed. There has been a notable lack of in-depth research focusing on democracy and the rule of law in Central and Eastern Europe, exploring mutual relationships and interactions between national levels and European institutions; such research could also produce normative proposals for the reforms necessary, which would also be applicable in comparative contexts. This gap is most notable and concerning in the field of law. A comprehensive approach to the problems analysed in this book is also necessary to ensure the presence of Slovenia in international discourse and analysis. The review of the leading international literature, which has been concerned with the transition of the post-communist states and their road to EU membership, demonstrates a curious absence of Slovenia and an absence of any analysis of the success or failure of European institutions in strengthening the rule of law and democracy in that country.[45] The international rule-of-law and democracy focus has mostly been on Hungary, Poland, Romania and Bulgaria, while the specific Slovenian problems have gone by undetected,[46] with some rare exceptions.[47] From the legal point of view most of the dimensions of Slovenian

[45] See eg Jacques Rupnik and Jan Zielonka, 'The State of Democracy 20 Years On: Domestic and External Factors' (2013) 27 *East European Politics and Societies* 3; Siobhan Kattago, *Memory and Representation in Contemporary Europe: The Persistence of the Past* (Farnham, Ashgate, 2012).

[46] See eg Müller (n 13); Gabor Halmai and Kim Lane Scheppele (eds), 'Opinion on Hungary's New Constitutional Order: Amicus Brief for the Venice Commission on the Transitional Provisions of the Fundamental Law and the Key Cardinal Laws', February 2012, http://lapa.princeton.edu/hosteddocs/hungary/Amicus_Cardinal_Laws_final.pdf (accessed 24 April 2019); Lane Scheppele (n 14). See also a vibrant debate at *Verfassungsblog*: 'Hungary: Taking Action' https://verfassungsblog.de/hungary-taking-action/ (accessed 24 April 2019); Mark Dawson and Elise Muir, 'Hungary and the Indirect Protection of EU Fundamental Rights and the Rule of Law' (2013) 14(10) *German Law Journal* 1959; Bugarič (n 12): Armin von Bogdandy and Pal Sonnevend (eds), *Constitutional Crisis in the European Constitutional Area: Theory, Law and Politics in Hungary and Romania* (Oxford, Hart Publishing, 2014); Kim Lane Scheppele and Vlad Perju, 'Separating Law and Politics in Romania' *New York Times* (12 July 2012) http://krugman.blogs.nytimes.com/2012/07/12/guest-post-separating-law-and-politics-in-romania/?_php=true&_type=blogs&_r=0 (accessed 24 April 2019); Kim Lane Scheppele, 'Romania Unravels the Rule of Law' *New York Times* (5 July 2012) http://krugman.blogs.nytimes.com/2012/07/05/guest-post-romania-unravels-the-rule-of-law/ (accessed 24 April 2019).

[47] See Matej Avbelj and Jernej Letnar Černič, 'Slovenia' in Leonard Hammer and Frank Emmert (eds), *The European Convention on Human Rights and Fundamental Freedoms in Central and Eastern Europe* (The Hague, Eleven International Publishing, 2012); Jan Zobec, 'Slovenia: Just a Glass Bead Game?' in Iulia Motoc and Ineta Ziemele (eds), *The Impact of the ECHR on Democratic Change in Central and Eastern Europe: Judicial Perspectives*, (Cambridge, Cambridge University Press, 2016); Jan Zobec and Jernej Letnar Černič, 'The Remains of the Authoritarian Mentality

democracy and the rule of law remain undertheorized and underresearched. Nor has much been written on the mutual relationships and influence between national levels and European institutions in Central and Eastern Europe.[48] This book is closing this gap by offering, for the first time in the global academic environment, a systematic and a comprehensive scrutiny of the state of the Slovenian constitutional democracy and the role of European institutions in it.

A comprehensive treatment of the reasons for the failure of the rule of law and democracy in Slovenia and failure of the European institutions is thus clearly lacking. This book therefore analyses several dimensions of Slovenian democracy and the rule of law that could be useful in the comparative contexts, which are at the moment missing from global academic discourse. To the extent that such literature exists, it is mostly concerned with endogenous factors. The book aims to remove all these gaps. Different sectors of the rule of law and democracy are interconnected. The present book brings out these connections, focuses on their advantages and disadvantages, and proposes a set of reforms from both an internal and an external perspective. Finally, it also for the first time in the global academic environment produces a systematic and comprehensive analysis of the consequences that deficiencies in democracy and the rule of law have for human rights protection in Slovenia and beyond.

The book is an example of legal research. This harbours its own specific 'scientific' approach, instruments and research methods, which are markedly different from those typical of natural sciences and even from those characteristic of social sciences and humanities. The methodological approach thus follows the established scheme of legal research. As a result, it is based on descriptive, explanatory and normative methods. The descriptive method aims at a comprehensive and undistorted representation of factual and legal context in order to delimit the object of research. The explanatory method concentrates on establishing the causal relations between the various constitutive elements of the social phenomenon under research. The most important method, however, is a normative method, which is a prerequisite of new and original scientific discoveries. This method critically evaluates the social phenomenon under investigation, sheds light on its drawbacks and disadvantages, and, most importantly, results in normative proposals for the possible reforms and improvements.

This book is, accordingly, structured in the following way. After this introductory chapter, Chapter 2 describes the genesis of the contemporary Slovenian state, the ideal and actual nature of its democracy and economic character, which determines the functioning of the country in practice. In so doing, the

within the Slovene Judiciary' in Michal Bobek (ed), *Central European Judges Under the European Influence: The Transformative Power of the EU Revisited* (Oxford, Hart Publishing, 2015).

[48] See Michal Bobek (ed), *Central European Judges Under the European Influence: The Transformative Power of the EU Revisited* (Oxford, Hart Publishing, 2015); Leonard Hammer and Frank Emmert (eds), *The European Convention on Human Rights and Fundamental Freedoms in Central and Eastern Europe* (The Hague, Eleven International Publishing, 2012).

parallels are drawn with other CEE Member States that have in recent years come under EU and international scrutiny. Chapter 3 explains the historical reasons for a discrepancy between Slovenian constitutional and rule-of-law ideals and actual practice by focusing closely on the challenges of transitional justice in Slovenia. A decisive factor in this discrepancy has also been a specific Slovenian model of economic governance, which has set Slovenia importantly apart from other CEE countries. The Slovenian model of economic gradualism marked by a notable absence of reforms is therefore analysed in Chapter 4. It is argued there that such a model of economic development has also been instrumental to the contemporary crisis of constitutional democracy in Slovenia. Chapter 5 moves the debate from the past to the present to discuss the several faces of the crisis of the rule of law and democracy in Slovenia. It concentrates on the problematique of human rights protection in Slovenia and the selective, perhaps even arbitrary, approach of state institutions and NGOs to these issues. Chapter 6 focuses on the rule of law problematique in Slovenia, more specifically on the functioning of the judiciary (*lato sensu*) and the role of European institutions in identifying as well as remedying these problems. Chapter 7 takes up the challenges of democratic governance in Slovenia, foremost in institutional terms – the tendency of the captured state, corruption, the implosion of the political system and populism, as well as unfair elections. The discussion of the democratic governance is followed, in Chapter 8, by an in-depth review of the problematique related to freedom of expression and media in Slovenia, and hate speech. Chapter 9 addresses the deficiencies of the Slovenian welfare state, which have been (in)directly caused by the constant crises of constitutional democracy and the rule of law. Finally, Chapter 10 takes a horizontal look across all the previously discussed domains of democracy and rule of law in Slovenia to study the impact of the Council of Europe on them in identifying as well as remedying these problems.

Chapter 11 does the same with respect to the influence of the European Union. Chapter 12 wraps up the discussion by drawing normative conclusions about the particularities of the Slovenian rule-of-law and democracy crisis and explains how the latter could be alleviated, also by involving EU institutions, and how the lessons hence learned could be extrapolated to the wider CEE region.

III. ACKNOWLEDGMENTS

This book has been written within the framework of a research project dedicated to the reform of the rule of law and democracy in Slovenia, which was generously supported by the Slovenian Research Agency[49] and New University.

[49] 'Reform of Democratic and Rule-of-law State in Slovenia', Research Project J5-7359 (A) ARRS (1 January 2016–31 December 2018) Slovenian Research Agency, Nova Univerza – Fakulteta za

Matej Avbelj is the author of chapters 2, 6, 7 and 11. Jernej Letnar Černič authored chapters 3, 5, 8, 9 and 10, while Gorazd Justinek contributed chapter 4. The first and last chapters have been coauthored by Avbelj and Letnar Černič. Several chapters draw upon or are inspired by the authors' previous publications, in particular: Matej Avbelj, 'Contextual Analysis of Judicial Governance in Slovenia' (2018) 17 *German Law Journal* 1901; Matej Avbelj, 'The Sociology of (Slovenian) Constitutional Democracy' (2017) 10 *Hague Journal on the Rule of Law* 35; Jernej Letnar Černič, 'Impact of the European Court of Human Rights on the Rule of Law in Central and Eastern Europe' (2018) 10(1) *Hague Journal on the Rule of Law* 111; Jernej Letnar Černič, 'The European Court of Human Rights in the States of the Former Yugoslavia' [1 September 2018] no 1 *East European Yearbook on Human Rights* 32; Jernej Letnar Černič, *Slovenija na razpotju: geneza varstva človekovih pravic v slovenski družbi* (Kranj: Nova univerza, Fakulteta za državne in evropske študije, 2018); and Jernej Letnar Černič, Matej Avbelj, Marko Novak ans Dejan Valentinčič, *Reforma demokratične in pravne države v Sloveniji* (Kranj: Nova univerza, Fakulteta za državne in evropske študije, 2018).

Over the last three years the questions, dilemmas and the arguments contained in this book were presented in numerous fora: universities, international workshops and conferences, including the international conferences 'How to Resolve the Crisis of Constitutional Democracy in Central Europe?', New University, Faculty of Government and European Studies and European Faculty of Law, Ljubljana, 9–10 December 2016; 'The Impact of the European Institutions on the Rule of Law and Human Rights Protection in Central and Eastern Europe', New University, Faculty of Government and European Studies and European Faculty of Law, Brdo pri Kranju, 10–11 November 2017; 'Oñati Workshop on the Rule of Law, Populism and Militant Democracy', Oñati, International Institute for the Sociology of Law, 12–13 April 2018; 'The Future of the Rule of Law and Democracy in Europe', New University, Faculty of Government and European Studies and European Faculty of Law, Ljubljana, 14 December 2018.

This book has benefited from the authors' short research stays at the following institutions: the European Human Rights Advocacy Centre, Middlesex University; the International Institute for the Sociology of Law (IISL), Oñati; the European University Viadrina, Frankfurt (Oder); WZB Berlin Social Science Center; Cleveland–Marshall College of Law, Cleveland State University; the Judicial Studies Institute, Masaryk University, Brno; the Indian Law Institute;

državne in evropske študije, www.fds.si/index.php/en/school/research-and-consulting/raziskovalna-skupina/research-projects/1232-reform-of-democratic-and-rule-of-law-state-in-slovenia (accessed 24 April 2019); 'Integral Theory of the Future of the European Union', Research Project J5-1791 (1 July 2019–30 June 2022) Slovenian Research Agency, Nova Univerza – Fakulteta za državne in evropske študije; Holistic approach to business and human rights: a normative reform of Slovenian and international legal order, Research Project J5-1790 (1 July 2019–30 June 2022) Slovenian Research Agency, Nova Univerza – Fakulteta za državne in evropske študije.

the Faculty of Law, Comenius University, Bratislava; the Faculty of Law, Ivan Franko National University, Lviv; the Romanian-American University, Bucharest; Dimitrie Cantemir University, Tagru Mares; the University of Latvia; the EU Fundamental Rights Agency; and the University of Zagreb. The authors would like to thank all institutions for providing facilities and intellectual space for research and debates.

The authors have thus benefited from discussions with many individuals – scholars and practitioners alike. The following colleagues and friends, however, deserve a special mention (in alphabetical order): Daniel Augenstein, Kamil Branik, Bojan Bugarič, Adam Czarnota, Anna Dolidze, Andrew Drzemczewski, Pietro Faraguna, Alun Gibbs, Igor Guardiancich, Gabor Halmai, Andras Jakab, Peter Jambrek, Jan Komárek, Dimitry Kochenov, David Kosar, Kriszta Kovács, Martin Krygier, Zdenek Kühn, Mattias Kumm, Konrad Lachmayer, Phillip Leach, Martins Mits, Iulia Motoc, Gianluigi Palombella, Wojciech Sadurski, Rok Svetlič, Andraž Teršek, Carmen Thiele, Jurij Toplak, Gabor Attila Toth, Žiga Turk, Alan Uzelac, Tara Van Ho, Maria Varaki, Katarina Vatovec, Jan Zobec, Miroslaw Wroblewski and Miroslaw Wyrzykowski. We would also like to thank Miren Cabada Rodriguez and Alesia Koletič for their invaluable editorial assistance. The authors would like to thank the New University, Slovenia, for providing facilities and intellectual space for the conclusion of this project. Finally, the authors would like to thank each other for hard work, mutual support and patience during the research for and writing of this book. All errors and inaccuracies, of course, remain the responsibility of the authors who dedicate this treatise to Jože Pučnik and Rudi Šeligo, Slovenian dissidents, who dreamt about a Slovenia based on constitutional democracy, the rule of law and human dignity.

Ljubljana
February 2020

2

The Genesis of Slovenian Constitutional Democracy

Yugoslavia is gone, now it's time for Slovenia.
Dr Jože Pučnik, Slovenian dissident

I. A PEOPLE THAT CAME FROM NOWHERE

THE REPUBLIC OF Slovenia declared its independence from the Socialist Federal Republic of Yugoslavia on 25 June 1991. The claim for sovereign statehood was supported by a plebiscite held a few months earlier by an overwhelming majority of Slovenians and other residents of the territory of the then Socialist Republic of Slovenia.[1] After hundreds of years Slovenians thus again made it to the world's political map. Those who later quipped that this country and its people came from nowhere were indeed not guilty of exaggeration. The one and only 'sovereign' political entity of the predecessors of contemporary Slovenians was the pre-medieval state of Carantania, which emerged in the 7th century and was taken over by the Carolingian Empire in 828.[2] Between then and 1918, ie for almost a thousand years, the Slovenian people were part of the Germanic political and cultural sphere. While historically the exact political formations of this part of Europe varied, towards the east its borders stayed mostly untouched. The territory populated by Slovenians, who first called themselves by this name only in the 16th century,[3] was delimited towards the east by the border that almost exactly follows the contemporary border between Slovenia and Croatia. This border, which is essentially a frontier that delimits Western Europe from its Eastern part, albeit not in Cold War terminology, was for the first time after hundreds of years changed in 1918 when the Slovenes, in the aftermath of World War I, opted to leave the defunct

[1] 88.5 per cent of all eligible voters supported independence.
[2] For a more in-depth discussion, see Peter Štih, Vasko Simoniti and Peter Vodopivec, *Slovenska zgodovina: družba, politika, kultura* (Ljubljana: Inštitut za novejšo zgodovino 2008) www. http://www.sistory.si/publikacije/prenos/?urn=SISTORY:ID:902, (accessed 9 September 2019).
[3] ibid 158.

Austro-Hungarian Empire for the future kingdom of Serbs, Croats and Slovenes that was soon thereafter transformed into Yugoslavia.[4]

Slovenia thus historically existed as a cultural and linguistic rather than a political community. Its people lived in a geographically condensed, but extremely diverse territory at the intersection of Germanic, Romanic, Slavic and Hungarian worlds and had frequently to change their national affiliations, official languages, currencies and other statal insignia. The unifying factor was the Slovenian language, the oldest Slavic language written in the Latin script,[5] which since the time of the Reformation was gradually turned also into a tool of political emancipation inside German Habsburg Austria. This development gained political momentum since 1848, following the Spring of Nations, after which much more politically conscious as well as self-confident emerging Slovenian politicians and intellectuals demanded their people's proper place in the European political sun. In pursuit of national homogeneity, which was *en vogue* in 19th-century Europe, Slovenians called for a United Slovenia[6] and were eager to integrate more closely with the peoples with whom they felt closest.

However, this was a complex choice to make and an even harder one to implement. In cultural identity terms, other than their language, Slovenians were indistinguishable from their German counterparts in Bavaria and Austria. For centuries geography, religion and tradition shaped a common identity of these peoples until the discovery of nationalism post 1848. It was after this point that the existing German political supremacy grew into a national one and resulted in the ambition of the so-called Germanisation that the Slovenians wanted to prevent or escape from. In this ambition they were joined by other Slavic peoples of Central Europe, in particular Slovaks, Czechs and also Poles whose shared identity and linguistic proximity made them a natural candidate for a joint political union of Central European Slavs inside Austria. However, it was Hungary that literally stood in the way of this union, both geographically and, in particular, politically. There had been no room for a Slavic political autonomy in the dualist Austro-Hungarian Empire until it was too late.

After World War I, geographically severed from their Central European Slavic counterparts, also under political duress and under threat of further fragmentation of their territory between Italy and German Austria, Slovenians decided to join the South Slavic peoples in the Balkans.[7] Slovenians admittedly shared linguistic roots with these peoples, but were simultaneously profoundly different from them in terms of tradition, culture, religion and hence overall identity. The South Slavic peoples east of the former border of the Holy Roman Empire of the German nationality for centuries lived under the oriental influence of

[4] ibid 332.
[5] ibid 29.
[6] ibid 268.
[7] ibid 326.

the Ottoman Empire and they, in particular the Serbs, sought to ally not with the West but with Orthodox Russia. The newly formed state of South Slavic peoples, who were thus in many respects literally worlds apart, was therefore quickly turned into a dictatorship under Serbian monarchical rule. The newly achieved relative political autonomy of Slovenians came under a fresh threat. The old, now diminished Austria, no longer felt so bad, but the Slovenians nevertheless consoled themselves that by joining Yugoslavia they became the most developed part of the country,[8] no longer trailing all the rest as had been the case before. Slovenian politicians also managed to obtain influential positions in the Yugoslav regime, but in the end the country, riven by ethnic tensions, political hostility, profound *Kulturkampf* and the collapsing peace in Europe succumbed to the German occupation immediately after the start of the World War II.

World War II was, as for the rest of Europe, a tragedy for Slovenia too. The fascist terror of Mussolini's Italy that the Slovenians in the western part of the country were subject to as long ago as the early 1920s now spread throughout the country. The present territory of Slovenia was divided among three occupying fascist regimes – Italy, Germany and Hungary. The suffering of the local population was exacerbated further by communist attacks on and assassinations of members of the old Slovenian political elite, intellectuals and ordinary citizens, who refused to convert to the communist ideology imported from Russia by a tiny, but extremely well-organized, cell of Slovenian communist activists.[9] As a result, in particular in Ljubljana province, a territory in contemporary central Slovenia under Italian occupation, a civil war between communists and their political opponents broke out. The former united, through political deceit, all other political and social groups in the so-called Liberation Front – a national resistance partisan movement – under exclusive communist rule.[10] Those social groups who did not join were declared traitors of the Slovenian people. The home guard, composed of individuals opposed to communism who were typically close to the Catholic Church, even took arms from the occupying forces to defend themselves against the communists. The shedding of blood inside the nation reached its climax after the war, when the defeated non-communist forces retreated to Austria only to be returned by the Allies to Slovenia. Thousands of them were extrajudicially executed by partisan forces controlled by the victorious communist regime led by local communists under the auspices of Marshall Tito.[11] Their bodies, together with those of thousands of other non-communist

[8] ibid 342.

[9] ibid 350.

[10] ibid 409–10.

[11] Jože Dežman, *Hudo zlo iz Hudih Jam: k ponatisu Poročila Komisije Vlade RS za reševanje vprašanj prikritih grobišč v mandatu 2005–2008* [*Terrible Evil from Caves of Evil: Appendix to the Reprint of the Report of the Committee of the Government of Slovenia for Resolving the Issue of Concealed Burial Sites in the 2005–2008 Mandate*] (Družina, 2009).

combatants and their family members from other parts of the former Yugoslavia who were fleeing to the West but were intercepted in Slovenia, were dropped into several hundred mass graves the locations of which remain only partially accounted for even today.[12]

This communist terror served the object and purpose of the revolution following the Soviet model, albeit without the Soviets. Unlike other parts of Central and Eastern Europe, Slovenia and other parts of the former Yugoslavia were not occupied by the Red Army. Tito and Stalin were firm allies in the immediate postwar period when the process of Sovietisation with confiscation and nationalisation of private property, collectivisation of agriculture, sham trials in front of kangaroo courts, persecution of political opponents and comprehensive suppression of pluralism in society were at its peak.[13] However, after Tito and Stalin fell out in 1953, a dispute motivated by Tito's desire for more political autonomy and by the Yugoslav need for foreign economic aid, the country departed from the most austere Soviet-type communism and embarked on its own course.[14] Internally, political opponents and intellectuals believed to be hostile to the regime were removed to the Goli otok and Grgur political prisons and labor camps.[15] Externally, a strategic decision was now taken in the context of the Cold War to thread a path in the middle between the two opposing grand powers and to form an unaligned movement, spearheaded by Yugoslavia and mostly composed of former colonies.[16] Slovenian communist intelligentsia and politicians played a decisive ideological role in this unique Yugoslav form of socialism with an allegedly human face, based on economic self-management, social property in the hands of workers and under the patronage of the all-encompassing Communist Party acting as a self-proclaimed avant-garde of the working class.[17]

The Yugoslav socialist experiment lasted for more than four decades. It was made possible by Tito's cult of personality, driven by the communist propaganda of brotherhood and unity among the Yugoslav nations. The state, fed by foreign loans which were generously granted to Yugoslavia to keep it off the Soviet course,[18] was omnipresent and ensured almost full employment, and free

[12] Jože Dežman in Pavel Jamnik, *Slovenija in vojna grobišča: dolga tranzicija* (Komisija Vlade RS za reševanje vprašanja prikritih grobišč 2017).

[13] Tamara Griesser Pečar, 'Značilnosti revolucionarnega sodstva' [2017] *Dileme: razprave o vprašanjih sodobne slovenske zgodovine* 119.

[14] Jeronim Perović, 'The Tito–Stalin Split: A Reassessment in Light of New Evidence' (2007) 9 *Journal of Cold War Studies* 32.

[15] Josip Zoretić, *Goli otok: Hell in the Adriatic* (Virtualbookworm.com Publishing 2011).

[16] Nataša Mišković, Herald Fischer-Tiné and Nada Boškovska, *The Non-Aligned Movement and the Cold War: Deli – Bandung – Belgrade* (Routledge, 2014).

[17] Edvard Kardelj, *Smeri razvoja političnega sistema samoupravljanja* (Komunist, 1977).

[18] Lorraine M Lees, *Keeping Tito Afloat: The United States, Yugoslavia and the Cold War* (Pennsylvania State University Press, 1997).

healthcare and educational systems. The wages were, admittedly, low; healthcare was simple, the education was modest too, so was the housing, but the Yugoslav nations under a relaxed communist regime did much better than their counterparts in Central and Eastern Europe. This was an important source of their pride, especially for Slovenians, who looked down on everything coming from Eastern Europe, even inventing a pejorative adjective for everything which is of poor quality as being Czech. What is more, the people of Yugoslavia were allowed to travel freely, which was, essentially, another economic tool for the country's survival. The mass labour migration to Germany and Austria starting in the 1960s eased the economic burden on Yugoslavia, which simultaneously benefited from the money that the *Gastarbeiter* were sending back to their relatives left behind. Weekend shopping in Trieste, Gorizia or Graz compensated for the lack of goods in Yugoslav stores. For apolitical members of the working class, who just minded their business and did not engage into public affairs, life was thus modest, but fairly uncomplicated, with basic goods at hand, including a week of summer holiday at the Adriatic coast spent in tourist facilities operated by trade unions or socialist companies.

However, besides this workers' reality, there were at least two other parallel and equally real realities. One was that of political opponents and the 'non-working', non-conformist intelligentsia. To send a message to the public at large, these persons were subject to strict sanctions, including prison sentences, and were ultimately forced to leave the country. Not just a free press, but journals and books, including those imported from abroad, were banned and confiscated and their owners or publishers thrown into jail.[19] This was made possible by a dense and extremely well organised network of secret police (UDBA) under the leadership of the Communist Party. The UDBA exercised comprehensive control over any hostile element both domestically and abroad.[20] It engaged in murders and terrorist acts against perceived political opponents across Europe.[21] Furthermore, the organisation ran its own parallel economy, involving banks and companies in neighbouring countries, some of them even collaborating closely with the Italian mafia.[22] The revenue from this illegal business was used to fund further UDBA activities as well as the luxury lifestyle of the communist elite.[23]

Tito's death in 1980 was a turning point in symbolic as well as practical terms. The cult of personality without a person is revealed to be a vacuum.

[19] Drago Jančar (ed), *Temna stran meseca* (Nova revija, 1998).

[20] Jože Pučnik (ed), *Iz arhivov slovenske politične policije* (Veda, 1996).

[21] Damjan Hančič, Boštjan Kolarič, Jernej Letnar Černič, Renato Podbersič and Andreja Valič, 'National Report of the Crimes of Communism in Slovenia' (2010) www.ustrcr.cz/data/pdf/konference/zlociny-komunismu/COUNTRY%20REPORT%20SLOVENIA.pdf, 13 (accessed 16 February 2019).

[22] Rado Pezdir, Intervju, 4d.rtvslo.si/arhiv/intervju-tv/174479889 (accessed 16 February 2019).

[23] ibid.

The propaganda of brotherhood and unity was recognised for what it was: simply propaganda, hardly distinguishable from that of Nazi Germany.[24] Political rivalry among the local communist parties and their leaders broke lose. Tensions grew with the economic decline of unsustainable Yugoslav socialism, which was being kept afloat by foreign loans. These were cut back when the Cold War subsided, as the Western allies lost interest in Yugoslavia. The economic and political crisis in Yugoslavia, also in the context of the increasingly unstable Eastern Communist bloc in the late 1980s, caused a reawakening of national tensions and hostilities between the South Slavic peoples in the Balkans. These tensions, existing from the time immemorial, had been forcefully suppressed by the velvet fist of the Tito regime. They were never eliminated, but left dormant, waiting for the right historical moment to be unleashed. What was for the Serbian regime under the patronage of Slobodan Milošević the chance for a final reunification of all Serbs in one Great Serbia,[25] was for the Slovenian people a historical window of opportunity to leave the Balkans and, for the first time in modern history, create their own independent state.

II. THE ROAD TO INDEPENDENCE AND CONSTRUCTION OF A NEW CONSTITUTIONAL LEGAL ORDER

In 1987 the Yugoslav communist regime proposed in its death throes a set of federal constitutional amendments the purpose of which was to prevent a seeming disintegration of the country by introducing more centralisation.[26] In Slovenia, this deepened the cleavage between members of the ruling communist political class, who were rather sympathetic to the announced federal constitutional reforms, and the nascent opposition. This was first limited to narrow intellectual circles, in particular writers and academics gathered around the *Nova Revija* journal.[27] Their activities marked the beginning of the rise of democratic civil society movements in Slovenia. In this reformist circle Dr Jože Pučnik played a decisive role. A Slovenian counterpart of the CEE anti-communist, dissident giants, in 1989 Pučnik returned to Slovenia from exile in Western Germany where he had been forced to go after more than six years of imprisonment by the Slovenian communist authorities for his public criticism of the communist economic and political system.[28] As a staunch man of

[24] Jaka Bartolj, 'A Slovenian Poster Challenged Yugoslavia's Communist Othodoxy' (*RTVSLO*, 12 August 2014) www.rtvslo.si/news-in-english/slovenia-revealed/a-slovenian-poster-challenged-yugoslavia-s-communist-orthodoxy/326571 (accessed 16 February 2019).

[25] Peter Jambrek, *Nation's Transitions: Social and Legal Issues of Slovenia's Transitions 1945–2105* (Graduate School of Government and European Studies, European Faculty of Law, 2014) 44–46.

[26] Peter Jambrek, *Ustava in svoboda: Ustavna ureditev Slovenije, izvori, temelji in razvoj* (Graduate School of Government and European Studies, European Faculty of Law, 2014) 31ff.

[27] Igor Omerza, *Veliki in dolgi pohod Nove revije* (Mohorjeva, 2015).

[28] Rosvita Pesek, *Pučnik* (Mohorjeva, 2013).

integrity and a social democrat, he was a champion of freedom and progress of individuals and nations, and was hence the main motor behind the Slovenian independence movement. A true Nestor of Slovenian independence.[29] He led the coalition of political parties assembled into the Democratic Opposition of Slovenia (known by its Slovenian acronym, Demos) which in 1990, at the first ever democratic election, defeated the ruling Communist Party. Afterwards this political bloc, hand in hand with progressive civil society groups, contributed to a constitutional moment which resulted in the new Constitution of the Republic of Slovenia.

In a unique way, a constitutional process in Slovenia thus emerged and was driven by civil society. The first constitutional draft was penned by the Slovenian Writers' Association and the Slovenian Sociological Association in opposition to the proposed centralising amendments to the federal constitution. The so-called Writers' Constitution, consisting of the normative theses for a new Slovenian constitution, was thus published in April 1988.[30] It was soon fiercely attacked by the leading constitutional scholars of the day, who decried the text for its bourgeois character and its total incompatibility with the then constitutional and political order.[31] Two years later, civil society's constitutional engagement was joined by the Slovenian democratic opposition which in a politically inclusive forum of the Assembly for the Constitution (Zbor za ustavo) authored the Demos Constitution.[32] This, itself based on the earlier Writers' Constitution, was then used as a working template by the leading Slovenian constitutional scholars gathered in a special constitutional commission led by Peter Jambrek. The outcome was the Constitution of Podvin, the draft of which was presented on 31 August 1990. This was a direct predecessor of the present Slovenian Constitution. The latter was, however, adopted more than a year later on 23 December 1991. The delay was due to political tactics and disputes in a divided National Assembly.[33]

Views had been split as to the exact legal strategy to achieve independence for Slovenia. The legal basis for the latter was undisputed. The Yugoslav Federal Constitution of 1974 in explicit terms stipulated the principle of national self-determination, which included the right to secession.[34] The political stakeholders thus had to weigh the choice between two models for proclaiming independence: it would either be proclaimed by the National Assembly issuing a Declaration of Independence, or independence would be declared following a popular vote

[29] As he was posthumously described by the then President of the Republic of Slovenia, Borut Pahor.

[30] Jambrek (n 26) 61–70.

[31] ibid 74.

[32] ibid.

[33] See Peter Jambrek, Dimitrij Rupel and Matej Avbelj, 'Ustavnost in suverenost v razmerju do zunanje oblasti – Slovenija v Jugoslaviji, Natu in Evropski uniji' in Matej Avbelj (ed), *Izzivi moderne države* (Fakulteta za državne in evropske študije, 2012).

[34] Constitution of a Socialist Federal Republic of Yugoslavia 1974, Art I.

in a referendum. The latter strategy won political support and the referendum was called for 23 December 1990. However, the exact formulation of the question to be decided in the referendum remained open until very late. Originally, it had been envisaged that a referendum would take the form of a constitutional referendum at which the people would endorse a new Constitution.[35] As this constitutional road to independence failed to materialise, due to delays in the political process, the referendum simply offered voters the choice of whether or not Slovenia should become a sovereign and independent state.[36]

Following overwhelming support for independence, the government was mandated to prepare within the following six months a legislative framework for implementing the will of the people. Slovenia thus effectuated its independence on 25 June 1991, not, however, by adopting a new Constitution, but rather by issuing a Basic Constitutional Charter (Temeljna ustavna listina). The Basic Constitutional Charter is a founding document of the Slovenian state that came into being on the basis of a plebiscite in the absence of a new Constitution. With its adoption the Republic of Slovenia irretrievably broke its ties with Yugoslavia and established itself as a sovereign state. As the Constitutional Court argued years later, the Basic Constitutional Charter represents a 'permanent and inexhaustible source of the statehood of the Republic of Slovenia'.[37] It is symbolically the highest source of the Slovenian constitutional order. The new Constitution was, eventually, adopted on 23 December 1991.

The new Constitution presented a clear and explicit formal and substantive value break with the former Yugoslav and Slovenian communist constitution. In the words of the Constitutional Court, by declaring independence and adopting a new constitutional order, Slovenia was being endowed with a new constitutional quality whose essence 'is the protection of human rights and fundamental freedoms to all persons in the territory of the Republic of Slovenia irrespective of their national origin, without any discrimination whatsoever'.[38] This was important since in Yugoslavia human rights had been grossly violated.[39] The object and purpose of Slovenian independence was therefore not only to sever federal links with Yugoslavia, but to effectuate an explicit 'fracture with the fundamental value concept of the constitutional order'.[40] The totalitarian communist regime, which was founded on 'murder, robbery, violence and culture

[35] Peter Jambrek, Dimitrij Rupel and Matej Avbelj, 'Ustavnost in suverenost v razmerju do zunanje oblasti – Slovenija v Jugoslaviji, Natu in Evropski uniji' in Matej Avbelj (ed), *Izzivi moderne države* (Fakulteta za državne in evropske študije, 2012).

[36] For a more in-depth discussion, see Rosvita Pesek, *Osamosvojitev Slovenije: ali naj Republika Slovenija postane samostojna in neodvisna država?* (Nova Revija, 2007).

[37] U-II-1/12, U-II-2/12 [2012].

[38] U-I-109/10 [2011] [7].

[39] Basic Constitutional Charter [*Temeljna ustavna listina*], para 3.

[40] U-I-109/10 [2011] [7].

of fear, deception and lies',[41] was to be substituted by a constitutional order based on democracy, human rights protection and the rule of law.

III. SLOVENIA AS A CONSTITUTIONAL DEMOCRACY

The ambitions for an independent Slovenia have certainly been achieved on the level of the new constitutional text. The new Slovenian Constitution has been modelled on modern Western European constitutional texts, in particular the German Constitution and the ECHR. The Constitution is embedded in the value-framework of a liberal democracy. Its structure thus reflects a typical organisation of a liberal-democratic constitution in which human rights come first, followed by the provisions for the organisation of the state. The Constitution defines Slovenia as a democratic republic, based on the principles of the rule of law and the welfare state.[42] A central place is awarded to the protection of human rights, which should be afforded the highest standard of protection.[43] In this context, a special role is played by the ECHR,[44] which is directly applicable in Slovenia[45] and hence binds all organs of the state.[46]

In a clear departure from its communist predecessor, the Constitution also inaugurates a system of separation of powers. Sovereignty is vested in the people and the citizens exercise it directly or through elections, consistent with the principle of the separation of legislative, executive and judicial powers.[47] Also by contrast with the former communist regime, the judiciary is now a distinctive and independent branch of government. Judges are to be independent in the performance of their judicial function and are bound exclusively by the Constitution and the statutes.[48] Judges are tenured and enjoy all the privileges and immunities typical of a constitutional democracy.[49] The highest court in the state is the Supreme Court.[50] Its role is to rule as a last instance in criminal and civil cases, commercial lawsuits, administrative review, and labour and social security disputes.

[41] Peter Jambrek, *Demokracija in država, Slovenija 1945–2015* (Fakulteta za državne in evropske študije, Evropska pravna fakulteta, 2014) 373.

[42] Constitution of the Republic of Slovenia 1991, 2016, Arts 1 and 2.

[43] ibid Art 15/5.

[44] For an overview of the role of the ECHR in Slovenia, see Matej Avbelj and Jernej Letnar Černič, 'Slovenia' in Leonard Hammer and Frank Emmert (eds), *The European Convention on Human Rights and Fundamental Freedoms in Central and Eastern Europe* (Eleven International Publishing, 2012) 527.

[45] Constitution of the Republic of Slovenia 1991, 2016, Art 8: 'Ratified and published treaties shall be applied directly.'

[46] This is drawing on Avbelj and Letnar Černič (n 44).

[47] Constitution of the Republic of Slovenia 1991, 2016, Art 3.

[48] ibid Art 125.

[49] ibid Art 129.

[50] ibid Art 127.

The Constitution also provides for a Constitutional Court as the supreme body of the judicial power for the protection of constitutionality, legality, human rights and fundamental freedoms.[51] The Constitutional Court is composed of nine judges, elected on the proposal of the President of the Republic by the National Assembly for a term of nine years and may not be re-elected.[52] It is endowed with important competences in relation to the executive and the legislative branch, as well as to the ordinary judiciary. It rules in, inter alia, disputes on constitutionality and legality, as well as in proceedings for human rights protection on the basis of constitutional complaints brought by individuals.[53] The Constitutional Court has played a central role in laying down and upholding the legal foundations of the Slovenian state. In particular, the composition of the Court in its first mandate made a lasting contribution. The justices, inspired by comparative constitutional law practices, introduced all the standards of constitutional review typical of modern constitutional democracies, not infrequently in the absence of any written legal basis in the Slovenian Constitution. Most importantly, the Constitutional Court has always regarded the Constitution as a living document.[54] Its approach to judicial decision-making has been creative, which has prompted, in particular, former communist lawyers, scholars and political stakeholders to accuse it of judicial activism.[55]

However, it is precisely due to this creative and influential role of the Constitutional Court that Slovenia should not be regarded as a mere formal democracy in which a popular majority of any kind may rule as it pleases, as long as it continues to represent a majority of votes. Rather than existing as a formal, majoritarian democracy, the Constitutional Court insisted on Slovenia being a constitutional democracy.[56] In this particular type of democracy, constitutionally protected values, especially fundamental rights and freedoms, prevail over the democratically adopted decisions of the majority.[57] Constitutional democracy as originally construed by the Slovenian Constitutional Court was hence conceived of in negative terms, as a constraint on majoritarian decision-making. This negative conception was relied upon by the Court to prevent requests for referenda, which could produce unconstitutional outcomes.[58] It was also employed to ensure the execution of rulings by the Court, which has, as a guardian of constitutional democracy, claimed a privileged position for itself in the

[51] Its more detailed regulation can be found in the Constitutional Court Act; Constitutional Court Act 1994, 2012, Art 1.

[52] Constitution of the Republic of Slovenia 1991, 2016, Art 165.

[53] ibid Art 160.

[54] Jambrek (n 26).

[55] See eg Ivan Kristan, 'Delitev oblasti ob ankaranski zgodbi' [2011] *XVII. dnevi javnega prava in javnega managementa* 25; for an overview, see also Marko Novak, *Delitev oblasti; medigra prava in politike* (Cankarjeva založba, 2003).

[56] This paragraphs draws on Matej Avbelj, 'The Sociology of (Slovenian) Constitutional Democracy' [2017] *Hague Journal on the Rule of Law* 40.

[57] Case U-I-111/04 [2004] [26].

[58] See cases U-II-1/09 [2009], U-II-2/09 [2009] and U-II-1/10 [2010].

national system of checks and balances.[59] However, the Tito Street case moved this jurisprudence to the next stage by introducing an affirmative conception of constitutional democracy.[60]

Rather than focusing on the constraining capacity of constitutional democracy, by denying the political majority the right to rule as it pleases, the Tito Street ruling advanced constitutional democracy as a vehicle for the protection and promotion of each individual's right to self-actualisation within the limits of the equal rights of others. Accordingly,

> The principle of democracy … in its substance and significance exceeds the definition of the state order as merely a formal democracy in which laws and other regulations are adopted in accordance with the rule of the majority. On the contrary, the principle of democracy substantively defines the Republic of Slovenia as a constitutional democracy, thus as a state in which the acts of authorities are legally limited by constitutional principles and human rights and fundamental freedoms, precisely because individuals and their dignity are at the centre of its existence and functioning.[61]

In so doing, the Constitutional Court rectified the human dignity deficit in the Slovenian Constitution. As explained by Jambrek, the founding fathers of the Slovenian constitutional order, following the constitutional texts of similarly historically traumatised political communities, in particular Germany, insisted that the Preamble to the Constitution should contain provisions on the sanctity of human life and the inviolability of human dignity.[62] However, the deeply ideologically split Slovenian political community failed to reach a consensus on this point and the proposal was eventually dropped.[63] In this way, paradoxically, 'an element of natural law [which] appeared initially as a source of inspiration for the whole constitutional text'[64] failed to enter the text itself. In the foundational value-sense, the Slovenian Constitution thus emerged as a truncated constitution. It took a further 20 years to reconstruct its normatively holistic character. In 2011 the Constitutional Court read into the existing Article 1 of the Constitution, which provides that Slovenia is a democratic republic, a conception of democracy whose foundation and normative ideal, deserving the highest constitutional protection, is equal human dignity.[65]

[59] Case U-I-109/10 [2011].

[60] ibid.

[61] Case U-I-109/10 [2011] [10].

[62] Jambrek (n 25) 361.

[63] ibid.

[64] ibid.

[65] Constitutional Court Case U-I-109/10 [2011]. See Avbelj, in Jambrek (n 25) 401; even this obvious, and in itself uncontroversial normative construction, supported by comparative constitutional law practices, did not find unanimous approval among Slovenian scholars. For two particularly harsh critiques, see Dragan Petrovec, 'Varuh iztaknjenih oči – Pandorina skrinjica ustavne odločbe' [2011] *Pravna praksa* 17; and Ljubo Bavcon, 'K odločbi Ustavnega sodišča o Titovi cesti' [2011] *Pravna praksa* 16.

It can be thus concluded that following its independence Slovenia formally engaged in the construction of a modern, liberal and pluralist constitutional democracy. The country's academic and intellectual elite who, assisted by civil society, initiated and facilitated Slovenia's relatively smooth exit from the Yugoslav imbroglio, emulated the comparative constitutional and institutional best practices found in Western Europe, in particular Germany. In that way, Slovenia has succeeded in setting up a formal institutional organisation of the state that should guarantee a relatively quick transition from its communist days to catch up with developed Western democracies. For its seeming success in building quickly, and apparently effectively, a formal institutional framework, without major domestic tensions, Slovenia had been perceived as the best disciple, as the poster child of the New Europe. This won the country, very early on, full membership of the European Union and NATO. The country has been praised for its soft transition,[66] which allegedly enabled it to draw on acquired social capital from the past. Unlike certain Central and Eastern European countries that required (economic) shock-therapies, Slovenia appeared to have made a straighforward transition to genuine democracy, the rule of law and an open-market economy in accordance with the Copenhagen criteria. This has turned out to be a false expectation, a myth. Instead, the Slovenian soft transition has come with a high price. This becomes clear as soon as an exclusive formal constitutional focus is supplemented by a more sociological approach.

IV. THE SOCIOLOGY OF SLOVENIAN CONSTITUTIONAL ORDER

In contrast to the rest of the communist CEE countries, Slovenia opted for a consensual model of a gradual and soft transition from communist regime to democracy. Effectively there was no lustration and the elite retention rate, reflecting the number of people who were in key societal positions in pre- and post-communist times, was consequently exceptionally high.[67] The reasons for that were manifold. The literature typically quotes the size of the country and the correspondingly narrow elite, which made it practically impossible to replace a communist elite with a non-communist one.[68] The latter simply did not exist in sufficient numbers. Its members were either killed or expelled during and immediately after World War II. The operational, political and economic know-how had been thus possessed by the communist party and its allies. The new political parties were mainly concerned with making an independent state and defending the country against Serbian aggression. In so doing,

[66] Anton Bebler, 'Slovenia's Smooth Transition' [2002] *Journal of Democracy* 127.

[67] Frane Adam and Matevž Tomšič, 'Transition Elites: Catalysts of Social Innovation or Rent Seekers' [2000] *Družboslovne razprave* 138.

[68] Drago Jančar (ed), *Temna stran meseca* (Nova revija, 1998).

the survival of the idea of an independent Slovenia was existentially dependent on domestic unity.

The Communist Party understood that well and its leaders, despite their profound lack of sympathy for the independence and democratisation movement, took the cue mainly to ensure their political and economic survival. Furthermore, in the late 1980s and early 1990s the emancipatory, progressive narrative in Slovenia, again different to that in other CEE countries, was much more directed against the crumbling Yugoslav socialist economic model, now personified by the nationalist aggressiveness of the Milošević regime, than against totalitarian communism. The imprisonment of four dissident politicians, journalists and activists (the so-called 'JBTZ affair') by the Secret Service and their trial in the heart of Ljubljana in front of a military court and in the Serbo-Croat language spontaneously ignited a Slovenian uprising against the federal government under Serbian control in defence, first, of Slovenian national identity, and then human rights and democracy. The rejection of the idea and practices of communism was then considered less important, and by significant strata of the population even unimportant, whereas the communist elites invested (at least) in their symbolic preservation.

Consequently, the essence of the qualitative change in the character of the Slovenian statehood, as perceived by the majority of its citizens and portrayed by the former Communist Party, its satellites and the media, in particular, existed in escaping from the Yugoslav state under Serbian rule, which increasingly threatened the national identity of Slovenia and its people. According to mainstream views, the problem of Yugoslavia and Slovenia was therefore not communism (or its softer version, socialism), it was its misapplication and distortion by the Great Serbian nationalistic ambition. This sentiment, which is still prevalent nowadays and might be even on the rise, to a certain extent at least belies the framers' intent that the new Constitution should represent an explicit 'fracture with the fundamental value concept of the constitutional order'.[69] In practice, however, the fracture in the popular mindset, orchestrated by the post-communist narrative, has been one with the Yugoslav statist form, but much less with its ideological substance.

Slovenia has thus failed to execute a decisive, symbolic, value-based rupture with the communist *ancien régime* as well as with its underlying economic system. The first fact is reflected in the quality of public discourse, which comprehensively translates down on the civic identity, the mind-set of every single individual in the country. Most importantly, the identity traits of *homo sovieticus* have neither been removed or undone. The four traits, typical of communist subjects – the exile, the honest crook, the actively obedient and the abusive mind-set[70] – are in deep and irreconcilable conflict with the civic identity

[69] Case U-I-109/10 [2011] [7].
[70] Avbelj (n 56).

presupposed and encouraged by a constitutional democracy. This explains why in the Slovenian polity, which was uniquely subject to three European totalitarian regimes, citizens report much weaker attachment to the values constitutive of a constitutional democracy as is the case, for instance, in Western Europe with its longer liberal constitutional tradition.[71]

Instead of freedom and equality, the self-conception of an individual as a responsible agent of change in a democratic polity,[72] trust and acceptance of others as equals,[73] the perception that public power is exercised in the name of and for the citizens,[74] rather than citizens being the instruments in the hands of the state,[75] it is general apathy, a sense of passivity, uninvolvement and civic infantilism that prevail.[76] The latter has been described as 'a limited understanding of other people, easily provoked aggression, an inferiority complex, a constant feeling of being dependent and managed by others'.[77] This produces 'double-think',[78] a schizophrenic public character, which constantly 'unifies things that cannot be unified'.[79] A central role in this proces is played by individuals' inherent and unavoidable continuing dependence on the state in the wake of communism. This attitude displays an entirely instrumentalist, indeed relative sense of her own individual being, which is simultaneously combined with an enormous distrust of anything related to the state and public power.[80] Such an intimately self-contradicting relationship between private and public autonomy in a post-communist citizen leads to (self-)loathing, resentment, a constant search for scapegoats and is anything but conducive to the development of a sound society. The latter, however, is a prerequisite for a genuine constitutional democracy.

The existence of constitutional democracy in practice depends on its institutionalisation, which is a function of a de facto acceptance of the constitutive values of constitutional democracy by the people in any given polity.

[71] ibid.

[72] More than 80 per cent of those surveyed find political engagement not important or not very important. See World Value Survey, Slovenia 2011.

[73] More than 79 per cent of those surveyed believe that one should be careful in trusting other people. See World Value Survey, Slovenia 2011.

[74] See eg Special Eurobarometer 461 (April 2017) 6, according to which the trust in national government among the EU Member States is the second lowest in Slovenia, while trust prevails among the Northern and Western member states, and declines toward the East and the South.

[75] It follows from the EBRD survey that 82 per cent of Slovenes would trade political freedom for economic growth; moreover only 56 per cent of Slovenes believe that democracy is preferable to any other political system, available at: www.ebrd.com/publications/life-in-transition-iii-slovenia.pdf

[76] Lev Dimitrievich Gudkov, '"Soviet Man" in the Sociology of Iurii Levada' (2008) 47(6) *Sociological Research* 6.

[77] ibid 22.

[78] ibid.

[79] ibid 16.

[80] See eg Special Eurobarometer 461, 6 whereby, with the exception of Hungary and Estonia, all other post-communist Member States' trust in their government is below the EU-28 average. In Slovenia, in particular, it is strikingly low, as only 17 per cent of Slovenian citizens trust their government. However, only 16 per cent of Slovenians trust the country's judicial system.

Following and paraphrasing Hart,[81] the actual institutionalisation of constitutional democracy in a polity depends on the activities and attitudes of two types of actors. Individuals who occupy institutional positions in a polity, in particular judges and officials, have a qualified duty to ensure a constitutional democracy functions.[82] This requires that they not only comply with its normative mandates, but also internalise these as part and parcel of their professional as well as personal ethos. On the other hand, all other individuals, citizens in a polity, should by and large understand and comply with the normative expectations of constitutional democracy too. A functioning constitutional democracy thus comes with constitutionally committed institutional actors and a critical mass of constitutionally complying citizens.

Since, as Habermas has argued, constitutional democracy represents 'a paradoxical union of contradictory principles',[83] a combination of popular sovereignty in the form of majoritarian decision-making and the rule of law as its constraining factor,[84] it requires for its existence a special character of citizenship and a correspondingly unique role for its citizens. In a constitutional democracy, as explained by Tully, citizens are not only the formal bearers of rights and duties under a constitution, but by exercising these rights in practice they also develop an actual identity as citizens, in the form of their self-awareness and self-formation.[85] In other words, citizens in a constitutional democracy develop and foster a special civic identity, a product of their 'citizenisation', which enables them to fruitfully participate in a historically self-correcting process between private and civic autonomy, a process that lies at the heart of a system of constitutional democracy.[86] As such civic identity is notably lacking in Slovenia, this presents a potent sociological obstacle to the evolution of a genuine constitutional democracy in this country.

Another empirical obstacle that hinders the evolution of a constitutional democracy in practice, and hence ensures a discrepancy between the normative ambition of the Slovenian Constitution and its functioning in practice, is the specific Slovenian post-communist economic model.[87] Unlike the rest of the CEE countries, Slovenia opted for an economic model of gradual transition, with limited privatisation and a large degree of state ownership.[88] This economic

[81] HLA Hart, *The Concept of Law* (Clarendon Press, 1905).

[82] ibid.

[83] Jürgen Habermas, 'Constitutional Democracy: A Paradoxical Union of Contradictory Principles' (2001) 29(6) *Political Theory* 766.

[84] ibid.

[85] ibid.

[86] ibid 768.

[87] The following three paragraphs draw on Matej Avbelj, 'Transformation in the Eye of the Beholder' in Michal Bobek (ed), *Central European Judges Under the European Influence: The Transformative Power of the EU Revisited* (Hart Publishing, 2015).

[88] See eg Matevž Tomšič and Lea Prijon, *Ideological Profile and Crisis Discourse of the Slovenian Elites*, www.eisa-net.org/be-bruga/eisa/files/events/warsaw2013/Tomsic%20Prijon_Ideological%20Profile%20and%20Crisis%20Discourse%20of%20Slovenian%20Elites.pdf (accessed 11 November 2014); also Rado Pezdir, *Slovenska tranzicija od Kardelja do Tajkunov* (Časnik Finance, 2008).

model initially ensured its citizens relatively high standards of living in comparison with other CEE countries, especially due to Slovenia's appreciable economic advantages over them.[89] However, this economic model in fact served to preserve the political and economic status quo and has effectively blocked the development of a genuine constitutional democracy in Slovenia.

Economic gradualism, closed to foreign investors, meant that half of the economy has been state owned and therefore run by the government in power, whereas the other half was privatised by insiders close to the very same government.[90] As a result, economic power became concentrated in the hands of a post-socialist elite, which gradually took control over all other sectors of society.[91] As explained by Bugarič:

> [M]any 'rule of law' institutions (courts, the civil service, and the media) have been deeply politicized by the former 'nomenclature officials.' Instead of defending the rule of law, these institutions, unable to withstand the strong political pressure of their 'principals,' were engaged in legal enforcement favouring partisan political interests. Since the left-liberal political bloc (former communists (Social Democrats, SD) and the reformed Communist Youth Organization (Liberal Democracy of Slovenia, LDS)) had dominated the political space for almost fourteen years, this strongly impacted the formation of the Slovenian elite in general. Consequently, the majority of Slovenian elites gravitated towards the 'retention' elite, represented by the LDS and SD political parties. This elite managed to create better contacts with the business sector, media, academia and, most importantly, with a substantial part of the public sector, including the judiciary, civil service, state-owned companies, etc.[92]

This elite's economic and political control over the media, however, proved decisive. For it was exactly the media with a strong left-centre bias[93] which facilitated, justified and defended the conquering of the Slovenian public and private sphere by the leftist post-socialist elite. It is the media that has been concealing rather than exposing the end result of the Slovenian success story in which 'cronyism'[94] and 'state capture' have become so widespread and 'internalised' that informal rules and habits are more important than formal rules.[95]

However, it would be wrong to conclude that this specific Slovenian economic model was a peculiar transitional, post-communist invention destined to reform

[89] Which has, however, almost disappeared in the last decade, see 'How "New Europe" Has Fared on its Tenth Birthday' *Economist* (1 May 2014) www.economist.com/blogs/graphicdetail/2014/05/daily-chart?fsrc=scn/fb/wl/dc/growingupfast (accessed 11 November 2014).

[90] The following three paragraphs draw on Matej Avbelj, 'How to Reform the Rule of Law in Slovenia' in Frane Adam (ed), *Slovenia: Social, Economic and Environmental Issues* (Nova Publishing, 2017).

[91] Frane Adam and Matevž Tomšič, 'The Dynamics of Elites and the Type of Capitalism: Slovenian Exceptionalism' [2012] *Historical Social Research* 63.

[92] Bojan Bugarič, 'Crisis of Constitutional Democracy in Post-Communist Europe: "Lands In-between" Democracy and Authoritarianism' [2015] *ICON* 219.

[93] For an overview of the state of the media in Slovenia, see the comprehensive multifaceted analysis in [2007] *Dignitas – Slovenian Journal of Human Rights* 33–36.

[94] See Tomšič and Prijon (n 88).

[95] Bugarič (n 92).

and ultimately give way with the passage of time to an open market economy, based on economic freedom and respect for private property. On the contrary, the present Slovenian economic, and consequently also political, model follows closely what Djilas described as the political economy of the 'New Class'. In his seminal work, published in 1957,[96] he argued that a communist revolution in practice betrayed all of the ideals preached by the communists and resulted in the creation of a new class. Its core is composed of former communist revolutionaries, party officials and extends to nepotistic networks and, finally, to everyone exhibiting devotion and loyalty in order to enjoy 'the special privileges and economic preference because of the administrative monopoly they hold'. In short: 'to live as parasites at the expense of others'.[97]

The 'insatiable' hunger for power and its unscrupulous use by the new class were indistinguishable from that of the deposed pre-revolutionary aristocratic or bourgeois regimes that the communists sought to replace.[98] Having done so, things have stayed the same, other than the new class was now absent of 'the [bourgeois] virtues of frugality and economy ... and [aristocratic] refinement and proud chivalry'.[99] It sought to conceal its true character under an omnipresent socialist phraseology. Hence, socialist or collective ownership was invented to serve as 'a disguise for the real ownership by the political bureaucracy'.[100] In the system governed by the new class 'the power and the government are identical with the use, enjoyment and disposition of almost all the nation's goods'.[101] This is why the ownership privilege of the new class 'extends from state administration and administration of economic enterprises to that of sports and humanitarian organisations'.[102] As described by Bugarič above, the model of political and economic governance in independent Slovenia has preserved most of the elements of a new class system, with the unimportant exception that under a liberal, modern constitution socialist property was replaced by a dominant model of state ownership.

This makes Slovenia essentially different from the other CEE countries. Slovenia's model of de facto political and economic continuity with the predemocratic system has permitted its elites to hold on to control of the country without any openly authoritarian tendencies, capture of the state or constitutional backsliding. Unlike Hungary and Poland, where the political elite had to engage in an overt attack on the constitutional and legal framework of the state in order to ensure that their loyalists penetrated the essential institutions and gained control over the economy, in Slovenia those loyalists and this control

[96] Milovan Djilas, *The New Class: An Analysis of the Communist System* (Thames & Hudson, 1957).
[97] ibid 46.
[98] ibid.
[99] ibid 60.
[100] ibid 47.
[101] ibid 46.
[102] ibid.

of the economy, perfectly legally on the basis of state ownership, have existed for decades. The dynamics of a political project in Slovenia is thus opposite to that in the currently backsliding CEE countries. Rather than seeking a profound change in the society, the political agenda of the contemporary Slovenian new class is the preservation of the status quo by all means.[103] As members of the elite have already been institutionalised, they only have to ensure that things remain as they have always been. The defence of the status quo, under the guise of stability, predictability and order, is thus the main policy, combined with the subtle reproduction of this elite through the monopolised education system and the all-encompassing welfare state. The latter, instead of alleviating the socio-economic hardship of those parts of society in need, has instead been used to benefit the existing kleptocratic allies and to recruit new ones.

V. A SEMI-PERMANENT TRANSITION AND THE NEW NORMAL

This chapter has outlined the genesis of the contemporary Slovenian constitutional order. We have seen that, staying faithful to the country's preamble to the Constitution, Slovenia's centuries-long struggle for national liberation formally resulted in a modern, liberal constitutional framework. On the basis of this constitutional order the country has achieved equally impressive foreign policy results, becoming a full member of the international community, including the EU and NATO, just a decade after winning independence. Economically, too, independent Slovenia began to catch up with the EU average development rate. This positive trend, however, stopped in 2008 with the outbreak of the global financial crisis, which revealed the unsustainability of the Slovenian economic, and hence also political, model. Falling output exposed the gap between the normative requirements of the Slovenian constitutional order as written and the actual existing (un)constitutional, (un)democratic practices. It turned out that a massive drop in the country's economic performance and the political fragility that followed were not a one-off event, caused by a hostile external environment. The causes of the crises that have engulfed Slovenia since 2008 were endogenous. They stemmed from systemic deficiencies in the building blocks of the country's constitutional democracy.

The following four chapters will thus demonstrate in more detail how the failure to engage seriously with Slovenia's painful history and to systemically invest in transitional justice aggravated historical problems; rather than learning from history, Slovenia imported its historical malaise not only into the present but also into the future. This has, inevitably, had negative, sometimes profoundly negative, consequences for the actual protection of human rights

[103] Which is the practice seen across Eastern European countries such as Bulgaria, Romania, the former Yugoslavia and former Soviet countries.

in the country; for the meaningful assurance of the rule of law by the judiciary; for the sound functioning of a democratic political process lato sensu as well as for the fair operation of the country's welfare state. While all of these normative ideals occupy the highest status in the Slovenian hierarchy of constitutional values, there exists a major and still growing discrepancy between ideals and actual practice. Due to Slovenia's tiny size, traditionally good (if not entirely deserved) international reputation, relative economic closure and poor international coverage of its domestic affairs, not to mention the country's quite exotic language, the Slovenian post-communist, left-liberal elite has been developing its 'neo-corporatist'[104] democracy largely in the isolation from external oversight and under the benign neglect of the international community. As the following chapters will show, the results in terms of the actual quality of constitutional democracy in Slovenia have been in many respects much worse and much more concerning than in other CEE countries which are presently subject to rule-of-law oversight by the EU. If this negative trend is to continue, Slovenia risks that its process of transition, now more than 25 years old, will simply become the new normal.[105]

[104] Bugarič (n 92).
[105] See also conclusion in Avbelj (n 87).

3

Historical Reasons for Failures of the Rule of Law and Constitutional Democracy in Slovenia

We thought we'd leave communism behind and everything would turn out fine. But it turns out you can't leave this and become free, because these people don't understand what freedom is.[1]

I. INTRODUCTION

THIS CHAPTER DESCRIBES and analyses the historical reasons for the deficiencies and failures of the rule of law and constitutional democracy in Slovenia, attempting to draw parallels with the rest of Central and Eastern Europe. Accordingly, it explores the transitional measures that have been employed to overcome such deficiencies. History has often haunted post-transitional societies in Central and Eastern Europe. Slovenia, not unlike many CEE countries, spent a good proportion of the 20th century behind the iron curtain under a communist regime that abused the rule of law and systematically violated human rights and fundamental freedoms.[2] After the creation of the newly independent CEE states, regional organisations and mature liberal democracies from the West and North embarked on the ambitious project of translating the tools, institutions and rules of constitutional democracy to the 'new' Europe.[3] However, this project has not proceeded without challenges as

[1] Svetlana Aleksijevič in Shaun Walter, 'Interview: Svetlana Aleksijevich: "After Communism we Thought Everything Would Be Fine. But People Don't Understand Freedom"' *The Guardian* (21 July 2017) www.theguardian.com/books/2017/jul/21/svetlana-alexievich-interview (accessed 24 April 2019).

[2] Jernej Letnar Černič, 'Consolidating Democracy Through Transitional Justice in Slovenia: Lessons Learnt?' in Agata Fijalkowski and Raluca Grosescu (eds), *Transitional Criminal Justice in Post-Dictatorial and Post-Conflict Societies* (Cambridge, Intersentia, 2015) 147–68.

[3] Jernej Letnar Černič and Matej Avbelj, 'Introduction to the Special Issue on the Crisis of Constitutional Democracy in Central and Eastern Europe' (2018) 10(1) *Hague Journal on the Rule of Law* 1; Matej Avbelj, 'The Sociology of (Slovenian) Constitutional Democracy' (2018) 10(1) *Hague Journal on the Rule of Law* 35.

the translation process has not from the outset run smoothly.[4] As a result, the values of constitutional democracy have been only partially translated into the life of the democratic institutions of Central and Eastern Europe. Although the CEE countries have established the institutions of modern constitutional democracies, they have not fully internalised these values, thereby subjecting themselves to the parochial interests of informal elites.[5] Criticism can therefore be levelled at those elites that derive their power from their privileged positions in the former totalitarian and authoritarian regimes.

For these reasons, most of the citizens of this part of Europe, including Slovenia, appear not to place substantial trust in any of the branches of government and public administration institutions.[6] This distrust is not structured only vertically between individuals and governmental elites, but can be discerned in the relationships between different branches of government, where cooperation has been lacking, as well as in the horizontal relationships between individuals and/or between companies.[7] On a declarative level, constitutional texts of CEE countries traditionally pronounce these countries to be constitutional democracies based on the rule of law and the values of liberal democracy.[8] However, in the everyday institutional life of the state and public administration constitutional values appear to have been subjected to parochial interests, thereby displacing common or public interests and disregarding the principles of the Weberian bureaucracy model.[9] In so doing, state institutions have been seized as an instrument for the protection of the narrow interests of state and

[4] See eg Jernej Letnar Černič, 'Impact of the European Court of Human Rights on the Rule of Law in Central and Eastern Europe' (2018) 10(1) *Hague Journal on the Rule of Law* 111.

[5] Zdeněk Kühn, *The Judiciary in Central and Eastern Europe: Mechanical Jurisprudence in Transformation?* (Leiden, Brill–Njihoff, 2011).

[6] Zsolt Boda and Gergő Medve-Bálint, 'The Politicised Nature of Many Eastern European Institutions Means that They Are Trusted Less than Those in Western Europe' London School of Economics and Political Science (21 August 2012) https://blogs.lse.ac.uk/europpblog/2012/08/21/institutional-trust-zsolt-boda/ (accessed 24 April 2019). See also Zsolt Boda and Gergő Medve-Bálint, 'Does Institutional Trust in East Central Europe Differ from Western Europe?' (2014) 3(2) *European Quarterly of Political Attitudes and Mentalities* 1; Simona Kukovič, '(Dis)trust in Political Institutions: Comparisons Between New Democracies of Central and Eastern Europe' (2013) 6 *Journal of Comparative Politics* 20; European Commission, 'The 2019 EU Justice Scoreboard' https://ec.europa.eu/info/sites/info/files/justice_scoreboard_2019_en.pdf (accessed 24 April 2019) Figure 47: 'Perceived independence of courts and judges among the general public', 44.

[7] Jernej Letnar Černič, 'Nezaupanje', *IUS-INFO*, 25 March 2013.

[8] Wojciech Sadurski, *Rights Before Courts: A Study of Constitutional Courts in Postcommunist States of Central and Eastern Europe*, 2th edn, (Dordrecht, Springer, 2014).

[9] Leonardo Morlino and Wojciech Sadurski (eds), *Democratization and the European Union: Comparing Central and Eastern European Post-communist Countries* (Abingdon, Routledge, 2010). See also András Sajó and Vera Losonci, 'Rule by Law in the East Central Europe: Is the Emperor's New Suit a Straitjacket?' in Douglas Greenberg, Stanlet N Katz, Melanie Beth Oliviero and Steven C Wheatley (eds), *Constitutionalism and Democracy: Transitions in the Contemporary World: The American Council of Learned Societies Comparative* (Oxford, Oxford University Press, 1993).

public administration elites, who have fiercely fought to retain their status quo.[10] Similar developments can be identified elsewhere in Central and Eastern Europe.[11] As a result, the absence of trust in institutions has prompted the formation of weak governing institutions.

Divided into four parts, this chapter begins in section II by examining the pitfalls of the past by describing and analysing the systematic and widespread human rights violations during the former Communist regime (1945–90) as the reasons for the present deficiencies of the rule of law in Slovenia. Section III then considers the application and effectiveness of transitional justice measures employed in the Slovenian context. In this respect, it first analyses the role of the Constitutional Court of Slovenia as a motor of transitional justice and then proceeds to examine the transitional justice measures, which consisted of opening the state security files, prosecution of alleged perpetrators of crimes against humanity and of other human rights violations, and lustration measures or the lack thereof. In so doing, it then critically considers the hurdles facing prosecutions of alleged perpetrators of crimes against humanity and gross human rights violations, and scrutinises the applicability of lustration measures (or the lack thereof). Section IV subsequently assesses the impact of unresolved past issues on the rule of law and democracy.

This chapter argues that the existence of historical failures reflecting in crimes against humanity and systematic human rights violations has contributed to the failures of the rule of law and constitutional democracy in Slovenia. Simultaneously, those historical failures have engendered a widespread belief that state institutions are neither fair nor professional, let alone impartial and independent in the execution of their competences.

[10] Letnar Černič (n 7).

[11] Sajó and Losonci (n 9) 321; Samuel Spac, 'Judiciary Development after the Breakdown of Communism in the Czech Republic and Slovakia' (2014) 9(3–4) *CEU Political Science Journal* 234; Alan Uzelac, 'Survival of the Third Legal Tradition?' (2010) 49 *Supreme Court Law Review* 377; Zoltán Fleck, 'Judicial Independence in Its Environment in Hungary' in Jiři Přibáň, Pauline Isobel Roberts and James Young (eds), *Systems of Justice in Transition Central European Experiences since 1989* (Dartmouth, Ashgate, 2003) 121; Peter Jambrek, 'Simbolna sporočila države in jedro slovenske ustavne identitete' *Delo-Sobotna priloga* (3 August 2013); Siniša Rodin, 'Functions of Judicial Opinion – A View from a Post-communist European State', www.pravo.unizg.hr/_download/repository/13_Rotterdam.pdf (accessed 24 April 2019); Zdeněk Kühn, 'The Authoritarian Legal Culture at Work: The Passivity of Parties and the Interpretational Statements of Supreme Courts' (2006) 2(2) *Croatian Yearbook of European Law and Policy* 19; Boštjan M Zupančič, 'Prolegomena to Comparative Law' in G Harutyunyan (ed), *New Millennium Constitutionalism: Paradigms of Reality and Challengens* (Yerevan, NJHAR, 2013) 367; Peter Jambrek, 'Pravice do svobode izobraževanja, do svobode znanosti in umetnosti ter do avtonomije univerze' (2012) 55/56 *Dignitas* 3–11; Igor Kaučič (ed), *Twenty years of the Constitution of the Republic of Slovenia: Significance of Constitutionality and Constitutional Democracy* (Ljubljana, Faculty of Law – Constitutional Court of the Republic of Slovenia, 2012); Andreas Voßkuhle, 'Quo Vadis, Europa?', Speech at Constitutional Court (Ljubljana, 19 December 2013).

II. THE PITFALLS OF THE PAST

A. Systematic and Widespread Human Rights Violations (1945–90)

The end of the World War II brought about one of the darkest chapters in recent Slovene history – crimes against humanity committed against civilians on Slovenian territory.[12] These postwar crimes were committed in over 700 different locations and resulted in the deaths of over 100,000 civilians.[13] These crimes against humanity were committed in clandestine locations – old mines, caves, forests and meadows – almost always hidden from the eyes of the public.[14] They were part of the systematic human rights violations committed across Slovenia during the Communist regime[15] as a general attack aimed at the civilian population. Ferenc argues 'it is not even known where [all these victims] lie, and they have never received a burial worthy of a human being'.[16] He continues that 'crimes were exacerbated by forced silence and suppression of the right to a grave' and that 'victims simply did not exist'.[17] Similarly, Dežman adds that:

> Killing civilians and prisoners of war after [the] Second World War is the greatest massacre of unarmed people of all [time] on Slovenian territory. Compared to Europe, the Yugoslav Communist massacres after the Second World War are probably right after the Stalinist purges and the Great Famine in the Ukraine. The number of those killed in Slovenia in [the] spring of 1945 can now be estimated at more than 100,000[.] Slovenia was the biggest post-War killing site in Europe. It was a mixture of events, when in Slovenia there are retreating German units, collaborator units, units of the Independent State of Croatia, Chetniks and Balkan civilians; more than 15,000 Slovenia inhabitants were murdered as well. Because of its brevity, number of casualties, way of execution and [enormous scale], it is an event that can be compared to the greatest crimes of Communism and National Socialism.[18]

[12] Jernej Letnar Černič, 'Od Barbarinega rova do rudnika Pečovnik', *IUS-INFO*, 4 November 2016.

[13] See Jože Dežman (ed) *Nemoč laži, Poročilo 4 Komisije Vlade RS za reševanje vprašanj prikritih grobišč* (Ljubljana, Družina doo, 2019). See also Pavel Jamnik, 'Post-World War Two Crimes on the Territory of Slovenia: Police Investigation and Proof Regarding Criminal Offences that Do Not Fall under the Statute of Limitations' in Peter Jambrek (ed), *Crimes Committed by Totalitarian Regimes* (Ljubljana, Slovenian Presidency of the Council of the European Union, 2008) 207. See also Jože Dežman, 'Communist Repression and Transitional Justice in Slovenia' in Jambrek (ibid) 204; and Jerca Vodušek Starič, 'Kako se čistila Jugoslavija?' (2004) 4/5 *Gordogan* 36–50. See also Jože Pučnik, 'Mass Post-War Killings' in Drago Jančar (ed), *The Dark Side of the Moon. A Short History of Totalitarianism in Slovenia 1945–1990* (Ljubljana, Museum of Recent History, 1998) 39–52.

[14] Mateja Jančar and Jernej Letnar Černič (eds), *Poročilo o pobojih: vmesno poročilo o raziskovanju povojnih množičnih pobojev Preiskovalne komisije Državnega zbora Republike Slovenije o raziskovanju povojnih množičnih pobojev, pravno dvomljivih procesov in drugih tovrstnih nepravilnosti, ki jo je vodil dr. Jože Pučnik*, (Ljubljana, Inštitut dr Jožeta Pučnika, 2010).

[15] Vladimir Tismaneanu, *The Devil in History: Communism, Fascism and Some Lessons of the Twentieth Century* (Berkeley, University of California Press, 2012).

[16] Mitja Ferenc, 'Secret World War Two Mass Graves in Slovenia' in Jambrek (n 13) 157.

[17] ibid.

[18] Dežman (n 13) 204.

Ferenc additionally observed that 'methodical record-keeping of secret mass graves only began in 2002, accompanied by a huge response in the media which was triggered by the recovery of 431 victims' bodies from two mineshafts in Zgornja Bistrica and in Štajerska'.[19] The Ministry of Labour, Family and Social Affairs of the Republic of Slovenia has catalogued 3,986 wartime graves and mass graves in Slovenia from World War II.[20] Additionally, the Commission for Settlement of Hidden Mass Gravesites of the Government of the Republic of Slovenia has so far identified over 700 secret post-World War II mass grave sites. (See Figure 3.1.)

Figure 3.1 Identified locations of mass killings on the territory of Slovenia, Source: Mitja Ferenc, *Topografija evidentiranih grobišč: Poročilo Komisije Vlade Republike Slovenije za reševanje vprašanj prikritih grobišč 2005–2008* (Ljubljana, Družina, 2008) 25.

These crimes were committed deliberately and systematically, and were part of a general state policy, ultimately directed against the civilian population.[21] Perhaps the most notorious instance of such crimes is the forced return in May 1945 of over 30,000 Slovenian refugees (mostly civilians, political opponents of the Communist Party from the British Occupation Zone in Carinthia who had been detained in a camp at Vetrinj) by British Army troops to Slovenian

[19] Ferenc (n 16) 158.

[20] ibid 155.

[21] For a detailed historical account, see Mitja Ferenc, *Topografija evidentiranih grobišč: Poročilo Komisije Vlade Republike Slovenije za reševanje vprašanj prikritih grobišč 2005–2008* (Ljubljana, Družina, 2008); Tamara Griesser-Pečar, *Razdvojeni narod: Slovenija 1941–1945, Okupacija, Kolaboracija, Državljanska Vojna, Revolucija* (Ljubljana, Mladinska knjiga, 2004). See also Public Exhibition, 'Prikrito in očem zakrito' (Ljubljana, Museum of Contemporary History, 2005). See also Lovro Šturm (ed), *Brez milosti: ranjeni, invalidni in bolni povojni ujetniki na Slovenskem* (Ljubljana, Nova revija, 2000).

partisans.[22] Most of them were later executed by Communist partisans in the forest of Kočevje.[23]

All 700-plus mass grave sites thus meet the criteria for crimes against humanity, and possibly even the chapeau requirements for the crime of genocide. The victorious side attempted to ensure unlimited power without any potential dissent, and therefore executed most of its potential opponents, irrespective of the fact that these mainly included the civilian population, women, the elderly and children.[24] They also exterminated the civilian population belonging to the German minority, although many of these had helped the partisan movement and opposed the national socialist ideology of the German occupiers. But little mercy was shown during this time.[25] As a rule, most people were executed as a warning to anyone thinking of opposing the communist regime. Despite some attempts, none of the perpetrators have been successfully prosecuted for these crimes.[26] In addition, several other systematic and general human rights violations were committed by the communist regime,[27] including show trials,[28] systematic violations of civil and political rights, and incarceration in concentration camps.[29] Nonetheless, the Slovenian authorities have so far in general turned a blind eye to such violations. As a result, the postwar atrocities have

[22] See Griesser-Pečar (n 21) 529.

[23] ibid 457. See also Anthony Cogwill, Thomas Brimelow and Christopher Booker, *The Repatriation from Austria in 1945. The Report of an Inquiry* (London, Sinclair Stevenson, 1990); Anthony Cogwill, *The Repatriation from Austria in 1945: Cowgill Inquiry: The Documentary Evidence Reproduced in Full from British, American, German and Yugoslav Sources* (London, Sinclair Stevenson, 1990); Ian David Mitchell, *The Cost of Reputation: Aldington Versus Tolstoy. The Causes, Course and Consequences of a Notorious Libel Case* (Edinburgh, Canongate, 1997); Nigel Nicholson, *Long Live* (New York, Putnam, 1998); John Corsellis and Marcus Ferrar, *Slovenia 1945: Memories of Death and Survival After World War II* (London, IB Tauris, 2005).

[24] Griesser-Pečar (n 21); Jančar and Letnar Černič (n 14).

[25] Šturm (ed) (n 21).

[26] See eg Jernej Letnar Černič, 'Supreme State Prosecutor v Ribičič (Mitja), Order on Whether to Open Pre-Trial Criminal Investigation', Ks 962/2006, *Oxford Reports on International Law in Domestic Courts* 523 (SI 2006) (Ljubljana, 27 June 2006) http://opil.ouplaw.com/view/10.1093/law:ildc/523si06.case.1/law-ildc-523si06 (accessed 24 April 2019).

[27] Lovro Šturm, 'O kratenju človekovih pravic in temeljnih svoboščin v Sloveniji v obdobju 1945–1950' in Drago Jančar (ed), *Temna stran meseca: kratka zgodovina totalitarizma v Sloveniji 1945–1990: Zbornik Člankov in dokumentov* (Ljubljana, Nova revija, 1998) 65–112; Tamara Griesser Pečar, 'Generalni register pojavov in žrtev totalitarizma' in Mateja Čoh, *Totalitarizmi-vprašanja in izzivi, Ob dvajsetletnici padca železne zavese v Evropi* (Ljubljana, Študijski center za narodno spravo, 2009) 33–46.

[28] Lovro Šturm, 'Revolucionarno kazensko pravo na Slovenskem po drugi svetovni vojni' in Mateja Čoh Kladnik (ed), *Brezpravje v imenu ljudstva: Zbirka Totalitarizmi- vprašanja in izzivi* 5 (Ljubljana, Študijski center za narodno spravo, 2016) 46–61. See also Gašper Dovžan and Urška Tekavec, 'Zgodovinski uvod v Komentar slovenske ustave. Temne strani slovenske pravne preteklosti v luči slovenske ustave: Argumenti Ustavnega sodišča Republike Slovenije o hudih množičnih in strukturnih kršitvah človekovih pravic in svoboščin v Sloveniji v času prevlade ideologije in prakse komunizma 1945–1990' (2001) 11/12 *Dignitas*.

[29] Peter Jambrek, 'Slovenska taborišča za prisilno delo – kdaj in zakaj' in Peter Jambrek (ed), *Ženska taborišča: ženska kazenska taborišča za prisilno delo v Sloveniji 1949–50* (Brdo pro Kranju, Fakulteta za državne in evropske študije, 2014) 13–20; Milko Mikola, *Kazenske ustanove in zaporniki v Sloveniji 1945–1951* (Ljubljana, Nova obzorja, 2016).

deeply impacted the daily functioning of Slovenian society and its constitutional democracy.

III. TRANSITIONAL JUSTICE MEASURES

After their democratisation, several CEE countries adopted effective measures to break away from the former totalitarian systems. Slovenia too has introduced a wide variety of formal transitional justice measures, both of individual and collective scope as well as of both a judicial and non-judicial nature. These have, inter alia, consisted of attempts to prosecute perpetrators of totalitarian crimes, to rehabilitate the victims of the totalitarian period and their relatives; to undertake restitution of the seized property, to undertake partial lustration measures, and opening of the state security files.[30] On a declarative level, those measures have facilitated the introduction of formal standards of constitutional democracy and the rule of law. The success rate of those measures has differed depending on their nature, scope, duration and objectives. The national transitional justice measures have been complemented by several ECtHR judgments addressing recent history, the rule of law and constitutional democracy.[31] Nonetheless, transitional justice in Slovenia has so far been ambivalent and inefficient. This section therefore examines selected national transitional justice measures. It first turns to the Constitutional Court of Slovenia as a motor of transitional justice.

A. The Constitutional Court as a Motor of Transitional Justice

The Slovenian Constitutional Court has, post-democratisation, taken up a seminal role in the country's transitional process, particularly in its first mandate immediately after democratisation in 1990–1. In so doing, it has joined other constitutional courts that have served as harbingers of democratic change and the rule of law in the past decades. For instance, the Colombian Constitutional Court is noted in the comparative constitutional practice for its successful role in the country's transitional process.[32] Daly notes that, in general, 'specialized

[30] See in detail Lovro Šturm, 'Ústavní souvislosti vyrovnávání se s totalitní minulostí ve Slovinsku' in Konference středoevropských ústavních soudů, *Vyrovnání se s komunistickou minulostí ve státech střední Evropy* (Brno, Linde Praha, 2003) 69–112.

[31] See eg cases such as: *Janowiec and others v Russia* (Grand Chamber) no 55508/07 and 29529/09 (ECtHR, 21 October 2013); *Naidin v Romania* no 38162/07 (ECtHR, 21 October 2014); *Ecaterina Mirea and Others v Romania* no 43626/13 et al (ECtHR, 12 April 2016); *Kolk and Kislyiy v Estonia* (Grand Chamber) no 23052/04 and 24018/04 (ECtHR, 17 January 2006).

[32] Rodrigo Uprimny, 'The Constitutional Court and Control of Presidential Extraordinary Powers in Colombia' in Siri Gloppen, Roberto Gargarella and Elin Skaar, *Democratization and the Judiciary: The Accountability Function of Courts in New Democracies* (London, Frank Cass, 2004); Rodrigo Uprimny, 'Judicialization of Politics in Colombia: Cases, Merits and Risks' (2007) 49(6) *SUR International Journal on Human Rights* 56–69.

constitutional courts have become a popular way of providing a new institution untainted by links with the prior regime, and avoiding the risk of politicization of the ordinary judiciary by giving the new court exclusive jurisdiction over constitutional questions'.[33] The rise of constitutional courts in Central and Eastern Europe since the 1990s has been a prime example of the former.[34] The Constitutional Court of Slovenia has long insisted that Slovenia is profoundly different from the former totalitarian Yugoslavia since it is based on the rule of law and protection of human rights. The Constitutional Court has, in particular, seeded rule-of-law de iure standards in the Slovenian constitutional system, contrary to what existed under the previous totalitarian regime. As a rule, the Slovenian Constitutional Court's jurisprudence on transitional justice is impressive. It has stressed the importance of the Basic Constitutional Charter on the Sovereignty and Independence of the Republic of Slovenia, which states that the former Yugoslavia 'does not function as a state governed by law and that within it human rights, national rights, and the rights of the republics and autonomous provinces are grossly violated'.[35] The Constitutional Court underlined that 'the former Yugoslav system … did not put human rights at the forefront and did not define any clear legal restrictions for the state authorities and their violence. Thus, it made arbitrary government possible.'[36] Individuals were 'subject to sustained and systematic threats to human rights and fundamental freedoms'.[37] More specifically, the Constitutional Court also declared that the former Yugoslavia was

> a state whose authorities had after the end of the war carried out mass executions of former military and current political opponents, legally unacceptable trials followed by death penalties, … thus making the injured parties afraid, with good reason, for their lives in case of residing in such a country.[38]

In this repect, the Constitutional Court identified the judiciary in the communist regimes as unfair and lacking in impartiality and independence. It stressed

[33] Tom Gerald Daly, 'The Judiciary and Constitutional Transitions', International Institute for Democracy and Electoral Assistance, Workshop Report, 14–15 November 2014, The Hague, 15.

[34] See eg Sadurski (n 8); See also Wojciech Sadurski, 'Transitional Constitutionalism versus the Rule of Law?' (2016) 8(2) *Hague Journal on the Rule of Law* 337; Wojciech Sadurski, 'A Response to Daniel Smilov and Michael Hein' (2015) 39(3) *Southeastern Europe* 431; Michel Rosenfeld, Wojciech Sadurski and Roberto Toniatti, 'Central and Eastern European Constitutionalism a Quarter Century After the Fall of the Berlin Wall: Introduction to the Symposium' (2015) 13(1) *International Journal of Constitutional Law* 119.

[35] The Basic Constitutional Charter on the Sovereignty and Independence of the Republic of Slovenia, Official Gazette of the Republic of Slovenia No 1I/1991, Preamble. See also Lovro Šturm, 'Pravna država' in Lovro Šturm (ed), *Komentar Ustave Republike Slovenie – Dopolnitev A* [*Commentary on the Constitution of the Republic of Slovenia – Supplement A*] (Ljubljana, Fakulteta za državne in evropske študije, 2011) 16–43. See also Lovro Šturm, *Omejitev oblasti: ustavna izhodišča javnega prava* (Ljubljana, Nova Revija, 1998) 23.

[36] Constitutional Court of Slovenia, Decision U-I-158/94, 9 March 1995, para 13.

[37] Constitutional Court of Slovenia, Decision U-I-121/97, 23 May 1997, separate opinion of Judge Lovro Šturm, para 2.

[38] Constitutional Court of Slovenia, Decision U-I-69/92, 10 December 1992, para 8.

in its decision U–I–107/96 that 'the courts at that time were not autonomous, independent and impartial. They were tools for carrying out the revolution, a whip in the hand of the people, effective means for the elimination of the people's enemies.'[39] It also declared in its decision U–I–247/96 that 'many political trials against industrialists and tradesmen were held, the purpose of which was confiscation of their property. There were also a number of proceedings against priests and monks … which were held to suppress verbal criticism of the authorities.'[40] As a rule, the law was used to protect and advance the interests of the governing totalitarian elites.

However, the primary landmark ruling of the Slovenian Constitutional Court in the field of transitional justice is the decision concerning Tito Street or more specifically the Ordinance on Determining and Changing the Names and Course of the Roads and Streets in the Territory of Ljubljana Municipality, where it upheld the individual but also the collective nature of human dignity.[41] The Court stipulated, in this decision, as already discussed in chapter 2, that:

> Human dignity is also at the centre of the constitutional order of the Republic of Slovenia. … Its ethical and constitutional significance already proceeds from the BCC [Basic Constitutional Charter], which is not only the constitutional foundation of Slovenian statehood, as also certain principles that demonstrate the fundamental legal and constitutional quality of the new independent and sovereign state are outlined therein. In its Preamble the BCC first proclaimed the fact that the SFRY [Socialist Federal Republic of Yugoslavia] did not function as a state governed by law and that within it human rights were grossly violated, while Section III, as the antipode to the above-mentioned, emphasized that the Republic of Slovenia would guarantee the protection of human rights and fundamental freedoms to all persons in the territory of the Republic of Slovenia irrespective of their national origin, without any discrimination whatsoever, in accordance with the Constitution of the Republic of Slovenia and the treaties in force. This new constitutional quality of the new state is even more clearly demonstrated in the Declaration of Independence.[42]

It further considered that 'differently than the former SFRY, the Republic of Slovenia is a state governed by the rule of law whose constitutional order proceeds from the principle of respect for human rights and fundamental freedoms already on the basis of the basic constitutional documents'.[43] It concluded its argumentation by affirming that:

> [T]he glorification of the Communist totalitarian regime by the authorities by naming a street after the leader of such regime is unconstitutional. Such new naming

[39] Constitutional Court of Slovenia, Decision U-I-107/96, 5 December 1996, para 29.

[40] Constitutional Court of Slovenia, Decision U-I-247/96, 22 October 1998, para 20.

[41] Constitutional Court of Slovenia, Decision U-I-109/10, 26 September 2011. See Chap 2 of this book for further analysis of this decision. See also also Jernej Letnar Černič, 'Človekovo dostojanstvo kot temelj vladavine prava v slovenski družbi' (2018) 78(1) *Bogoslovni vestnik* 147.

[42] Constitutional Court of Slovenia, Decision U-I-109/10, para 7.

[43] ibid, para 8.

> of a street no longer has a place here and now, as it is contrary to the principle of respect for human dignity, which is at the very core of the constitutional order of the Republic of Slovenia. Naming a street after Josip Broz Tito namely does not entail preserving a name from the former system and which today would only be a part of history. The challenged Ordinance was issued in 2009, eighteen years after Slovenia declared independence and established the constitutional order, which is based on constitutional values that are the opposite of the values of the regime before independence. Not only the victims or opponents of the former regime, but also other members of the public can understand such act of the authority at issue in the present time as newly emerged official support for the former Communist regime. Such act is contrary to the values on which the Constitution is based.[44]

The Slovenian Constitutional Court has therefore in several cases declared human rights violations committed by the previous regime as unconstitutional and contrary to the rule of law. It has thus joined other CEE constitutional courts, in particular that of Hungary,[45] in playing an important role in the transitional process. It has served as a transitory mediator, bridging the gap to the former totalitarian and undemocratic systems. Accordingly, Šturm rightly argues that 'the role of constitutional justice in new democracies is an indispensable constituent part of the process of transforming the post-totalitarian regime into a system of constitutional democracy with a free democratic society'.[46] The Slovenian Constitutional Court has therefore contributed to the formation of the formal standards of the rule of law and human rights, deriving them from those found in mature European liberal democracies.[47] It has introduced formal, fully fledged standards of constitutional democracy and the rule of law. On the other hand, its impact on the reform of the mentality of civil servants, public employees and holders of public offices and the daily application of the rule of law in practice has so far been limited. Encouraged by the Constitutional Court, the Supreme Court of Slovenia too has since democratisation rehabilitated several victims of human rights abuses, who were erroneously convicted under the former totalitarian regime. Moreover, Šturm notes that the Constitutional Court not only legally, but also symbolically attempted to remedy past injustices:

> The Constitutional Court, having its headquarters in Plečnik's palace, where the former Chamber of Trade, Crafts and Industry was located, on 28 October 1997 on the ground floor of the court located at Beethovnova ulica 10 in Ljubljana solemnly

[44] ibid, para 18.

[45] Gabor Halmai and Kim Scheppele, 'Living Well Is the Best Revenge: The Hungarian Approach to Judging the Past' in A James McAdams (ed), *Transitional Justice and the Rule of Law in New Democracies* (Notre Dame, University of Notre Dame Press, 1997).

[46] Lovro Šturm, Constitutional Court review of mass and systematic violations of human rights and redress of injustices, Ljubljana, November 2016, on file with authors, 1.

[47] Lech Garlicki, 'Cooperation of Courts: The Role of Supranational Jurisdictions in Europe' (2008) 6 *International Journal of Constitutional Law* 509.

> erected a permanent memorial plaque to members of the chamber who were victims of the revolutionary terror after 1945. Because they were denied free entrepreneurial initiative and their property was seized, their human dignity trampled on or personal freedom taken, 40,000 members of the former chamber were affected; when taking into account their family members, more than 150,000 people were harmed. To intimidate the people, at that time very striking death penalties were passed and executed immediately. By erecting the plaque as a sign of reverence for the victims, their complete rehabilitation was made at a symbolic level.[48]

Similar developments can be observed across Central and Eastern Europe.[49] Nonetheless, the developments elsewhere in the region are not conclusive.[50] Halmai argues that in Central and Eastern Europe 'transitional justice became a substitute idealism for trying to invigorate new democratic regimes without strong democratic prehistory relatively quickly after transitions'.[51] He adds that 'the Central European experience shows that it is relatively easy to introduce institutions of constitutional law, such as those of transitional justice, but they cannot work without constitutional culture'.[52] In this vein, Kuti, for instance, argues that constitutional courts remained 'far from consequent and conclusive, as they sometimes either upheld problematic provisions, or contributed, through their decisions, to the enhancement of confusion and perpetuation of injustice'.[53] As a result, constitutional courts have through their impact on at least the de jure rule of law fostered their legitimacy in new liberal democracies.[54] Another similar observation has been made by Svetlana Aleksijevič, which was quoted at the start of this chapter. Slovenia, as most CEE countries, therefore appears to suffer from the fact that liberal democratic values have not been fully internalised due to resistance from institutional elites and ordinary people. We can agree with Sadurski, who finds that 'the "record card" of constitutional courts in Central and Eastern Europe, as far as the protection of constitutional rights and the policing of constitutional allocation of powers are concerned, is on

[48] Lovro Šturm, 'Slovenia. Law and Non-Law after 1941' (2016) on file with authors, 14.

[49] Renata Uitz, 'Constitutional Courts and the Past in Democratic Transition' in Adam Czarnota, Martin Krygier and Wojciech Sadurdski (eds), *Rethinking the Rule of Law after Communism* (Budapest, Central European University Press, 2005).

[50] Leonard M Hammer and Frank Emmert (eds), *The European Convention on Human Rights and Fundamental Freedoms in Central and Eastern Europe* (The Hague, Eleven International Publishing, 2012).

[51] Gabor Halmai, 'The Role of Constitutionalism in Central Europe's Transitional Justice Processes', paper prepared for ICTJ, 2005, EUI Working Paper https://me.eui.eu/gabor-halmai/wp-content/uploads/sites/385/2016/10/constitutions_and_tj_halmai_longacceptedallchanges.pdf, 43 (accessed 24 April 2019).

[52] ibid. See also Letnar Černič (n 4).

[53] Csongor Kuti, *Post-Communist Restitution and the Rule of Law* (Budapest, Central European University Press, 2009) 292, 293.

[54] Wojciech Sadurski (ed), *Constitutional Justice, East and West: Democratic Legitimacy and Constitutional Courts in Post-Communist Europe in a Comparative Perspective* (The Hague, Kluwer Law International, 2003); Sadurski (n 8).

balance positive'.[55] Perhaps the impact of the Constitutional Court of Slovenia could be rated in terms of its positive contribution to the rule of law in the Slovenian constitutional system even more positively than its CEE counterparts.

B. Opening of the State Security Archives

Free access to archives has proved crucial for the functioning of a state based on constitutional democracy and the rule of law. In order to protect human dignity, it is important to protect the personal data of victims of totalitarian systems. Access to the archives of non-democratic regimes realises the fundamental principles of constitutional democracy, including transparency, accountability, the rule of law and respect for fundamental human rights.[56] The Principles of Access to Archives of the International Archives Council provide in Article 1 that 'The public has the right of access to archives of public bodies. Both public and private entities should open their archives to the greatest extent possible.'[57] Article 2 stipulates that 'institutions holding archives make known the existence of the archives, including the existence of closed materials, and disclose the existence of restrictions that affect access to the archives'.[58] In Slovenia access to archives has been particularly important as they contain materials from the secretive official journals of the former regime and supervision reports of the UDBA, who supervised and spied on the lives of thousands.[59] However, most of the UDBA archives have been destroyed or stolen, with only a few files left intact.[60] As it stands, access to the archives is regulated by the Act on the Protection of Documentary and Archival Materials and Archives, which provides in section 1 of Article 63 that 'public archival material … in archives on the basis of a written request for use or through online publication is accessible to everyone'. Yet in practice even professional researchers have encountered difficulties in accessing the archival materials.[61] The Act, for instance, notes in section 1 of Article 65 that 'public archives containing information relating to state and public security, defence, foreign affairs or intelligence and security activity of

[55] Wojciech Sadurski, 'Postcommunist Constitutional Courts in Search of Political Legitimacy', EUI LAW Working Paper no 2001/11, p. 52.

[56] Jernej Letnar Černič, 'Ustavnopravni in mednarodni vidiki svobode do dostopa do arhivov' in Damjan Hančič, Gregor Jenuš and Neža Strajnar (eds), *Odstiranje zamolčanega: Zbornik prispevkov. Zbirka Totalitarizmi – vprašanja in izzivi*, 3 (Ljubljana, Študijski center za narodno spravo, 2013) 338–560.

[57] International Council on Archives, Principles of Access to Archives, principle 1 www.ica.org/en/principles-access-archives (accessed 24 April 2019).

[58] ibid, principle 2.

[59] See eg Jernej Letnar Černič, Svoboda dostopa do arhivov (2011) 9 *Pravna praksa* 20.

[60] Jože Pučnik, *Iz arhivov slovenske politične policije* (Ljubljana, Veda, 1996).

[61] Act Amending the Protection of Documents and Archives and Archival Institutions, Official Gazette of the Republic of Slovenia No 51/14.

a State ... become available for use, as a rule, no later than 40 years after the occurrence'.[62] As a result, the conditions for accessing the archives have been quite rigorous thereby limiting full access to the existing archives of the former regime. Nonetheless, the opening of the archives has at least partially afforded a glimpse of the modus operandi of the former totalitarian regime and of the individuals who continue to hold public functions in the newly created democratic institutions.

C. Prosecution of Alleged Perpetrators of Crimes against Humanity and Human Rights Violations

State authorities are obliged to conduct careful and objective investigations into genocide and crimes against humanity that occurred after World War II and the individual responsibility of their perpetrators.[63] They are obliged to do whatever possible to identify which individuals in the former communist regime are responsible for committing any crimes against humanity.[64] Such obligations not only derive from public interest but also from the right of victims' families to know how a systematic and universal plan for the killing of thousands took place.[65] The state obligation to investigate and prosecute is a positive obligation that requires active measures and action.[66] As a rule, the Slovenian authorities have so far not been very successful in prosecuting the perpetrators of crimes against humanity and systematic human rights violations.[67] Although some attempts have been made to prosecute those responsible for crimes against humanity, only a few cases have in fact been considered by the prosecution and even fewer have been brought before the courts. Perhaps the most notorious has been the case of *Prosecutor v Ribičič*.[68] As we have already described elsewhere:

> The Investigating Court found that no investigation could be opened against Ribičič on two grounds: legal and evidential. First, the investigating court argued that Ribičič could not be tried for crimes against humanity, since Article 3 of the Criminal Code provides that the perpetrator of a criminal offence be subject to the statutory provisions applicable at the time the offence was committed. Second, the investigating judge opined that no strong evidence had been submitted indicating Ribičič's influence in deciding whether a certain group of people should be killed, as the prosecution failed to present evidence amounting to probable cause that Mitja Ribičič had played a significant role in issuing the orders for the commission of mass killings. The Chamber of the High Court of Republic Slovenia in Ljubljana examined the appeal

[62] ibid.
[63] Letnar Černič (n 12).
[64] ibid.
[65] ibid.
[66] ibid.
[67] ibid.
[68] Letnar Černič (n 26).

> filed by the Supreme State Prosecutor and analysed the decision of the investigating magistrate of the District Court. It held that there were in fact legal grounds to try Ribičič for crimes against humanity given sufficient evidence, but nevertheless agreed with the Investigating Court that the prosecution had failed to meet this standard. The Decree on Military Courts of 24 May 1944 already provided legal basis for prosecution of war crimes and crimes against humanity as it was in 1994 confirmed by decision of the Constitutional Court of Republic of Slovenia.[69]

However, we noted in 2014 that 'opening the investigation for crimes committed so many decades ago would deepen disagreement between different parts of Slovenian society and would hinder the path towards reconciliation between members of the former Communist Party and the rest of the society'.[70] Additionally, several indirect perpetrators from among the highest ranks of the then authorities, who allegedly ordered the killings, have already died, making prosecutions more difficult.[71]

State investigation of these worst crimes on Slovenian territory has been deficient.[72] It seems more appropriate to leave such investigations and potential prosecutions to the reputable, independent and impartial foreign police and criminal prosecution experts who would work immune from the daily pressures faced by Slovenian judicial authorities.[73] As state authorities have been unable or unwilling to conduct proper investigations, civil society initiatives and enthusiastic individuals and experts have stepped in to carry the majority of the burden.[74] In particular, the Slovenian judiciary could have been more actively involved in securing diligent and effective investigations.[75] Nonetheless, the procedural obligations under the right to life require that when excavating and burying the victims' remains, genuine efforts must be made to investigate all the circumstances surrounding postwar homicides and to identify the responsible, whether alive or already dead.[76] Undoubtedly, crimes against humanity serve as a reminder that such heinous acts are never again to be repeated.[77] Until then, civil society will continue to draw the attention of Slovenian authorities to their unfulfilled procedural obligations.[78]

[69] Jernej Letnar Černič, 'Consolidating Democracy Through Transitional Justice in Slovenia: Lessons Learnt?' in Agata Fijalkowski and Raluca Grosescu (eds), *Transitional Criminal Justice in Post-Dictatorial and Post-Conflict Societies* (Cambridge, Intersentia, 2015) 153.

[70] ibid 157. See also attempts to prosecute other allegedly responsible individuals, namely Vinko Kosovel: Anton Kosovel and Vladimir Kavčič(eds), *Zločin brez kazni* (Ljubljana, Slovenska matica, 2003); and Martin Štorgelj: Martin Ozmec, 'Zaradi pomanjkanja dokazov je sodišče zadevo ustavilo' *Štajerski tednik* (30 January 2014), https://sterntal.wordpress.com/2014/02/03/zaradi-pomanjkanja-dokazov-je-sodisce-zadevo-ustavilo/ (accessed 24 April 2019).

[71] Letnar Černič (n 69) 157.

[72] ibid.

[73] ibid.

[74] ibid.

[75] ibid.

[76] ibid.

[77] ibid.

[78] ibid.

D. Lustration Measures (or the Lack Thereof)

The prohibition of public officials and politicians in the totalitarian regimes from taking up posts in state institutions and public administration in the new constitutional democracies has been one of most popular measures potentially contributing to the construction of the rule of law in transitional societies. For instance, the Parliamentary Assembly of the Council of Europe stated in its Resolution 1096 (1996) that lustration measures are employed 'to exclude persons from exercising governmental power if they cannot be trusted to exercise it in compliance with democratic principles, as they have shown no commitment to or belief in them in the past'.[79] However, it noted that 'measures can be compatible with a democratic state under the rule of law if several criteria are met. Firstly, guilt, being individual, rather than collective, must be proven in each individual case.'[80] It added that 'secondly, the right of defence, the presumption of innocence until proven guilty, and the right to appeal to a court of law must be guaranteed'.[81] Interestingly, Slovenia has so far also employed some minimal measures to limit the members of the former communist regime from accessing public functions in the newly formed democracy. However, its lustration measures have not been as wide reaching as in some other CEE countries. Generally, the ECtHR has allowed state parties a wide margin of appreciation concerning lustration measures. It observed in *Naidin v Romania* that: 'States have a legitimate interest in regulating the conditions and access to jobs in public administration. The democratic state has the right to demand from its employees that they are loyal to the constitutional principles that justify them.'[82]

Slovenia has not introduced any prohibition on former officials of the totalitarian regime accessing public functions in the executive and legislative branches of the newly formed democratic state. No prohibitions have been so far imposed even for the agents of the former state security police. Nor has any prohibition been adopted for any teaching staff, from primary school to university, which is a far cry from the measures adopted, for example, throughout East Germany after democratisation and unification. All professors who had taught at universities in the communist regime retained their posts, even though since the 1970s the communist authorities had conducted purges among the university professors

[79] Council of Europe, Parlimentary Assembly, Resolution 1096 (1996) on Measures to dismantle the heritage of former communist totalitarian systems, 27 June 1996, para 11.

[80] ibid, para 12.

[81] ibid.

[82] *Naidin v Romania* no 38162/07 (ECtHR, 21 October 2014). See also *Sidabras and Džiautas v Lithuania* no 55480/00 and 59330/00 (ECtHR, 27 July 2004); *Vogt v Germany* no 17851/91 (ECtHR, 26 September 1995); *Ždanoka v Latvia* (Grand Chamber) no 58278/00 (ECtHR, 16 March 2006); *Rainys and Gasparavičius v Lithuania* no 70665/01 and 74345/01 (ECtHR, 7 April 2005); *Turek v Slovakia* no 58278/00 (ECtHR, 14 February 2006); *Matyjek v Poland* no 38184/03 (ECtHR, 24 April 2007).

to ensure the desired ideological homogeneity.[83] The absence of any lustration measures in the executive and legislative branches reveals the nature and scope of the informal networks of the members of the former totalitarian regimes who successfully lobbied against the imposition of any bans. Such lack of any prohibition caused long-lasting consequences in the first decade of the institutional life of the newly democratised and independent state, which fought at that time against the capture of the state by the elites of the former totalitarian regimes.[84] The only exception to the general amnesty of public officials has been the judiciary. On a declarative level, the Judicial Service Act provided in paragraph 3 of Article 8 that:

> Judges who have tried or ruled in investigative and judicial proceedings in which the fundamental human rights and freedoms were violated by a judgment, after the expiry of their term of office, do not fulfil the conditions for election to judicial office.[85]

This provision, also known as the Pučnik Amendment, was also subject to review and was upheld by the Constitutional Court, which held that:

> [I]t is evident that, from the point of view of the principle of the state governed by the rule of law, it is on the one hand impossible to contest the legitimacy of the lawgiver in the transitional period to set such a condition for the performance of judicial functions, while it is on the other hand necessary to ensure that such a condition will be interpreted and applied only in accordance with constitutionally admissible interpretation, as is required by the principle of the state governed by the rule of law, so as to ensure the protection of rights and prevent any abuse of such provision. From the foregoing it is evident that this has been ensured by the legal regulation, which is why the disputed provision is not in conflict with Article 2 of the Constitution.[86]

However, despite the existence of an explicit legal basis for the lustration of the judiciary, it was applied only in very few cases. This has prompted Zobec and Letnar Černič to conclude that 'the judicial transition to a liberal democracy based on the rule of law has therefore taken place with the old personnel (trained in socialism)'.[87] All of this has affected the current state of the rule of

[83] Manja Klemenčič, Sjur Bergan and Rok Primožič, *Student Engagement in Europe: Society, Higher Education and Student Governance* (Strasbourg, Council of Europe Higher Education Series no 20, 2015) 73.

[84] See eg '"Pravnik v današnjem času" (uvodno predavanje na 30. Dnevih slovenskih pravnikov) ["Lawyer in Current Times", The Introductory Lecture at the 30th Day of Slovene Lawyers]' (2004) 36 Pravna praksa 4; Vladimira Dvořáková and Anđelko Milardović (eds), *Lustration and Consolidation of Democracy and the Rule of Law in Central and Eastern Europe* (Zagreb, Political Science Research Centre, 2007) 169.

[85] Judicial Service Act, Official Gazette of the Republic of Slovenia No 94/07, official consolidated text 91/09, 33/11, 46/13, 63/13, 69/13 amend, 95/14–ZUPPJS15, 17/15 and 23/17, Art 8(3).

[86] Constitutional Court of Slovenia, Decision U-I-83/94, 14 July 1994, s 1.

[87] Jan Zobec and Jernej Letnar Černič, 'The Remains of the Authoritarian Mentality Within the Slovene Judiciary' in Michal Bobek (ed), *Central European Judges Under the European Influence: The Transformative Power of the EU Revisited* (Oxford, Hart Publishing, 2015) 125, 136.

law in Slovenia as the human resources have not substantially changed since the democratisation. As a result, it has been very difficult to move from the rule of law de jure to the rule of law de facto in the life of democratic institutions of transitional states.

IV. THE IMPACT OF THE UNRESOLVED PAST ON THE RULE OF LAW AND DEMOCRACY

The undemocratic past has certainly affected the quality of the rule of law and constitutional democracy in Slovenia. It appears that Slovenia and beyond are still haunted by the spirit of Václav Havel's 1979 essay 'The Power of the Powerless'.[88] His metaphor of a kiosk owner who sells fruit and vegetables still holds weight in most CEE societies. This greengrocer puts on a window sill of his kiosk, beside the onions and carrots, a flyer with the slogan: 'Workers of the world, unite!'[89] Havel asks why the seller placed the flyer on the window sill?[90] What does he wish to communicate?[91] Does he really care about workers around the world? An office worker who displays a poster on the internal and external walls of their office is no different from the vegetable seller. The posters which are displayed are both interrelated and interdependent.[92] One would not exist without the other. Everything, says Havel, is in place to maintain stability, peace and public order.[93] The seller and employee at the same time become a victim of the system and its key components. Havel maintains that this is social totalitarianism which does not come from top down, but works the other way around: from the bottom up. In such a system, all persons are required to maintain the system and the level of their individual responsibility only depends on their position in the system hierarchy. The system does not compel greater obedience since it creates itself.

Whereas Slovenia has on its initiative and due to the influences of various European institutions introduced formal rule-of-law reforms and structured its institutions following the model of established Western liberal democracies, it appears to have failed to fully internalise the rule-of-law values in its institutional life. As it stands, its people have not been able to fully change all their old habits of 'dirty togetherness' into practices of integrity and transparency working for the common good. Moreover, the Parliamentary Assembly of the Council of Europe has observed in its Resolution 1481 (2006), which has yet to be adopted by the Slovenian Parliament, that 'the fall of totalitarian Communist

[88] Václav Havel, 'Power of Powerless', Letter, October 1978.
[89] ibid, 1–2.
[90] ibid.
[91] ibid.
[92] ibid.
[93] ibid.

regimes ... has not been followed in all cases by an international investigation of the crimes committed by them. ... [T]he authors of these crimes have not been brought to trial by the international community'.[94] It added that 'public awareness of crimes committed by totalitarian Communist regimes is very poor'[95] and 'moral assessment and condemnation of crimes committed play an important role in the education of young generations'.[96] However, recent history holds Slovenian society a prisoner as its everyday decisions remain subject to different interpretations of past violations. As a rule, abuses from the past are, with some exceptions,[97] missing from textbooks on recent history in primary and secondary schools. The same applies to the presentation of the unresolved past in state museums or the presence of past totalitarian symbols in the names of the cities, squares, streets and schools. The crimes and human rights violations from the unresolved past, particularly those committed under the communist regime, have therefore been disappearing from the collective memory. In spite of this, most of population has not subscribed to the old practices often connected with state elites and their networks. The post-totalitarian elites have continued to be influential in the social, economic and cultural life of Slovenian society. As a result, democratisation and independence have not been able to unilaterally fully instrument the reform of elites as informal networks have managed to maintain the status quo and retain their positions. Moreover, the former communist elites have almost completely usurped the public institutions where they have advanced their own arbitrary interests.

Nonetheless, the transitional measures described above have to some extent affected the rule of law in Slovenia, mostly under the influence of Western European institutions.[98] The impact has been threefold. First, the transitional justice measures have produced both positive and negative individual and general impacts. In this respect, it seems that the individual measures taken to achieve transitional justice have generated a wider impact, particularly as there was no consensus on general measures to prosecute perpetrators of systematic human rights violations. Particularly successful were measures concerning rehabilitation of the victims of the totalitarian system and denationalisation (which is still ongoing) aimed at the return of confiscated property to its rightful owners. However, those measures could only have been invoked by the surviving victims and their relatives. Those who died or were arbitrarily killed and had no relatives to make claims were denied any justice. The perpetrators and their relatives

[94] Council of Europe, Parliamentary Assembly, 'Need for International Condemnation of Crimes of Totalitarian Communist Regimes', Resolution 1481 (2006), Assembly debate on 25 January 2006.

[95] ibid, para 6.

[96] ibid, para 7.

[97] See eg Daša Ganna Mahmoud, Elissa Tawitian and Mateja Zupančič, *Jaz, Midva, Mi* (Ljubljana, Rokus Klett, 2018).

[98] Wojciech Sadurski, 'Partnering with Strasbourg: Constitutionalisation of the European Court of Human Rights, the Accession of Central and East European States to the Council of Europe, and the Idea of Pilot Judgements' (2009) 9(3) *Human Rights Law Review* 397.

have in some cases occupied properties arbitrarily seized from their rightful owners after World War II. As a result, such facts still cause and maintain a deep sense of injustice not only among several social groups in Slovenia, but also in the Slovenian diaspora around the world. The suffering of victims and relatives has been, on the other hand, exploited and manipulated by various centre-right political forces, most often to mobilise their traditional electorate. Second, the Constitutional Court of the Republic of Slovenia, was able, as pointed out in detail above, to condemn the abuses of the rule of law and the systematic violations of human rights and fundamental freedoms in the totalitarian system. It has in several cases clarified that the newly formed Slovenian state and its legal system are qualitatively better and different from the former totalitarian legal system. Less successful have been attempts to prosecute the perpetrators of crimes against humanity and systematic human rights violations, where prosecutions have yet, due to a number of obstacles, to result in criminal convictions. The same applies for lustration measures to prohibit former public officials or functionaries of the communist regimes from accessing positions in state institutions. As noted, only a few persons have been successfully removed from the judiciary. Third, the opening of the state security files has been partially successful. Victims and researchers have been able to access only some files, although the vast majority has been destroyed.

As a result, these transitional justice measures have due to their piecemeal nature negatively affected the institutional life of the Slovenian state during the first three decades of democracy. In this respect, three categories of criticism can be levelled. First, people who previously in the totalitarian state occupied public functions have in most cases maintained their positions after democratisation, particularly in the judiciary, given the absence of effective lustration measures immediately after democratisation. Human factors have therefore impeded any break from practices of the former totalitarian regimes. What has attracted the attention of external observers is that individuals who violated human rights under the previous regime, still in 2019, almost 30 years after democratisation, occupy some of the highest posts in all three branches of government.[99] Second, a culture of impunity and fear has been created, where perpetrators of the most heinous acts have gone unpunished and the victims or their relatives have lived in fear or have been forced to leave Slovenia. This culture of impunity and fear has subconsciously affected the functioning of the society as a whole and created a resistance against the introduction of liberal values, and particularly against their internalisation in many aspects of daily life. Third, the rule of law has, due to the above two factors, been subjected to clientelistic and nepotistic interests of different informal groups and to partisanship of governmental elites deriving from the former system.[100] Zobec and Černič have therefore in

[99] See eg Jernej Kosec, 'How Communist Is the Judiciary in Slovenia? A Survey', CRCE Briefing Paper, July 2018.

[100] France Bučar, *Demokracija in kriza naših ustavnih institucij* (Ljubljana, Nova revija, 1998) 134, 135.

respect of the judiciary observed that 'nearly twenty-five years since the judiciary became a sovereign and independent branch of power, the remnants of the old mentality, based on authoritarian culture ... remain'.[101] They added that 'even a gradual influx of new judges does not significantly alter the legacy of the (pre)dominant corporate and authoritative mind-set that was inherited from the totalitarian period. ... The forma mentis of the Slovene judiciary remains always the same.'[102] Other authors have reported similar developments elsewhere in Central and Eastern Europe.[103]

Its totalitarian past has undoubtedly affected the daily functioning of the rule of law within Slovenia's state institutions. First, it has turned the rule of law in institutions of all three branches into rule by law at least in the formal de jure perspective.[104] Second, it has influenced the protection of human rights and fundamental freedoms in Slovenia, which has remained ineffective, selective and unequal, and has often, despite the equal nature of human rights, given priority to those human rights violations that are closer to the dominant ideology of the state institutions and of the informal groups connected with them.[105] Third, the application and interpretation of the rule of law de jure appears to have been in the everyday practice of Slovenian institutions subjected to parochial interests, which have often blocked the necessary reforms.[106] Fourth, Slovenia, like most other CEE countries, has introduced a modern constitutional democracy and the rule of law. However, such developments have not been joined by a change in the mentality of the institutional elites. As a result, although human dignity was formally translated in Slovenian society, it has not been internalised by the vast majority of the population as an individual and collective value that underpins its daily functioning. Civil and political rights have therefore been made available, but have been frequently manipulated by the major media outlets backed by the government and informal networks.[107]

More specifically, as described in the previous chapter,[108] the elites of the former totalitarian regime have since democratisation given the appearance of embracing democracy and the rule of law. However, in the reality they have not relinquished the arbitrary practices of the former regime.[109] In short, the rule of law and human rights protections have been regularly and systematically

[101] Zobec and Letnar Černič (n 87) 148.
[102] ibid.
[103] Spac (n 11) 24ff; see Uzelac (n 11) 388; Zdeněk Kühn (n 5) 147.
[104] András Sajó and Vera Losonci (n 9) 322.
[105] See eg Avbelj (n 3); and Jernej Letnar Černič, *Slovenija na razpotju: Geneza varstva človekovih pravic v slovenski družbi* (Kranj, Nova univerza – Fakulteta za državne in evropske študije, 2018).
[106] See Chap 2 of this book.
[107] ibid.
[108] ibid. See also Avbelj (n 3).
[109] Jernej Letnar Černič, 'Petindvajset let kasneje' in Dean Komel and Tomaž Zalaznik (eds), *Spoprijem z razmerami in razmerji v Sloveniji* (Ljubljana, Inštitut Nove Revije, 2017). See also Chaps 10 and 11 of this book.

employed in political and ideological disputes as instruments for the realisation of parochial interests.[110] As a result, our conclusions are not based solely on the analysis in the ensuing chapters but also on reports of international organisations and judgments of the European courts.[111]

V. CONCLUSION

Slovenian society and the institutions of constitutional democracy have long suffered from systematic and overwhelming human rights violations. In general, these violations have been only partially and arbitrarily addressed following democratisation. However, a fully developed response has been absent. The rules, tools and institutions for transitional justice have been indeed seeded in the Slovenian domestic legal system, but they have not been properly applied. They have failed to displace the old mentality of 'business as usual' in Slovenian institutions, public administration and beyond. The past therefore remains deeply present in the everyday life of Slovenian society. Clearly, the rule of law cannot function properly only on a de jure level.[112] It needs to be introduced also into the practice of the institutions of any state that elects to follow the rule of law. In this respect, it has to be translated from books to the values and mentality of individuals who occupy essential functions in all three branches of government, public administration and also in the private sphere. Slovenia has, in general, been slow in its attempts to prosecute perpetrators of totalitarian crimes, to rehabilitate the victims of the totalitarian period and their relatives, in undertaking lustration, and in opening up the state security files, but has proved to be pioneer in responding to the unresolved past through the decisions of its Constitutional Court.

[110] ibid.

[111] ibid.

[112] cf Bojan Bugarič and Alenka Kuhelj, 'Slovenia in Crisis: A Tale of Unfinished Democratization in East-Central Europe' (2015) 48(4) *Communist and Post-Communist Studies* 273; and Matej Avbelj, 'Zadeva Patria – (ne)pravo v kontekstu' (2014) 26 *Pravna Praksa* II.

4

The (Non) Reforms of Slovenia's Economy

The right to choose. The rule of law. We need even more than these to promote and protect liberty.[1]

I. INTRODUCTION

SLOVENIA'S ECONOMY EXPERIENCED various ups and downs before and after the beginning of the 20th century, when it was part of the Austro-Hungarian (Habsburg) empire. Afterwards it was part of various[2] South Slavic entities,[3] and during this period experienced rapid economic growth until the 1930s. After World War II, however, as part of the Socialist Federal Republic of Yugoslavia (SFRY), it started stagnating and eventually began to lag behind.[4]

Nevertheless, compared to other members of the federation, Slovenia was in a privileged position at the end of the 1980s, when the SFRY started falling apart. It was the wealthiest and most Western-oriented member of the SFRY, generating 18 per cent of the federation's social production and 20 per cent of its industrial production with only 8 per cent of the population. Its unemployment rate, at 3.2 per cent, was about one-fifth that of the SFRY as a whole, and productivity was at least twice the national average. Slovenia was also SFRY's window to the Western world.[5]

[1] Margaret Thatcher, Speech at Monash University, 1981 Sir Robert Menzies Lecture (Melbourne, 6 October 1981).

[2] First it was the less-known State of Slovenes, Croats and Serbs, established on 29 October 1918. The new state only actually existed for just over a month, but politically and administratively it was a 'confederal republic', in which Slovenes governed themselves for the first time. After that (December 1918) it was the Kingdom of Serbs, Croats and Slovenes. This was discussed further in Chap 2.

[3] Peter Štih, Vasko Simoniti and Peter Vodopivec, *A Slovene History. Society, Politics, Culture* (Ljubljana, Inštitut za novejšo zgodovino, 2009).

[4] Gorazd Justinek and Katja Lautar, 'Slovensko gospodarstvo med preteklostjo in prihodnostjo' in M Avbelj et al. (ed), *Evropska Slovenija* (Ljubljana, Inštitut Nove revije, zavod za humanistiko, 2013).

[5] Carlos Silva-Jáuregui, 'Macroeconomic Stabilization and Sustainable Growth' in M Mrak et al (ed), *Slovenia: From Yugoslavia to the European Union* (Washington, DC, World Bank, 2004) 116.

When Slovenia gained independence in 1991, the country's entire economic and monetary system[6] experienced a shock, since it had to change from a centrally planned to a free market economy.[7] Yet, as already mentioned, compared to other transitional economies (Slovakia, the Czech Republic, the Baltic states) at the beginning of the 1990s, Slovenia was fortunately much more developed and economically advanced,[8] which was mostly due to past economic development and reforms already carried out during the Habsburg era. Consequently, it was in a position to choose whether this transition should be achieved through gradualism or shock therapy. The first concept prevailed, for inter alia economic reasons, and gave relatively good results at the beginning of the 1990s. However, in the following years, this approach began to hinder any serious systemic reforms, especially in the judiciary, labour market, pensions system, healthcare, etc.

Nevertheless, Slovenia achieved all its important political, economic and diplomatic goals in its first 15 years of independence. It became a full EU member in May 2004, the first of the former SFRY republics to do so. In 2007 it fulfilled the Maastricht criteria as the first 'new' EU Member State and joined the eurozone.[9] In 2008 Slovenia took over the presidency of the EU Council, again as the first 'new' Member State to do so, and at that time had already reached 90 per cent of the average development of EU Member States, measured in GDP per capita.[10]

However, with the end of 2008 all the dreams of the best 'student', as Slovenia was often referred to, collapsed. Slovenia's economy was completely unprepared for the global financial and economic crisis, and recorded one of the largest falls in economic growth of the EU Member States in 2009, namely a fall of 7.8 per cent.[11] In the following years Slovenia was almost going towards the Greek scenario of a bailout, but escaped the claws of the debt crisis at the last minute, mainly due to the excellent performance of its exporters and a more positive global economic climate.[12] Guardiancich[13] also believed that the country seriously risked becoming the next in line for an international bailout, a puzzling scenario for a country that until then was considered the most prosperous and stable of the post-socialist states.

[6] Andrej Rant, 'Establishing Monetary Sovereignty' in Mrak et al, ibid 84.

[7] Jože P Damijan, 'Reentering the Markets of the Former Yugoslavia' in Mrak et al, ibid 336.

[8] Agnus Madison, *The World Economy: A Millennial Perspective*, Historical Statistics Vol 2 (Paris, OECD, 2007) 172–77.

[9] Janez Potočnik and Jaime Garcia Lombardero, 'Slovenia's Road to Membership in the European Union' in Mrak et al (n 5) 368.

[10] Gorazd Justinek, 'The Slovenian Economy: Yesterday and Today' in F Adam (ed), *Slovenia: Social, Economic and Environmental Issues* (New York, Nova Science, 2017) 120.

[11] www.stat.si.

[12] Gorazd Justinek, 'Izvoz rešuje slovensko rast' (2015) 23(2) *Ocena konjukturnih gibanj za Slovenijo* 23–24.

[13] Igor Guardiancich, 'Slovenia: The End of a Success Story? When a Partial Reform Equilibrium Turns Bad' (2016) 68(2) *Europe-Asia Studies* 205.

Nevertheless, since its independence Slovenia's economy has, comparatively speaking, been losing against other transitional economies; or more precisely, other economies have been catching up much faster. Bearing all this in mind, and looking at the data for 2017 and 2018, we can see that some other transitional economies that were lagging far behind Slovenia's development in 1991 have now almost caught up.[14]

What, therefore, has happened to Slovenia in the last quarter century? Why, despite a relatively advanced (compared to other transitional economies) and developed economy at the beginning of the 1990s, did the country get hit so hard by the last financial crisis and in comparative terms lose pace against other transitional economies, such as Slovakia, the Czech Republic or various Baltic states?

In this regard the focus of this chapter will be to comparatively analyse the economic performance of Slovenia and some other selected transitional economies. For our research we have preliminarily chosen Slovakia, Latvia, Estonia and Hungary. These are all relatively comparable transitional economies in terms of size and economic openness. We will analyse the economic growth performance of these countries and point out which country has been growing faster over the last 25 years. Furthermore, we will analyse the level of development by looking at GDP per capita, where we will be interested in which country is catching up fastest to the EU average.

Having obtained all these results, we will look at different policies and segments of the selected economies, such as foreign direct investment, privatisation, monetary policy and the performance of their legal systems, which have all differed considerably in the countries investigated. Using these results, we will search for any correlation between these implemented policies and the economic performance of the selected economies.

Finally, concrete proposals and policy recommendations will be provided.

II. SLOVENIA'S ECONOMY IN THE 19TH AND THE EARLY 20TH CENTURY

Before analysing Slovenia's economic policies over the last 25 years, it is also important to understand how development has evolved since the industrial revolution took place in the 19th century and how it transferred to other regions of Europe, and for our purposes especially to Slovenia.

Due to the end of the Napoleonic wars and the progress of the industrial revolution, towards the end of the 19th century European countries were progressing quite rapidly. The Habsburg monarchy was one of the largest states in Europe at that time, and included regions of today's Ukraine, Serbia, Austria,

[14] See Figure 4.1.

Hungary, Slovenia, Croatia, Romania, northern Italy, etc, although there were huge differences between the regions.

In 1910 the Slovenian provinces were not an exception. In 1910, the coastal provinces (Trieste) recorded about 109 per cent of the average development of the empire, and were one of its most developed parts. Štajerska (Maribor), on the other hand, recorded just 89 per cent of the average, while Kranjska (Kranj, Ljubljana) recorded only 71 per cent, which was comparable to regions in the Hungarian part of the empire.[15] In this regard it is interesting to note that, just before the beginning of World War I, Slovenia had achieved 66.1 per cent of the GDP per capita of Sweden (the whole Habsburg empire stood at 70.8 per cent, the Austrian part of the empire 78.3 per cent and the UK[16] 166.7 per cent). It is interesting to note that Slovenia's development was completely comparable to the development of Finland at that time.[17] All this has had, of course, an immense influence on the future developments of Slovenia's economy – even during the socialist times of the SFRY.

After World War I Slovenia joined the Kingdom of Yugoslavia and experienced an economic boost, which was mainly due to the reforms carried out earlier in the time of the monarchy. Thus, for example, the period between the two world wars witnessed the construction of 403 factories in Slovenia, or 18 per cent of the total number in the kingdom (8 per cent of the population), 635 in Croatia, or 29 per cent of the total (24.1 per cent of the population), 390 factories in Vojvodina, or 17.8 per cent (12 per cent of the population) and 428 factories in Serbia, or 19.5 per cent (24.2 per cent of the population). Half of all engaged capital was in Slovenia and Croatia, while Bosnia and Herzegovina, Montenegro, Macedonia, and Kosovo together held just over 10 per cent. The area north of the Sava and Danube rivers (Slovenia, Croatia and Vojvodina) accounted for around 64 per cent of industry, 85 per cent of bank capital and more than 67 per cent of agricultural production (in terms of value).[18] These figures clearly show that Slovenia was well ahead of the other southern Slavic territories in terms of the development of industry and the capital market.

It should be noted that in 1939[19] wages in Slovenia were almost converging with those in Austria, indicating that Slovenia was advancing relatively well during the first phase of industrialisation. It can be argued that it was well ahead of other southern provinces, even ahead of those provinces that were in the

[15] David F Good, 'The Economic Lag of Central and Eastern Europe: Income Estimates for the Habsburg Successor States, 1870–1910' (1994) 54(4) *Journal of Economic History* 877.

[16] The UK was at that moment in time the most industrialised economy in the world.

[17] Good (n 15) 886.

[18] Teo Zalar, *Značilnosti slovenskega gospodarstva v obdobju med prvo in drugo svetovno vojno-diplomsko delo* (Ljubljana, Ekonomska fakulteta, 2008) 16.

[19] Rok Spruk, 'Primerjalna gospodarska uspešnost Slovenije po 20 letih' (2011) https://sites.google.com/site/rokspruk/research/primerjalna-gospodarska-uspesnost-slovenije (accessed 16.6.2019).

Hungarian part of the empire. However, after World War II, Slovenia became part of the SFRY and began to lag behind economically.[20]

III. THE CENTRALLY PLANNED TIMES OF THE SFRY AND THE PRETRANSITION ERA

With the integration of the Slovenian economy into the SFRY's centrally planned economy everything changed. Several hundred years of cultural, economic and political relations with Central/Western Europe were replaced with southern Slavic relations. The centre of regional geopolitics shifted from Vienna towards Belgrade. However, it should be noted that the economic approach of the SFRY still differed slightly from those of other countries on the eastern side of the iron curtain.[21]

Economic reform in the SFRY (including Slovenia) began in the 1950s, long before it did in other socialist and communist countries. After 1945, four distinct 'socialisms', defined in terms of the formal allocation of decision-making authority in the economy, can be distinguished in the SFRY's history: 'administrative socialism' (1945–52), 'administrative market socialism' (1953–62), 'market socialism' (1963–73) and 'contractual socialism' (1974–88). The last of these rejected both the market as the basic mechanism of resource allocation, and macroeconomic policy as the means of indirect regulation of economic activity. Instead it insisted that these be substituted by other mechanisms: social contracts, enterprise self-management agreements and social planning.[22] All this of course neglected previous economic concepts of market economy. However, even the government in Belgrade understood that exports provide an inflow of foreign currency, of which the SFRY was desperately in need.[23] Thus, some market-oriented concepts continued to operate in Slovenia, which was not the case in other republics of the SFRY.

Moreover, it should also be noted that the Slovenian communists also advocated economic reforms[24] in the direction of market socialism at the federal level and a greater decentralisation of decision-making. In this regard Slovenia

[20] Glenn Eldon, *Country Studies: Former Yugoslavia* (Washington, DC, Library of Congress, 1992).

[21] Winston Churchill used this term in a speech 'The Sinews of Peace', Westminster College, Fulton, MO, after receiving an honorary degree on 5 March 1946.

[22] Jože Mencinger, 'Transition to a National and a Market Economy: A Gradualist Approach' in Mrak et al (n 5) 68.

[23] Having in mind that inflation was at the end of the 1980s over 3,000% in the SFRY. Additionally, from the early 1960s onward, banks were obliged to accept foreign currency deposits but were prohibited from extending foreign currency loans or taking other measures to protect themselves from exchange rate risk. More in Ivan Ribnikar and Tomaž Košak, 'Monetary System and Monetary Policy' in Mrak et al (n 5) 152.

[24] An often heard comment was that 'laws are written in Belgrade, read in Zagreb and implemented in Ljubljana'.

was not only the most developed part of the former SFRY, and indeed of the whole socialist bloc, but also the one where economic reform in the pretransition period went the furthest. Producing the lion's share of the SFRY's exports to Western markets, Slovenia's economy had been relatively open for a long time before transition.[25]

Slovenia had numerous specific advantages: it was the richest part of Eastern Europe, with an ethnically and socially homogeneous population, a diversified manufacturing sector, predominantly private agriculture, a partly privately owned services sector, well-established economic links with Western markets, and a good geographic position. Furthermore, Slovenia was never fully integrated into the SFRY; it was quite autonomous in terms of infrastructure, with its own access to the sea as well as its own pipelines, railways, telecommunications and electrical grid, and its trade patterns with the rest of the SFRY resembled its trade patterns with the rest of the world.[26] It can even be said that Slovenia's economy never really fitted into the SFRY concept. It is interesting to note that even today regions and cities such as Pula (now in Croatia) have direct railway links only towards the north, via Slovenia. Pula still does not have a direct railway link with other Croatian cities.

All these aforementioned facts confirm our thesis that after World War II the Slovenian economy was well ahead when compared to other transitional economies in the East, not to mention the other countries subsumed in the SFRY. However, other CEE countries under the 'influence' of the Soviet bloc during the Cold War experienced extreme setbacks with regard to economic development. On the other hand, Slovenia, as a part of the SFRY, did experience some economic development during these decades. This was still far behind the development of Austria, with whom Slovenia had for centuries compared itself, but was still better compared to other former Habsburg countries that 'stayed' under the Eastern bloc.

Nevertheless, the breakdown of contractual socialism and the political vacuum after Tito's death in 1980, the rise in oil prices, and the tightening of world financial markets set in motion what, in the early 1980s, developed into a deep economic, social and political crisis in the SFRY. The economic situation worsened and economic growth disappeared, while inflation and unemployment rose and the current account deficit grew. Various attempts to change the economic system were accompanied by political changes. In fact, the SFRY ceased to exist as a functioning economic entity, since taxes were not collected, money was 'printed' elsewhere (the required reserve ratios were ignored), and special duties were assessed on 'imports' from other republics. In addition, the republics began to frame their own economic systems, which differed considerably. In the autumn of 1990, the SFRY began to collapse as

[25] Janez Šušteršič, 'Political Economy of Slovenia's Transition' in Mrak et al (n 5) 402.
[26] Mencinger (n 22) 72–73.

a country as well[27] and Slovenia started on its own path, for the first time in history, as a fully independent state.

The main questions in this regard were, of course, how to transform the economic and monetary system from a centrally planned concept into a competitive Western-oriented market economy. There were many different views in this regard among experts as well as politicians in Slovenia. In the end, Slovenia took a slightly different road compared to other Eastern countries. In the following sections we consider what the key differences were and what kind of results they brought in the following decades.

IV. STATE OF PLAY AFTER INDEPENDENCE

So, where are we today when speaking about the economic development of Slovenia? Let us first take a look at the data for GDP per capita for the last 25 years. As Figure 4.1 shows, Austria is, as expected, by far the most developed economy among those considered here. According to the data in Figure 4.1, the least developed economies were the Baltic states, especially Latvia with just slightly over the US$5,500 per capita in 1995, while Slovenia was already at the level of US$13,500 per capita at that time.

Hungary was the third most developed country among the observed economies at the beginning of 1990s. However, around 2005 and especially after the 2008 global financial crisis, Slovakia and even Estonia (coming from far behind) overtook it.

Figure 4.1 also clearly presents the results of different economic (and political) systems in play over the past century. Keeping in mind that just before World War II some regions of Slovenia were almost around the average economic development of other Austrian provinces, and especially having in mind the fact that wages in Slovenia were almost converging with those in Austria, we see the result of different political and economic models after just 50 years.

During these 50 years the Austrian economy evolved and today Austrian citizens (as well as Finnish) are among the wealthiest in the world. Yet Slovenia took another path after World War II and joined the SFRY with its non-democratic political system and a non-market economic system, which over the following half century pushed Slovenia far behind Austria.

Yet, from Figure 4.1, another important finding emerges. If at the beginning of the 1990s the observed countries were ranked as follows: Austria, Slovenia, Hungary, Slovakia, Estonia and Latvia, just two decades later this order had changed quite a bit with Austria still taking the lead and Slovenia

[27] ibid 68–70.

Figure 4.1 GDP per capita (US$) for selected economies, 1990–2017

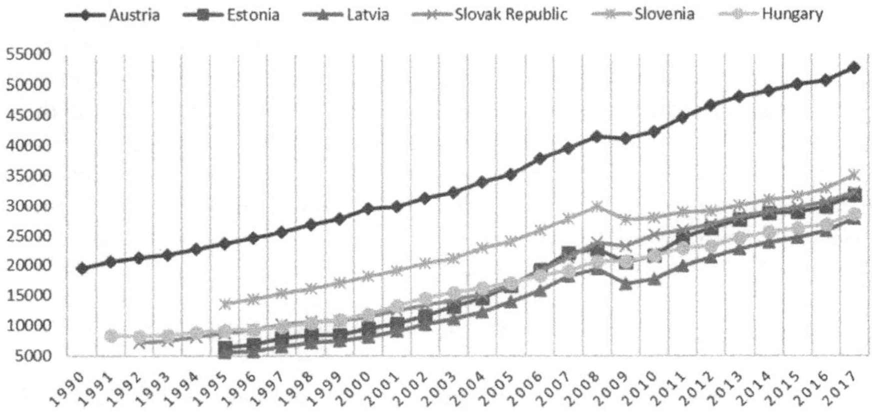

Source: Own calculations on the basis of World Development Indicators (World Bank).

still in second place, while in third place we could already see Slovakia and Estonia coming close behind and Hungary and Latvia not far away (Figure 4.1).

Throughout the observed timeframe we can find Slovenia stable in second place. Yet what is more important is the trend. As already mentioned, Slovenia was declining in comparison with other transitional economies. This was especially the case after the 2008 global financial crisis, when other economies were catching up much faster compared to Slovenia.

Thus, in Figure 4.2, we will take a closer look at this period in time. If we focus only on the years after the global financial crisis, we can observe the impressive economic performance of Slovakia and especially of Estonia, which recorded the highest rise of GDP per capita. It is also interesting to note that although Hungary actually did not experience any significant economic downturn in 2008 and later, Estonia nevertheless overtook it in 2010.

With regard to Slovenia and Slovakia, we should observe that in 2017 the difference in GDP per capita was only US$2,691, while in 1995 the difference was almost double (US$4,916). If we compare Slovenia and Estonia, we see that in 1995 the difference between the two countries was US$7,272, while in 2017 the difference was only US$3,164.

We can conclude that Slovenia was relatively speaking losing pace in terms of development and population wealth compared to certain other transitional economies (in particular, Slovakia and Estonia).

Why was this so? We will analyse these three economies and some of the policies their governments have implemented in recent decades, which have resulted in the different levels of economic development.

Figure 4.2 GDP per capita (US$) for selected economies, 2008 onwards

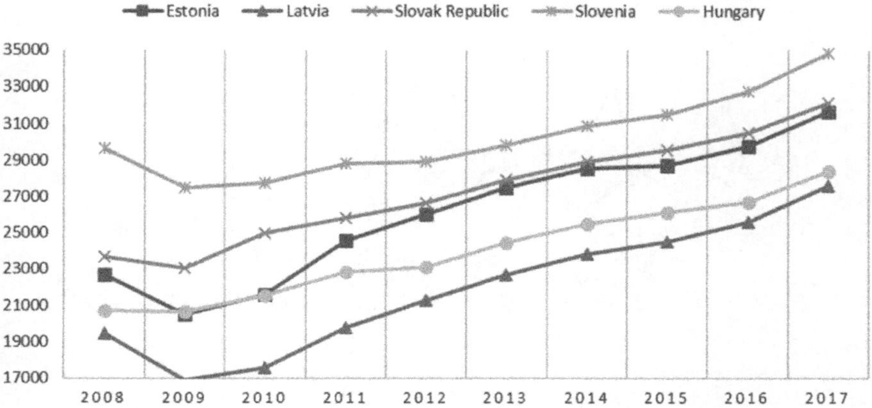

Source: Own calculations based on World Development Indicators (World Bank).

V. THE CRASH: THE 2008 GLOBAL FINANCIAL CRISIS

As we saw in the previous section, differences in the dynamics of GDP per capita were quite noticeable among the observed economies over the last 25 years. However, if we look at GDP growth (Figure 4.3), we can observe similar oscillations as in the previous section.

Estonia presented some huge oscillations, topping 10 per cent of annual growth in the mid-1990s and similar in 2000 and 2006. Nevertheless, it also showed the highest fall in GDP growth during the time of the global financial crisis with almost a 15 per cent negative downturn.

On the other hand, Slovakia was struggling towards 1999, but after the turn of the millennium started to grow steadily until the beginning of the global financial crisis in 2008.

Slovenia, on the other hand, grew stably and constantly (albeit gradually) until the beginning of the global financial crisis. Yet it struggled with growth after 2009, and recorded another recession in 2012 and 2013.

We can observe that Slovenia escaped the grip of the global financial crisis only in 2014, while the other two countries discussed here were already out of economic trouble in 2010. Comparatively speaking, Slovenia lost almost four years in terms of development vis-a-vis these other countries, since it was not able to implement policies that would put the country's growth back on the right track.

We can thus summarise that Slovenia's economy declined the most, comparatively speaking in regard to other observed countries, immediately after the global financial crisis, and then needed almost four years to record positive economic growth again.

Figure 4.3 GDP growth (%) for selected economies.

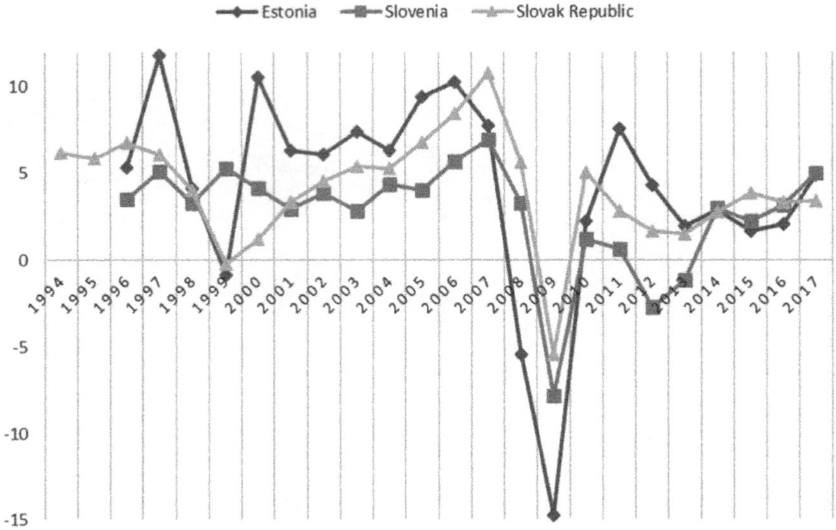

Source: Own calculations on the basis of World Development Indicators (World Bank).

The other countries studied here needed only one year to regenerate their economies. The reasons for Slovenia's slow recovery will be the focus of our analysis in the following sections.

VI. DIFFERENCES IN SOME POLICIES

A. Fiscal Policy (Public Debt)

Let us therefore take a look at some differences in economic policies among the economies studied here. If we first take a look at public debt (Figure 4.4), we can observe huge differences in the fiscal policies of the observed economies.

To date, Estonia has accumulated almost zero public debt and during the crisis did not increase it at all. In this regard Estonia is one of the few countries in the EU with such low public debt and is thus very well prepared for a potential new recession. Slovakia, on the other hand, started the crisis with a debt of around 30 per cent and has increased it to slightly over 50 per cent of GDP.

As shown in Figure 4.4, Slovenia started the crisis in relatively good shape with only around 20 per cent of GDP public debt, but by 2015 this had increased to over 82 per cent of GDP. This represents one of the largest

Figure 4.4 Public debt as a percentage of GDP for selected economies

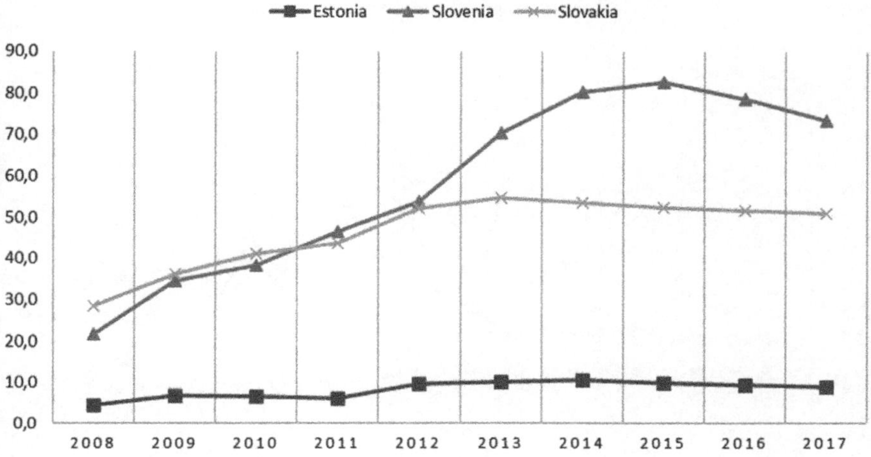

Source: Own calculations on the basis of Eurostat data.

public debt growths among the EU countries.[28] Slovenia only started lowering its debt in 2016, when the majority of observed economies had already been recording stable economic growth for some years.

In this regard Slovenia lost another comparable advantage (public indebtedness) relative to the observed economies, since the present high public debt puts its future fiscal policy on shakey ground. This will especially be a problem in the event of another potential recession.

B. Openness to Foreign Capital – Foreign Direct Investment

The second policy in which Slovenia differs from other transitional countries is the field of foreign direct investment (FDI). In this regard Slovenia records one of the lowest shares of FDI among the OECD countries. Figure 4.5 clearly shows the low levels of FDI in the case of Slovenia, compared to Slovakia or Estonia.

For instance, Slovakia received almost as much inward capital from abroad in just one year (2002), as Slovenia did in the whole observed period of 25 years. Slovakia, of course, also continued with records of high inward investments throughout the observed period. Estonia, on the other hand, witnessed a similar inflow of foreign capital, as did Slovakia, and thus already outperformed Slovenia by 2005.

[28] European Commission, *Report on Public Finances in EMU 2017* (Brussels, European Commission, 2018) 69.

Figure 4.5 Foreign direct investment, net inflows (BoP, in current US$ bn)

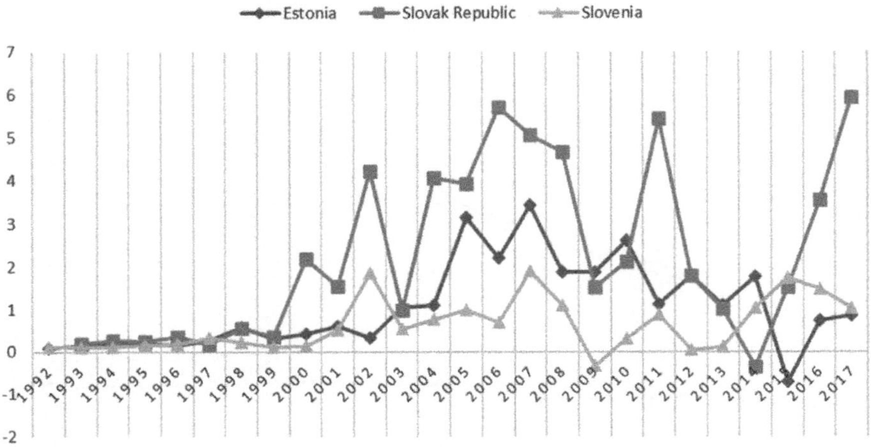

Source: Own calculations on the basis of World Development Indicators (World Bank).

It is thus interesting to note that Slovenia declares itself to be an FDI-friendly country,[29] and yet a huge share of the national economy is still run by state-owned companies.

In accordance with the results presented in Table 4.1, it can be seen that Slovenia has the highest number of majority state-owned companies among the observed economies. The same applies to minority-owned listed companies, as well as majority-owned, non-listed companies, where the Czech Republic has indeed a higher number of companies (89), but has fewer people employed in these companies compared to Slovenia.

We also wanted to include data for Slovakia, but unfortunately the OECD does not have comparable data for this economy. Consequently, we included data for the Czech Republic. When analysing the data, we again note huge differences when comparing Slovenia with Estonia, which has practically no state-owned companies.

However, the difference would be even more visible if we were to relativise the acquired data in per-capita terms or compare it to the size of the economy; this calculation would indicate that the state-owned sector in Slovenia is even larger. These findings accord with previous FDI data observations, however, since by having the economy relatively closed to foreign capital, the state can still run the majority of the economy, meaning that the transition from a centrally planned economy where all the economic decisions were made in 'planning offices' is still not yet finished. To this day, politics in Slovenia still plays an important role in the economy, as well as in day-to-day business decisions. This, of course, presents a number of issues from the point of view of constitutional

[29] SPIRIT, Public Agency of the Republic of Slovenia for foreign direct investments, www.investslovenia.si.

democracy, as well as the entire rule-of-law concept, especially when speaking about competitiveness, entrepreneurship and the relationship between public/private spheres.

Table 4.1 State-owned enterprises for selected OECD countries

	Majority-owned listed entities				Minority-owned listed entities				Majority-owned non-listed enterprises		
			Value of enterprises (mio USD)				Value of enterprises (mio USD)				
	No of enterprises	No of employees	Market	Book equity	No of enterprises	No of employees	Market	Book equity	No of enterprises	No of employees	Value of enterprises (mio USD)
Slovenia	4	11,502	1,486	2,267	16	30,570	3,497	4,037	35	40,537	11,153
Estonia	–	–	–	–	–	–	–	–	29	16,046	3,555
Austria	2	26,281	11,142	7,465	2	45,104	14,794	19,751	6	47,872	9,709
Czech Republic	1	31,300	18,589	13,012	–	–	–	–	89	33,900	12,511

Source: Own presentation on the basis of OECD Dataset on the Size and Sectoral Composition of National Sectors (2012).

Yet this should not come as a surprise, since for the majority of the last 25 years, the leading economic doctrine in Slovenia has been the concept of gradualism,[30] meaning that certain changes and reforms have been introduced progressively.

On the basis that gradualism was an appropriate concept in the first phase of transition, mostly due to the relatively advanced economy and overall development in Slovenia, we argue that towards the end of the 1990s a shift in the concept should have taken place. Consequently, no serious reforms have been introduced since Slovenia's integration into the EU, despite the awareness that certain sectors (labour market, pensions system, health system, judiciary), are strongly in need of them. This was seen very clearly during and after the global financial crisis, when the government had practically no room to manoeuvre to react to the new global market conditions.

In a time of crisis, managers and governments need to react quickly and swiftly. In tough times a gradual approach, with many consultations, many decision-makers (lots of coalition partners, trade unions, business community, NGOs, etc) and high levels of coordination is more a setback than an advantage. The companies and countries that had the capacity to react quickly gained certain advantage.

C. Doing Business – The Rule of Law

The final policy that we compared among the observed countries was the rule of law in relation to doing business. The World Bank's annual 'Ease of Doing

[30] Justinek and Lautar (n 4).

Business' report analyses various data from different policies for almost all the world's countries and compares these data among economies. From the data in 2019,[31] according to which Slovenia is performing extremely poorly, is a section entitled 'Enforcing Contracts'.

The enforcing contracts indicator measures the time and cost for resolving a commercial dispute through a local court of first instance, and the quality of the judicial processes index, evaluating whether each economy has adopted a series of good practices that promote quality and efficiency in the court system.

The data in the first column of Table 4.2 present the time needed to resolve a commercial dispute. The results for Slovenia are devastating, since they show that it takes over three years for a commercial dispute to be resolved in a local court of first instance. Here Slovenia shares its place with countries such as Gabon or Myanmar and in this regard ranks among the least developed countries in the world.

Table 4.2 Ease of doing business, judiciary

	Time taken for process (days)	Cost (% of claim value)	Quality of judicial processes index (0–18)
Slovenia	1160	12.7	11.5
Austria	397	20.6	13.0
Finland	485	16.2	8.5
Hungary	605	15.0	12.5
Estonia	455	21.9	13.5
Lithuania	370	23.6	15
Slovak Republic	775	20.5	13.5
Gabon	1160	34.3	4

Source: World Bank (Doing Business Report 2019).

However, in the field of costs, the Slovenian judiciary surpasses all the observed economies, since it takes the lowest percentage of the claim value of the disputed contract. Furthermore, with regard to the overall judicial processes index, Slovenia ranks relatively well. It is lagging behind some of the other observed economies, which record indexes of around 13, while Slovenia records only 11.5, but this gap between Slovenia and the others is not fundamental.

Nevertheless, the time needed for resolving a legal dispute is the most crucial indicator. This, especially, is of the utmost importance for the business community, since companies have to react quickly to market changes and certainly do

[31] More at www.doingbusiness.org/.

not have the time to wait three years or more for a court decision. The length of decision-making in the courts in Slovenia is elaborated in detail in other chapters of this book, especially in the light of the many rulings by the ECtHR.

The rule of law and successful enforcement of contracts is one of the key prerequisites for business and thus also greenfield investments. These are the investments that bring additional added value, new capital, new know-how, new jobs and new technology to countries. This is what Slovenia's economy chronically lacks.

With high probability we can directly link the poor performance of Slovenia in the field of the rule of law and the amount of inward FDI. Consequently, Slovenia records one of the largest shares of state-owned economy, which is again closely linked to the lack of foreign investments and foreign capital itself in the economy. If we also bear in mind that until recently the majority of the banking system in Slovenia was also state owned, then the circle is closed. High public debt that was accumulated after the global financial crisis was also mainly the consequence of the required capitalisation of the key state-owned banks. The three major state-owned banks (NLB, NKBM, Abanka) alone required a capital injection worth €3.012 billion in the years after the crisis.[32]

VII. ANALYSIS OF DIFFERENT ECONOMIC CONCEPTS

So, what went wrong? We have presented in depth the good starting position of Slovenia as it entered independence. According to Guardiancich, Slovenia was the most successful of all post-socialist countries. Slovenian GDP grew on average by 4.5 per cent per annum between 1993 and 2008. Per capita income rose from less than half the Western European average to around 90 per cent of the EU27 average by 2009. Slovenia's public finances underwent only mild deterioration after the early 2000s. Public debt never rose above 27.8 per cent of GDP, and the average yearly budget and current account deficits between 1995 and 2008 were 2.6 and 1.5 per cent of GDP, respectively. Low unemployment rates, averaging 6.3 per cent between 1996 and 2008, and relatively high employment rates, which climbed from 61.7 to 68.6 per cent during the same period (the EU average was 65.8 per cent in 2008), underpinned the years of buoyant growth.[33] In summary, it can be said that Slovenia was performing like an 'A-grade student' until 2008, when all the hidden problems started falling out of the 'non-reform' closet.

As is evident from our analysis, the main difference between the observed countries, on the one side Slovenia and on the other side Estonia and Slovakia,

[32] Bank of Slovenia, *Full Report on the Comprehensive Review of the Banking System* (Ljubljana, Bank of Slovenia, 2013).

[33] Guardiancich (n 13) 207.

was in the predominant concepts of economic transition. In Slovenia the concept of gradualism prevailed.

The main assumption supporting the superiority of a gradual approach is that, in the short term, it produces winners who gain a stake in the reform process.[34] However, it can also be the reverse. Hellman, among others, has warned that gradualism may have negative long-term consequences as 'short-term winners stall the economy in a partial reform equilibrium that generates concentrated rents for themselves, while imposing high costs on the rest of society'.[35] Rojec et al have identifies various reasons for the choice of gradualism in Slovenia: consensual decision-making; the early, endogenous transition; a high starting point of development; and the dissolution of the SFRY and ensuing unstable politics, which cautioned against 'shock therapy'.[36]

In this regard, it is also important to understand the slightly different political backgrounds among the observed countries. Unlike in some other Central and Eastern European countries where the main impulse for the breakdown of the socialist regime came from the outside, the transition in Slovenia was (also) endogenous. The key difference was in the behaviour of the established political elites. In some countries these elites stuck to the unreformed centrally planned system until the very end, and the breakdown thus came unexpectedly for them as a result of international developments and domestic pressures. In other countries, including Hungary and Russia as well as Slovenia, the established elites anticipated the possible breakdown and tried to prepare themselves for the coming changes. To secure their future in the new system, they had to obtain private economic and political capital. They did so in two important ways. First, they acquired economic assets[37] through what has been called 'spontaneous privatisation', using the laws adopted in the final years of the socialist system to appropriate the resources of viable enterprises for themselves. Second, they acquired political capital by presenting themselves as 'reform communists', initiating some cautious changes toward market socialism and pluralistic democracy.[38]

From the point of view of our research, the most important point is the acquisition of economic assets, which were accumulated predominantly in the hands of people close to internal information – elites. In this sense, the concept of gradualism was an excellent tool for enabling these people to gain, accumulate and maintain the economic power within their hands and their influential circles.

[34] ibid 206.

[35] Joel S Hellman, 'Winners Take All: The Politics of Partial Reform in Post-Communist Transitions' (1998) 50(2) *World Politics* 204–05.

[36] Matija Rojec, Janez Šušteršič, Boštjan Vasle, Maja Bednaš and Slavica Jurančič, 'The Rise and Decline of Gradualism in Slovenia' (2004) 16(4) *Post-Communist Economies* 461.

[37] See Chap 8.

[38] Šušteršič (n 25) 401.

In this regard, despite the normative changes in the legislation, many elements, such as practices, people and concepts, and even informal networks of power, stayed the same. As already mentioned, the concept of gradualism was probably the right decision for the first years of transition due to Slovenia's relatively good economic development. Even economists in Slovenia who are not in favour of gradualism partly agree with this notion.[39] However, after the turn of the millennium, the gradualist approach started to hinder urgently needed reforms in many spheres.

This was especially the case in the field of privatisation which was never really implemented and internalised among people in Slovenia. This has led to a large share of state-owned enterprises and a very low share of FDI. The Ownership Transformation Act passed at the beginning of independence particularly favoured various forms of insider privatisation.[40] The state and quasi-state institutions obtained the biggest stake in capital-intensive and export-oriented companies.[41] In summary, the gradualist approach to transformation backed up by consensual politics and functioning neocorporatism sustained and stabilised the growth of Slovenia's economy.[42]

Another important aspect of the problem, closely related to lack of foreign capital, elites, networks of informal power and inside information were management buyouts. The main instrument in Slovenia was the Lombard loan. Managers were granted credit by banks against pledged companies in the form of securities that could be readily marketed (stock), or by using real estate as collateral.[43] All these management buyouts were largely supported by the (at that time) state-owned banks. The majority of these actions would probably have been successful if the financial crisis had not struck at the end of 2008.

The country's GDP suffered a significant decline, the unemployment more than doubled and the public deficit mounted. Slovenia swiftly became one of the worst performers within the EU. With the collapse of the stock market and the rise of interest rates, the share of non-performing loans started growing and companies started collapsing. In the case of Slovenia, even some banks (mostly state-owned ones) were close to the brink.

Here, again, politics and the gradualist economists[44] came under the spotlight. Persuaded by the argument of national interest by influential gradualist

[39] ibid 400.

[40] Guardiancich (n 13) 210.

[41] Marko Simoneti, Matija Rojec and Aleksandra Gregorič, 'Privatisation, Restructuring, and Corporate Governance of the Enterprise Sector' in Mrak et al (n 5) 231.

[42] Guardiancich (n 13) 211.

[43] ibid 219.

[44] The Minister of Finance in the years 2008–11 was Dr France Križanič, from the Social Democrat party and one of the well-known and influential economists supporting the gradualist approach. Together with Dr Jože Mencinger, who was the first Minister of the Economy after independence and one of the most important gradualist economists in Slovenia, they shared ownership in the most influential privately owned economic think-thank in Slovenia, namely the Economic institute of the Law Faculty (EIPF).

economists, the government approved recapitalisation of the largest state-owned banks, which triggered problems with public debt. Past recapitalisations and growing concerns over the conditions of Slovenian financial institutions led to credit rating downgrades of both the largest state-owned banks (NLB and NKBM) and the state. Slovenian bonds were downgraded between 2006 and 2014 from Aa2 (positive) to Ba1 by Moody's; from AA to A– by Standard & Poor's; and from AA to BBB+ (negative) by Fitch.[45]

All this led to a huge crisis in which Slovenia started losing the most, compared with other transitional economies. Between 2008 and 2011, Slovenia lost 15.9 per cent of its world merchandise market share and 6.7 per cent with its most important trade partners. Slovenian exports, the main driver of a small open economy, grew more slowly than the recovery in global trade, and the Visegrád countries have all performed better.[46]

The global financial crisis in fact confronted the Slovenian economy with all the problems that had been accumulating over the past 20 years. The economic concept of gradualisation left many elements of the economy as 'business as usual', untouched or just slightly modified. The pragmatic leadership of Slovenian coalition governments has implemented only those reforms urgently needed in order to participate in European integration (where usually just the legislative framework was enough), while all the rest (how things really work in practice) was left waiting.

The 'homework' was still waiting to be done in 2008, when the 'final exam' came around, and as we have seen in this chapter, despite a considerably inferior starting point, the other students from the 'East' performed better. The gradualist approach, which enabled some positive externalities at the beginning,[47] was also responsible for the negative ones in the following years.[48]

VIII. CONCLUSION

The focus of this chapter was to comparatively analyse the economic performances of Slovenia and certain other selected transitional economies and

[45] IMAD, *Development Report 2014* (Ljubljana, Institute for Macroeconomic Analysis and Development, 2014) 109.

[46] European Commission, *European Economy: Macroeconomic Imbalances Slovenia 2014*, Occasional Papers 187 (Brussels, European Commission, Directorate General for Economic and Financial Affairs, 2014) 29–31.

[47] Slovenia's Gini coefficient (after taxes and transfers) was 0.242 in 2004, lower than in any other EU Member State, except Sweden. More in: OECD, *OECD Income Distribution Database (IDD): Gini, Poverty, Income, Methods and Concepts* (Paris, OECD, 2015); see also Chap 9.

[48] Low inflow of foreign capital, informal networks of economic powers, no structural reforms, privatisation with inside information, management buyouts, non-performing loans in state-owned banks, recapitalisation of state-owned banks, fall of GDP, rise in public debt and the most important setback in the field of competitiveness, compared to other countries that were 25 years ago, and even before (in the time of the monarchy), far behind.

present the key differences in transitional policies that are reflected today in their levels of economic development. For the preliminary research we selected Slovakia, Latvia, Estonia and Hungary, since they are all relatively comparable economies in regard of size and economic openness. However, the GDP per capita analysis demonstrated that Slovakia and Estonia have outperformed Slovenia in many economic fields.

Thus, a more detailed economic analysis of these three countries was carried out. In this regard, we analysed economic growth in recent years, where it can be seen that Slovenia was most affected, due to the global financial crisis.

We argue that this is mainly due to non-reformistic economic and other policies (the gradualist approach) which in 2008 and beyond left the Slovenian government without any instruments to tackle the crisis. Therefore, Slovenia recovered from the crisis some four years later than the other economies studied here. Slovenia, in fact, lost four years of economic development and growth.

Yet Slovenia survived the crisis without the need for a bailout, although this dark scenario came very close. Nevertheless, the country paid a high price – public debt rose from 20 to over 80 per cent of GDP, meaning that future Slovenian governments will have very little room to manoeuvre should a new recession appear on the horizon.

It should be noted that the Bank for International Settlements puts global debt at an eye-watering 217 per cent of GDP at the end of 2017, which is over 20 per cent more than in 2007. In emerging markets, debt is even 50 per cent higher. Since rising interest rates and soaring debt are a toxic combination,[49] Slovenia has a lot to consider.

However, as we have pointed out, the key difference in some policies among the observed economies lies in the attitude towards foreign capital, which Slovenia is (still) crucially lacking. Slovenia is one of the OECD economies that records the lowest share of FDI and consequently records one of the highest shares of state-owned enterprises.

We have tried to analytically argue why is this the case. The first reason is the different concept of transition: in Slovenia the concept of gradualism, national interest and state-owned enterprises prevailed. All this led to many consequences, discussed above. However, another key difference we found when comparing Slovenia to the other observed economies was the ease of doing business – especially in the field of the rule of law.

In terms of the time needed for resolving a commercial dispute, Slovenia ranks alongside the least developed countries in the world, since it takes more than three years to get a standard commercial dispute through a local court of first instance.[50]

[49] Leo Abruzzese, 'Economic Trouble Ahead' *The Economist* (January 2019) https://worldin2019.economist.com/endofthebullrun (accessed 31 August 2019).

[50] See Chap 5.

We argue that this is one of the main obstacles today for foreign capital and foreign investors to invest in Slovenia. These investors are, of course, much needed, not only in the sense of bringing fresh new capital to the financial markets, but mainly due to new technologies that they bring, along with new know-how and new jobs. Slovakia and Estonia have both benefited heavily from FDI in this regard.

On the other hand, due to the lack of foreign investors and foreign capital, Slovenia runs a conglomerate of state-owned companies and enterprises, which are very much dependent on day-to-day politics, or different centres of power. Guardiancich[51] agrees with Damijan[52] and states that in the name of defending national interests the privatisation of state-owned enterprises and of state-owned banks slowed down, effectively cutting out foreign investors, concentrating the Slovenian economy in the hands of a few politically connected (and controlled) managers and bankers and establishing a variety of state-managerial capitalism that systematically manipulated market forces.

This was one of the reasons why Slovenia had to pay a price to the tune of 60 per cent of GDP public debt, which was due to 'homework not done' before the crisis, since the majority of these funds were related to the much-needed recapitalisations of the largest state-owned banks.

In short, reforms in Slovenia are much needed in practically all spheres (healthcare, the pensions system, public affairs, and the legal system).

The reform of the Slovenian judiciary is, in particular, much needed in the sense of ensuring a stable economic background for the business environment and consequently development. Once a normally functioning legal system is enforced (especially in the sense of timely procedures), foreign investors will have more impetus to invest in Slovenia, and consequently, the share of state-owned companies could shrink to encompass only strategic investments and public debt could be lowered. The informal circles of economic power could disperse and more competition could be presented on all levels, especially concerning the relationship between the public and private in subsystems such as healthcare, education, etc.

An effective concept of the rule of law in Slovenia is thus much needed and many reforms need to be carried out, since Slovenia has to be prepared for the next cyclical global downturn, when a new 60 per cent of GDP indebtedness will not be sustainable as in the years after the 2008 crisis.

Thus, groundwork in regard to economic policy needs to be done before that occurs, and certain reforms need to be implemented, starting with the reform of the judiciary.

[51] Guardiancich (n 13) 206.

[52] Jože P Damijan, 'Kučan in Janša – botra slovenskih oligarhov' *Razgledi.net* (20 August 2007) http://razgledi.net/2007/08/20/kucan-in-jansa-botra-slovenskih-oligarhov/ (accessed 10 September 2019).

5

The Current Crises of Human Rights Protection, the Rule of Law and Democracy in Slovenia

O you, hundred thirty five constitutional bodies,
or what to do with the carrion cat in order not to have it stink,
O you, revolution of all the people's masses,
or where is the sanatorium to cure us of impotence.[1]

I. INTRODUCTION

THE PRECEDING CHAPTERS have outlined and analysed the genesis of the contemporary Slovenian constitutional democracy, the historical reasons for a discrepancy between Slovenian constitutional and rule-of-law ideals and have also provided a critical account of the country's economic model. As noted in those chapters, Slovenia has since the early 1990s turned into an economically relatively developed country. It is ranked 25th overall on the UN Human Development Index measuring socioeconomic development.[2] Some commentators have even described Slovenia as the 'post-communist "success story"'.[3] However, the past and current crises and practices of its constitutional democracy testify that it has struggled to incorporate and internalise modern standards of the rule of law and human rights protection. In line with similar developments in Central and Eastern Europe, Slovenia has since its

[1] Tomaž Šalamun, 'Thought' 64' ('Duma' 64'), Centre for Romanian Studies, 'Poetry in Translation (CLXXXVIII): Tomaž ŠALAMUN, (b. 1941) Slovenian Poet, "Thought '64", "Gând '64"' http://romanianstudies.org/content/2013/04/22/poetry-in-translation-clxxxvii-tomaz-salamun-b-1941-slovenian-poet-thought-64-gand-64/ (accessed 24 April 2019) in Tomaž Šalamun, *Four Questions of Melancholy: New & Selected Poems*, trans Michael Biggins (New York, White Pine Press, 1996).

[2] United Nations Development Programme, Human Development Reports, Human Development Indicators 2018, Slovenia, http://hdr.undp.org/en/countries/profiles/SVN (accessed 24 April 2019).

[3] Matej Makarovič, Lea Prijon, Mateja Rek and Matevž Tomšič, 'The Strength of Pro-European Consensus among Slovenian Political Elites' (2016) 41(4) *Historical Social Research* 195.

democratisation in 1990 and independence in 1991 experienced constant crises of human rights protection, the rule of law and democracy.[4] As a result, the socioeconomic development of the country has not been followed by a corresponding development in realising and upholding the principal values of constitutional democracies.[5]

In order to understand the current crises of human rights protection, the rule of law and democracy in Slovenia, it is first necessary to grasp the country's recent history, particularly the wealth of evidence documenting systematic and general abuses during all three totalitarian regimes – fascism, nazism and communism – to which Slovenia has been subject. As we have explained in Chapter 3, the communist regime has had, due to its longevity, nature and scope, the most wide-ranging and deep-reaching negative consequences for the rule of law and human rights protections in present-day Slovenia. In particular, it is indispensable for a reader to grasp that the fundamental values of every constitutional democracy – human dignity, pluralism, freedom, equality, solidarity and the rule of law – were trampled upon during the communist regime, which over many decades directly destroyed the individual and collective dimension of human dignity. Jože Pučnik, a Slovenian dissent, sociologist and founder of the modern-day Slovenian state, has accurately observed that 'the search for freedom is the common thread in the search for European culture, the common thread in the history of its nascence and generation'.[6] Pučnik subsequently produced one of the most accurate descriptions of present-day Slovenia. He argued in 1999 that:

> The chronic lethargy of legal, political, and moral measures is causing an erosion of the rule of law and presents a threat to the democratic system. The cause does not lie only in the negligence and irresponsibility of individuals because both are already the consequence of the general value lethargy of the Slovenian public and the institutions of the state. This lethargy enables the spread of an insincere relation towards reality, the falsification of facts, and public appearances, in which the people assuming the key positions in our country are lying to your face while at the same time looking into your eyes. … Not only politicians do this, but also people in journalism, science, business, and government.[7]

He added that 'even worse: some people are trying to theoretically justify that consistency and moral values have no place within an efficient public activity, for there, so they say, "elasticity," "pragmatism," "adjustability," and "efficiency"

[4] For a good overview, see Matej Avbelj, 'The Sociology of (Slovenian) Constitutional Democracy' (2018) 10(1) *Hague Journal on the Rule of Law* 35.

[5] Frane Adam, *Na razpotju družbene krize: quo vadis, Slovenija* (Ljubljana, IRSA – Inštitut za razvojne in strateške analize, 2013). See chapters 3 and 9 of the current book.

[6] Jože Pučnik, *Članki in spomini 1957–1985* (Maribor, Obzorja, 1986) 29, quoted in Dean Komel, 'Jože Pučnik: Personal Freedom, Culture, and Politics' (2014) 43(1) *Traditiones* 125, 126. See also Jože Pučnik, *Kultura, družba in tehnologija* (Maribor, Obzorja, 1988).

[7] Jože Pučnik, 'Kulturna prenova Slovenije', in Niko Grafenauer (ed), *Sproščena Slovenija: Obračun za prihodnost* (Ljubljana, Nova revija, 1999) 46, quoted in Komel (n 6) 132 and 133.

must prevail'.[8] Pučnik's description very accurately describes the main challenges to human rights protection, the rule of law and democracy in Slovenia. They are basically equivalent to what Adam Podgorecki observed about the unhealthy closeness of institutional and societal elites in Poland.[9] Similarly, Adam Czarnota explained the rise 'informal operations due to the distrust of authorities'.[10] The informal networks of different origins have been present in all layers of Slovenian society. As it stands, they have aimed to protect the status quo and the old or established ways of doing business that are embedded in all aspects of daily lives in Slovenian society. Some have perceived the values of constitutional democracy as foreign and intrusive to the established practices and mentality of Slovenian society.[11] As a result, the elites in state institutions and public administration have so far not been prepared to internalise the values of constitutional democracies as they have so far been more concerned with the preservation of the status quo, particularly of their financial interests.[12]

The overall objective of this chapter is therefore to analyse the current crises, the reasons for them, and to explain how they may be overcome. Slovenia's state institutions have, despite the wide-ranging normative influence of European institutions, primarily the Council of Europe and the European Union, failed to move beyond the simple translation of the normative standards of mature European constitutional democracies into Slovenian constitutional law.[13] Eroding the rule of law and democracy, and reform of the *homo sovieticus* mentality of the persons holding public office remain outstanding issues. Similar problems can be observed in the private sphere, where business has been proceeding as usual by often maintaining the old and corrupt practices and informal networks with questionable objectives. Chapter 3 portrayed some of the instances of systematic and general human rights violations that occurred in Slovenia in the past and suggested that the unresolved past has been one of the reasons why the normative standards of constitutional democracy have not so far borne any long-lasting fruit. The reminder of this chapter is divided in three sections. Section II first deals with the current crises of human rights protection in Slovenia, examining various facets of the crises from institutional limitations to ideological bias.

[8] Makarovič et al (n 3).

[9] Adam Podgorecki, 'Polish Society: A Sociological Analysis' (1987) 7(1) *Praxis International* 57. See also Bálint Magyar, *Post-Communist Mafia State: The Case of Hungary* (Budapest, Central European University and Noran Libro, 2016).

[10] Quoted in Martin Krygier, 'Introduction' in Wojciech Sadurski, Adam Czarnota and Martin Krygier (eds), *Spreading Democracy and the Rule of Law? The Impact of EU Enlargement on the Rule of Law, Democracy and Constitutionalism in Post-Communist Legal Orders* (Dordrecht, Springer, 2006) 21.

[11] Matej Makarovič and Matevž Tomšič, 'Democrats, Authoritarians and Nostalgics: Slovenian Attitudes Toward Democracy' (2015) 8(3) *Innovative Issues and Approaches in Social Sciences* 8.

[12] Matevž Tomšič and Lea Prijon, 'Elites, Ideologies and Crisis in Slovenia' (2003) 6(2) *Raziskave in Razprave*, 71.

[13] See Chap 10 below.

Section III then deals with the current crises of the rule of law and constitutional democracy and their practices in Slovenia. Finally, section IV analyses reasons for the current state-of-affairs.

II. THE CURRENT CRISES OF HUMAN RIGHTS PROTECTION IN SLOVENIA

A. Backdrop

Individuals and groups have in the domestic constitutional system of Slovenia enjoyed almost exemplary normative human rights safeguards. They include domestic constitutional and statutory human rights protections available to individuals and groups residing in Slovenia. Arguably, the text of the Constitution of the Republic of Slovenia is quite modern and in some instances even more advanced than the constitutional texts of mature constitutional democracies.[14] The strong domestic normative system has been complemented by regional and international frameworks such as the Council of Europe, the EU and the UN. Nonetheless, human rights protection in Slovenia has been so far unequal, selective and inefficient, and has not appropriately protected the human dignity of individuals and groups.[15] The protections of individual and group rights have often depended on the ideological and/or societal position of the duty-holders. As a result, this approach has so far undermined human dignity as an individual and collective core value of Slovenian society.[16] State authorities are theoretically obliged to guarantee equal, efficient and objective protection of human rights and fundamental freedoms. However, the daily practice of state institutions and civil society demonstrates deeply divided approaches to human rights protection.

The Slovenian government seems at least at the rhetorical level committed to ensuring respect for human rights via a variety of policies and decisions implemented through its executive, legislative and judicial branches. The rule of law and human rights protections in the judiciary, including the quintessential role of the Constitutional Court, have been addressed in Chapter 3 and will be further elaborated on Chapters 6 and 10. The legislative branch ensures that all statutes that the National Assembly approves have to pass the through a due-diligence compliance procedure in accordance with national constitution and human rights treaties within the Legal Office of the National Assembly. The executive branch of the government has often prided itself on placing great emphasis on the effective protection of human rights in Slovenia, with all major international human rights treaties being ratified and forming part of Slovenian law.[17] For instance, the

[14] Peter Jambrek, *Ustava in svoboda* (Nova Gorica, Brdo pri Kranju, Evropska Pravna Fakulteta and Fakulteta za Državne in Evropske Študije, 2014).

[15] Jernej Letnar Černič, *Slovenija na razpotju: Geneza varstva človekovih pravic v slovenski družbi* (Kranj, Nova Univerza – Fakulteta za Državne in Evropske Študije, 2018).

[16] ibid.

[17] ibid.

Permanent Mission of the Republic of Slovenia to the United Nations has submitted in 2015 that 'respect for human rights is a pivotal founding principle of the Slovenian State'.[18] It further added that 'as a Council member, we will continue our efforts to promote human rights in a fair and objective manner'.[19] Accordingly, the Slovenian government has by such promising rhetorical commitments set the bar of effective human rights protection very high. Such statements have obliged the Slovenian authorities to move beyond window-dressing policies on human rights protections and rule of law. However, as shown below, these policies are quite far removed from the daily reality of human rights protection in Slovenia, which has been often subjected to partiality and bias based on ideology and private interests.

B. Institutional Protections

Several Slovenian public administration institutions work in the wider field of human rights protections. The state institution with the widest mandate is the Office of the National Ombudsman, which has enjoyed a constitutionally protected mandate. More specifically, section 1 of Article 159 of the Constitution of Slovenia provides that 'in order to protect human rights and fundamental freedoms ... the office of the ombudsman for the rights of citizens shall be established by law'.[20] The ombudsman can accept complaints, but does not have wide-ranging normative powers to influence state institutions to change their arbitrary practices or to remedy the victims.[21] A former ombudswoman has interpreted such provision to mean that that the mandate of the office applies human rights protections also to private relationships.[22] The ombudsmen have so far often shown political bias in the choice, scope and treatment of human rights as they have mostly concentrated on socioeconomic rights and the rights of selected vulnerable groups such as the 'erased', migrants and asylum applicants, Roma, and the new ethnic minorities in Slovenia.[23] Therefore, they have attracted justified criticism of their often unequal, selective and inefficient approach to human rights violations in Slovenia.[24] However, ensuring pluralism

[18] 'Annex to the note verbale dated 16 July 2015 from the Permanent Mission of Slovenia to the United Nations addressed to the President of the General Assembly, Candidacy of Slovenia for the Human Rights Council, 2016–2018', A/70/358, 3 September 2015, 2.

[19] ibid 3.

[20] Constitution of the Republic of Slovenia, Official Gazette of the Republic of Slovenia No 33/91-I, 42/97, 66/2000, 24/03, 69/04, 68/06, 47/13, and 75/16, Art 159(1). See generally on the nature of ombudsman institution, Thomas Bull, 'Rapports: Sweden: The Original Ombudsman: Blueprint in Need of Revision or a Concept with More to Offer?' (2000) 6(3) *European Public Law* 334.

[21] Jernej Letnar Černič, 'Kritična ocena dosedanjega delovanja slovenskega varuha človekovih pravic' (2014) 14(4) *Hrvatska i komparativna javna uprava* 921.

[22] ibid.

[23] See Annual Reports of the Human Rights Ombudsman of the Republic of Slovenia 1994–2017.

[24] See eg Jambrek (n 14).

in national human rights settings has often been one of the most difficult challenges facing national human rights institutions in Central and Eastern Europe.[25]

In order for constitutional democracy and the rule of law to function properly it is crucial that state institutions afford equal attention to the choice, scope and treatment of all issues of concern in society. Otherwise, state national human rights institutions, such the Office of the National Ombudsman of the Republic of Slovenia, can quickly lose their credibility and legitimacy. A politically biased choice of topics can cause difficulties in the exercise of their constitutional functions and particularly in the acceptance of their work in society.[26] We have argued before that 'the power of the Ombudsman … is also conditioned by the previous reputation and work of an individual occupying such a function'.[27] In this line the Constitutional Court of the Republic of Slovenia stipulated in case U-I-10/08-19 that 'the Ombudsman acts primarily with his influence and with the reputation that gives rise to the power of his authority'.[28] It added that 'the ombudsman can act only in a democratic environment where the responsible government and advanced officials are genuinely prepared to deal with unintentionally caused violations and deficiencies'.[29]

The Paris Principles on the Status of State Institutions for the Promotion and Protection of Human Rights accordingly stipulate in Principle 3 that national institutions for the protection of human rights must function independently and ensure the pluralistic treatment of human rights issues.[30] More specifically, they recommend that states ensure that 'the composition of the national institution and the appointment of its members … shall … ensure the pluralist representation of the social forces (of civilian society) involved in the protection and promotion of human rights'.[31] However, an ombudsman should not only ensure pluralism in the composition of the national human rights institution, but also in its remit. National human rights institutions are obliged to act on the basis of pluralism, without supporting any particular ideological position in society. We have previously argued that the Ombudsman Office of the Republic Slovenia 'must avoid the unequal, selective and arbitrary protection of human rights,

[25] See eg Richard Carver, 'National Human Rights Institutions in Central and Eastern Europe: The Ombudsman as Agent of International Law' in Ryan Goodman and Thomas Pegram (eds), *Human Rights, State Compliance, and Social Change: Assessing National Human Rights Institutions* (Cambridge, Cambridge University Press, 2012).

[26] Gorazd Trpin, 'Komentar 159. člena ustave' in Lovro Šturm (ed), *Komentar Ustave Republike Slovenije* (Ljubljana, Fakulteta za podiplomske državne in evropske študije, 2002).

[27] Letnar Černič (n 21) 922.

[28] Constitutional Court of the Republic of Slovenia, Decision U-I-10/08-19, 9 December 2009, para 17.

[29] ibid.

[30] United Nations Principles relating to the Status of National Institutions (the 'Paris Principles'), General Assembly Resolution 48/134, 20 December 1993, www.ohchr.org/EN/ProfessionalInterest/Pages/StatusOfNationalInstitutions.aspx (accessed 24 April 2019).

[31] ibid, principle 3(1).

since only in this way can the public be convinced of their actions'.[32] The state and public institutions that broadly work on human rights, such as the Study Centre for National Reconciliation, the Office of the Advocate of the Principle of Equality and the Office for National Minorities of the Republic of Slovenia, have faced similar difficulties in exercising their mandate, although their influence has so far been marginal. The Study Centre for National Reconciliation, on one hand, deals primarily with the preservation of memory and transitional justice and does not have powers to accept complaints. Nonetheless, the incumbent leadership of this organisation appears to have several times treated human rights violations from the past unequally, which perhaps calls for more external oversight. On the other hand, the Office of the Advocate of the Principle of Equality has only recently started substantial work and enjoys only minor decision-making powers on the basis of the Administrative Procedure Act. The Office for National Minorities of the Republic of Slovenia performs a policy role and assists the government of the Republic of Slovenia with implementing the rights of the Italian and Hungarian national communities and the Roma community and assisting different levels of public administration with discharging their responsibilities relating to those minorities.[33]

In sum, therefore, institutions of all branches of the Slovenian government have in the country's constitutional order rhetorically committed to protect constitutional and international human rights. Interestingly, their daily actions illustrate that their practice has been far removed from their rhetorical commitments, thereby often curtailing the rule of law and democracy. As it stands some of the pertinent daily challenges facing human rights protections include: the non-plural composition of state institutions; the selective, unequal and non-plural choice and treatment of human rights concerns; the institutional lack of knowledge of the standards and the case-law of major international and regional human rights bodies; the lack of institutional capacity and knowledge; the ideological treatment and interpretation of human rights norms; and finally resistance by institutional elites to the internalisation of liberal values of international and regional human rights treaties.[34]

C. Civil Society

Outside the institutional sphere, civil society itself has been deeply divided, often employing a parochial approach, omitting dialogue and preferring a

[32] Jernej Letnar Černič, 'Komentar 159. člena ustave' in Matej Avbelj (ed), *Komentar Ustave Republike Slovenije* (Nova Gorica, Nova Univerza – Evropska Pravna Fakulteta, 2019).

[33] The Decree on the establishment of the Office of the Government of the Republic of Slovenia for Nationalities, Official Gazette of the Republic of Slovenia No 57/13 and 9/17.

[34] See eg Frane Adam and Matevž Tomšič, 'The Dynamics of Elites and the Type of Capitalism: Slovenian Exceptionalism?' (2012) 37(2) *Historical Social Research* 53.

particular human rights issue over others.[35] Some organisations, for example, have focused on the rights of asylum applicants and migrants, the 'erased', the LGTB community, Roma, hate speech and workers' rights.[36] On the other hand, they have often turned a blind eye to civil and political rights and the rule of law such as the right to a fair, independent and impartial judiciary, and transitional justice and prosecutions of crimes against humanity after World War II and the memory thereof.[37] Similar criticism can be levelled against the work agenda of civil society organisations from the opposite ideological side, which have often focused only on transitional justice, pro-life and similar issues.[38] Certainly, both set of organisations exhibit the diversity, plurality and richness of the human rights landscape in Slovenia. Nonetheless, NGOs from all sides at times appear to argue that their particular view on human rights situation is unique, exclusive and objective.[39] Given the specific Slovenian context, some issues attract more attention than others; for instance, it seems that the rights of asylum applicants and migrants, the 'erased', the LGTB community, Roma, hate speech and socio-economic rights have often been more visible than, for example, the (un)fair functioning of the Slovenian judiciary. On the other hand, some civil society organisations have not paid much, or indeed any, attention to transitional justice issues,[40] with few exceptions at most.[41] Such divisions have created a culture of misunderstanding and fear, which does not foster dialogue and debate.[42] Disturbingly, some NGOs have even been spreading hatred towards civil society organisations from the opposite pole, trying thereby to exclude them from public debate and in even some cases calling for the state censure of their work.[43]

[35] Jernej Letnar Černič, 'Vizija učinkovitega varovanja človekovih pravic v slovenski družbi' in Matej Avbelj, Gašper Dovžan, Jernej Letnar Černič and Miha Movrin (eds), *Evropska Slovenija* (Ljubljana, Inštitut Nove revije, 2013) 52–76.

[36] ibid.

[37] ibid.

[38] ibid.

[39] See eg Milan Zver (ed), *Človekove pravice in svoboščine v tranziciji: primer Slovenije* (National Council of the Republic of Slovenia, Office of the Ombudsman, Ljubljana, 1998). See also Andraž Teršek, *Etika politike: Esejistični komentar ustave, z novo ustavo* (Ljubljana, UMco, 2018).

[40] Jernej Letnar Černič, 'Rămăşiţele identitaţii comuniste in Slovenia: justiţia de tranziţie – potenţialul, capcanele şi viitorul său' in Cosmin Budeanca and Florentin Olteanu (eds), *Stalinizare şi destalinizare: Evoluţii instituţionale şi impact social* (Bucharest, Polirom, 2014).

[41] Jernej Letnar Černič, 'Primerjava med slovensko in špansko tranzicijsko izkušnjo' in Mateja Čoh Kladnik and Neža Strajnar (eds), *Represivne metode totalitarnih režimov: Zbornik prispevkov z mednarodnega znanstvenega posveta, Zbirka Totalitarizmi – vprašanja in izzivi*, 2 (Ljubljana, Študijski center za narodno spravo, 2012). Andreja Valič Zver, Damjan Hančič, Boštjan Kolarič, Jernej Letnar Černič and Renato Podbrešič, 'National Report on the Crimes of Communism in Slovenia: Country Report' in David Svoboda, Cóilín O'Connor and Jiří Liška (eds), *Crimes of the Communist Regimes: International Conference: An Assessment by Historians and Legal Experts: Proceedings* (Prague, Institute for the Study of Totalitarian Regimes, 2011).

[42] Jernej Letnar Černič, 'Culture of Fear in Slovenian Society' in Janez Juhant and Bojan Žalec (eds), *From Culture of Fear to Society of Trust* (Zürich, Lit Verlag, 2013).

[43] For more detail, see Letnar Černič (n 15).

As a rule, those NGOs have been trying to present themselves as a unique source of facts, and indeed of ultimate truth. In this way, they have employed their privileged – publicly funded – positions to exclude different opinions and viewpoints from the public debate. As a result, a plural civil society in Slovenia exists primarily on paper. It has through its nature and activities essentially only paid-lip service to its financial sources, mostly the state annual budget. This has resulted in the political ideals of incumbent local and central governments being promoted, thereby entirely contravening the pluralistic foundations of the country's constitutional democracy.

D. Regional and International Human Rights Bodies

Interestingly, the UN international human rights bodies have to a large extent reflected the divisive approach to human rights protection in Slovenia described above. As a result, the UN bodies have expressed concerns about the rights of migrants, refugees and asylum seekers,[44] the erased,[45] prison and detention conditions,[46] conditions in psychiatric institutions,[47] domestic violence,[48] Roma rights[49] and others. However, they have to a lesser extent addressed also rule-of-law issues and freedom of expression and other civil and political rights. The Working Group of the UN Human Rights Council on the Universal Periodic Review has in its 2014 report on Slovenia highlighted several issues, including the ongoing situations of 'erased' persons, the rights of children and elderly persons, and Roma rights.[50] For instance, it urged the Slovenian authorities to 'strengthen the mandates of the Ombudsman for Human Rights and the Defender of the Principle of Equality and avoid any overlap in the execution of their respective mandates (Morocco)';[51] to 'accelerate the process of reform of the Ombudsman for Human Rights in order to comply with the Paris Principles (Tunisia)';[52]

[44] United Nations, 'Consideration of Reports Submitted by States Parties under Article 19 of the Convention: Slovenia', CAT/C/SVN/CO/3/Add.1, 29 August 2012, paras 7, 9 and 17. See also, United Nations, 'Concluding Observations on the Combined Third and Fourth Periodic Reports of Slovenia', CRC/C/SVN/CO/3–4, 8 July 2013, paras 3(a) and 3(d).

[45] United Nations, Human Rights Council, Working Group on the Universal Periodic Review, 'Compilation prepared by the Office of the United Nations, High Commissioner for Human Rights in accordance with paragraph 15 (b) of the annex to Human Rights Council resolution 5/1 and paragraph 5 of the annex to Council resolution 16/21: Slovenia', A/HRC/WG.6/20/SVN/2, 18 August 2014, paras 14–18.

[46] ibid para 22.

[47] ibid para 23.

[48] ibid paras 24 and 25.

[49] ibid paras 28 and 30.

[50] United Nations, Human Rights Council, 'Report of the Working Group on the Universal Periodic Review: Slovenia', A/HRC/28/15, 10 December 2014.

[51] ibid 115.34.

[52] ibid 115.35.

to 'bring the national human rights institution into compliance with the Paris Principles and broaden its mandate to carry out investigations into allegations of torture and ill-treatment (Ukraine)';[53] and to 'create the conditions that allow the Human Rights Ombudsperson to acquire A status according to the Paris Principles … (Chile)'.[54] As for Roma rights, it recommended the Slovenian government 'measurably improve access to the legal system for Roma individuals and other individuals belonging to groups facing discrimination … (United Kingdom of Great Britain and Northern Ireland)'.[55] On a declarative level, the UN Human Rights Council pinpointed a plethora of issues; however, it appears to have turned a blind eye to challenges relating, for instance, to the incorporation of efficient transitional justice measures and to ensuring the right to fair, independent and impartial trials before Slovenian courts.

In contrast, the UN Human Rights Committee has in its 2016 report drawn attention to the erosion of various civil and political rights in Slovenia. It urged the Slovenian authorities to 'expedite efforts to improve the living conditions in detention facilities in line with the Covenant and the United Nations Standard Minimum Rules for the Treatment of Prisoners'.[56] As for the role of judiciary, it observed that 'the State party should adopt a comprehensive strategy to address the backlog of cases throughout the judiciary, particularly in the labour and social courts, and ensure the right to a fair trial without undue delay'.[57] Concerning freedom of expression, it stated that 'the State party should reconsider decriminalizing defamation and restrict the application of criminal law to the most serious cases, bearing in mind that imprisonment is never an appropriate punishment in such cases'.[58] As it stands, the ECtHR has so far delivered 337 judgments against Slovenia, finding at least one violation of the ECHR,[59] particularly highlighting deficiencies to ensure human dignity through state obligations under the right to life and prohibition of torture, inhuman and degrading treatment and/or punishment and the right to fair trial.[60]

[53] ibid 155.36.
[54] ibid 155.37.
[55] ibid 115.73.
[56] Human Rights Committee, 'Concluding Observations on the Third Periodic Report of Slovenia', CCPR/C/SVN/CO/3, 21 April 2016, para 26.
[57] ibid para 26.
[58] ibid para 32.
[59] European Court of Human Rights, Hudoc database, https://hudoc.echr.coe.int/eng#{"documentcollectionid2":["GRANDCHAMBER","CHAMBER"]} (accessed 1 July 2019). See Jernej Letnar Černič et al, *Slovenija pred Evropskim Sodiščem za Človekove Pravice (1994–2016)* (Ljubljana, Fakulteta za Državne in Evropske Študije, 2017); Jan Zobec, 'Slovenia: Just a Glass Bead Game?' in Iulia Motoc and Ineta Ziemele (eds), *The Impact of the ECHR on Democratic Change in Central and Eastern Europe: Judicial Perspectives* (Cambridge, Cambridge University Press, 2016). Republic of Slovenia, Ministry of Justice, Implementation of Judgements of the European Court of Human Rights, www.mp.gov.si/si/delovna_podrocja/aktivnosti_na_podrocju_clovekovih_pravic_in_izvrsevanja_sodb_evropskega_sodisca_za_clovekove_pravice/izvrsevanje_sodb_evropskega_sodisca_za_clovekove_pravice/ (accessed 24 April 2019).
[60] See Chaps 6 and 10 below.

Overall, one can discern heterogeneity in the pronouncements of the various regional and international human rights bodies as to human rights crises in Slovenia. The majority of these bodies have too often only pinpointed recurring themes always highlighted by ministries and publicly funded NGOs. For those reasons, some of them have turned a blind eye to practices affecting fundamental human rights issues such as the right to fair, independent and impartial trial, protections of human dignity against the abuses of state authorities, and the lack of transitional justice measures, all of which certainly call for more examination and attention. This unequal approach has contributed to the creation of a public image that only certain human rights issues are of concern in Slovenia and therefore merit detailed examination. Moreover, such a selective approach has certainly been politically biased, unequal and inefficient. As it stands this approach has also disregarded the indispensable protection of human dignity as an individual and collective value across Slovenian society. On the contrary, state authorities carry negative and positive obligations to investigate, examine and prevent all human rights violations, whether of socioeconomic, civil and political rights. To be clear, only a holistic approach to human rights protections in Slovenia will effectively realise the individual and collective nature of human dignity.

III. THE CURRENT CRISES OF THE RULE OF LAW AND CONSTITUTIONAL DEMOCRACY IN SLOVENIA

Constitutional democracy and the rule of law have been under stress in Slovenia since its democratization, as elsewhere in most of Central and Eastern Europe. Indeed, the current Hungarian and Polish governments have employed a number of wide-ranging normative measures that have undermined the foundations of any state based on the rule of law and constitutional democracy. Those and similar practices have directly blurred constitutional separations between the executive and the legislative power and the judiciary. These governments have carried out systematic and wide-reaching reforms of the judiciary and have forcibly replaced dissident judges particularly at the highest levels of respective judiciaries, namely the Supreme Court and Constitutional Tribunal.[61] Additionally, they have directed attacks at those whom they were not able easily to replace.[62] Any student of law would note that the separation of powers has

[61] See eg Bugarič and Kuhelj (n 71).

[62] Jan Zobec, 'Odziv Jana Zobca: Policistovo ukrepanje zoper mene sem ocenil kot napad', *Delo (Sobotna priloga)* (23 June 2018) www.delo.si/sobotna-priloga/odziv-jana-zobca-policistovo-ukrepanje-zoper-mene-sem-ocenil-kot-napad-62246.html (accessed 24 April 2019); N Ž, 'V bran vrhovnemu sodniku Janu Zobcu stopili priznani slovenski pravniki Teršek, Avbelj in Letnar Černič, ki so izrazili zgroženost nad pogromom mainstream medijev!', *Nova 24 TV* (8 June 2018) http://nova24tv.si/slovenija/v-bran-vrhovnemu-sodniku-janu-zobcu-stopili-priznani-slovenski-pravniki-tersek-avbelj-in-letnar-cernic-ki-so-izrazili-zgrozenost-nad-pogromom-mainstream-medijev/ (accessed 24 April 2019).

been for centuries the quintessential principle of any modern democracy as it prevents elites from applying power arbitrarily.[63]

If the recent constitutional and statutory reforms in Hungary and Poland have been described as constitutional backsliding,[64] it appears that several CEE countries have been witnessing a constant backsliding since democratisation onwards. One could argue that similar or worse events than the recent infringements of the rule of law in Hungary and Poland have been for years a well-established practice in Slovenia and elsewhere, where old arbitrary practices have been taken up by the post-communist transitional elites, which have translated them to all layers of the public and institutional life of the Slovenian state.[65] As a result, Transparency International accordingly ranks Slovenia 36th on its annual corruption perception index.[66] Further, the Economist Intelligence Unit's Democracy Index (EIU DI) ranks Slovenia 36th, describing it as a flawed democracy.[67] As it stands, informal elites have through state authorities governed society not entirely on the foundations of the rule of law, but through rule by law, which they have created and interpreted according to their parochial interests.[68] It is no surprise that Slovenian state institutions have not internalised the values of constitutional democracy, the rule of law and human dignity.[69] Their decision-making has been therefore subjected to the wide-ranging influence of transitional post-communist and other informal elites, who have since democratisation occupied most positions in state institutions and public administration and who have traditionally divided their 'prize' after every election.[70] This preservation and restoration of the status quo has served the interest of the institutional elites, who have sold it to the ordinary people via a media apparatus operating under pressure from their informal networks.[71]

A. The Legislative Branch

The legislative branch of the Slovenian constitutional democracy has so far perhaps most directly represented the popular will. It is divided into two tiers,

[63] Martin Krygier, 'The Rule of Law: Legality, Teleology, Sociology' in Gianluigi Palombella and Neil Walker (eds), *Re-Locating the Rule of Law* (Oxford, Hart Publishing, 2008).

[64] See eg Laurent Pech and Kim Scheppele, 'Illiberalism Within: Rule of Law Backsliding in the EU' (2017) 19 *Cambridge Yearbook of European Legal Studies* 3.

[65] Jernej Letnar Černič, 'Vzpon "novoreka"', *Slovenski čas-Družina* (30 September 2018).

[66] Transparency International, 'Corruption Perception Index 2018', www.transparency.org/cpi2018 (accessed 24 April 2019).

[67] *The Economist*, Intelligence Unit, 'Democracy Index 2017: Free Speech Under Attack', www.eiu.com/Handlers/WhitepaperHandler.ashx?fi=Democracy_Index_2018.pdf&mode=wp&campaignid=Democracy2018 (accessed 24 June 2019), 17.

[68] ibid.

[69] ibid. See eg Bojan Bugarič, 'Administrative Law Developments in Post-Communist Slovenia: Between West European Ideals and East European Reality' (2016) 22(1) *European Public Law* 25.

[70] ibid.

[71] Bojan Bugarič and Alenka Kuhelj, 'Slovenia in Crisis: A Tale of Unfinished Democratization in East-Central Europe' (2015) 48(4) *Communist and Post-Communist Studies* 273.

namely the National Assembly and the National Council, with the latter having only limited law-making competences. The Slovenian Constitution grants the legislative branch the highest position in drafting and adopting binding sources of law. However, its members have traditionally not enjoyed very high esteem, nor have they generated much confidence in their work. The majority of the electorate remains generally unfamiliar with their parliamentary representatives; hardly anybody in Slovenia would be able to name the member of the parliament who represents them from their electoral district.[72] This disconnect goes back to the legal nature of the current electoral system, which is based on proportional representation.[73] More specifically, the current model of the electoral system for the National Assembly is centred on the political parties. Accordingly, it has not allowed individuals even to cast preferential votes within the electoral lists of political parties. It has even permitted electoral districts of immensely different sizes or those without any representation in parliament. As a result, the Constitutional Court declared in November 2018 such legal arrangements found in Article 4 of the Act Establishing Constituencies for the Election of Deputies to the National Assembly, which provides for electoral districts, as unconstitutional and called for their revision within two years.[74]

Such normative arrangements have fostered a the culture of non-accountability and the lack of direct relationships of elected members of parliament with their constituencies.[75] These legal frameworks prompted the creation of this culture of non-accountability as almost none of the decisions made by sitting deputies in the parliament can be traced back to promises they made during the electoral campaign. The legislative branch has also experienced difficulties in understanding the separation of powers as one of the core principles of the rule of law as 14 decisions of the Constitutional Court remain non-executed.[76] By refusing to execute the decisions of the Slovenian Constitutional Court the legislative branch has thereby turned a blind eye to the rule-of-law principle.[77] What is more, the legislative branch has so far walked up a cul-de-sac concerning combating the presence of actual or perceived conflicts of interest, corruption and nepotism. For instance, the Freedom House has in its report 'Nations in Transit 2018 – Confronting Illiberalism' noted that 'Members of the National Assembly made no progress in adopting a code of ethics. … The preparatory activities for adopting the code, which commenced at the beginning of the government's

[72] Jernej Letnar Černič, 'Umanjkanje demokracije' *IUS-INFO* (23 March 2018).

[73] ibid.

[74] Constitutional Court of the Republic of Slovenia, Decision U-I-32/15-65, 26 November 2018.

[75] ibid.

[76] See eg Matej Avbelj, Andraž Teršek, Jurij Toplak, Verica Trstenjak, Veronika Fikfak, Bojan Bugarič and Jernej Letnar Černič, 'Dvojna zloraba prava' *Večer* (29 November 2017) www.vecer.com/krsitev-ustavnosti-in-teptanje-ustavne-demokracije-v-drzavnem-zboru-6357244 (accessed 24 April 2019); Constitutional Court of the Republic of Slovenia, Annual Report 2018, www.us-rs.si/media/porocilo.o.delu.za.leto.2018.pdf (accessed 24 April 2019).

[77] See eg Constitutional Court of the Republic of Slovenia, Decision U-I-269/12-24, 4 December 2014.

mandate, have at the moment halted.'[78] Among the most unfortunate practices of the legislative branch are decisions from 2013 and 2014, where the National Assembly and the National Council, in the absence of any legal basis, withdrew the mandate of an elected deputy and a member of the National Council. As a result, those decisions prompted the Constitutional Court to first suspend and thereafter declare these decisions as arbitrary and therefore unconstitutional.[79]

As it stands, one of the strongest powers held by the legislative branch as regards the rule of law are theoretically the Parliamentary Inquiry Commissions, which have quasi-judicial powers to investigate issues of particular concern. However, their final reports have been in the past rarely executed, mostly due to pressure exercised by informal networks at the practice of the police or prosecutions organs.[80] Overall, it appears that the deputies have only rarely shown any capacity to grasp the essence of the notions of constitutional democracy and therefore have not been able or willing to act accordingly.

B. The Executive Branch

The executive branch of the Slovenian constitutional democracy is the branch of government with the most impact as it oversees the daily functioning of the entire state apparatus and public administration. It is divided into a political part and a part encompassing the state and public administration. It has not been functioning according to the Weberian model of public administration, which requires strict integrity, meritocracy and transparency in the execution of the function of the state institutions and public administration. The daily workings of Slovenian public administration appear not to follow a model based on meritocracy, but that of vested interests, corruption, nepotism and clientelism. Decisions are often adopted in a non-transparent and formalistic manner, contradicting the public interest and advancing only the particular interests of the privileged institutional elites.[81] For instance, the government in autumn 2017 allocated funds for

[78] Marko Lovec, Report on 'Nations in Transit 2018 – Slovenia', Freedom House, https://freedomhouse.org/report/nations-transit/2018/slovenia (accessed 24 April 2019).

[79] Constitutional Court of the Republic of Slovenia, Decision Mp-1/12-13, 21 February 2013; Constitutional Court of the Republic of Slovenia, Decision Up-790/14-19, U-I-227/14-2, 21 November 2014.

[80] See, for example, final reports by Commission of Inquiry to determine abuses in the Slovenian banking system and to determine the causes of and responsibilities for the second rehabilitation of the banking system in independent Slovenia, Official Gazette of the Republic of Slovenia 30/15, www.dz-rs.si/wps/portal/Home/deloDZ/zakonodaja/izbranZakonAkt?uid=C1257A70003EE749C125826C003D5065&db=kon_akt&mandat=VII (accessed 24 April 2019).

[81] See eg Franci Demšar, *Transparentnost in skrb za denar davkoplačevalcev* (Ljubljana, Mladinska knjiga, 2013). See also Polonca Kovač, 'Openness and Transparency in (Slovene) Administrative Procedures as Fundamental European Principles' (2016/2017) 9(2) *NISPAcee Journal of Public Administration and Policy* 49.

a referendum campaign about a second railway link between Koper and Divača only to itself and not to the opposing campaign. This arrangement was later declared an arbitrary exercise of executive power and a direct abuse of the rule of law by the Supreme Court of the Republic of Slovenia.[82] Additionally, it is widely accepted that recruitment and promotion within the public administration is based on political and interest-group connections, leaving qualified candidates who lack connections empty-handed.[83] However, some commentators have also argued that informal elites, and allegedly even organised crime groups, have been present in the functioning of the government, particularly relating to state-owned enterprises, banks and large infrastructure projects.[84] As a result, some researchers have therefore suggested that informal networks constitute a fifth branch of government as they have advanced their parochial interests through the three main branches of government and the media.[85] The shortcomings of the executive branch are therefore general and systematic in nature and scope, and hence require deep and structural reforms at all levels.

C. The Judicial Branch

Across Central and Eastern Europe, as discussed in Chapter 2, institutional elites have attempted to blur the lines separating the three main branches of government. The Slovenian judiciary has in recent decades expressed concerns over attempts by the political class, particularly the legislative and executive branches, to take control of the judiciary. However, even though such minor attempts have occurred in the past, the real problem lies elsewhere. As will be discussed in detail in Chapter 6, the judiciary in Slovenia has since democratisation and independence faced the dilemma of how to achieve internal and external independence and impartiality in order to provide individuals with the right to a fair trial.[86] As it stands, it has suffered from the monopoly of power exercised by the post-communist elites and other informal networks over the highest branches of the judiciary. More specifically, the former communist judicial elites have since democratization broadly maintained control of the judiciary. The limited transitional measures have resulted in hardly any lustration measures

[82] Supreme Court of Slovenia, Decision Uv-10/2017, 14 March 2017.

[83] Franci Demšar and Renata Zatler, *Javna hiša Slovenija: politično kadrovanje* (Ljubljana, Cankarjeva založba, 2018).

[84] Katja Eman, Tine Furdi, Rok Hacin and Bojan Dobovšek, 'Discourse on the Gray Economy, Corruption, and Organized Crime in Slovenia' in Maximilian Edelbacher, Peter C Kratcoski and Bojan Dobovšek (eds) *Corruption, Fraud, Organized Crime, and the Shadow Economy* (Boca Raton, FL, CRC Press, 2015).

[85] Bojan Dobovšek, *Peta veja oblasti* (Ljubljana, eBesede – Dobra država, 2016).

[86] Jan Zobec and Jernej Letnar Černič, 'The Remains of the Authoritarian Mentality within the Slovene Judiciary' in Michal Bobek (ed), *Central European Judges Under the European Influence: The Transformative Power of the EU Revisited* (Oxford, Hart Publishing, 2015).

being brought to completion.[87] Recent examples, further elaborated in Chapter 6, such as the nomination of the former head of public relations of the Supreme Court as vice-minister on the behalf of the Social-Democratic Party, a successor to the Communist Party, illustrate the symbiosis between the highest levels of the judiciary and daily politics.[88] The judges at the highest levels of judiciary often observe that they decide cases neutrally and objectively. However, unlike the Slovenian Constitutional Court, the Supreme Court has been described as a spider's web of informal – political – networks connected with the post-communist elites, which still decide cases on the basis of power or even telephone calls.[89] Such political networks have influenced the recruitment, the election and promotion of judges, and the elections of the presidents of the courts.[90]

Judicial decision-making has therefore been characterized by an authoritarian mentality, formalism, and a lack of meritocracy and transparency. For instance, the public cannot witness sessions of the Judiciary Council and the Supreme Court as they take part behind closed doors.[91] The few judges who have been courageous enough to pinpoint malpractices have thereafter been publicly ostracised.[92] International surveys have also shown that the Slovenian judiciary has yet to fully grasp the essence of the rule of law in its daily practice. The Freedom House report 'Nations in Transit 2018 – Confronting Illiberalism' noted that 'the judiciary continued to face low public trust due to perceptions of inequality before the law and poor effectiveness in prosecuting important and well-connected individuals'.[93] Trust in the judiciary has traditionally been very low due to the existence of informal networks, both internal and external, resulting in decisions being based on private objectives, most often to protect financial interests.[94]

[87] Alan Uzelac, for example, argues that 'the integrity of those who are "lustrating" can be warranted if they are impeccable; if they are not, the vicious circle of "lustrating lustrators" appears, as one of the fundamental paradoxes that are related to the personal element of the lustration practices'. Alan Uzelac, '(In)Surpassable Barriers to Lustration: Quis Custodiet Ipsos Custodes?' in Vladimira Dvořáková and Anđelko Milardović (ed), *Lustration and Consolidation of Democracy and the Rule of Law in Central and Eastern Europe* (Zagreb, Political Science Research Centre Zagreb, 2007), 57–58.

[88] Jernej Letnar Černič, Matjaž Nahtigal, Boštjan Udovič and Iztok Mirošič, Broadcast 'Future of Europe', *Radio Slovenija-Prvi* (20 September 2018) https://4d.rtvslo.si/arhiv/studio-ob-17h/174563533 (accessed 24 April 2019).

[89] Jan Zobec, 'Telefonska justica po slovensko' *IUS-INFO* (30 April 2018).

[90] See eg Barbara Zobec, 'Ponižano Vrhovno sodišče' *Finance* (19 September 2016); Matej Avbelj, 'Izbiranje predsednika Vrhovnega sodišča – slovenski sodni svet je farsa' *Finance* (19 September 2016); Matej Avbelj, 'Bo sodni svet zdaj odstopil?' *Finance* (17 December 2016).

[91] Matej Avbelj, 'Judicial Self-Government in Slovenia', draft prepared for a workshop organised by David Kosař on 'The Rise of Judicial Self-Government: Changing the Architecture of Separation of Powers without an Architect', Prague, September 2017 (unpublished manuscript on file with author). See generally, David Kosař, *Perils of Judicial Self-Government in Transitional Societies* (Cambridge, Cambridge University Press, 2016).

[92] See eg Zobec (n 62).

[93] Lovec (n 78).

[94] European Commission, 'Communication from the Commission to the European Parliament, the Council, the European Central Bank, the European Economic and Social Committee and the Committee of the Regions – The 2018 EU Justice Scoreboard', COM(2018) 364 final, Brussels, 28 May 2018, figure 57.

Figure 5.1 Perceived independence of courts and judges among companies

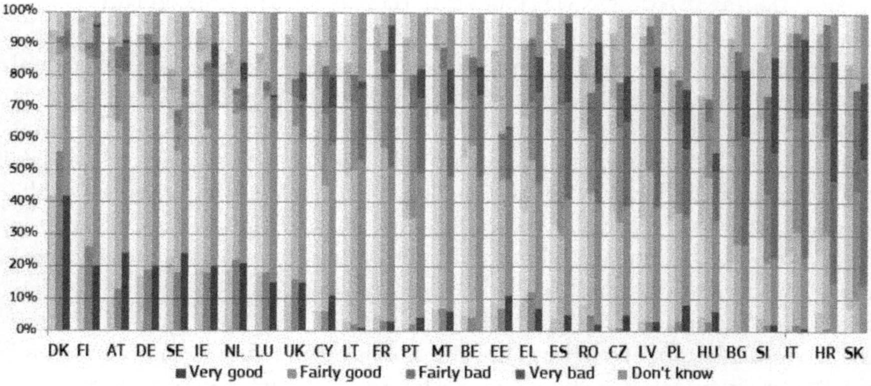

Source: Eurobarometer, European Commission, 'Communication from the Commission to the European Parliament, the Council, the European Central Bank, the European Economic and Social Committee and the Committee of the Regions – The 2018 EU Justice Scoreboard', COM(2018) 364 final, Brussels, 28 May 2018, 42, figure 57, https://ec.europa.eu/info/sites/info/files/justice_scoreboard_2018_en.pdf (accessed 24 April 2019) – light colours, 2016 and 2017; dark colours, 2018.

The EU Justice Scoreboard clearly illustrates that the perceived independence of Slovenian courts and judges among the general public[95] and the perceived independence of courts and judges among companies[96] are among the worst five EU Member States (see Figure 5.1). The reasons for this low trust lie in the presence of informal networks advancing vested interests and in political interference from outside and within.[97] Another negative trait of the Slovenian judiciary has been the constant and persistence resistance, as will be explained in Chapters 10 and 11, towards normative and sociolegal reforms influenced by the ECtHR and the CJEU. Accordingly, judges at the highest levels appear not to consider themselves bound by ECtHR judgments. They perceive these judgments as recommendations that can be followed or not, even in the most straightforward cases where there clearly exists a statutory basis for their execution as in the Criminal Procedure Acts, which allows for the reopening of proceedings on the basis of an ECtHR judgment.[98] For above reasons the current state of the rule of law and constitutional democracy in Slovenia leaves much to be desired. Not only normative but in particular sociolegal reforms are required to respond to current deficiencies in the exercise of the rule of law and constitutional democracy, which has triggered the current distrust of professionals and the lay public in the Slovenian judiciary.

[95] ibid figure 55.
[96] ibid figure 57.
[97] ibid figure 56.
[98] See *Koprivnikar v Slovenia* no 67503/13 (ECtHR, 24 January 2017).

IV. THEORISING REASONS FOR THE CURRENT CRISES OF THE RULE OF LAW AND CONSTITUTIONAL DEMOCRACY IN SLOVENIA

As explained, the normative protections of human rights and fundamental freedoms and the rule of law are quite advanced in Slovenia. What has been lacking has been the effective execution and enforcement of such protections in practice. The enforcement of human rights protections and the rule of law has unfortunately been part of the ideological struggle in the Slovenian public sphere. Accordingly, certain interest groups and individuals have attempted to monopolise the human rights movement by concentrating only on selected topics, which are closer to their ideological positions.[99] The rule of law has been often interpreted as the rule by law and has been employed to advance the narrow interests of institutional elites, contrary to the common good and the Weberian model of bureaucracy. Such struggles appear to have been thereafter repeated in reports by various international bodies on the human rights situation and the rule of law in Slovenia. There are manifold reasons for such traits: institutional limitations; lack of capacity; resistance to the influence of European institutions due to parochial interests and the desire to preserve the status quo; ideological bias and division; lack of internalization of human rights values; lack of economic pluralism; and lack of periodic change in government. This section first explores the traits behind the current crises of the rule of law and constitutional democracy in Slovenia, whereas the lack of economic pluralism and crises of democracy are respectively explored in Chapters 4 and 7.

A. Institutional Limitations, the Lack of Capacity and Resistance to the Influence of European Institutions

State institutions in Slovenia have traditionally been weak, generally showing a lack of meritocracy, integrity, transparency and respect for the rule of law. Most individuals working in public administration and occupying the highest positions would not be able to explain the meaning of the rule of law, the application of which in Slovenia has been subject to powerful interests of informal parallel networks.[100] Consequently, those institutions have been hotbeds of corrupt practices, which have bred constant conflicts of interest and/or appearances thereof.[101] In line with this modus operandi, civil servants and public

99 Avbelj (n 4). See also Zobec and Letnar Černič (n 86).

100 See eg Frane Adam and Matevž Tomšič, 'Elite (Re)Configuration and Politico-Economic Performance in Post-Socialist Countries' (2002) 54(3) *Europe-Asia Studies* 435; Frane Adam and Matevž Tomšič, 'Elites, Democracy and Development in Post-Socialist Transition' (2002) 31(1) *Österreichische Zeitschrift für Politikwissenschaft* 99. See also Ali Žerdin, *Ujetniki omrežij* (Ljubljana, UMco, 2018).

101 See in detail Demšar and Zatler (n 83).

employees have maintained their status quo, with few individuals committed to working for the common good in line with constitutional principles and values. The Weberian model of public administration has thus been translated only formally to Slovenia's public administration. The reason for this deficiency in the exercise of the rule of law is not so much the absence of effective transitional justice measures as the direct lack of internalisation of the values of constitutional democracy among civil servants, public employees and public officials. As a result, this modus operandi has left the door open to corruptive and arbitrary practices.

As far as normative human rights protections are concerned, Slovenia still lacks a proper national human rights institution, which would fulfil the criteria of the Paris Principles relating to the status of national institutions,[102] despite many calls from international bodies to establish one. The UN Human Rights Committee noted in its 2016 report on Slovenia that: 'The State party should take measures to establish a fully functioning and independent national human rights institution with a broad-based human rights mandate and provide it with adequate financial and human resources.'[103] Accordingly, the Slovenian parliament in 2017 adopted an amended Human Rights Ombudsman Act,[104] which attempted to place the Office of the National Ombudsman in the line with the Paris Principles. These inter alia require national institutions to proceed on the basis of independence and pluralism without any government involvement.[105] They are obliged to reflect pluralist views both in the composition of institutions and also in the selection of topics for investigation and examination. States are to ensure that national human rights institutions are equipped with adequate resources and that they enjoy a broad mandate, which gives them the competence to conduct efficient and adequate investigations.[106] Further, several other similar institutions in public administration have been under-equipped to appropriately deal with the rule of law and effective human rights protection. The judiciary has often, particularly at both the lowest and highest branches, demonstrated a lack of knowledge of the case-law of the highest European judicial organs.

The influence of European institutions has been welcome on the normative level, although less in practice, particularly within the judiciary. For instance, the Slovenian Supreme Court has in several cases refused to follow ECtHR judgments.[107] Makarovič et al therefore rightfully observed that post communist elites 'cannot ignore the international institutional frame-work in which the country is integrated. … Nevertheless, if these recommendations or even

[102] United Nations Paris Principles (n 30).

[103] United Nations, Human Rights Committee, 'Concluding Observations on the Third Periodic Report of Slovenia', CCPR/C/SVN/CO/3, 21 April 2016, para 6.

[104] Human Rights Ombudsman Act, Official Gazette of the Republic of Slovenia No 69/17 – official consolidated text.

[105] United Nations Paris Principles (n 30).

[106] ibid.

[107] See Chaps 6 and 10 below.

demands challenged some entrenched interests, they could provoke tensions or even revolts among their protagonists.'[108] They add that 'Slovenian political elites are still pro-European, but often in mere pro-forma fashion.'[109] As a rule, the values of constitutional democracy have yet to be fully internalized in the institutional life of Slovenian society. This modus operandi reflects the apparent lack of knowledge as to the core objectives and goals of human rights protections and the rule of law. It illustrates resistance towards internalization of such values in domestic settings. Those values have had to take a backseat to more pertinent concerns about the status quo, old practices, informal networks, parochial interests, corruption, nepotism, clientelism and the exercise of 'dirty togetherness'. As a consequence, such practices have interfered with the need for the rule of law and human rights to be equally, efficiently and impartially employed and protected.

B. Ideological Bias and Divisions

One of the major reasons for the inefficient, ineffective and unequal protections afforded human rights and the rule of law in Slovenia has been the political bias of the majority of actors – from both government and civil society – involved in their realisation. These actors have protected and interpreted the rule of law and human rights through their particular ideological lenses, thereby attempting through media propaganda to present them as neutral and objective. This approach has created the impression that human rights aim to protect a particular ideology or worldview and that they are not about protecting vulnerable individuals; and moreover that no significant challenges to the rule of law have occurred. For instance, the Slovenian judiciary has rarely been challenged by publicly funded NGOs about its independence and impartiality. Amnesty International Slovenia has chosen to focus on the rights of asylum applicants, Roma, 'erased' persons and migrant workers, as well as on gender rights.[110] However, it has never explained in detail why it has paid hardly any attention to the civil and political rights of ordinary Slovenians such as the right to a fair trial, the protection of human dignity against the arbitrary denial of life or the prohibition of torture, inhumane and degrading treatment or punishment. The lack of any critical view of the rule of law and human rights protections is also standard practice at public educational institutions, particularly the universities of Ljubljana and Maribor.[111]

[108] Makarovič et al (n 3) 210.
[109] ibid.
[110] Amnesty International Slovenia, Campaigns, www.amnesty.si (accessed 24 April 2019).
[111] See eg Lovro Šturm, 'Začetek revolucionarnega kazenskega prava na Slovenskem in njegovi odmevi po drugi svetovni vojni in po demokratizaciji in osamosvojitvi Slovenije' (2017) 25(3) *Acta Histriae* 719.

Due to their majoritarian position state institutions have generally followed such trends. They have similarly emphasised protection of socioeconomic rights and the issues raised by publicly financed NGOs. Such practices have often been characterised by a politically biased and partial approach to the application of the rule of law and human rights protection. However, this approach has undermined the credibility and legitimacy of these institutions in the society, which has perceived such institutions as politically illegitimate, leaving their official position and credibility shattered. Such practices have created vicious circles where all seems fine and well, particularly to external observers. Therefore, what has been lacking is a balanced, holistic and pluralistic approach to human rights protection, which would treat all human rights concerns equally and afford equal protection to victims of any kind of human rights violation.

Civil society organisations in Slovenia have therefore been subject to heavy criticisms influenced by the ideological bias that favours the policies of transitional elites. These ideological biases can be clearly seen from their work programmes, reports, media interventions, etc. There is nothing wrong with political bias per se; however, the lack of clarity and the presence of actual or perceived conflicts of interest of public employees and officials in decision-making are highly undesirable. Interestingly, some civil servants and public employees at various levels have often chosen not to disclose their actual or perceived conflicts of interest. Most civil society organisations are able to function only because of governmental financial support, with some exceptions, eg Amnesty International Slovenia. Interestingly, most NGOs working in the field of human rights have been, controversially, publicly funded. One survey reports that 30 of the largest NGOs have been allocated €50 million in the last 10 years.[112] Therefore, it comes as no surprise that these NGOs rarely level criticism at government policies, and if they do, their criticism is generally only moderate.

NGOs have therefore mostly not been critical of the weak rule of law and constitutional democracy in Slovenia, as they have tended to concentrate on socioeconomic rights; they have paid little attention to civil and political rights and only when these have been connected to the rights of certain vulnerable groups.[113] Crimes against humanity or fairness of judicial proceedings have often been forgotten, secondary human rights topics in Slovenia.[114] For these reasons, Slovenian civil society organisations should not be considered as proper civil society organisations, but rather as an extension of government or even as part of the public administration. Clearly, with their carefully chosen ideologies

[112] Uredništvo, '55 milijonov evrov, ki jih namenjate aktivistom za odstavitev Damirja Črnčeca' *Domovina.je* (22 September 2018) www.domovina.je/55-milijonov-evrov-ki-jih-namenjate-aktivistom-za-odstavitev-damirja-crnceca/ (accessed 24 April 2019).

[113] Letnar Černič (n 15).

[114] Lovro Šturm, 'O kratenju človekovih pravic in temeljnih svoboščin v Sloveniji v obdobju 1945–1950' in Drago Jančar (ed), *Temna stran meseca: kratka zgodovina totalitarizma v Sloveniji 1945–1990: Zbornik Člankov in dokumentov* (Ljubljana, Nova revija, 1998).

and political objectives they cannot be described as independent and impartial actors. Therefore, despite advances in the formal frameworks of such protections, they have often in practice protected human rights unequally, selectively and inefficiently.[115]

C. Weak Internalisation of the Values of the Rule of Law and Human Rights Protection

The values of the rule of law and human rights protection have not been fully internalised in state institutions, public administration and generally in Slovenian society.[116] As a rule, this deficiency has been particularly observed within the judiciary which finds it difficult to internalise the liberal values of a modern constitutional democracy. We have previously submitted that 'the institutional elites in some CEE states demonstrate that those standards have been unwelcome in most cases, even though subsidiarity is the main pillar of the Convention system' and that 'the rule of law de iure frameworks … have not been translated into practice and translated in the rule of law de facto'.[117] As a result, there has been an apparent resistance to the transition of the values of constitutional democracy into the daily institutional lives of the current democracy and the rule of law. The values and narratives of human dignity, pluralism, tolerance, equality, freedom and solidarity have been only partially taken up by persons performing public functions in Slovenia's public administration. State institutions and public administration may have developed ethics codes,[118] but these have remained only paper exercises, lacking any proper application in practice.[119] Moreover, Slovenian society has not as whole internalised the values of compassion and empathy.[120] The narrative of the rule of law has not been incorporated in Slovenian society as a tool to preclude the arbitrary use of power by the institutional elites but as a technical tool to apply often unjust statutory provisions. Nevertheless, Slovenia's constitutional democracy and its institutions could in the long term be reformed through education.[121] However, even educational institutions such as the schools of law of

[115] Ibid 211.

[116] See generally Jeffrey L Dunoff and Joel P Trachtman (eds), *Ruling the World? Constitutionalism, International Law, and Global Governance* (Cambridge, Cambridge University Press, 2009).

[117] Jernej Letnar Černič, 'Impact of the European Court of Human Rights on the Rule of Law in Central and Eastern Europe' (2018) 10(1) *Hague Journal on the Rule of Law* 111, 133.

[118] Code of Ethics for Public Servants in State Bodies and Local Communities, 11 April 2011, www.mpju.gov.si/fileadmin/mpju.gov.si/pageuploads/Uradniski_svet/Code_of_ethics.pdf (accessed 24 April 2019).

[119] Vojko Strahovnik and Gašper Škarja, 'Upravljanje etike in integritete ter etični kodeksi v upravi' (2014) 14(4) *Hrvatska i komparativna javna uprava* 905.

[120] Janez Juhant, 'Resnica in sočutje se odpirata na bregovih večnosti' (2015) 75(2) *Bogoslovni vestnik* 199; Janez Juhant, 'Nasilje in sočutje v ideologijah in religijah in slovenska tranzicijska resničnost' 2014 74(2) *Bogoslovni vestnik* 175.

[121] Vojko Strahovnik, 'Pomen moralne teorije za etično vzgojo' (2017) 28(1/2) *Šolsko polje* 45.

the universities of Ljubljana and Maribor have in some instances not shown leadership in the introduction of such values. They have continued to invite as guest speakers persons known to have violated human rights and the rule of law.[122] They have turned a blind eye rather than questioning systematic abuses of the rule of law and human rights.

V. CONCLUSION

The various facets, traits and narratives of the crises in constitutional democracy, human rights protection and the rule of law in Slovenia are complex and diverse; however, state institutions have not afforded equal attention to all of them. This chapter has painted the landscape of these crises, thereby analysing the reasons for the current crises in human rights protection and the rule of law as the main pillars of constitutional democracy in Slovenia. In so doing it has provided a descriptive-analytical account of the current crises and has investigated the direct and indirect reasons why a proper, fully fledged constitutional democracy has not been established in Slovenia. As it stands, the formal normative architecture required for the realisation of the rule of law and human rights protection has been, with few exceptions, well established in Slovenia. It is comparable to any modern and mature European constitutional democracy. However, the normative design and its application have in practice acted like estranged distant cousins. The modern normative architecture has not been diligently translated into the daily practice of public institutions and in some instances even in the private sector. In some aspects, it appears to have been held hostage by the powerful interests of well-established networks deriving from as far back as the totalitarian system and beyond. As a rule, human rights protection and the rule of law have not been applied based on the principles of transparency, fairness, independence and meritocracy; rather, they have too often been subject to 'dirty-togetherness', nepotism and informal post-communist networks and other informal networks. Protections of human rights and the exercise of the rule of law have often been applied unequally, selectively and inefficiently. As a result, the arbitrary, efficient and transparent application of human rights protection and the rule of law has in the Slovenian public space created the appearance that constitutional democracy and the rule of law are legal concepts open to subjective interpretations by different groups who can tailor these to their own needs. This approach has had deep and long-lasting negative consequences for the daily functioning of state institutions, public administration and wider Slovenian society. The next chapter now turns to the crises of constitutional democracy and how to address these.

[122] See eg Damijan Florjančič (President of the Supreme Court of the Republic of Slovenia), lecture at University of Maribor, Faculty of Law, 25 October 2018.

6

The Judiciary and the Rule of Law in Slovenia

'Everyone strives to attain the Law,' answers the man, 'how does it come about, then, that in all these years no one has come seeking admittance but me?' The doorkeeper perceives that the man is nearing his end and his hearing is failing, so he bellows in his ear: 'No one but you could gain admittance through this door, since this door was intended for you. I am now going to shut it.'

Franz Kafka, *The Trial*

I. INTRODUCTION

THE PROTECTION OF the rule of law stands at the forefront of the Slovenian Constitution.[1] This is not a coincidence, but a deliberate choice. It was the absence of the rule of law in Yugoslavia, gross violations of human rights and the rights of national minorities that were the principal reasons[2] setting Slovenia on the path to independence. The new Constitution, drawing on the discontinuity function of modern constitutionalism,[3] sought to create a clear rupture with the past, which, naturally, involved the transformation of the old authoritarian regime into democracy and the rule of law. If the existence and quality of democracy is traditionally associated with and dependent on a political process, in which political parties, civil society and the media play a role, the rule of law is conventionally understood as an (exclusive) realm of the judiciary. In a constitutional democracy, of course, as Chapter 2 has shown, democracy and the rule of law, the political process and adjudication, do not constitute two separate, unconnected worlds, but stand for two distinct discursive practices that are subject to differing substantive and procedural discursive constraints. However, they still make up a holistic, constitutionally democratic

[1] Constitution of Republic of Slovenia 1991, 2016, Art 2, declares that Slovenia is a country based on the rule of law.

[2] Basic Constitutional Charter 1991.

[3] James Tully, *Strange Multiplicity – Constitutionalism in an Age of Diversity* (Cambridge, Cambridge University Press, 1995) 64; U-I-109/10 [2011] [7].

whole. Therefore, while admittedly in what follows this chapter will focus exclusively on the contribution of the judiciary to the rule of law in Slovenia, this is not to suggest that the remaining two branches of power and the political process in general have no role to play in sustaining and fostering, or conversely undermining, the rule of law. On the contrary, as democracy and the rule of law are intrinsically connected in a constitutional democracy, it is the political democratic process which affects the law, as much as the (rule of) law impacts back on the quality of democracy. This, for now theoretical, claim will also be illuminated with the help of some empirical examples taken from Slovenian political and judicial practice over the past three decades.

Under the new constitutional system of Slovenia, different to its socialist past, the judiciary has been elevated to a separate branch of power. The Yugoslav system of undivided powers has been replaced by a system that divides powers between legislative, executive and judicial branches.[4] The three branches do not exist side by side in mutual isolation, but are linked in a complex system of checks and balances ensuring that none of the branches prevails over the other; that the powers are exercised in a non-arbitrary manner; and, most importantly, that the equal freedom of every individual is respected.[5] With respect to the judiciary, the Constitution provides that judges shall be independent in their performance of their judicial function and that they shall be bound by the Constitution and statutes.[6] In this way, the Constitution guarantees the judges, and the judiciary as a whole, a special, independent constitutional status, protecting them from inappropriate political and executive interference. This constitutional status of an independent judiciary simultaneously confers certain individual human rights. Accordingly, everyone in Slovenia has the right to a trial without undue delay, by an independent and impartial statutory court[7] in front of a lawful, natural judge.[8]

However, constitutional regulation and the status of the judiciary is one thing in writing; what matters for the actual rule of law is translating these normative ideals into practice. In the case of the Slovenian judiciary a notable gap between the normative ideals prescribed by the Constitution and their actual operationalization in practice can be observed. The most important principles of a well-functioning judiciary, the prerequisites of a fair trial, such as the length of proceedings, the independence of judges, their impartiality, the capacity and willingness to protect human rights of individuals and, eventually, trust in the judicial system, exhibit major weaknesses and shortcomings in actual practice. This is not a value judgement of the present authors, but a fact corroborated

[4] Constitution of Republic of Slovenia 1991, 2016, Art 3.

[5] See Christoph Mollers, *The Three Branches: A Comparative Model of Separation of Powers* (Oxford, Oxford University Press, 2013).

[6] Constitution of Republic of Slovenia 1991, 2016, Art 125.

[7] ibid Art 23/1.

[8] ibid Art 23/2.

by the judicial practice, expert reports and (trans)national rankings, including those by the EU and the Council of Europe. In what follows, we describe the most important deficiencies in the functioning of the Slovenian judiciary with regard to the central principles stipulated above, and analyse the main causes for this state of affairs.

II. SYSTEMIC VIOLATION OF THE RIGHT TO A TRIAL IN A REASONABLE TIME

In October 2005 the ECtHR handed down its decision in *Lukenda*.[9] It ruled that the Slovenian courts, by taking more than five years to decide on the petitioner's claim to an increased disability benefit, violated the petitioner's right to a hearing in a reasonable time as ensured by Article 6(1) ECHR. However, the ruling went beyond the conclusion on the facts of that particular case, since the ECtHR, flooded by similar cases from Slovenia,[10] stressed that the present case was not

> an isolated incident, but a systemic problem that has resulted from inadequate legislation and inefficiency in the administration of justice. The problem continues to present a danger affecting every person seeking judicial protection of their rights.[11]

Between 1994 and 2018 the ECtHR rendered 263 judgments against Slovenia for failing to respect the right to a trial in a reasonable time.[12] This statistic confirms that since the independence of Slovenia, and especially after the judicial reforms between 1994 and 1997, the excessive duration of trials has been one of the main problems facing the Slovenian judiciary. Since 1995 the Ombudsman, under pressure from individual complaints, has continually warned about this systemic problem, calling on the representatives of all three branches to adopt the necessary measures.[13] The issue was of great concern especially since the backlogs in the period between 1991 and 2000 were increasing, while the number of new cases reaching the courts was actually in decline.[14] The courts themselves were not up to the challenge – neither the ordinary courts, which caused

[9] *Lukenda v Slovenia* App no 23032/02 (ECtHR, 6 October 2005).

[10] Slovenia was convicted in 263 cases for the violation of the right to a trial in a reasonable time, www.echr.coe.int/Documents/Stats_violation_1959_2017_ENG.pdf (accessed 16 February 2019).

[11] See *Lukenda v Slovenia* App no 23032/02 (ECtHR, 6 October 2005).

[12] Annual Report 2018 of the European Court of Human Rights, Council of Europe. available at: www.echr.coe.int/Documents/Annual_report_2018_ENG.pdf (accessed 16 February 2019).

[13] Ivan Šelih, 'Dolgotrajnost sodnih postopkov skozi letna poročila varuha' *Varuh človekovih pravic RS* (24 August 2018) www.varuh-rs.si/medijsko-sredisce/aktualni-primeri/novice/detajl/dolgotrajnost-sodnih-postopkov-skozi-letna-porocila-varuha-1/?cHash=fec54496b45dc0aea9299bdcd053fbd7 (accessed 16 February 2019); '20 let varuha človekovih pravic' www.varuh-rs.si/fileadmin/user_upload/pdf/Razne_publikacije/20let_VCP_a_www.pdf (accessed 16 February 2019).

[14] Vlada RS, Vrhovno sodišče RS, 'Sodni zaostanki v Republiki Sloveniji (analiza vzrokov in predlogi za zmanjšanje in odpravo)' 7.

the increasing delays in the judicial system, nor the Constitutional Court which failed to prescribe an adequate remedy for an ongoing systemic violation of the right to a trial in a reasonable time.

Up until 2005 the Constitutional Court consistently ruled that in cases of violation of the right to a trial in a reasonable time the aggrieved individuals had to apply to the administrative courts.[15] They were competent to review such complaints in cases that were still pending.[16] No complaints, except in cases of the alleged violation of this right before the Supreme Court, were admissible at the Constitutional Court.[17] Furthermore, in cases of excessively long, but already completed trials, the administrative courts as well the Constitutional Court refused their jurisdiction.[18] As the alleged violation of the right to a trial in a reasonable time ceased with the conclusion of a trial, the case was considered moot and the petitioner could only sue for damages, either material or immaterial, in a new trial before the civil courts.[19] Eventually, after having taken this second round of judicial proceedings and after having exhausted all the remedies, he could turn to the Constitutional Court. In short, for 15 years the Constitutional Court preserved a system in which the violation of the right to a trial in a reasonable time could only be protected by another trial, potentially also a protracted one, and in which, moreover, the petitioner stood very little chance of success. He had to prove the state's responsibility for damages according to the general principles of tort law, including an unlawful action by the ruling judge.[20] The Slovenian legal system, as upheld by the Constitutional Court, thus provided neither for an efficient procedure to ensure the protection of the right to a trial in a reasonable time, nor could such proceedings, even if completed, result in a just compensation as prescribed by the ECtHR. As succinctly put by the Ljubljana Court of Appeals, the right to a trial in a reasonable time was until 2006 effectively just a dead letter.[21]

Interestingly, the Constitutional Court changed its established case-law literally at the eleventh hour, just two weeks before the above-mentioned *Lukenda* ruling by the ECtHR,[22] and clearly in its anticipation. Drawing closely on the ECtHR jurisprudence, especially on the case of *Kudla v Poland*,[23] the Constitutional Court reversed itself by issuing a declaratory ruling in which it found

[15] Up-369/97 [1998].
[16] U-I-65/05 [2005].
[17] Up-277/96 [1996].
[18] Up-73/97 [2000].
[19] ibid.
[20] For the state's and the judge's individual responsibility for damages, see: Damjan Možina, 'Odškodninska odgovornost države' [2013] *Pravni letopis* 162; Jan Zobec, 'Odškodninska odgovornost sodnika in odgovornost države zanj' [2013] *Pravni letopis* 185.
[21] VSL Sklep I Cpg 493/2007 [2007].
[22] The decision of the Constitutional Court in case U-I-65/05, Ur l 92/05. was adopted on 22 September 2005, while the ECtHR ruled in *Lukenda* on 6 October 2005.
[23] *Kudła v Poland*, App no 30210/96 (ECtHR, 20 October 2000).

the Slovenian system of protection of the right to a trial in a reasonable time unconstitutional and ordered the legislature to fill the systemic gap by adopting legislative changes.[24] This resulted in the adoption of the Protection of Right to Trial without Undue Delay Act.[25] The Act introduced the means for parties to a case to request acceleration of delayed proceedings[26] and to obtain just compensation in form of a pecuniary redress, a written statement or a publication of the ruling in case of violation of the right.[27]

The ECtHR *Lukenda* case prompted the then government to initiate a comprehensive 'Lukenda project' to eliminate all cases of judicial delays by the end of 2010. The project was preceded by other reform attempts to increase the quantity and quality output of the Slovenian judiciary. However, as the success of the Herkules, Matra and Matra Flex projects was relatively moderate,[28] the Lukenda project was more ambitious. Its objectives were to ensure better judicial facilities; appoint new judges, expert and administrative staff; provide for stimulating remuneration; simplification of legislation; complete informatisation of the judiciary; and additional training of judicial staff as well as reorganisation and better administration of courts.[29] The outcome has been mixed. The trend of growing judicial delays has clearly been reversed and for several years now the courts have been reported to resolve more cases as these are annually received.[30] Also, the focus has been gradually moved from a mere quantity of resolved cases to their quality too. The number of judges, expert and administrative staff has been increased significantly.[31]

As a result, the number of convictions of Slovenia in front of the ECtHR for violation of the right to a trial in a reasonable time has since dropped significantly and the Committee of Ministers of the Council of Europe declared in 2016 that judicial delays no longer pose a systemic problem in Slovenia.[32] This

[24] U-I-65/05 [2005] [14].

[25] Protection of Right to Trial without Undue Delay Act 2006 (Zakon o varstvu pravice do sojenja brez nepotrebnega odlašanja).

[26] ibid Arts 5 and 8.

[27] ibid Arts 15–18.

[28] Court of Auditors RS, *Revision Report on Judicial Delays* (Ljubljana, 16 March 2011).

[29] Government RS, 'Poročilo o izvajanju Programa za povečanje učinkovitosti sodstva in odprave sodnih zaostankov – projekt Lukenda', www.vlada.si/fileadmin/dokumenti/cns/doc/0811071528505_a185v2cc.doc (accessed 16 February 2019).

[30] Vrhovno sodišče, 'Letno poročilo o učinkovitosti in uspešnosti sodišč' (Ljubljana 2018).

[31] In order to accelerate the decrease in the number of judicial delays in the period between 2005 and 2008 the number of judges rose by 147 from 939 to 1086 (eg by 15.6 per cent), the number of judicial staff was increased by 677 from 2539 to 3216 (eg by 26.7 per cent). The number of state prosecutors increased from 174 to 181, their assistants from 20 to 23 and of the other personnel from 204 to 256, which means 15.6 per cent altogether. The number of state attorneys rose by 63.6 per cent from 33 to 54, www.vlada.si/fileadmin/dokumenti/cns/doc/0811071528505_a185v2cc.doc (accessed 16 February 2019).

[32] 'Fewer Rulings against Slovenia at European Court of Human Rights' (*RTVSLO* 28 January 2017) www.rtvslo.si/news-in-english/fewer-rulings-against-slovenia-at-european-court-of-human-rights/413615 (accessed 16 February 2019).

being the case, it does not mean that the problem of excessive duration of trials no longer exists. On the contrary, the annual statistics published by the Supreme Court demonstrate that while the courts are now able to control their dockets[33] and they do resolve more cases as these are actually received on a yearly basis,[34] these statistical findings do not apply to the hard and complex cases, in particular not in the field of criminal law.[35] There the efficiency trend has been one of stagnation or even explicit deterioration. The president of the District Court of Ljubljana, which is the largest Slovenian court, thus warned in February 2018 that unless reforms were implemented in a month, the criminal system would collapse, as in a year or two the management of criminal law cases would become impossible.[36] The European Commission too has stressed the criminal justice efficiency challenges in Slovenia.[37] It has also noted other delays in the planned reforms of the judicial system.[38] According to the EU Justice scoreboard, measuring the efficiency of trials across the Member States, Slovenia ranks 17th in litigious civil and commercial cases[39] and 9th in administrative cases,[40] while the ranking for criminal law trials is not available. Most importantly, the ultimate goal of the Lukenda project, to eliminate all judicial delays by 2010, has not been met. In 2017 the backlog of all Slovenian courts consisted of almost 160,000 cases,[41] among which 72,000 qualified as judicial delays. In 14,686 cases the trial has lasted longer than 5 years and in 2,699 cases even more than 10 years.[42]

The statistical data thus corroborate the Council of Europe's finding that judicial delays no longer pose a systemic and general problem in Slovenia. This general conclusion, however, neither means that in individual cases the right to a trial in a reasonable time is no longer violated nor suggests that the Slovenian judiciary is efficient enough.[43] The above stipulated lack of efficiency in the

[33] Vrhovno sodišče, 'Letno poročilo o učinkovitosti in uspešnosti sodišč' (Ljubljana 2018) 67–71.

[34] ibid.

[35] ibid.

[36] Majda Vukelić, 'Pred kolapsom sodnega sistema' *Delo* (23 February 2018) /www.delo.si/novice/slovenija/pred-kolapsom-sodnega-sistema.html (accessed 16 February 2019).

[37] European Commission, '2018 European Semester: Assessment of progress on structural reforms, prevention and correction of macroeconomic imbalances, and results of in-depth reviews under Regulation (EU) No 1176/2011, – Report on Slovenia' COM(2018) 120 final, <ec.europa.eu/info/sites/info/files/2018-european-semester-country-report-slovenia-en.pdf> (accessed 16 February 2019).

[38] ibid: 'Additional projects are being implemented to further improve the quality of justice, but the judicial map reform is facing delays. Several projects, including on publishing all first instance judgments and on informing parties about the progress of their case, are being implemented. However, the judicial map reform, currently in consultation with the courts, is facing delays and risks remaining unfinished during Parliament's current term. Timeframes will be further enhanced by judges calculating the optimal length of different types of cases, based on procedural phases.'

[39] ibid 12.

[40] ibid 13.

[41] Supreme Court of Slovenia, Annual Report (2017) 25.

[42] ibid 65.

[43] 'The Wheels of Justice Grind Slow' *The Economist* (18 February 2016) www.economist.com/europe/2016/02/18/the-wheels-of-justice-grind-slow (accessed 16 February 2019).

so-called hard and complex, in particular criminal cases, rather suggests that the judicial system might be skewed in favour of influential individuals, white-collar crime, and crime with major economic and financial repercussions. For these cases are considered hard and complex and take much longer, quite often reaching no judicial epilogue, while petty crimes, typically committed by ordinary people, tend to be judicially disposed with much more swiftly. This disequilibrium in the courts' efficiency in trying grave and less grave crimes merits our attention given that, according to the European Commission's report, economic crime and corruption have caused significant financial damage in Slovenia, eg €2.29 billion or 81.7% of all recorded criminal pecuniary damage for the period 2009–14.[44] This might suggest that certain, but not exclusively, extrajudicial factors influence the functioning of the judiciary in important cases to the detriment of its efficiency to ensure de jure or de facto impunity of formal and informal power-holders.[45] Testing this hypothesis invites us to explore the problems related to judicial independence and impartiality in Slovenia.

III. CHALLENGES TO JUDICIAL INDEPENDENCE

Judicial independence is a prerogative of a judicial branch of power and simultaneously an individual human right in terms of ensuring a fair trial. Judicial independence has a collective-institutional dimension as well as an individual dimension.[46] Independence pertains to the judiciary as an institution, as well as to each individual judge separately. Judges are entitled to be independent from the legislative and executive branches. The two are prohibited from meddling in the functioning of the judiciary on a systemic level, as this would place the judicial system under political, economic or administrative pressures to bend in favour of the standing government or (in)formal power structures.[47] The legislative and executive branches are absolutely prohibited from interfering in individual cases and with individual judges. The latter, however, are independent not just from the legislative and the executive branch, but also from the judiciary as a whole and individual judicial colleagues. The individual independence of a single judge entails that he ought to be free of formal and informal institutional pressures to decide a given case as he or she finds it best legally fit.

[44] European Semester, Country Report: Slovenia, <ec.europa.eu/info/sites/info/files/2018-european-semester-country-report-slovenia-en.pdf, 46 (accessed 16 February 2019).

[45] For a critical discussion, see Anže Voh Boštic, 'Zakaj močnim, bogatim in vplivnim uspe prelisičiti pravno državo' *Pod črto* (7 December 2017) podcrto.si/zakaj-mocnim-bogatim-in-vplivnim-uspe-prelisiciti-pravno-drzavo (accessed 16 February 2019).

[46] For a more in-depth discussion, see eg John Ferejohn, 'Independent Judges, Dependent Judiciary: Explaining Judicial Independence' [2001] *Southern California Law Review* 353.

[47] See also Frank Cross, 'Judicial Independence' in Gregory A Caldeira, R Daniel Kelemen and Keith E Whittington (eds), *The Oxford Handbook of Law and Politics* (Oxford, Oxford University Press, 2009).

The constitutional mechanisms for ensuring the described judicial independence on the institutional and individual level consist of prescribed appointment and dismissal procedures for judges, immunity guarantees and tenure, judicial self-governance and financing. These judicial independence-securing mechanisms do not absolve judges from institutional responsibility. On the contrary, they are part and parcel of a complex web of checks and balances in which the three branches of power cooperate as well as mutually control each other, which also ensures the legal and democratic accountability of the judiciary and individual judges alike. As in the case of the right to a trial in a reasonable time, for which a written guarantee alone is insufficient, judicial independence too must be ensured both formally and in practice.[48]

The formal dimension of judicial independence in Slovenia is well established.[49] Three strands of criticism can, however, be identified. The first relates to the appointment procedure. The Slovenian system for appointing judges presents a notable exception in the EU. Whereas in most EU Member States judges are almost always[50] appointed by the executive or by a special (judicial) independent body,[51] in Slovenia the judges are appointed by the parliament (the National Assembly). This is a remnant of the communist past, of its system of undivided powers in which all important decisions had to be taken, at least formally, by the then socialist parliamentary assembly. On the other hand, this particular system of parliamentary appointment of judges is also a product of a political compromise between the new and old political forces at the time of independence. While the old communist forces strived to preserve as much as possible the institutional solutions of the old system, the new forces wanted to avoid the continuous influence of the old forces over the judiciary. Since the new forces at the time were in the majority in the parliament, while the office of the President of the Republic was occupied by the former president of the Communist Party, a compromise was made to divest the President of his institutional role of appointing judges and to leave this competence with the parliament.[52]

This constitutional solution has ever since been criticised by the judiciary, by the main organ of judicial self-government, the Judicial Council, as well as by most academics.[53] These critical voices feared the potential politicisation of the process of judicial appointments. Until recently, the fears were mostly

[48] Bernd Hayo and Stefan Voigt, 'Explaining De Facto Judicial Independence' [2007] *International Review of Law and Economics* 269.

[49] What follows draws heavily on Matej Avbelj, 'Contextual Analysis of Judicial Governance in Slovenia' [2018] *German Law Journal* 1901.

[50] In Latvia and Poland too judges are appointed by parliament.

[51] Justice Scoreboard 2018, 45.

[52] Avbelj (n 49).

[53] Marko Novak, 'Nevarno razmerje: politika nad Sodnim svetom' *IUS-info* (2016); also Marko Novak, 'Volitve sodnikov – mora Slovenija ostati evropska izjema?' *IUS-info* (2016); but see: Jernej Letnar Černič, 'Kako izvoliti sodnike' *IUS-info* (2016); Tone Jerovšek, 'Ustavna ureditev sodstva' (2001) VII *Dnevi javnega prava* 47.

unfounded, as the parliament has exercised its constitutional competence more like a notary duty,[54] automatically voting in all the proposals received by the Judicial Council.[55] However, in 2015 the National Assembly rejected two reasoned proposals by the Judicial Council,[56] which put the practice of automatic approvals of judicial appointments by parliament to an end. This has reinforced the initial criticisms, which have nevertheless not led to any institutional reforms.

The second strand of a criticism relates to the establishment of the Office for the Supervision of the Management of the Courts.[57] This was created within the Ministry of Justice to review whether the administrative management of the courts met the prescribed quality standards.[58] The judiciary and several legal experts have argued that this newly instituted administrative supervision, irrespective of the fact that it is headed by a judge appointed by the Judicial Council,[59] poses the risk of substantive interference in judicial decision-making and hence presents a threat to judicial independence.[60] For now, in the absence of much practice, it is still too early to tell whether or not these critiques are well founded.

Finally, the last issue which has emerged with regard to the formal independence of judiciary relates to judicial remuneration. As part of the Lukenda reform project discussed above, the government in 2006 proposed a judicial salary reform, which would introduce a financial stimulus for more productive judges, but simultaneously reduce the salaries of other, less deserving judges. The Constitutional Court struck the reform down for formal and substantive reasons. Formally, the government's reform did not meet the requirements of the principle of legality, as the judicial salaries had not been determined in a statute, but in a special parliamentary Act. On substantive grounds, however, the Court found that the reform had undermined the economic independence of judges and put them in an unequal position with other branches of power in terms of their remuneration.[61] After a lengthy strike, the judiciary secured most of its demands and, with the assistance of the Constitutional Court, secured its economic independence.

[54] Luka Vavken, 'Delovanje in upravljanje sistema rednega sodstva' (master's thesis, University of Ljubljana Faculty of Law, 2016) 101.

[55] Jerovšek (n 53) 53, who reports that in the first ten years of Slovenian independence the National Assembly refused to appoint three candidates, which were eventually nevertheless appointed upon the repeated proposal by the Judicial Council.

[56] In 2015 the National Assembly unanimously refused the proposal of the Judicial Council to appoint a practising attorney at law as a Court of Appeals judge. Later in 2015, it also refused by an ordinary majority to elect an acting Court of Appeals judge to the Supreme Court. See Avbelj (n 49) 1913.

[57] Služba za nadzor organizacije poslovanja sodišč, www.mp.gov.si/si/delovna_podrocja/sluzba_za_nadzor_organizacije_poslovanja_sodisc (accessed 16 February 2019).

[58] Courts Act 1994, 2018, Art 65a.

[59] This position is currently held by a designated judge, Miran Jazbinšek.

[60] Vavken (n 54) 81.

[61] Constitutional Court U-I-60/06 [2006]; U-I-159/08 [2008]. For a comment, see Gregor Virant, 'Sodstvo – močna veja oblasti in hkrati učinkovit servis' [2007] *Pravna praksa* 6–7.

Other than these three instances of imperfect legal arrangements, formal independence of the judiciary and judges has not posed any problems and is entirely comparable to the regulation existing in other well-ordered democracies. The judges are appointed through a prescribed procedure, they are tenured and enjoy full professional immunity.[62] They can be dismissed only on the basis of carefully crafted legislative conditions in cases of serious violations of judicial duties upon a proposal from the Judicial Council.[63] The latter is the main body of judicial self-governance, which formally decides on all the important aspects of judicial office. It prescribes the criteria for and decides on the selection, appointment and dismissal of judges, presidents and vice-presidents of the courts.[64] It evaluates the work of judges and makes decisions on their promotion as well as sanctioning in disciplinary proceedings.[65] Out of 11 members of the Judicial Council, 6 are judges who are thus in the majority, and the judiciary, hence, literally governs itself. However, this solution, which formally works in favour of judicial independence, is not necessarily conducive to such results in practice.

There are several problems with de facto judicial independence in Slovenia. We can distinguish between historical, institutional and operational failures as well as the lack of professional integrity that have in practice led to the undermining of judicial independence. Historical problems relate to the specificities of the Slovenian transition from the totalitarian communist regime to democracy. In 1991 the then socialist judges with a limited tenure were turned en masse, as if in a judge-making factory, into democratic judges with permanent tenure.[66] The limited lustration clause that ought to have prevented the judges who violated human rights under communism from continuing to occupy their posts in democratic Slovenia was essentially left unapplied.[67] This occurred for personal, collegiate reasons – it was judges in the Judicial Council who were deciding on the future fate of their colleagues and friends – as well as for political reasons. The politically unseated communists worked in favour of as soft and as 'smooth' a transition as possible,[68] to ensure that their political loss would

[62] Constitution of the Republic of Slovenia 1991, 2016, Art 134.
[63] ibid Arts 130 and 132.
[64] Judicial Council Act 2017 Art 23/1.
[65] ibid Art. 23/3.
[66] Alenka Leskovic, 'Deset let pozneje' [1999] *Pravna praksa* 33.
[67] See further Jan Zobec and Jernej Letnar Černič, 'The Remains of the Authoritarian Mentality within the Slovene Judiciary' in Michal Bobek (ed), *Central European Judges under the European Influence* (Oxford, Hart Publishing, 2015) 126, who point out that the entire body of lawyers was implicated in the previous regime and quote the following fitting paragraph by France Bučar: '[W]ith their often unnecessary or at least excessive meekness … they themselves have strengthened the totalitarian system, as by their conduct and laxness they were giving it justification of at least acceptability, if not legitimacy, and thus inadvertently confirming that it is right and simultaneously giving it an absolution for its violations of fundamental human rights.' France Bučar, '"Pravnik v današnjem času" (uvodno predavanje na 30. Dnevih slovenskih pravnikov)' ['"Lawyer in Current Times": The Introductory Lecture at the 30th Day of Slovene Lawyers]' [2004] *Pravna praksa* 6.
[68] Anton Bebler, 'Slovenia's Smooth Transition' [2002] *Journal of Democracy* 127.

not be translated into any decline of their influence in the other institutions of the state, the economy, and hence in society as a whole. Keeping the judiciary as unchanged as possible was seen as a guarantee that the criminal economic activities mostly pursued by the post-communist elite would go unsanctioned during the transition period. As this intention has materialised to a great extent, the judiciary has increasingly been perceived by the general public as an ally of the old communist forces and hence clearly politicised. It has been even argued that the courts, unable to withstand strong political pressure, have through their actions furthered partisan political interests rather than the rule of law.[69]

The appointments of the highest judicial functionaries deepened that impression of the political dependency of the judiciary further. The most illustrative example is the case of Mr Branko Masleša, a highly controversial political and legal figure.[70] The centre-right post-communist parties claimed that before independence he was, as a local communist functionary and a criminal judge in Koper, an avid supporter of the Yugoslav (later occupying) Army and a critic of the independence movement. He also took part in a trial that rendered the last death sentence in the Socialist Republic of Slovenia. Also, public charges were made against him that during the communist regime he participated at verifications of killings of renegades on the Yugoslav– Italy border.[71] For these reasons, Mr Masleša faced considerable hurdles in the process of his appointment to the Supreme Court in 2000. His candidacy was first refused and was successful only on a rerun. However, only a few years later, in 2010 he became a president of the Judicial Council and was shortly thereafter, while still in that position, appointed President of the Supreme Court. The allegations against him were repeated and this time even corroborated by the Constitutional Court Justice and two Supreme Court judges, but to no avail. They were dismissed by the Judicial Council, chaired by Miro Cerar (who later became Prime Minister), as a clear sign of disrespect for professional ethics.[72]

The peculiarity of the appointment of Mr Masleša as the President of the Supreme Court, who heads and represents the entire Slovenian judiciary, was not an isolated example. In fact, the opposite is true. Since the independence of Slovenia the presidency of the Supreme Court has either been repeatedly mired in controversy or the role has simply been left vacant.[73] Most significantly, the first president of the Supreme Court of the Republic of Slovenia was simply the last president of the Supreme Court of the Socialist Republic of Slovenia. Until 1993, almost three years after the fall of the communist regime, the Slovenian judiciary

[69] Bojan Bugarič, 'Crisis of Constitutional Democracy in Post-Communist Europe: "Lands In-between" Democracy and Authoritarianism' [2015] *ICON* 229.

[70] For a more in-depth discussion, see Avbelj (n 49).

[71] Mr Masleša has, however, repeatedly refuted these allegations as false and malicious.

[72] 'Sodni svet, Zavarovanje dostojanstva in sodnikov in sodstva' [2010] *Pravna praksa* 36.

[73] The Supreme Court was thus without a President first for three years, then for nine months and most recently for three months. For a more in-depth discussion, see Avbelj (n 49) 1920.

thus continued to be headed by a high communist functionary, a member of the central committee of the Communist Party of Slovenia. This is important not just for symbolic reasons, but also for very practical, operational reasons that go to the heart of the actual independence of the judiciary in Slovenia, or its lack thereof.

The court presidents and, in particular the President of the Supreme Court, play a very powerful, indeed a decisive, role in the actual set-up of the Slovenian judiciary. This power derives in large part from the extreme institutional weakness of the main body of judicial self-governance, the Judicial Council. While the latter is a constitutionally mandated body and has been endowed with far-reaching statutory competences designed to ensure the independence of judiciary, in practice the decisions formally taken by the Judicial Council are made elsewhere. As the Judicial Council lacks material, IT, and personnel support, and none of its members conducts his or her role professionally, decisions are effectively made by those who prepare the files that the Judicial Council votes on, typically behind closed doors.[74] The files on promotion and career development of judges are prepared by the Personnel Councils of the respective courts, which are chaired by the presidents of these courts. These presidents also preselect the candidates for a judicial function. They thus essentially filter those who are allowed to enter the judiciary, determine the career prospects of existing judges and, finally, structure the overall working environment.[75]

From socialist times, this judicial working environment has been strictly hierarchical and very bureaucratic. It is worth noting that, unlike in many other EU Member States, the Slovenian courts and their presidents are also in charge of the so-called judicial administration.[76] This provides them not just with control over the quality of judicial work of the lower judges in the process of the appellate judicial review, but also with the tools of administrative formal and informal control over the judges of the lower courts and especially over those who are at the beginning of their career. The judiciary in Slovenia is conceived of as a collectivist system, run by the presidents of the courts and ultimately by the President of the Supreme Court. It is a vast system of judges, the second highest per capita in the EU.[77] The huge number of judges reduces the importance of a single judge. In the judicial body of almost 1,000 judges in a country of two million people, what matters is the judiciary as a whole, represented by the leading judicial functionaries, whereas each individual judge is just a small piece in the overall judicial mosaic that he or she should serve.

A Slovenian judge thus resembles much more a civil servant in a hierarchical bureaucratic structure than an independent, highly professional lawyer

[74] Nevenka Šorli, 'Odstopna izjava članice Sodnega Sveta' [2003] *Odvetnik* 31.

[75] Avbelj (n 49).

[76] For a comprehensive comparative discussion on judicial self-governance in Europe, see David Kosar (ed), 'Judicial Self-Governance in Europe' [2018] *German Law Journal* 1567.

[77] Justice Scoreboard 2018, 31.

with an established reputation. Slovenian judges, not unlike other civil servants, consequently and understandably strive for anonymity and have been very reluctant to ensure more transparency, which would enable the professional and lay public to familiarise itself with their professional backgrounds, judicial achievements through the publication of all their rulings and to ensure a better media oversight.[78] The status of a judge as conceived of in Slovenia has consequently also attracted individuals who prefer conformity to independence; and who stress fidelity to the system rather than building their own jurisprudence on the basis of their best understanding of the law. As Slovenian judges are also relatively poorly remunerated, as their judicial facilities are old and inadequate, and as the expert and administrative support they receive is insufficient, the job of a judge is unappealing and has been attracting lawyers with below-average qualifications.[79] These individuals are much more compatible with the existing system than highly qualified lawyers, who would, as professionally conscious individuals with high judicial integrity, also function personally independently.

However, to ensure that everyone is properly integrated into the system, the Supreme Court in 2017 launched an EU-funded project, 'Let's Adjudicate Together'. This implements a mentoring programme for newly appointed judges by senior judges to ensure that the newcomers quickly become accustomed to the modalities of the system.[80] This project reveals, in the best manner possible, the inbuilt comprehensive self-understanding of the Slovenian judiciary. This ought to be a collectively independent system against the other two branches of power and the public at large, but it is simultaneously made of hundreds of dependent judges as parts of this large, hierarchically structured system, pervaded by a bureaucratic mind-set. Not only has such a system been chronically inefficient, as we have seen above, but its de facto independence has essentially been taken away due to the compact, hierarchic structure headed by the so-called judicial oligarchy,[81] composed of the court presidents, the President of the Supreme Court and their close and loyal administrative staff, which renders the system generally porous and open to political or other influence.[82]

In a judicial system, such as that of Slovenia, which is labour intensive, and composed of many dependent, bureaucratically minded and typically very black-letter judges, the question of who appoints the presidents of the courts and who these individuals are becomes crucial. Those who control these individuals, essentially hold de facto control over the Slovenian judicial system.[83] The independence of the judiciary as a whole clearly cannot exist if judges are

[78] www.mp.gov.si/si/medijsko_sredisce/novica/7248 (accessed 16 February 2019).

[79] Janko Marinko in an interview, podcrto.si/sodni-zaostanki-zakaj-so-nastali-in-kako-dolgotrajni-so-postopki-pred-slovenskimi-sodisci-danes (accessed 16 February 2019).

[80] Avbelj (n 49) 1913.

[81] Jan Zobec, 'Sodniški novi razred' [2018] *Finance*, www.finance.si/8848227 (accessed 9 September 2019).

[82] Marko Šorli, 'Neučinkovit sodni sistem – uspešno vodenje?' [2013] *Pravna praksa* 1.

[83] Matej Avbelj, 'Pravni mit 5: Zakaj slovensko sodstvo ne more biti neodvisno' [2016] *Finance* https://www.finance.si/8844169 (accessed 28 October 2019).

not individually independent or where the judicial system as a whole acts to the detriment of the individual independence of judges. This is confirmed by the international rankings of the Slovenian judiciary in terms of its independence. Both the EU and the Council of Europe's reports demonstrate that Slovenia ranks comparatively very low with regard to the perceived independence of its judiciary.[84] More than half of the responses find the independence of judges in Slovenia fairly bad or very bad, which puts the country in 24th position out of 28 Member States. These reports quote the inadequate status of judges,[85] interference from economic or other specific interests,[86] and interference or pressure from government and politicians as the most important reasons for the perceived lack of independence.[87] The business community sees the independence of the Slovenian judiciary in even worse terms, so that almost two-thirds of respondents evaluate independence as fairly bad or very bad.[88] Finally, in the judges' own evaluation judicial independence fares even worse, as only Latvian and Lithuanian judges judge their independence less favourably than their Slovenian counterparts.[89] This disquieting fact, however, does not come as a surprise especially when taking into account that individual judges have claimed that the privacy of their mail has been violated, their files have been subject to illegal searches, and their personal dossiers have been tampered with to hinder their promotion.[90] However, these claims have not been taken seriously either by the judiciary or the media, while the Office of the President of the Supreme Court has flatly rejected them.[91]

IV. IMPARTIALITY OF THE JUDICIARY

The de facto lack of judicial independence in Slovenia translates also into a lack of impartiality. The two principles, although not the same, are intrinsically connected. Both function to ensure a free trial, and while the principle of judicial independence acts as a shield against the two other branches of power, the principle of impartiality applies to the actual parties in the case. They have the right to be treated equally, free of any subjective bias on the part of the judge or, indeed, of any judicial behaviour that could distort the very appearance of impartiality.[92]

[84] Slovenia ranks 24 out of 28 EU contries, EU Justice Scoreboard 2018, 40.
[85] More than 30 per cent of respondents share this opinion; ibid 41.
[86] More than 40 per cent of respondents share this opinion, ibid.
[87] Almost 50 per cent of the respondents share this opinion, ibid.
[88] ibid 42.
[89] ibid 44.
[90] Jan Zobec, 'Kot smetana na torti' [2018] *Pravna praksa* 1; Matej Avbelj, 'Srhljivke iz slovenskega sodstva' *Finance* (19 January 2019) www.finance.si/8943642 (accessed 16 February 2019).
[91] Peter Lovšin, 'Sodišče zavrača Zobčeve očitke o vdorih v pošto, brskanju po kabinetih in podtikanju dokumentov' *Dnevnik* (26 January 2019) www.dnevnik.si/1042859589 (accessed 16 February 2019).
[92] See eg cases *Hit doo v Slovenia* and *Perak v Slovenia*, App no 37903/09 (ECtHR, 1 March 2016) in which the ECtHR has found that the same judge sat on two different instances.

In short, 'Not only must justice be done; it must also be seen to be done.'[93] This section emphasises two methodologically distinct instances of the lack of judicial impartiality which, taken together, cast a fuller, if not yet complete, light on this important element of judicial functioning in Slovenia. The first relates to the judicial behaviour in the notorious Patria trial.

The lengthy Patria case began to unfold in Slovenia in 2006. It was a case against Mr Janez Janša, the leader of the main Slovenian opposition party, who was accused and convicted on all three charges, and imprisoned just days before the general parliamentary elections in 2014, for having accepted the promise of an unknown reward at a vaguely determined time, at an undetermined place and by an undetermined mode of communication to use his influence, then as Prime Minister, to have a military contract awarded to the Finnish company Patria.[94] The case was from the very beginning conducted in an extremely unusual way, raising suspicions that this was a politically motivated persecution of a leading political opponent. It started by way of a direct indictment and hence avoided the procedural guarantees of an appellate review that an ordinary indictment is subject to. The trial on all instances lasted for almost a decade and it had through media orchestration distorting effects on three general elections to the National Assembly, local elections as well as elections to the European Parliament.[95]

In the meantime and as the case was pending, a Higher Court judge, Vesna Rakočević Bergant, in her academic extrajudicial writing publicly congratulated the District Court judge for the courageous sentencing (then not yet final) of the accused.[96] She likened the protests by Janša's supporters in front of court to the hysterical reactions of North Korean children at visits by Kim Jong Un.[97] The trial at the Supreme Court was, however, presided over by the aforementioned Mr Masleša who, in order to ensure that he would actually sit on the case, appointed himself as president over all criminal cases that would take place up to the end of that judicial year. In so doing, Mr Masleša selected cases for himself, and through his previous public appearances he marred the appearance of judicial impartiality even further. In front of a crowd of judges gathered at the annual 'Days of Judiciary' event Mr Masleša used the occasion to launch tirades against both the defendant, who at the time had an open deadline for a request for extraordinary legal remedy at the Supreme Court, as well as against one of the Constitutional Court judges.[98] In addition, the very same supreme

[93] *The King v Sussex Justices, ex parte McCarthy* [1924] [1924] KB 256, [1923] EWHC KB 1.

[94] For an in-depth analysis of the case, see Matej Avbelj, *Nepravna država* (GV Založba, 2015).

[95] Matej Avbelj, 'How to Reform the Rule of Law in Slovenia' in Frane Adam (ed), *Slovenia: Social, Economic and Environmental Issues* (Nova Science Publishers 2017).

[96] Vesna Rakočević Bergant, 'Zakaj meni nihče ne piše sodb v Murglah?' [2013] *Pravna praksa* 33.

[97] ibid 33.

[98] Avbelj, Matej, 'Failed Democracy: The Slovenian Patria Case – (Non)Law in Context' (4 July 2014), originally published in Slovenian as Matej Avbelj, 'Zadeva Patria – (ne)pravo v kontekstu' [2014] *Pravna praksa*, available at papers.ssrn.com/sol3/papers.cfm?abstract_id=2462613 or dx.doi.org/10.2139/ssrn.2462613.

public prosecutor who then gave the final sentence in the Patria case was taking part in the event.[99]

The final ruling in the Patria case was, eventually, voided by a unanimous decision of the Constitutional Court. The Constitutional Court found that the defendant had been convicted of an abstract criminal act, that the judges at all instances violated the principles of *lex certa*, *lex scripta* and *lex stricta* in criminal law and that, furthermore, Mr Masleša, as the President of the Supreme Court and of the trial chamber himself, also violated the requirement of impartiality and hence the constitutional guarantee of a fair trial.[100] However, in response to the Constitutional Court's decision, the Supreme Court,[101] the County Court of Ljubljana[102] and the Office of the State Prosecutor General in three separate but very similar public statements, expressed their disagreement with the decision, arguing that the Constitutional Court by way of its hierarchic supremacy simply arrived at a different interpretation of the law and in so doing even imperilled the prosecution of the crimes of corruption in the future.[103] The Constitutional Court, however, did not rule on the merits of the case, but ordered a retrial by giving clear constitutional guidance as to how the case ought to be decided on the first level to which it was remanded. The first-instance judge let the statute of limitation pass and issued a procedural verdict. This led most of the media, as well as leading politicians, to conclude that the accused ultimately failed to prove his innocence. Finally, when Janša and his political party sued for damages from the actual judges and a prosecutor whose actions had been found unconstitutional, the President of the Slovenian Judicial Association intervened in the media to send a message that judges in such a case cannot be held to account.[104] The case, which was still pending when this public statement was made, which was itself a clear violation of judicial impartiality, was subsequently indeed resolved by the first- and second-instance court against the petitioner's political party whose claim for damages was rejected.[105]

Of course, by focusing on a single case no general conclusions on the state of impartiality of Slovenian courts can be made. However, the uniqueness of this case, the parties involved, the enormously high political stakes, the behaviour of senior judges and, eventually, the unconstitutional conduct of the President of the Supreme Court himself and the absence of the required follow-up to the

[99] See the official report from the event, at www.sodisce.si/vsrs/objave/2014060616053789/.

[100] Up-879/14 [2014], Up-883-14 [2014], Up-889/14 [2015].

[101] www.sodisce.si/vsrs/objave/2015042415373322/ (accessed 16 February 2019).

[102] www.sodisce.si/mma_bin2.php?nid=2015042414201349&static_id=20150424141742 (accessed 16 February 2019).

[103] Matej Avbelj, 'Slovenia Constitutionally Reloaded but Still Failing' *Verfassungsblog* (25 April 2015) verfassungsblog.de/slovenia-constitutionally-reloaded-but-still-failing/#.VUskk_ntlBc.

[104] Andrej Petelinšek, 'Sodniško društvo zavrača možnost odškodninskih tožb zoper sodnike' *Večer* (12 April 2018) www.vecer.com/sodnisko-drustvo-zavraca-moznost-odskoninskih-tozb-zopoer-sodnike-6444352 (accessed 16 February 2019).

[105] Decision of the Maribor Court of Appeals I Cp 291/2019, 7 May 2019.

decision of the Constitutional Court by the ordinary courts, allow us to peer into the actual functioning of the Slovenian judiciary and its (in)capacity to guarantee the impartiality of trials in the most important cases.

The second instance illustrating the lack of judicial impartiality in Slovenia makes a more systemic, sociological argument, zooming into the very small Slovenian legal community, which might per se, conceptually and ab initio, prevent the actual existence of judicial impartiality. The main systemic obstacle in its way is the so-called 'legal homeliness'.[106] The term refers to a system of informal connections between the main actors in the Slovenian justice system, which can significantly and not infrequently impact decisively on the outcome of judicial procedures that on their face and in the eyes of external observers strictly follow the letter of the law and meet the highest standards of judicial independence and impartiality.[107] These connections take place across several dimensions, between family members, friends, business partners and influential politicians. Their existence and relative influence is made possible and facilitated by the following factors: the Slovenian legal community is tiny and ideologically quite homogeneous; awareness of the importance of professional ethics is low; and peer solidarity reigns in cases that call for sanctioning of deviations. All of this is turning the legal community overall into an example of 'dirty togetherness'.[108] This has been famously defined by Adam Podgorecki as

> perverse forms of loyalty based on a matrix of different, more or less connected, partnership aimed at making use of all formal and official structures in order to take them over for private goals, taking advantage of their administrative position and formal power.[109]

The number of practical examples of this phenomenon is very high, but there is one in particular that deserves our attention. This is the case of a secretary-general of the former government of Miro Cerar, who was appointed to that position from his previous role as a judge, a role that was suspended for the duration of his secretary-generalship. However, while he was a secretary-general, and a suspended judge, he also acted as an attorney in a trial in the case of a private business dispute involving his wife. And in this case, acting from the highest office of the government to defend his family business interests in the court, he even filed a motion that all Slovenian judges ought to recuse themselves from his case as they, as state employees, could not rule independently and impartially in his wife's dispute with the state. It took several weeks and mounting media pressure before the secretary-general eventually stepped down, during

[106] Matej Avbelj, 'Pravni mit 5: Zakaj slovensko sodstvo ne more biti neodvisno' [2016] *Finance* https://www.finance.si/8844169 (accessed 28 October 2019).

[107] ibid.

[108] Janine R Wedel, 'Dirty Togetherness: Institutional Nomads, Networks, and the State–Private Interface in Central and Eastern Europe and the Former Soviet Union' [2003] *Polish Sociological Review* 139.

[109] Adam Podgorecki, 'Polish Society: A Sociological Analysis' [1987] *Praxis International* [1987] 7 Praxis International 57.

which period he continued to enjoy the full support of his Prime Minister.[110] This was a case in which legal homeliness, combined with the occupation of the very high administrative office, was completely transparent. However, there are many more cases where dirty togetherness acts behind the scenes and is much less visible to the public eye.

An acute, but little discussed, impartiality problem is the fact that the law in Slovenia is often, not unlike in other countries, a family business. However, due to Slovenia's small size, different members of the same family not infrequently run an influential law firm and occupy important positions in the prosecutor's office, the state attorney's office, in the courts and even in the Constitutional Court. Such close family relations even in an ideal situation, let alone a transitional post-communist country with a very poor legal culture, create appearances of conflict of interests and raise concerns about their impact on the impartiality of judges and the capacity to conduct trials in an impartial manner. Furthermore, it is important to note that for the 40 years after World War II there was only one law school in Slovenia, which means that lawyers in important, as well as less important, positions all know each other. The informal ties engendered by this legal collegiality, which have been created over the years, are in many cases more significant than the formal rules and procedures of the law. It is the form of the law that is instrumentalised to the furtherance of informal family, economic and political interests. The law is taken as a constraint, to which 'connected' lawyers have to adapt, not because the law stands for what is right, but because it is necessary to create the mere appearance that the letter of the law is formally followed.

Finally, a historical source of impartiality in the communist regimes of the CEE countries was also the so-called telephone law. This was a well-known practice across Central and Eastern Europe in which influential communist party leaders or their loyal bureaucrats instructed 'independent' judges as well as prosecutors how to decide a particular case. As this practice had become embedded, the judges themselves too were making calls to their superiors in the ministries and elsewhere to get their cases right.[111] Since 1991 this practice has, however, declined significantly in Slovenia. With the adoption of the new Constitution and the proclamation of the rule of law, it has been found increasingly inappropriate, and to the extent that legal deals are still negotiated, they are no longer done so openly on the telephone, but in a more clandestine matter. However, as a remnant of the communist past and its lack of separation of powers, the practice of direct telephone communication between judges and prosecutors to discuss the details of a particular criminal case, especially the

[110] See Simona Toplak, 'Norost v vladi Mira Cerarja – generalni sekretar vlade Darko Krašovec zahteva: Vsi slovenski sodniki in sodišča, izločite se!' *Finance* (20 April 2016) www.finance.si/8844060.

[111] See eg Alena Ledeneva, 'Telephone Justice in Russia' [2008] *Post-Soviet Affairs* 324.

sentencing details, has remained widespread. There even exists a final ruling of the Supreme Court in which the latter established that its President informally, by telephone, intervened with the Public Prosecutor General to resume a halted criminal procedure.[112] It goes without saying that such practice is incompatible with the requirement of equality of arms in criminal cases and hence does not meet the conditions of impartiality of a judge in relation to a defendant.

V. ORDINARY COURTS AND HUMAN RIGHTS PROTECTION

If the preceding discussion on the excessive duration of legal processes, problems with the lack of independence, and the impartiality of judges has a bearing on the quality of judicial proceedings in Slovenia, this section looks briefly into the outcome produced by the courts. The cause for concern in this domain are the unfavourable statistics published by the ECtHR according to which Slovenia was found to have violated the Convention in 334 cases up to 2018.[113] In absolute terms, this is a comparatively very high number, taking into account that Slovenia has been a member of the Council of Europe only since 1993 and that with its population of two million is one of the smaller Member States. In relative terms, however, Slovenia ranks first in the number of identified violations of the ECHR per capita.[114] Although these data ought to be inviting institutions and scholars alike to take the problem seriously, analyse its actual extent and dig into its deeper causes, little actual research has been undertaken in this field. However, to the extent this research has been done, it has, as a rule, been greeted with much scepticism and criticism by the judiciary. The spokesperson of the Supreme Court, for example, argued against the over-simplistic interpretation of the Slovenian statistics in front of the ECtHR and insisted that these data were too often used in a deceptive and tendentious manner to turn the Slovenian judiciary into a scapegoat for all the violations committed by the state.[115]

When in 2014 research was published demonstrating that between 2004 and 2013 the Constitutional Court has found violation of human rights protection in more than 400 trials,[116] the Supreme Court rejected the methodology of the

[112] Supreme Court ruling I Ips 32088/2011 [2016]; see also Jan Zobec, 'Telefonska justica po slovensko' *IUS-info* (30 April 2018) www.iusinfo.si/medijsko-sredisce/kolumne/219023 (accessed 16 February 2019).

[113] ECHR Annual Report 2018, www.echr.coe.int/Documents/Annual_report_2018_ENG.pdf, 179 (accessed 16 February 2019).

[114] 'Slovenia Top in ECHR Report by Human Rights Violation Rate' *Slovenia Times* (18 August 2015) www.sloveniatimes.com/slovenia-top-in-echr-report-by-human-rights-violation-rate (accessed 16 February 2019).

[115] Gregor Strojin as quoted in siol.net/novice/slovenija/sramotna-statistika-stevilo-krsitev-clovekovih-pravic-v-sloveniji-narasca-390019 (accessed 16 February 2019).

[116] Lovro Šturm, 'Analiza kršitev človekovih pravic in temeljnih svoboščin. Vmesno poročilo. Prikaz raziskave za obdobje 2004–2013' (Zbor za republiko, 2015) zborzarepubliko.si/wp-content/uploads/2015/09/US.Up_.Analiza-krsitev-CP.doc (accessed 16 February 2019).

research, denying its capacity to contribute to expert discussion or to lend itself to a meaningful interpretation of the data.[117] The Supreme Court argued that the rate of successful constitutional complaints in Slovenia, finding a constitutional violation of human rights by the ordinary courts, is comparable to that of Germany.[118] The President of the Judicial Council also intervened, in his words to prevent the deception of the public, and warned against across-the-board criticisms of alleged human rights violations by the courts. He insisted that not all identified constitutional violations are also human rights violations and that, in any case, not all human rights violations are equally pernicious so that lines should be drawn between 'the strongest' violation, a 'strong' violation and 'a mere' violation of human rights.[119] A very similar exchange occurred three years later, when two researchers published their analysis on the basis of publicly available statistics, according to which of all the judicial districts in Slovenia, the courts in Maribor are most likely to engage into human rights violations.[120] The President of the Supreme Court, again, downplayed the results, claiming that the sample was simply too small for any immediate and far-reaching conclusions on the performance of certain courts or even of individual judges.[121]

These two examples already hint at judicial complacency in Slovenia and a tendency of its leaders, as well as of the head of judicial self-government, to minimise any allegations of weak performance of the Slovenian courts in terms of human rights protection. This observation could, however, be undermined by insisting that the research produced was indeed not of a sufficient quality and that the critical reaction of those subject to the critique was justified. However, a conclusion of this sort does not appear to be warranted. This is demonstrated by the Supreme Court's critical engagement with the jurisprudence of the Constitutional Court. When in 2015 the latter reversed 56 decisions of the Supreme Court and in several of those cases determined that the Supreme Court acted arbitrarily and patently unconstitutionally, the Supreme Court assembled a working group to respond to the mounting public criticism as a result of these statistics. The outcome was not very different from the position taken to the critical academic research presented above. The Supreme Court indicated that the Constitutional Court might have overstepped its judicial competences and

[117] Vrhovno sodišče, 'Odziv na raziskavo dr Šturma o kršitvah človekovih pravic' (2014) www.sodisce.si/sodni_postopki/objave/2014072513084464/ (accessed 16 February 2019).

[118] Vrhovno sodišče, 'Odziv na raziskavo dr Šturma o kršitvah človekovih pravic' (2014) http://www.sodisce.si/vsrs/objave/2014072412023169/ (accessed 16 February 2019).

[119] Marko Novak, 'Kršitve človekovih pravic in zavajanje javnosti' *IUS-info* (7 November 2016) www.iusinfo.si/DnevneVsebine/Kolumna.aspx?id=181814 (accessed 16 February 2019).

[120] Andraž Teršek and Jurij Toplak, 'Kje v Sloveniji sodišča kršijo ustavne pravice – kršitve ustavnih pravic po območjih višjih sodišč' [2017] *Pravna praksa* 25.

[121] Urška Makovec, 'Sodišča na območju Maribora šestkrat bolj kršijo človekove pravice kot sodišča na Celjskem' *Siol* (28 September 2017) siol.net/novice/slovenija/sodisca-na-obmocju-maribora-sestkrat-bolj-krsijo-clovekove-pravice-kot-sodisca-na-celjskem-447993 (accessed 16 February 2019).

interfered with the statutory interpretation, which is the exclusive competence of the ordinary judiciary and on which the Supreme Court has the final say.[122] While the Supreme Court admitted that there remained some room for improvement on its side, it called for a dialogue with the Constitutional Court in which the relationship between the two institutions should be rethought. In particular, the Constitutional Court should have been more careful in applying its verdicts of arbitrariness or patent wrongfulness to the decisions of the Supreme Court lest it risked its own jurisprudence committing arbitrariness. The latter is, in the eyes of the Supreme Court's Working Group, a much greater danger for legal certainty than an incorrect decision of the (Supreme) court.[123] The Constitutional Court, however, insisted that the only permitted form of dialogue is through the judicial decisions of the two courts and therefore refused to engage in any extrajudicial debate with the Supreme Court.[124]

Despite the ongoing critical academic reactions to the described and growing complacency on behalf of the presiding judges at the Supreme Court, the latter went even further by rejecting the decision of the ECtHR in *Produkcija plus storitveno podjetje doo v Slovenia* (no 47072/15) as unpersuasive and indicated that the decision would not be respected and integrated in its jurisprudence.[125] For the second time in a row Slovenia had been convicted by the ECtHR, since its courts (in administrative procedures) were not conducting oral hearings. The response of the Administrative Court in the *Mirovni inštitut* case (no 32303/13) was almost identical: we have followed the statute and therefore could not be held accountable for a violation of the right to a fair trial. Due to a strong academic rebuke as well as political criticism, the Supreme Court retracted its announcement, described the situation as a misunderstanding and refused to hold anyone to account. However, it is safe to argue that this reaction of the Supreme Court was not just an isolated incident, or a coincidental professional slip, rather it was an example of a systemic attitude of the Supreme Court, most notably its presiding structure, that has been marked by complacency, self-aggrandisement and, ultimately, a lack of understanding as to what is required from a supreme court in a constitutional democracy in the context of a European constitutional space.

This analysis has demonstrated two difficulties the Slovenian judiciary faces in the field of human rights protection. The first is objective: the country has

[122] Vrhovno sodišče, 'Poročilo o odločbah Ustavnega sodišča, s katerimi so bile razveljavljene odločbe Vrhovnega sodišča', www.sodisce.si/mma_bin2.php?nid=2017091111092486&static_id=20170911090104 (accessed 16 February 2019).

[123] ibid.

[124] Stališče Ustavnega sodišča o Poročilu Vrhovnega sodišča o odločbah Ustavnega sodišča, s katerimi so bile razveljavljene odločbe Vrhovnega sodišča, www.us-rs.si/aktualno/novice/stalisce-ustavnega-sodisca-o-porocilu-vrhovnega-sodisca-o-odlocbah-ustavnega-sodisca-s-katerimi-so-b/ (accessed 16 February 2019).

[125] For a report, see Matej Avbelj, 'Slovenia's Supreme Court Rejects the European Court of Human Rights' *Verfassungsblog* (26 October 2018) verfassungsblog.de/slovenias-supreme-court-rejects-the-european-court-of-human-rights/ (accessed 16 February 2019).

had a poor record in front of the ECtHR, while domestically too the number of human rights violations by the courts has raised concerns, at least in some academic circles. Subjectively, however, the Slovenian judiciary, especially its leading representatives, has been reluctant to address this objective problem and has rather engaged in criticism of the published research and, eventually, even of the Constitutional Court itself for an alleged overstepping of its judicial competences. The fact that the ordinary judiciary has seen its role limited to the ambit of statutory interpretation and application, whereas the Constitution and human rights protection belong to the realm of the Constitutional Court, accentuates this subjective problem. It demonstrates that contrary to the requirement of the Slovenian constitutional democracy, the Constitution and its values have failed – due to the reluctant reception by the ordinary judiciary – to permeate the entire legal system. Admittedly, all of this has not contributed to the ethos of human rights protection in Slovenia, whose presence is relatively weak in the courts, but even more so in the sphere of the administrative branch and the police.[126] Instead, it has strengthened the impression of courts as increasingly self-serving institutions, in which human rights often play an ancillary, sometimes even just a mere formal and declaratory role. This has, eventually, contributed to a growing distrust in the Slovenian system of justice.

VI. DISTRUST OF THE JUDICIARY

Since 2007 public trust in the Slovenian judiciary has been in a persistent decline.[127] Today it is the lowest among all EU Member States with only 16 per cent of Slovenian citizens expressing their confidence in the judiciary.[128] Moreover, even the members of the professional legal community (advocates, state advocates and prosecutors) express very little trust in the judiciary and assess its reputation to be equally low.[129] This is an alarming figure since the courts, unlike the legislative and executive branches, possess neither the power nor the financial means to enforce their rulings. The only resource at their disposal is reason-giving, argumentation and justification aimed at convincing the relevant audience. If the latter, as is the case in Slovenia, has no, or very little, trust in the judiciary, the process of persuasion has a very small chance of success. Given such deep distrust, the courts are not received as a legitimate authority, which turns them either into weak or oppressive institutions, or both. As the distrustful

[126] For a critical account with a number of empirical evidence of the lack of human rights ethos among the Slovenian authorities, see Andraž Teršek, *Pravna ignoranca škodi: kritika pravne prakse 1, 2* (Univerzitetna založba Annales, 2015).

[127] Miro Haček, '(Dis)trust into the Rule of Law in Slovenia' [2013] *Political Preferences* 9, 19.

[128] Special Eurobarometer 461: Designing Europe's Future, ec.europa.eu/commfrontoffice/publicopinion/index.cfm/ResultDoc/download/DocumentKy/78720 (accessed 16 February 2019).

[129] Supreme Court, Annual Report 2017, 101.

addressees of judicial rulings are unwilling to accept the decisions of the courts as good reasons for their behaviour in cases that ought to have been judicially and hence peacefully resolved, it is not just the efficiency but also the effectiveness of the judiciary that becomes seriously undermined. If the judicial rulings are thus, as a consequence, not followed, the rule of law increasingly remains on paper only.

The dramatically low trust in the Slovenian judiciary can be explained by the fact that judicial legitimacy has been undermined across all of its three dimensions. Judicial input legitimacy, which stands for the quality and reputation of judges in the judicial system, has been principally undercut by the above-described modality of a de facto automatic appointment of judges under communism into the courts of the independent state, based on the rule of law and democracy. Due to the ordinary cycle of career development – the most experienced judges are also the oldest judges who began their career long back in the communist system – this communist judicial continuity has had the strongest negative impact on the courts which are higher in the judicial hierarchy and, in particular, on the Supreme Court. Moreover, the judicial human resources policy in the two decades after independence failed to attract the most qualified lawyers into the judicial system. Even with the huge increase in the number of judges produced by implementation of the Lukenda reform project there were not even enough qualified candidates to fill all judicial posts, especially in the less attractive courts in less urban areas.[130]

The throughput legitimacy, reflecting the procedural fairness of trials, has also been suffering due to the above-described weak judicial independence, the problems surrounding the impartiality of judges, and continual, albeit no longer systemic, issues related to the excessive duration of trials. Moreover, an impression of deep procedural unfairness has been created by the fact that trials against certain influential Slovenian figures start only after long delays, or even not at all; and that not infrequently such trials end without a true conclusion, precluded by the statute of limitations due to the lethargy of the courts, the prosecution and the police.[131] This phenomenon has been described as the existence of two rule-of-law states. The strict one acts for the common people and the lenient one works for the privileged classes. Finally, the outcome legitimacy of the judiciary, which is expressed in the quality and quantity of judicial work, has been kept low as well. The above-described frequent violations of human rights by the ordinary judiciary combined with an unwillingness to address problems effectively and at their roots; judicial failures, sometimes little short

[130] Rok Praprotnik, interviewing Marjan Pogačnik, 'Žal mi je, da sodniška toga najboljših študentov ne zanima' *Dnevnik* (1 April 2006) www.dnevnik.si/173264 (accessed 16 February 2019).

[131] Anže Voh Boštic, 'Zakaj močnim, bogatim in vplivnim uspe prelisičiti pravno državo' *Pod črto* (7 December 2017) podcrto.si/zakaj-mocnim-bogatim-in-vplivnim-uspe-prelisiciti-pravno-drzavo (accessed 16 February 2019).

of scandal, in landmark cases; the embedded practice of avoiding decisions on merits in appellate procedures and the ordering of repetitive retrials, explain in objective and subjective terms the dwindling output legitimacy of the Slovenian judiciary. The low input, throughput and output legitimacies have ultimately translated into the described low trust in the Slovenian judiciary.

VII. CONCLUSION

The actual existence of the rule of law to a great extent depends on the performance of the judiciary. It is in the practice of judges, as HLA Hart famously argued in his sociological account of the concept of law,[132] that the rule of recognition, on the basis of which a legal system exists and functions as a legal system, can be identified. If the performance of the judicial function is poor; if justice is (systematically) delayed; if judicial independence and impartiality as well as the judges' attitude towards human rights protection is as fragile as in the case of Slovenia, no trust can develop in the overall system of justice. This results in the existence of the rule of law being either extremely precarious or, in parts, lacking. Most importantly, the absence of a commitment to strengthening and furthering the rule of law in the courts, which are by their very nature the rule-of-law institutions par excellence, is sending a negative signal about the importance of the protection of the rule of law to the other institutions of the state as well as to the citizens at large. A vicious circle of disrespect for the rule of law is created instead. This stimulates practices that are the opposite of the rule of law, which open the gates to arbitrariness, corruption and widespread political influence into spheres where the rule of law, legality and legal certainty should normally reign.

It is important to understand that the above-described systemic rule-of-law shortcomings of the Slovenian judiciary are neither haphazard nor of a temporary transitional character, so that they will disappear, by some evolutionary necessity, with time. On the contrary, the described problems are endemic. They are systemically engraved into the character of the Slovenian judiciary. They are part of its very nature. This is confirmed, if nothing else, by the fact that the problems of the Slovenian system of justice have been known for a very long time; they have been treated by governments of all political orientations, and yet no major breakthrough, no real systemic improvement has ever been achieved. This is so because the overall institutional set-up, modus operandi, material conditions and, finally, the mind-set of the people working in the Slovenian judiciary are, ultimately, not conducive to the kind of system of justice required by the rule of law in so-called well-ordered states. As the judicial system in toto is incompatible with the idea of a well-functioning judiciary in

[132] HLA Hart, *The Concept of Law* (Oxford, Clarendon Press, 1905).

the rule-of-law system, it is, of course, unsurprising that partial solutions, incremental reforms that have been implemented to extinguish the most critical and burning problems, cannot deliver the desired result. Provided, of course, that a well-functioning judiciary and, on its basis, an actually existing rule of law is desired in the first place.

That actual (governmental) interest in ensuring the rule of law, inter alia, through a functioning judiciary, is equivocal underlines why political and legal practice over the last 30 years has failed to carry out any genuine judicial reform with a lasting rule-of-law contribution. The overall political tendency, irrespective of the ideological orientation of the political parties in power, has instead worked in favour of the status quo. The latter, however, means that the type of judiciary created in the former communist Yugoslavia continues to be preserved in democratic Slovenia as well. If this is the case, it is important to understand that the Yugoslav communist judiciary, and the Slovenian judiciary as its subpart, had been deliberately designed in a way to prevent the emergence of the actual rule of law. In a one-party totalitarian system it is, of course, impossible to require that everyone is under the law. In a totalitarian state, it is not the law that governs, but the party as an avant-garde of the working people governs with the law. The main role of the courts in such a system is not to protect the rights of individuals, but to shield the state against such individuals whose activities appear a threat to the system.

This explains why the Yugoslav, and hence also the Slovenian, judiciary was established as a hierarchic bureaucratic structure, controlled by the courts' presidents and the President of the Supreme Court, who was, of course, a high communist functionary, reporting directly to the Communist Party's central committee. The need to have the judiciary under political check explains why it was created as a mass organisation, in which the individual judges counted little and in which they needed to develop an understanding that their role was to serve and defend the system, rather than upholding the law. The judges were not supposed to stand out. That is why they were more than happy to play the role of faceless bureaucrats who stuck to the black letter of the law, avoided any kind of judicial creativity, let alone activism, to be on the safe side, to ensure that they get their case 'right' and not risk (political) accountability from acting independently and making potentially 'wrong' decisions.[133] This self-censorship reflex, as well explained by Uzelac, also taught the judges that the fewer decisions they actually made, the lower risk for (political) sanction they incurred.[134] This explains why judges in the communist system resisted decision-making and why the practice of continuous ping-pong between the first-instance and the reversing second-instance courts, instead of the latter simply deciding the case on the merits, was so widespread. Furthermore, it was already part of the Yugoslav

[133] Zdenek Kuhn, *The Judiciary in Central and Eastern Europe* (Brill, 2011).

[134] Alan Uzelac, 'Survival of the Third Legal Tradition' (2010) 49 *Supreme Court Law Review* 377.

judicial structure that the judicial function was, for obvious reasons, not a job with a very high reputation. Moreover, as again reported by Uzelac, a specific division of labour developed in Yugoslav lawyer families.[135] The men would work long and hard as advocates, whereas their wives would take up much more cosy, less stressful positions as judges, with clearly determined and relatively short working hours, which would enable them to take care of their home and families. In this way too, already in Yugoslavia, the reputation of the judiciary was low, it did not attract the best lawyers, but rather those who sought a more (family-)friendly working environment, which they indeed obtained, provided that they had developed the degree of conformism expected from them by the system.

Most of the described traits of the communist judiciary have been preserved to the present day. While the personal structure of the judiciary, other than in the several top positions of the Supreme Court, is no longer the same as in Yugoslav times, the infrastructure, the way things have always been done and the mind-set has stayed very much the same.[136] This is, again, not surprising. Systems are, in general, reluctant to change and boast of a high degree of autopoiesis. In a system such as the judiciary, which is by its nature conservative, this effect is even more accentuated. Moreover, due to the above-described 'legal homeliness' there is little internal incentive to change. The cosiness associated with the judicial function is something that sociologically, from the most banal human perspective, will be traded for major change only with great reluctance, even if the system is patently not functioning well and such a change is clearly overdue. Furthermore, the degree and extent of 'dirty togetherness' inside the judicial system, the fact that not infrequently the appointments of judges and other personnel is not based on the meritocratic criteria, but on family, political, ideological and economic connections, act against such change as well. Pushing for a change would bring the cases of 'dirty togetherness' out into the light and call for their revision and removal. This is not in the interest of those many who are already complicit in such a system or who might become so, out of solidarity or in pursuit of their personal interest, in the future.

Similarly, there has been little external pressure on the judicial system to undergo the required reforms. Slovenian politics has only acted when it came under pressure from the Council of Europe or was under the formal or informal oversight of the European Union. Beyond those absolutely necessary measures, to save the face of Slovenia abroad, the reforms have not been implemented. This suggests that, not unlike in the former Yugoslavia, a weak, inefficient, dependent and partial, under-resourced judiciary with a bad reputation and literally no

[135] ibid.

[136] Slovenia is only one of such examples. The very poor statistics of the former Yugoslavian republics in front of the ECtHR proves that the Yugoslav judicial model has left lasting negative consequences on the judiciary in this part of Europe.

public trust is in the interest of those who wield, either formally or informally, power in Slovenia. The scope of the actual rule of law in Slovenia hence clearly trails the one that exists on paper.

The judicial system, those who are in charge of it, as well as those who are constitutionally mandated to create the necessary conditions for a successful functioning of a judiciary, eg the legislative and executive branches, carry the brunt of responsibility for this state of affairs. Contrary to the mainstream narrative in influential judicial circles, it is not the media, politicians and querulant citizens who are to blame for the failings of the Slovenian system of justice; the responsibility lies primarily with those who exercise judicial powers, ie the judges themselves. Nevertheless, citizens indeed bear some responsibility as well. This is not, contrary to the conventional narrative, because they are turning in too high numbers to the courts, flooding them with their cases, but because they – as voters – despite their huge distrust in the Slovenian judiciary, keep electing those very politicians and political parties who have either caused or tolerated this negative state of affairs. However, reference to voters invites us to look at the overall state of democracy in Slovenia. It is to this topic that the next chapter turns.

7

The Vicious Circle of Slovenian Democracy

Many forms of Government have been tried, and will be tried in this world of sin and woe. No one pretends that democracy is perfect or all-wise. Indeed it has been said that democracy is the worst form of Government except for all those other forms that have been tried from time to time.

Winston S Churchill, 11 November 1947

I. INTRODUCTION

ADDRESSING THE ILLS and virtues of democracy in Slovenia requires first explaining the meaning of democracy. Democracy is one of the systems of legitimation of power, which uniquely, unlike any other system of political legitimation, draws its legitimacy from the people, understood as free and equals.[1] In democracy it is the people that rule in the name of the people, not because they are richer, older, cleverer, carry the right blood or are even sent by god, but because they are equal. For the sake of convenience, the decisions in a democracy are normally taken by a majority, following procedural and substantive conditions prescribed by a constitution. The democracy that this chapter builds upon is thus not a majoritarian democracy, but a constitutional democracy as expounded in Chapter 2. Constitutional democracy can be, borrowing from Scharpf,[2] analytically presented as the composition of three elements that are constitutive of a democratic legitimacy lato sensu: input legitimacy, throughput legitimacy and output legitimacy.[3]

Input legitimacy is structured around the concept of demos or the people from which democratic political authority ensues. Ideally, demos shall be defined

[1] This is the gist of the Western form of political liberalism and constitutionalism stretching from Locke, Rousseau, Rawls, Dworkin, Habermas, etc.

[2] Fritz W Scharpf, 'Problem-Solving Effectiveness and Democratic Accountability in the EU' (2003) MPIfG working paper 03/1.

[3] See also See Matej Avbelj, 'Crises and Perspectives of Building a European Nation – The Case of Slovenia' in Peter Jambrek (ed), *Nation's Transitions: Social and Legal Issues of Slovenia's Transitions: 1945–2015 (Slovenia 1945–2015)* (Graduate School of Government and European Studies, European Faculty of Law, 2014).

as inclusively as possible in order to ensure a comprehensive self-determination of everyone living under a particular democratic rule. Having put the concept of demos in place, the political democratic process needs to be launched. Its trigger and the essential institute of a democratic governance is an election. In a well-functioning democracy, the election needs to be general, equal, direct, free and with a secret ballot.[4] The fulfilment of these 'ideal' electoral criteria entails robust political parties, free and pluralist media as well as a vibrant civil society. It also, and foremost, requires active citizens, cognizant of and with an interest in public affairs.

After the electoral process has been successfully carried out, input legitimacy moves onto the next stage of a democratic process: throughput legitimacy. Here the main role is played by the institutions of the state, and in particular the legislative branch. It is the parliamentary process through which the political interests advocated by the ruling political parties, which in turn represent the interests of the people as expressed in the election, get filtered into binding legislation. The democratic legitimacy of the adopted laws requires the parliament to adhere to certain constitutional and statutory rules, as well as to the good practices associated with parliamentarism as ideally conceived of. Accordingly, the composition of the parliament shall, as much as possible, reflect the plurality existing in a given democratic society. The political parties in the parliament will be, typically, divided into two groupings: the coalition, supporting the government, and the opposition, which by criticising the existing government tries to build its own way into power after the next election. While parliamentary debates will be often rife with conflicts, these need to be conducted in a mutually respectful manner, with an emphasis on a genuine dialogue between the competing political blocs. The parliamentary process shall be under a close scrutiny by the media as well as by the civil society, which can, either by the means of informal public pressure or by formal means of calling a referendum, prevent the ruling political majority from steering too far off the political course that it campaigned upon; from the actual will of the people; or even from the permissible bounds of the constitution. Shall the latter happen, in a constitutional democracy it is the constitutional court that will have a final say.

Lastly, any system of government, including a democracy, is expected to deliver certain outcomes for those that it is governing for. This is what lies at the bottom of the output legitimacy, which measures the scope of 'utility' produced by the government. Any utility produced must be in line with the constitutional requirements. As long as that is the case, politics, with its contestation can freely take place, and depending on the shifting majorities within demos the next round of elections may bring a new electoral result, providing a fresh

[4] For a comprehensive overview of all international electoral standards, see European External Action Service, *Compendium of International Standards for Elections* (Luxembourg: Publication Office of the European Union, 2016).

stimulus for a new democratic cycle, composed of input, throughput and output legitimacy.

Against this ideal framework of democracy, which is by no means uncontested, this chapter will address the most significant shortcomings, indeed systemic flaws, in the Slovenian system of democracy. As our discussion will concentrate on all three elements of democratic legitimacy, the argument that follows will be broken down into three parts. The first part will address the deficiencies in the Slovenian input democracy through a historical lens, starting with the problem of the 'erased', continuing with the ensuing constitutional controversies regarding the adoption of an electoral system, and rounding off the discussion by examining the (un)fairness of the elections, in particular under the impact of the notorious Patria case. The second part will dwell on the throughput legitimacy, examining the increasingly pronounced implosion of the political system in Slovenia. The chapter will, finally, move to the output legitimacy, explaining how the gradual, but determinate, weakening of the political process is a sign of a captured state, of a country increasingly functioning as a kleptocracy, in which under a deformed media landscape and politically dependent civil society, the apathy of voters reigns, and, in so doing, continues to fuel the vicious circle of a democracy in retreat.

II. THREE CRISES OF INPUT LEGITIMACY

A. The Nature and Scope of the Demos in Slovenia

The input legitimacy of democracy in Slovenia has so far been subject to at least three major crises. The first relates to the nature and scope of demos in whose name Slovenian democracy is to be executed. The Slovenian Constitution defines the notion of demos, of the people, in inclusive terms. Article 3 declares that Slovenia is a state of all its citizens, founded on the permanent and inalienable right of the Slovenian nation to self-determination.[5] The Constitution thus grants a special symbolic position to the Slovenian people in ethnic terms out of recognition of the centuries-long struggle for national liberation by the Slovenes. However, the Slovenian democracy does not derive from an ethnic conception of demos, rather it belongs to all individuals who have met the requirements of the Citizenship Act, free of any arbitrary discrimination, including that based on ethnic terms.[6] Furthermore, the autochthonous ethnic Italian and Hungarian national communities are afforded a special constitutional protection.[7] As the Slovenian model of nationalism has historically been of a defensive character, shielding the relatively small Slovenian cultural

[5] Constitution of the Republic of Slovenia 1991, 2016, Art 3.
[6] ibid Art 14.
[7] ibid Art 64.

community against its far stronger neighbours, this did not change at the moment of state-building either. Slovenian nationalism did not take an exclusionary turn. On the contrary, in its Statement of Good Intentions the National Assembly (Skupščina) stressed explicitly that the process of independence is 'is committed to the best traditions of humanism and civilisation, Slovenian and European history, and a pleasant future for Slovenes and other citizens of the Republic of Slovenia'.[8]

This commitment has been realised by the referendum on independence in which the right to vote was accorded not only to Slovenian citizens, but to all residents in Slovenia, including individuals carrying a citizenship of the other Yugoslav republics from which Slovenia was effectively claiming independence.[9] These individuals were, furthermore, granted a special statutory privilege to obtain Slovenian citizenship, without meeting any specific substantive statutory requirements, provided that they were residents of Slovenia on 23 December 1990, that they actually lived there and that they filed an application to opt into Slovenian citizenship within six months upon adoption of the new Citizenship Act.[10] Again, this intention had been already announced in the aforementioned 'Statement of Good Intentions', in which Slovenia declared that all persons with permanent residence on the Slovenian territory would be enabled to acquire Slovenian citizenship if they so desired.[11]

Indeed, more than 170,000 citizens of the other former Yugoslav republics residing in Slovenia opted for and were granted Slovenian citizenship on the basis of this statutory privilege.[12] Almost 11,000 individuals decided to leave Slovenia, while around 25,000 individuals from the former Yugoslav republics, residing in Slovenia, for a variety of reasons failed to avail themselves of the granted statutory option.[13] After the expiry of the statutory period, the Ministry of Interior ordered the transfer of their data from the register of permanent residents to the register of aliens without a residence permit. These individuals have ever since been known as the 'erased'. The erasure from the register of permanent residents deprived them of their official residential status, and thereby also of many, especially welfare-state-related, rights, whose enjoyment depends on either citizenship or residence.[14] Many were therefore compelled to leave Slovenia; a few were even deported. Furthermore, not infrequently the erased were even rendered stateless. They did not obtain Slovenian citizenship,

[8] Statement of Good Intentions, www.slovenija2001.gov.si/10years/path/documents/good-intent/ (accessed 16 February 2019).

[9] Plebiscite on the Sovereignty and Independence of the Republic of Slovenia Act 1990, Art 6.

[10] The Act was adopted on 5 June 1991.

[11] Statement of Good Intentions, www.slovenija2001.gov.si/10years/path/documents/good-intent/ (accessed 16 February 2019).

[12] *Kurić v Slovenia* App no 26828/06 (ECtHR, 26 June 2012) [26].

[13] ibid.

[14] For a comprehensive overview of injustices suffered by the erased, see Neža Kogovšek and Brankica Petković (eds), *Brazgotine izbrisa, Prispevek h kritičnemu razumevanju izbrisa iz registra stalnega prebivalstva Republike Slovenije* (Mirovni inštitut 2010).

because they had not opted into it. They lost Yugoslav citizenship, because the country collapsed; and they failed to retain citizenship of any former Yugoslav republics, because, as residents in Slovenia, they did not settle their status in their republic of origin in good time.

This erasure has caused many personal tragedies and human rights violations to the individuals concerned. However, rather than concentrating on remedying the consequences of this wrongdoing, the problem of the erased was turned into one of the biggest political fights in the first two decades of Slovenian independence. This political conflict has marred not just the nature but also the actual practice of Slovenian input as well as, incidentally, throughput democracy. There have been two clashing narratives. The post-communist centre-right political parties, who were the engine of the independence movement, claimed that the erasure was a political manipulation of the post-communist centre-left, who wanted to taint independence by portraying the acts of Slovenian state-building as a means of exclusion or even retaliation over the citizens of the former Yugoslav republics. Indeed, the Montenegrin and Slovenian judges at the ECtHR even described the act of erasure as an (attempt) at 'legalistic means of ethnic cleansing'.[15] This fed nicely in the narrative of the post-communist left, according to which there was no difference between the acts of the communist authorities in 1945, who in an attempt to create the Socialist Republic of Slovenia as part of the newly formed SFRY extrajudicially executed thousands of its ideological opponents, and the acts of the post-communist pro-independence political parties in 1992, which resulted in the erasure, and hence the 'administrative genocide', of over 25,000 individuals.

This acute ideological conflict prevented any rational political and hence adequate constitutional solution for more than two decades. A post-communist centre-right political bloc claimed that Slovenia had been anyhow extremely generous in granting citizenship, on the basis of hardly any requirements, to more than 170,000 individuals. All those who failed to use this opportunity had only themselves to blame. According to this view, the system of transition from Yugoslav to Slovenian citizenship was generally sound. Had there been any constitutional or statutory lacunae, these ought to have been remedied on a case-by-case basis, and it was for the affected individuals to carry their burden of proof.[16] On the other hand, the post-communist centre-left argued that there had clearly been a gross constitutional violation, which should be remedied on a general, rather than individual, level by the state as it had had caused it.[17] Again, the opposing political camp and its supporters largely understood this

[15] See partly concurring, partly dissenting opinion of Judge Vučinić and a concurring opinion of Judge Zupančič, *Kurić v Slovenia* App no 26828/06 (ECtHR, 26 June 2012).

[16] This was a position of the Slovenian Democratic Party, see 'Naj odškodnine plačajo tisti, ki so lagali, da jih ne bo' *Siol* (2 July 2012) siol.net/novice/slovenija/sds-naj-placajo-odskodnine-tisti-ki-so-lagali-da-jih-ne-bo-230950 (accessed 16 February 2019).

[17] See Chapter 4 on the current crises of human rights protection and the rule of law.

move as a political attempt to appeal to the new Slovenian citizens of Yugoslav ethnic origin to increase the centre-left's electoral base by up to 10 per cent of the electorate.

The fight over the erased grew fiercer over the years, with increasing politicisation glossing over the complexity of the matter; eventually the problem was presented almost exclusively in black and white political terms. In this context, it was also litigated in the courts, advocated by NGOs, and eventually decided by the Constitutional Court. The latter issued a number of decisions, in which it declared the unconstitutionality of several provisions of the Slovenian legislation leading to the erasure and creating the precarious status of the erased.[18] To remedy their status comprehensively, a statute would need to be adopted, but the political will was missing. The Constitutional Court thus even ordered resident permits to be issued to the erased on the basis of its own decision, in the absence of a special statute, and it also had to preclude a referendum called by the National Assembly against this decision.[19] The judicial epilogue was finally reached by the ECtHR Grand Chamber decision in the case of *Kurić*. The Court, essentially only confirming the preceding decisions of the Slovenian Constitutional Court, found that a blanket measure of erasure, the failure to comply with the Constitutional Court's rulings and to put in place adequate and effective remedies for the caused situation, amounted to a violation of Articles 13 and 14 in conjunction with Article 8 of the ECHR.[20] Slovenia has implemented the ruling, on the one hand, by amending the Legal Status Act which enabled the acquisition of permanent residence both ex nunc and ex tunc; and, on the other hand, by adopting a new Act on Compensation for Damage to Persons Erased from the Register of Permanent Residents providing a legal basis for a just compensation.[21] On 25 May 2019 the Committee of Ministers of the Council of Europe expressed its satisfaction with the implementation and closed the case.[22]

B. The Electoral System in Dispute

Another heavily disputed matter, occurring simultaneously with the issue of the erased, was a constitutional controversy related to the electoral system.

[18] Decisions of the Constitutional Court: U-I-284/94 [1999]; U-I-246/02 [2003]; U-I-295/99 [2000]; Up-333/96 [1999]; Up-60/97 [1999]; Up-20/97 [1999]; Up-152/97 [1999]; Up-336/98 [2001]; Up-119/99 [2001]; Up-211/04 [2006]. For a more in-depth discussion, see www.mirovni-institut.si/izbrisani/en/constitutional-court-decisions (accessed 16 February 2019).

[19] See decisions U-II-3/03-15 [2003]; U-II-1/04 [2004]; U-II-3/04-7 [2004]; U-I-257/03-14 [2004] in U-II-1/10-25 [2010].

[20] *Kurić v Slovenia* App no 26828/06 (ECtHR, 26 June 2012) [368].

[21] ibid, state of the closed case: hudoc.exec.coe.int/eng?i=004-12107 (accessed 16 February 2019).

[22] Resolution CM/ResDH (2016) 112, execution of the judgments of the ECtHR in Kurić and others against Slovenia, search.coe.int/cm/Pages/result_details.aspx?ObjectId=090000168064ee8b (accessed 16 February 2019).

Article 80 of the Slovenian Constitution prescribes that members of parliament are elected according to the principle of proportional representation with a 4 per cent threshold required for election to the National Assembly, with due consideration that voters have a decisive influence on the allocation of seats to the candidates.[23] This provision, in itself formally entirely unobjectionable, was an outcome of another major political and constitutional conflict taking place in the second half of the 1990s in Slovenia. After the dissolution of the Demos coalition, in 1992 the first election was called to the newly constituted National Assembly. The electoral system based on proportional representation resulted in a fragmented parliamentary composition, consisting of eight political parties and two members of the Italian and Hungarian national minorities. This made coalition-building extremely arduous and consequently led to weak governments, often engulfed in internal disputes.

A deep division in the political spectrum between the post-communist centre-right and centre-left further decreased the capacity to govern. The system privileged small political parties over bigger ones, and moreover 'depersonalised' the elections. The voters were given the impression that they were selecting the actual candidate in their electoral district, while the votes were in fact distributed among the political parties on a national level. As a result, the high number of, especially small, political parties in the parliament reduced the transparency of the system of government and undermined political accountability. Dissatisfaction with the then existing electoral system was therefore growing, but not equally in all corners of the political spectrum, and most importantly there was no consensus about electoral reform, in which a compromise was sought between the proponents of a fully proportional system on the one hand, and the advocates of a two-round majoritarian system on the other.

Initiatives were therefore developed to settle the matter by turning to the people, but the then ruling coalition pushed hard to ensure that the referendum was called only about its own proposal. The State Council and the Social Democratic Party, defending their proposals, turned to the Constitutional Court, which in several decisions removed the legislative obstacles to a fair referendum in which the electorate could choose between all three proposals for a new electoral law.[24] Eventually, a referendum was called and the voters were faced with a ballot consisting of three questions, asking them to support one of the three possible electoral systems. The mixed proportionality–majoritarian system, proposed by the State Council, and the proposal of the ruling coalition to turn Slovenia into a single electoral unit, failed to win the support of the voters. The two-round majoritarian system, however, was approved by voters, but as the threshold for the success of the referendum, according to which the referendum needs to be supported by a majority of all voters taking part in it,

[23] Constitution of the Republic of Slovenia 1991, 2016, Art 80.

[24] Constitutional Court decisions: U-I-201/96 [1996]; U-I-266/96 [1996]; U-I-279/96 [1996]; U-I-304/96 [1996].

was not met, the Electoral Commission just reported the number of votes cast in favour or against each of the referendum questions, without declaring an official result. Consequently, the Constitutional Court was seized again. It found the situation unconstitutional and declared that the two-round majoritarian electoral system had been selected at the referendum, legally obliging the Parliament to turn its ruling confirming the referendum result into law.[25]

The decision of the Court was subject to fierce criticism, which blamed the Court not just for judicial activism, but even for overstepping the limits of its constitutional competences and for offering a helping hand to the Social Democratic Party and the electoral system proposed by it.[26] The Court, on the other hand, adopted a contextual and teleological approach, arguing that its decision compensates for the illegal inaction of the Electoral Commission as well for the National Assembly's overt attempt to undermine the referendum. Putting three questions on a single referendum forced voters to support only one of the three systems proposed, assuming that they oppose the remaining two systems on offer.[27] Moreover, having three questions in a single referendum contributed to splitting the votes in order to ensure that no proposal could obtain the required statutory majority and that the status quo was preserved.[28] If the political developments preceding the decision of the Court offered credence to the Court's contextual construction, the developments that followed strengthened the validity of its decision even further.

Faced with a constitutional obligation to implement the two-round majoritarian electoral system, the majority of political parties, fully aware that this reform would bring an imminent end to the highly fragmented, non-transparent and unaccountable political landscape, refused to comply with the decision of the Constitutional Court and to implement the will of the people, expressed at the referendum. On the contrary, a wide coalition stretching across the entire political spectrum amended the Constitution instead, thereby overriding the referendum result and the decision of the Constitutional Court. In a move that the Venice Commission declared, in a highly decontextualised and highly formalised opinion, as being in compliance with European constitutional standards,[29] the ruling political class entrenched in the Constitution a

[25] Constitutional Court decision: U-I-12/97 [1998].

[26] For a critique along these lines, see Ivan Kristan, 'Pravna država in ustavno sodišče: na rob odločbi o referendumu o volilnem sistemu' [1999] *Pravna praksa* 32; Matevž Krivic, 'Memorandum o ustavnopravnih vprašanjih v zvezi z odločbo US RS št U-I-12/97 [1999] *Pravna praksa* 36.

[27] Decision U-I-12/97 in which the Constitutional Court draws on the decision of the Constitutional Court of Bavaria (BayVerfGH, E v 30.5.1968, E 21 II, 110, quoted in Stefan Przygode, *Die deutsche Rechtsprechung zur unmittelbaren Demokratie* (Nomos Verlagsgesellschaft, 1995) 227). The latter also argued, like the Constitutional Court in its case U-I-266/96 [1996], that a regulation which would count a vote in favour of one question as necessarily opposing the other questions on the ballot as unconstitutional.

[28] See decision of the Constitutional Court U-I-12/97 [1998].

[29] CDL-INF(2000)013-e, Opinion on the constitutional amendments concerning legislative elections in the Republic of Slovenia, www.venice.coe.int/webforms/documents/?pdf=CDL-INF(2000)013-e (accessed 16 February 2019).

proportional electoral system, with a low parliamentary threshold, declaring that it ensures a decisive influence of the voters over the selection of candidates. However, to the present day it is the political parties that de facto make the selection of candidates by discriminating between the electoral districts where the candidates have actual chances of election and all those in which such a chance does not exist. The party favourites are nominated in the former, while the candidates with a lower party ranking end up in the latter. The voters are given merely 'an impression' of actually influencing the selection of individual candidates. Whether this complies with the letter of the Constitution, requiring 'a decisive influence on the allocation of seats to the candidates' by the voters, or not, is a question that has been recently submitted to the Constitutional Court. This declared, in a highly restrained ruling, that other than the size of the electoral units, which have been made too unequal due to demographic and administrative changes over the last 20 years, the electoral system in Slovenia is compliant with the Constitution.[30] Nevertheless, as the identified unconstitutionality will need to be removed in two years, potentially a new constitutional crisis with regard to the electoral law will erupt.

This short discussion of the constitutional controversies relating to the reform of the electoral system in Slovenia cannot, of course, do full justice to the overall political and democratic importance of the matter. The electoral system is the main component of the input democracy. The prolonged political conflicts, overriding the will of the people, and disrespect for the decision of the Constitutional Court all confirm that the ruling political class in the 1990s was deeply aware of the importance of the electoral system – not for the overall sound functioning of democracy in Slovenia, but rather for furthering their partisan political interests. The political coalition formed to amend the Constitution in 2000 was motivated by the participating parties' short- and medium-term desire to at least preserve the electoral status quo. The low parliamentary threshold ensured a large number of small political parties in parliament, which on the one hand wielded too much influence, given their electoral result, and hence acted to the detriment of the influence of the bigger political parties. However, the bigger political parties could rely on the smaller ones to avoid accountability for the lack of political progress in government by putting the responsibility on their numerous, tiny, but highly demanding coalition partners. In that way, the new electoral system entrenched in the Constitution ensured the status quo. It served basically everyone in the political arena, whose weakness, as a result of political fragmentation and complex governing, also served powerful informal interests of influential informal, especially economic, actors outside of democratic political control. Only the voters, despite the explicit constitutional language speaking to the contrary, have remained without any decisive influence. In the following two decades the Constitutional amendment of 2000 has led to the

[30] U-I-32/15 [2018].

balkanisation of the Slovenian political landscape and its gradual implosion, amidst the growing apathy of voters. However, this already touches on elements of the throughput legitimacy, to which we turn in section III. But before doing so, we must consider input legitimacy further by focusing on the decade-long disruption in the fairness of the electoral process (on the top of the constitutionally and democratically problematic electoral system) under the impact of the *Patria* case.

C. The Limping Fairness of Elections in Slovenia

In 2014 Slovenia, still embroiled in an economic crisis, was heading for a snap election, the second in less than three years. However, the circumstances of the election this time around were more than unusual. Three weeks before the election the leader of the main opposition party, Mr Janez Janša, had to start serving a two-year prison sentence. The County Court of Ljubljana had convicted him, and the Court of Appeals confirmed the decision with the force of res judicata, of committing a crime of accepting gifts for illegal intermediation pursuant to Article 269 of the Slovenian Penal Code.[31] The crime had been, literally, committed on an undetermined date, at an undetermined place and through an undetermined method of communication.[32] The indictment was brought by a state prosecutor, who was the wife of an agent of the Slovenian communist secret police who had arrested Mr Janša as a political dissident during the communist regime in the late 1980s. The case was brought to the lowest County Criminal Court for a shortened criminal procedure, suggesting factual clarity and a matter of lesser importance, on the basis of a direct indictment, avoiding control by an investigative judge. Nevertheless, the County Court carried out 21 hearings between September 2011 and June 2013. The appeal to the Court of Appeals and the extraordinary appeal to the Supreme Court were both unsuccessful. At the Supreme Court, as explained in Chapter 6, the president of the Supreme Court even publicly criticised the defendant and ensured by a procedural motion that he sat on the trial.

When the defendant, in order to ensure that he was at liberty at the time of the election, appealed his undoubtedly constitutionally suspect sentencing to the Constitutional Court prior to exhausting all his remedies, the Constitutional Court refused his constitutional complaint. It argued that the alleged violation of his rights, while serious, was not manifest enough to merit an

[31] Ruling of the Court of Appeals, Ljubljana II Kp 2457/2010 [2014], available at: siol.sdn.si/sn/doc/2014/4/patria.pdf (accessed 7 February 2019).

[32] For a more in-depth discussion, see Matej Avbelj, 'Failed Democracy: The Slovenian Patria Case – (Non)Law in Context' (2014), originally published in Slovenian as Matej Avbelj, 'Zadeva Patria – (ne)pravo v kontekstu' [2014] *Pravna praksa*, available at ssrn.com/abstract=2462613 or dx.doi.org/10.2139/ssrn.2462613 (accessed 16 February 2019).

exceptional admission of the constitutional complaint prior to the exhaustion of all other remedies.[33] The Constitutional Court hence directed the defendant to the Supreme Court, which could have still suspended the prison sentence before the election took place and until ruling on the merits of the case. However, the Supreme Court refused to do so. The judge rapporteur went on a previously planned vacation. The Supreme Court announced that while the case was of a multidimensional and absolute importance, no special treatment was justified.[34] Furthermore, the Supreme Court stressed that the defendant could have requested the suspension of the sentence by turning to the District Court.

While the courts were thus passing the case as a hot potato between different instances, as a result, the leader of the main opposition party stood in the parliamentary election from jail. He won strong support, but his party lost a lot of votes, and came second, unable to form a coalition, since other political parties were unwilling to collaborate with a party whose leader was convicted of graft. As the Slovenian electoral legislation does not prohibit individuals who are finally convicted of a crime to stand for election, Mr Janša was validly elected and parliament had to confirm his parliamentary mandate. Nevertheless, while being in prison, he was at first unable to attend parliamentary sessions and later the new parliamentary coalition voted on a proposal not to deprive (*sic!*) him of his seat in parliament. As this motion did not win majority support, Mr Janša was stripped of his parliamentary mandate, despite being elected entirely in accordance with the law. Meanwhile the Supreme Court also confirmed his sentence and the case again reached the Constitutional Court. This time around, almost one year later after Mr Janša had already served several months in prison, his political party suffered an electoral defeat and he was even stripped of his parliamentary mandate. The Constitutional Court, which had before found that the violation of his defendant's rights were not sufficiently manifest, ruled unanimously that the defendant had been convicted of an abstract criminal act, that the judges at all instances violated the principles of *lex certa*, *lex scripta* and *lex stricta* in criminal law and that, furthermore, the President of the Supreme Court and of the trial chamber himself also violated the requirement of impartiality and hence the constitutional guarantee of a fair trial.[35] The Constitutional Court hence ordered a retrial, but the County Court, to which the case was remanded, let the statute of limitation pass. Also, in a separate appeal, the Constitutional Court ruled that the parliamentary mandate had been taken away from Mr Janša unconstitutionally.[36]

The legitimacy and fairness of the 2014 election were thus, due to the described judicial and political treatment of the Patria case, clearly marred, not

[33] ibid.
[34] ibid.
[35] Constitutional Court decisions: Up-879/14 [2015]; Up-883/14 [2015]; Up-889/14 [2015].
[36] Constitutional Court, U-I-227/14, Up-790/14 [2015].

just from the perspective of the defendant and his political party, but indeed from the vantage point of all voters. Removing one's own political opponent, by placing him or her under custody a few weeks before the election, is a well-known strategy of authoritarian regimes that is clearly incompatible with the very idea of a fair election.[37] A protracted criminal case in the context of a heavily partial and biased media is also irreconcilable with a free election.[38] It is part and parcel of fair elections that they are actually free in the sense that the voters have unhindered access to an inclusive range of undistorted information on the political candidates. Since 2011 the Slovenian judicial system, either through its unconstitutional treatment of a leading opposition politician, or through its unwillingness to remedy the violated rights while that was necessary and still possible, permitted or even contributed to the manipulation of public affairs with regard to the (non-)existence of a crime of political corruption. However, the 2014 election was only the tip of an iceberg. The Patria affair politically commenced already in September 2008, three weeks before the parliamentary election, when Slovenian national television showed a Finnish documentary claiming that Mr Janša, then Prime Minister, was bribed by the Finnish arms corporation Patria, which was consequently awarded a military contract with the Slovenian government. The documentary identified the recipient of the bribe only by the letter J, which a couple of years later turned out to stand not for Mr Janša, but for a Croatian businessman, Mr Jerković. Nevertheless, a huge political controversy understandably broke loose, so much so that the Slovenian public sphere has for almost a decade been entirely absorbed with the Patria affair.[39]

The Patria case has been reported by the media in a very partial, often also straightforwardly untruthful manner.[40] It has also been utterly politicised. This is not necessarily to suggest that the case itself had been politically motivated, which certainly cannot be excluded either, rather that the case has caused huge political turbulences, essentially influencing – and as the absence of the judicial epilogue to the case confirms – distorting voters' preferences in at least three parliamentary elections in the last decade. It is beyond doubt that political opponents of Mr Janša have used the Patria affair, relying on the support of the Slovenian system of justice, to weaken him and his political party in order to politically capitalise on this situation. Eventually, however, this has had profound economic and political consequences for the country. Behind the smokescreen of the Patria case the country had effectively been politically and economically mismanaged, which in 2011 resulted in one of the biggest

[37] For an overview, see the ECtHR case-law on the basis of Art 18 ECHR, in particular Case 72508/13 *Merabishvili v Georgia*; and Cases 11082/06 and 13772/05 *Khodorkovskiy and Lebedev v Russia*.

[38] See ECtHR case-law: 20899/03 *GCP v Romania*; 9912/82 *Lutz v Germany*.

[39] For a wider discussion, see Matej Avbelj, *(Ne)pravna država* (GV Založba, 2015).

[40] See Chapter 8 on the freedom of press under stress in Slovenia.

economic crises in Slovenian history.[41] It was only with great difficulties that Slovenia evaded an EU bailout scheme and troika oversight.[42] On the other hand, this period simultaneously marked the decline of the established political parties, their institutional pauperisation and radicalisation. The eventual outcome has been an increasingly toxic democratic environment and the implosion of the Slovenian political landscape.

III. THE CRISIS OF THROUGHPUT DEMOCRATIC LEGITIMACY

Theories of democracy insist that a well-functioning democracy requires stable political parties, which act as institutions.[43] Jean Monnet is often quoted as saying that while nothing is possible without men, nothing lasts without institutions. Applied to political parties, this means that a political party as an institution is more than the sum of its actual members, and its institutional essence cannot be exhausted by its current leadership either. A political party devoted to influencing and developing politics in accordance with its ideology, which as a discursive practice is a perpetual task in *res publica*, must be conceived of as a long-term enterprise. A political party therefore requires a well-organised internal structure; transparent, pluralist and internally democratic functioning of its organs; financial autonomy, which is a precondition of the party's political autonomy; and independence from the (potentially corruptive) influence of potent factions beyond the political realm. A political party needs to be connected to its base, to the citizens in their local communities, as well as to a vibrant civil society, which acts as a bridge between exclusively self-interested individuals at one end and politicians on the other, fostering so-called 'active citizenship'. In other words, a political party has to be rooted in society, being at once its creation and a means of its representation.[44]

A political party is necessarily ideological in the sense that it harbours a clear and well-developed, relatively comprehensive political set of ideas, a normative programme for shaping and guiding the polity as a whole.[45]

[41] Igor Guardiancich, 'Slovenia: The End of a Success Story? When a Partial Reform Equilibrium Turns Bad' [2016] *Europe-Asia Studies* 205, 215.

[42] Alex Barker, 'Slovenia Struggles to Avoid EU Bailout' *Financial Times* (20. 11. 2013) www.ft.com/content/1d17fdd6-5053-11e3-9f0d-00144feabdc0 (accessed 16 February 2019).

[43] For a classical account, see Martin Seymour Lipset, 'The Social Requisites of Democracy Revisited' [1994] *American Sociological Review* 14.

[44] For a good overview of the literature discussing the role and functions of political parties in a democracy, see Janos Simón, 'The Change of Function of Political Parties at the Turn of Millennium' *ICPS* (2003) 18, https://www.icps.cat/archivos/WorkingPapers/wp221.pdf?noga=1 (accessed 7 February 2019).

[45] Otto Kirchheimer, 'The Transformation of Western European Party Systems' in Joseph La Palombara and Myron Wiener (eds), *Political Parties and Political Development* (Princeton University Press, 1966) 177–200, who describes a transition from the more ideologically narrow-minded political parties to the so-called 'catch-all' political parties.

In other words, political parties, unlike civil society associations, are not interest-based groupings, maximising insular societal interests.[46] Finally, political parties are created to get into power, to turn their political programmes into practice through the process of institutionalisation. However, in pursuit of this ambition, a political party as an institution simultaneously plays a very important role of democratic political socialisation.[47] In the broadest meaning of the term, political parties thus educate citizens in public, political affairs, thereby contributing to the political awareness of society as a whole, as well as to a professional, merits-based political class that a political party can rely upon in terms of cadres when in power to ensure an effective, productive and accountable government.[48]

In a totalitarian communist system, from which Slovenia emerged in the late 1980s, the above-described preconditions for a democratic party political system did not exist. Neither were these, admittedly, really present before in the illiberal last decades of the Habsburg empire or in the dictatorial system of the kingdom of Yugoslavia.[49] However, to the extent the democratic party political landscape managed to start forming in the late 1930s, this development came to an abrupt end with the outbreak of World War II, and especially in its aftermath. Soon after the war, political parties and political pluralism in Slovenia were effectively eliminated under the newly established Communist Party monopoly.[50] In lieu of a system of general democratic representation, a system representing, within the limits permitted by the Communist Party's central committee, the specific interests of workers, local self-governance and societal-political interests was developed.[51] Politics in a conventional democratic understanding and the political parties as its constitutive part were discredited as a relic of a bourgeois past and were portrayed as something negative that decent, law-abiding citizens stay away from as far as possible.[52]

In the late 1980s, in anticipation of the collapse of the communist regime and in the run up to the first democratic election, the process of creating political parties was initiated.[53] The then political parties were explicitly modelled

[46] See also Philippe C Schmitter, 'Intermediaries in the Consolidation of Neodemocracies: The Role of Parties, Associations and Movements' (1997) EUI SPS Working Paper no 130, 32.

[47] Janos Simón, 'The Change of Function of Political Parties at the Turn of Millennium' (*ICPS* 2003) 19, https://www.icps.cat/archivos/WorkingPapers/wp221.pdf?noga=1 (accessed 7 February 2019).

[48] See also Larry Diamond and Richard Gunther (eds), *Political Parties and Democracy* (John Hopkins University Press and the National Endowment for Democracy, 2001).

[49] Peter Štih, Vasko Simoniti and Peter Vodopivec, *Slovenska zgodovina: družba, politika, kultura* (Inštitut za novejšo zgodovino, 2008) 301ff, available at: www.sistory.si/publikacije/pdf/zgodovina/Slovenska-zgodovina-SLO.pdf (accessed 16 February 2019).

[50] ibid 429.

[51] See Chap 3 above.

[52] Matej Avbelj, 'Mit 10: Politika ni kurba' *Finance* (2 July 2016) www.finance.si/8846859 (accessed 16 February 2019).

[53] Rosvita Pesek, *Osamosvojitev Slovenije* (Nova Revija, 2007) 79–123.

after established democracies where broadly three ideological camps have traditionally existed: the social-democratic, the liberal and the Christian democratic bloc, with some political parties with a more fluid political identity occupying political spaces at the intersection of these three major ideological political movements. The continuing formal, but even more so informal, domination of the former communists, who rebranded themselves overnight into allegedly modern social and/or liberal democrats, as well as the rudimentary political identity of the newly emerged political parties, which were still in *statu nascendi*, prevented a reliable application of the traditional categories of the left and right on the Slovenian political spectrum. Nevertheless the tag of progressive political left was monopolised by former communists and their successors; while the label of conservative political right has been attached to those political parties that have been formed in opposition to the former communists. In many ways, if not entirely, this branding of the political landscape has been in the political interest of the dominant structures in the society and has obliterated the real ideological and interest-based divisions that particular political parties have been representative of. Most importantly, the political parties that have now been proudly acting under a self-ascribed modernist banner of political progressivism are effectively the most conservative, trying to preserve as much as possible of the overall societal arrangements from the previous totalitarian regime, and vice versa.

However, despite unsettled political identities, the consequent fluidity of the political landscape and a misfit between traditional and actually existing political categories in Slovenia, the Slovenian political parties in the 1990s and the early 2000s still, by and large, tried to emulate their political counterparts in established democracies. Even in this period, however, the political system was marked by political oddities, for example in the form of political parties established for the old, namely pensioners, as well as for the young. The former entered parliament in 1996, the latter in 2000, being established in very narrow circles of former student functionaries just weeks before the election. These single-interest political parties, formed in preparation for a particular election, were forebears of a political trend that prevailed after the country's admission to the EU in 2004. In the October election of that year the Liberal Democratic Party of Slovenia, a conglomerate of post-communist centre-left political parties that had been in power almost without interruption for 12 years, lost the election to the Slovenian Democratic Party, a leading post-communist centre-right political force. Only seven years later, in 2011, the Liberal Democratic Party, despite its history as Slovenia's strongest political party, failed entirely to enter parliament and disappeared from the Slovenian political landscape. This has left a profound void in the centre between the more left and right wing oriented political parties. In the 2008 election, the main political parties, the Slovenian Democrats and the Social Democrats still competed for the political centre, but later, under the impact of the economic crisis and the turmoil caused by the Patria affair, with declining output legitimacy, support for these two political parties started to wane as well, and the electorate was desperately looking for a political solution, preferably a political messiah to bring about a salvation from the accumulated crises.

The search for a political solution out of the unenviable circumstances in which Slovenia found itself at the end of 2000s, however, was taking place in a very specific discursive context. The Slovenian electorate has been for years 'educated' that the original problem of Slovenian democracy is that the latter is not ruled by the people, but rather by the political parties. This system has been pejoratively called 'partitocracy' and the argument has been that the power of the political parties has grown beyond what is still acceptable in a democracy. The rule of the political parties was allegedly pervasive, extending into the tiniest corners of Slovenian society.[54] Nothing could be, however, further from the truth. The political parties in Slovenia are extremely weak – according to the most generous assessment at present there are not more than three political parties that could be classified as such within the established meaning of the term. Moreover, even those political parties rooted in the beginnings of Slovenian democratisation lack financial autonomy, internal political pluralism and are increasingly dominated by their leaders and the loyalists assembled around them. However, since the 2011 election, the 'established' political parties have increasingly been pushed back by newly created, explicitly apolitical political parties. The so-called lists are almost exclusively known for their leaders, while the rest of the party apparatus as well as the elected deputies are basically anonymous. These self-branded apolitical lists have been established ad hoc, for the purposes of a particular election, and build on the public popularity of their leaders (a notorious businessman, popular university professor, a bureaucrat made into a prime minister overnight, or a profane local comedian) and the simultaneous anonymity of the remaining party apparatus, including the elected deputies. These apolitical lists are priding themselves for being explicitly nonideological and as a rule they do not have (a well-developed) political programme, they lack any kind of local political infrastructure or connection to the base, and have never invested in the meritocratic build-up of political professionals.[55]

And yet, in a social environment, such as the Slovenian, that has been 'fighting' partitocracy these new political initiatives have been repeatedly successful

[54] This argument has been, in particular, defended by France Bučar, a political dissident and the first president of Slovenia's democratic parliament; see France Bučar, *Temelji naše državnosti* (Mladinska knjiga, 2012); also France Bučar, *Slovenci in prihodnost* (Didakta, 2009).

[55] For a more in-depth and comparative discussion, see Matevž Tomšič, 'Decline of Elite Consensus and Destabilisation of Political Space in East-Central Europe' [2017] *Corvinus Journal of Sociology and Social Policy* 151, table, https://pdfs.semanticscholar.org/5c3b/628ffe149e787e7be165bd636acac93cb9c3.pdf (accessed 16 February 2019); Ladislav Cabada and Matevž Tomšič, 'The Rise of Person-Based Politics in the New Democracies: The Czech Republic and Slovenia' (2016) *Politics in Central Europe* 29–50; Matevž Tomšič and Lea Prijon, 'Person-Based Politics in Italy and Slovenia: Comparing Cases of Leadership's Individualisation' (2013) *International Social Science Journal* 237.

precisely because of their alleged apolitical and unideological nature, so much so that they emerged victorious in the 2011 and 2014 elections. In so doing, they have also drawn upon and further stimulated a populist narrative. Populism has existed in Slovenia since independence and has been growing over the years.[56] The sharp division between the right people and the 'traitors' stretches back to the civil war during World War II and was especially ignited in the *Kulturkampf* between the former communist forces and their overall social establishment and the opposition in the 1990s. The ensuing public and political discourses and practices have had all the elements of populism, as defined by Jan-Werner Muller.[57] There were good and bad people; fear has been constantly spread against the representatives of the respective sides; politics has relied upon and been driven by emotions and the cult of personality; the discourse has been profoundly anti-elitist and nationalist, the latter particularly in economic terms; and each side professed the moral and ethical cleansing of the society through the fight against corruption, to remove 'dirt' accumulated by the other side, while simultaneously forgiving their own people and their leaders any misconduct, no matter how grave. Unsurprisingly, the political rule of the apolitical political lists in this populist environment, often characterised by many farcical elements, has ultimately proven unsuccessful and most of these lists also disappeared after the next election in the same way as they emerged – almost instantly – only to be replaced by a new apolitical list, typically even more bizarre than its predecessors.

This political race to the bottom has led to a growing apathy among voters and a persistent decline in the turnout in elections.[58] This has, in turn, meant that moderate voters have been increasingly staying at home, creating even more room for instant political projects. These are then successful not only due to the aforementioned propagated animosity toward partitocracy, but also due to the orchestrated support by the media and (with them connected) factional interest groups who, directly or indirectly, participate in the management and extraction of the Slovenian predominantly state-owned economy.[59] The investment into ad-hoc, instant political parties, which are – especially, but not exclusively, at the moment of their creation *ex nihilo* – necessarily as understaffed as they are under-resourced and hence entirely dependent on their sponsors, comes with a double return. First, the political landscape under the leadership of such instant political parties is weak, reducing the likelihood of a democratic political process keeping in check private interests from parasitising not only the common good

[56] Matej Avbelj, 'Naše pravo in pravo ljudstvo: kako braniti ustavno demokracijo pred populizmom' [2016] *Dnevi slovenskih pravnikov, Podjetje in delo* 1221.

[57] Jan-Werner Muller, *What Is Populism* (University of Pennsylvania Press, 2016).

[58] The turnout has been in decline since the first democratic election: 1992, 86.5%; 1996 73.7%; 2000, 70.1%; 2004, 60.4%; 2008, 63.1%; 2011, 65.6%; 2014, 51.7%; 2018, 51.5%; see 'Volilna udeležna na parlamentarnih volitvah pada' *STA* (3 June 2018) www.sta.si/2520667/volilna-udelezba-na-parlamentarnih-volitvah-pada (accessed 19 February 2019).

[59] See Chap 4 above.

but in particular the state-owned economy. Second, once created and in power, these weak instant political groups continue to lack resources and professional staff, which opens a legitimate avenue for their sponsors outside the political sphere to make direct inroads into the formal structures of the state by, very generously, offering a helping hand in form of 'their own people'.

Such a system, while superficially entirely democratic, with periodic elections (albeit sometimes admittedly unfair), is increasingly controlled by and tilted to favour not the people, but pervasive formal and informal networks of vested interests. The product of democratic outcome legitimacy is thus increasingly not available to those in whose name and for whom democracy is nominally exercised. On the contrary, it is increasingly used by some narrow, powerful social circles, which have managed to twist the system representing the many to work in favour of the few. Such a description of the imploded Slovenian political system and of democracy based on it suggests the existence of elements of a captured state with a kleptocratic modus operandi. The final section, looking into the vices of Slovenian output legitimacy, therefore turns to the analysis of this phenomenon.

IV. THE CRISIS OF OUTPUT LEGITIMACY

The essence of an output legitimacy in a democracy, following its utilitarian guise, is to create the greatest utility for the greatest number. Any government is established with an aim, underlying the authorisation of those in power, to generate certain benefits for the governed. Should these benefits not emerge, the governed will, at the next election, replace those currently in power with successors who typically campaign on a promise of a more effective government than that of their predecessors. This is a typical democratic cycle, which, by enabling voters to throw the scoundrels out, ensures and demonstrates that it is the people who drive the democratic process and are ultimately in control of their polity. Should the opposite be the case, namely that elections do not change much, or indeed anything; and that, despite new faces being constantly elected to parliament and entrusted with the most responsible institutional positions, the country stays firmly on the same increasingly disadvantageous course (in terms of the view of the majority), the people and through them the elected political parties as well as the formal institutions of the state, in which they operate, are obviously not in control of their allegedly democratic polity. Somebody else, who stands beyond the official democratic process, apparently is. In this case, this is no longer a democracy, but a captured state.[60]

[60] On state capture, especially in transitional societies, see Joel S Hellman, Geraint Jones and Daniel Kaufmann, 'Seize the State, Seize the Day: State Capture, Corruption and Influence in Transition' (2000) Policy Research Working Paper Working Paper no 2444, 1–11, The World Bank, World Bank Institute: Governance, Regulation and Finance Division, Europe and Central Asia Region

Due to its peculiarly soft political transition and a specific model of state-owned economy under capitalism, Slovenia has always predominantly functioned as a captured state, but the extent of the capture, indeed the capture itself, became visible to layman's eyes only after 2004, with the decline of the Liberal Democratic Party, followed by the outbreak of the economic crisis in 2008 and the ensuing implosion of the political landscape as described in the previous section. As already indicated in Chapter 2, Slovenian sociologists have been warning from the beginning of the 1990s that due to the soft transition, the elite retention rate (ie the number of individuals who occupied important, indeed controlling functions under the old totalitarian regime and retained these roles in the new, formally democratic system) remained exceptionally high. The formal change of the regime and the 1990 election enabled the democratic political parties to win a majority in parliament and to carry out executive tasks for two years, until the democratic coalition dissolved itself. This time, however, was much too short to effectively take control over the country away from the former communist elites. The creation of the Liberal Democratic Party, with the Communist Party reforming itself into the Social Democrats, effectively enabled a comeback of the old guard. The Liberal Democratic Party, in particular, functioned as a conglomerate of interests of the old guard and its rule, which lasted for more than a decade, cemented Slovenia as a 'neo-corporatist' democracy.[61]

As reported by Bugarič and Kuhelj, the 'political elites, primarily former communists, sometimes directly, sometimes indirectly, using the parallel network of informal rules and practices, practically "control" the democracy'.[62] The same people have held sway over the courts, civil service and the media, which have all been 'deeply politicized by the cadre from the old political nomenclature'.[63] They have appointed their people and loyalists literally to all corners of Slovenian society, ranging from the overinflated public-sector, state-owned corporations to civil society, NGOs, including the Red Cross and the leading sporting organisations. However, even as the members of the old communist guard are gradually leaving the scene, they

> skilfully deploy their economic and political power and often enlist much younger cadres who then do work for the old elites. As a result, these new younger elites owe their existence to the older elites, making generational change less important than it appears if judged only from the structure of cadres currently in power.[64]

Public Sector Group, and European Bank of Reconstruction and Development, Office of the Chief Economist.

[61] Bojan Bugarič, 'Crisis of Constitutional Democracy in Post-Communist Europe: "Lands In-between" Democracy and Authoritarianism' [2015] *ICON* 221.

[62] Bojan Bugarič and Alenka Kuhelj, 'Slovenia in Crisis: A Tale of Unfinished Democratization in East-Central Europe' [2015] *Communist and Post-Communist Studies* 275.

[63] ibid 277.

[64] ibid 275.

Nevertheless, as the creation of the instant apolitical lists demonstrates, the younger elites, who have been skilfully 'appointed' by their older communist patrons, are patently less skilful than their predecessors. Neither the political nor the state-owned business enterprises they have been in charge of have seen much success. The political failures, however, have been compensated for by launching ever-new political faces, while the mismanagement of state-owned corporations, especially banks, has been repeatedly (three times already in Slovenia's short post-independence history) placed on the taxpayers' shoulders.[65] The apparent lack of experience and blatant incompetency of the instant politicians,[66] continuously invented by the post-communist elites, has inevitably led to the weakening of the formal political process in Slovenia. This, again, is neither an accidental nor an isolated phenomenon. The weak formal institutions of the state strengthen the bearers of informal powers in a polity. For them, in order to preserve the power relations they informally established under communism and in the transitional period that followed, it is essential to maintain the status quo. There is no better means of ensuring that than by keeping the formal institutions of the state weak and even leaving them to further decay. As already explained in Chapter 6, the fragility of the formal institutions is not just present in the democratic processes relating to the legislative branch, where the implosion of the political landscape is obvious and clear, but also in the judicial branch and indeed in the overall system of justice, which ought to ensure that those who exercise power, both inside the institutions and beyond them, are subject to the law. To the extent the institutions do exercise their competences, the fact that they have been for decades packed with loyalists minimises the risk of their meaningful interference with the status quo as well.

The described system of a captured state or controlled democracy is extremely hard to undo, especially in good times. The Slovenian political and the economic system, which has clearly been catering to the few; which has been unjust to the majority of people; which has been several times bailed out by taxpayers; and which has obviously been run by incompetent stake-holders is extremely resilient because it operates as a kleptocracy.[67] Research into kleptocratic regimes has demonstrated that their sustainability depends on the extent to which the kleptocratic circle is able to buy off, literally bribe, the pivotal groups in society and play them off against each other so that they, despite representing the majority in the state, become engulfed in internal strife, usually over petty matters, that exhaust their capacity to mobilise against the few who have been economically benefiting at the expense of the many.[68] The same research also stresses

[65] Guardiancich (n 41) 215.

[66] See the CV of the current Prime Minister: www.vlada.si/en/prime_minister/prime_minister.

[67] Acemoglu Daron, James Robinson and Thierry Verdier, 'Kleptocracy and Divide-and-Rule: A Model of Personal Rule. The Alfred Marshall Lecture' [2004] *Journal of the European Economic Association Papers and Proceedings* 162.

[68] ibid 164.

that a kleptocracy is more likely to succeed when the pivotal groups in society are myopic about democracy, discounting its long-term returns, in conditions of low inequality, since it is the more creative, and therefore also less equal, sectors of society whose interests the creation of a genuine democracy actually serves.[69] Provided these conditions are in place, the kleptocratic circle only requires the resources to bribe the pivotal actors who otherwise might imperil their positions. In economically good times, as indicated at the beginning, the availability of such sources is normally not a problem.

Slovenia meets most of the sociopolitical conditions for functioning as a kleptocracy. Almost one-fifth of the Slovenian workforce is employed in the public sector[70] and they receive on average 20 per cent higher salaries than workers in the private sector.[71] One-third of the entire Slovenian population are pensioners,[72] many citizens also depend on or are the recipients of welfare state transfers.[73] This part of the population, which forms a clear majority in the electorate, is thus dependent on public money. They have learned that loyalty to the system does not make them rich, but provides them with a fairly good quality of life, with little or no economic risks to themselves and their families. As under socialism, in a post-communist Slovenia too, a welfare state has been used as a means of upholding a kleptocracy, as a bribe for the electorate. It has been in the name of the preservation of the welfare state that the increasingly unjust captured state has been preserved and the oppositional spectrum of Slovenian politics villified for its allegedly neoliberal political agenda, destructive of the welfare state. The private sector has consequently remained small and politically uninfluential. Its calls for a more business-friendly environment have been presented as an attempt to undermine equality in society. Slovenia has the second lowest Gini coefficient among the OECD countries.[74] Income inequality therefore remains very low, chiefly due to the use of over-taxation as a means of weakening the productive sectors of the society, but also by stimulating migration from Slovenia in pursuit of better economic conditions, which again contributes to the strengthening of the environment favouring a kleptocracy

Another, even more important and influential, source of bribing the pivotal actors in society is presented by the state-owned economy, which provides a lot of opportunity for employment or contracting with those who have proven loyal

[69] ibid 165.

[70] Število zaposlenih v javnem sektorju 2007–2011, www.ajpes.si/doc/Statistike/Place_javni_sektor/Porocila/Stevilo_zaposlenih_javni_sektor_2007-2011.pdf (accessed 16 February 2019).

[71] www.umar.gov.si/fileadmin/user_upload/publikacije/izzivi/2018/EI2018_onepager.pdf accessed (16 February 2019).

[72] Najvišja pokojnina – december 2017, www.seniorji.info/POKOJNINE,_FINANCE_IN_PRAVNI_NASVETI_Najvisja_pokojnina_-_december_2017 (accessed 16 February 2019).

[73] Cca. 52,000 recipients each month, www.mddsz.gov.si/si/uveljavljanje_pravic/statistika/denarna_socialna_pomoc/ (accessed 16 February 2019).

[74] www.oecd.org/social/OECD2016-Income-Inequality-Update.pdf (accessed 16 February 2019).

in the past or will do so in the future. The *Kulturkampf*, the World War II-based division of the nation between the supporters of communist partisans and the fascist quislings is another efficient mechanism for clouding, indeed ideologically poisoning, public discourse and steering critical attention away from kleptocratic practices. The politically hostile environment, filled with distrust and often justified political paranoia, has similarly made the opposition to the post-communist political elite its worst enemy. Rather than investing into political alliances to build reform coalitions in the future, the main opposition party is striving to grow into a hegemon on its own side of the political spectrum to govern, more or less alone, in the future when their time comes. In so doing, party political self-interest is being elevated over the objective of building a genuine democracy first, just as in a kleptocracy. Accordingly, the political parties on the oppositional side of the political landscape, which are anyhow under-staffed, under-resourced and under-institutionalized, lacking access to the resources of the captured state, such as the broad media and NGO support built upon the state-owned and controlled economy, remain fragile and unable to form a broad political movement to counteract the process of a state capture.

Finally, according to the theories of kleptocracy, the latter ultimately depends on the ongoing availability of resources for bribing the pivotal actors. As Slovenia has no such natural resources, the system has been dependent, just as in socialist Yugoslavia, on foreign credit. In order to compensate for the lack of the structural reforms, public debt in Slovenia has in just seven years, from 2008 to 2015, risen from 21.8 to 82.6 per cent. The reforms, while necessary, have by and large not been carried out during and in the aftermath of the economic crisis, since they would, while contributing to the sustainability of the economy in the longer run, simultaneously disrupt the existing economic and therefore also political status quo. In this way, economic, political and social conditions remain in place, which in terms of the output legitimacy, enable Slovenia to function as a captured state, based on a kleptocratic modus operandi.

V. CONCLUSION

This chapter has striven to present the most important shortcomings in the functioning of democracy in Slovenia. These have, unfortunately, been identified in all three elements of a democratic process, its input, throughput and output legitimacy. Several instances of bad democratic practices, including those not been mentioned in this chapter for reasons of space, are not uncharacteristic of a polity at the early stages of its state and democracy building. Admittedly, as proved by historic experience, especially of countries emerging from previous undemocratic, totalitarian regimes, the process of democratic consolidation is laborious, not always exclusively unidirectional and certainly not definitely bound to succeed. Nevertheless, this chapter resists arriving at the conclusion that the democratic infelicities in Slovenia can be simply, or even exclusively, understood as a 'childhood disease', and as such something harmless and normal, which will go away by itself.

The conclusion emerging from the preceding discussion is rather the opposite. The shortcomings of the Slovenian democracy are of a systemic and general character and have been the product of a deliberate, orchestrated set of actions geared to preserve the described systemic flaws in the democracy, as well as to weaken the system even further, especially in its throughput legitimacy leg. The controversies surrounding the reform of the electoral system and its still contested constitutionality, but in particular the hugely controversial Patria affair, have demonstrated that over two decades an organised political action has been taking place, inside and outside of the formal democratic process, including with the involvement of the judiciary, to create an environment that distorts voters' preferences, radicalises political debate, turns voters away from participation in the political process, contributes to the implosion of political parties (in the making) and thereby systematically weakens the Slovenian system of democracy.

A weak democratic system is a reflection of a strong informal system of power, built upon the infrastructure of the state-owned economy and the looming public sector in Slovenia, which has always been under the control of the communist elite and their successors. Unlike the other CEE countries that have been identified as democratically backsliding, power in Slovenia rests not in the formal institutions of the state, but in its informal infrastructure and state-run economy. The ambition of the ruling elites therefore no longer necessarily is to be formally in power, but simply to ensure that those who are in power, either de facto or de jure, lack the means of undoing the informal substructure of the Slovenian state. The implosion of the political space and growing apathy among voters are therefore an expected result, and one that is desirable for those wishing the captured, klepocratic state to thrive or at least endure. Democracy in such terms is, of course, a seeming democracy at best.

8

Freedom of Press under Stress in Slovenia

> Anyone who challenges the prevailing orthodoxy finds himself silenced with surprising effectiveness. A genuinely unfashionable opinion is almost never given a fair hearing, either in the popular press or in the highbrow periodicals.[1]

I. INTRODUCTION

FREEDOM OF THE press has been described as the backbone of constitutional democracy.[2] Justice Frankfurter has observed that a 'free press is indispensable to the workings of our democratic society'.[3] The media has often also been labelled as a 'public watchdog' or as a fourth branch (the 'fourth estate') of government, whose role is to supervise the other three branches.[4] The media will be particularly able to perform its role as the fourth estate if the environment is conducive to investigative journalism. As a result, the media has obligations to promote and protect the values and objectives of constitutional democracy and the rule of law.[5] Baker has argued that 'democracy needs competing media to develop and promote alternatives' and 'both pluralist and complex democracy also require a segmented, partisan, mobilizing press'.[6] A free pluralistic press remains a principal constitutional precondition for the

[1] George Orwell, 'The Freedom of the Press', unused preface to *Animal Farm* published in *The Times Literary Supplement* (15 September 1972).

[2] See eg Jan Oster, *Media Freedom as a Fundamental Right* (Cambridge, Cambridge University Press, 2015).

[3] *Associated Press v United States* 326 US 1, 28 (1945) (concurrence of Frankfurter).

[4] See also James Weinstein, 'An Overview of American Free Speech Doctrine and its Application to Extreme Speech' in Ivan Hare and James Weinstein (eds), *Extreme Speech and Democracy* (Oxford, Oxford University Press, 2009) 81–91.

[5] See eg Richard Cullen, 'Freedom of the Press and the Rule of Law' in Steve Tsang (ed), *Judicial independence and the Rule of Law in Hong Kong* (New York, Palgrave, 2001) 157–79.

[6] C Edwin Baker, *Media, Markets and Democracy* (Cambridge, Cambridge University Press, 2002) 158.

functioning of free society and constitutional democracy,[7] despite the changing and complex forms of delivering information and communication.[8] If it is not guaranteed in its entirety, not only will the functioning of constitutional democracy be distorted, but also the life of society at large, as many examples from Slovenia testify.

Media outlets, both public and private, therefore have social responsibilities and human rights obligations, whereas public media in particular has a fortiori an essential role in ensuring space for a pluralistic debate in a democratic society. Baker concisely notes that 'a monopoly public-affairs media will (even if unconsciously) suppress differences – claiming objectivity for what is really a partisan vision'.[9] The false objectivity or perception of reality has been one of the principal features of the newly established constitutional democracies. Such traits have been particularly problematic in environments where journalists have mostly not been independent from government. Not unlike other CEE countries, Slovenia too has so far had little experience with investigative journalism as much of the traditional media landscape has been connected with state-owned companies and their marketing budgets, thereby advancing the interests and preserving the status quo of the societal and governing elites, belonging mostly to the post-communist spheres of society.[10] Therefore, the lack of a proper free press has adversely affected the workings of Slovenia's constitutional democracy by narrowing the space for pluralistic debate in its public sphere. Rosenfeld aptly argues that 'democracy cannot function without political will-formation or without open and wide-ranging discussion of political alternatives'.[11] Pluralistic debates have therefore been an essential prerequisite for transiting from authoritarian and totalitarian regimes to constitutional democracy based on the rule of law. The ECtHR observed in *Mladina v Slovenia* that 'though journalists are required to respect certain boundaries … their duty is nevertheless to impart – in a manner consistent with their obligations and responsibilities – information and ideas on all matters of public interest'.[12] As a rule, media outlets are at least theoretically

[7] See eg Martin Löffler, *Presserecht: Kommentar zu den deutschen Landespressegesetzen mit systematischen Darstellungen zum pressebezogenen Standesrecht, Anzeigenrecht, Werbe- und Wettbewerbsrecht, Urheber- und Verlagsrecht, Arbeitsrecht, Titelschutz, Mediendatenschutz, Jugendmedienschutz und Steuerrecht*, 6th edn, (Munich, Beck, 2015).

[8] Christian Katzenbach, Christian Pentzold, Sigrid Kannengießer, Marian Adolf and Monika Taddicken (eds), *Neue Komplexitäten für Kommunikationsforschung und Medienanalyse: Analytische Zugänge und empirische Studien, Schriftenreihe Digital Communication Research* 4, (Berlin, 2018).

[9] Baker (n 6) 158.

[10] See eg John Downey and Sabina Mihelj (eds), *Central and Eastern European Media in Comparative Perspective: Politics, Economy and Culture* (Farnham, Ashgate, 2012).

[11] Michael Rosenfeld, 'A Pluralist Theory of Political Rights in Times of Stress' in Wojciech Sadurski (ed), *Political Rights under Stress in 21st Century Europe* (Oxford, Oxford University Press, 2006) 12–54, 41.

[12] *Mladina dd Ljubljana v Slovenia* no 20981/10 (ECtHR, 17 April 2018) para 39. See also *Narodni List DD v Croatia* no 2782/12 (ECtHR 8 November 2018); and Andraž Teršek, 'Razumevanje

charged in this way to stimulate public debate on the issues of public concern, thereby providing an environment conducive to the functioning of constitutional democracy.

In the last two decades the media in Central and Eastern Europe have been placed under immense pressure by political parties[13] and informal networks of business corporations, who have sought to turn it into an instrument for not only preserving, but also advancing, their private interests.[14] The constitutional quality of the media in Central and Eastern Europe admittedly varies,[15] but Slovenia has been a textbook example of how the freedom of press can be used to protect and/or advance various interests of informal networks. Those economic and political networks have influenced media outlets to publish or not to publish information concerning individuals, businesses and others. In most cases, they appear to have aimed to support corrupt and arbitrary practices of local kleptocracy.[16] The population has therefore been extremely wary and distrustful of reporting in the media. Consequently, the media has not been perceived as independent and trustworthy.[17] The media has been directly used by informal networks to influence the dynamics of institutional elites, thereby affecting the observance of the rule of law. Slovenia has been no exception to such developments.[18] Freedom House reported in 2015 that 'while media content generally represents a range of opinions and information, some reporters have also complained that the country's major dailies tend to represent a left-leaning point of view, and that the right lacks sufficient representation in

svobode izražanja in svobode tiska: konceptualizacija ob sodnem primeru Grims proti Mladini (2016)' (2017) 3/4 *Javna uprava* 5–44.

[13] See eg Peter Bajomi-Lázár, *Party Colonisation of the Media in Central and Eastern Europe* (Budapest, Central European University Press, 2014), who uses the term 'colonisation' for (in)direct political pressures in Central and Eastern Europe.

[14] Richard L Bairett, 'Executive Power and Media Freedom in Central and Eastern Europe' (2015) 48(10) *Comparative Political Studies* 1260. See also Aukse Balčytiene, 'The Price of Liberalisation and Other Strains on Democracy and Media Freedom in Central and Eastern Europe' in Terry Flew, Petros Iosifidis and Jeanette Steemer (eds), *Global Media and National Policies: The Return of the State* (London, Palgrave Macmillan, 2016).

[15] See eg Boguslawa Dobek-Ostrowska, '25 Years after Communism: Four Models of Media and Politics in Central and Eastern Europe' in Boguslawa Dobek-Ostrowska and Michal Glowacki (eds), *Democracy and Media in Central and Eastern Europe 25 Years On* (New York, Peter Lang, 2015).

[16] Ivanka Pjesivac, Katerina Spasovska and Iveta Imre, 'The Truth Between the Lines: Conceptualization of Trust in News Media in Serbia, Macedonia, and Croatia', (2016) 19(3) *Mass Communication and Society* 323. See also Peter Bajomi-Lázár, 'Variations in Media Freedom: Why Some Governments in Central and Eastern Europe Respect Media Freedom More than Others' (2015) 8(1) *Central European Journal of Communication* 4.

[17] Ivanka Pjesivac, Katerina Spasovska and Iveta Imre, 'Attribution of global ethical norms: Perceptions of journalistic independence and integrity in Serbia, Macedonia, and Croatia' (2017) 13(2) *Global Media and Communication* 157.

[18] See eg Karol Jakubowicz, 'Post-Communist Political Systems and Media Freedom and Independence' in John Downey and Sabina Mihelj (eds), *Central and Eastern European Media in Comparative Perspective: Politics, Economy and Culture* (Farnham, Ashgate, 2012) 15.

the print media'.[19] Nonetheless, Reporters without Borders ranks Slovenia 32nd out of 180 states with a score of 21.69 on the 2018 World Press Freedom Index.[20] However, such scores do not convey much without knowledge of the societal and institutional background in Slovenia. This chapter will argue that Slovenia's major media outlets have been controlled by economic and political networks under the influence of transitional elites, thereby affecting the electoral processes and, ultimately, Slovenian constitutional democracy as such. It will explore and scrutinise the situation concerning the realisation of press freedom in Slovenia. Freedom of the press has been under stress in Slovenia both from the state interference, but also from the concentration of power in the non-transparent and informal private networks.[21] Section II therefore sets out the constitutional and institutional frameworks of press freedom in Slovenia and analyses them from the perspective of the jurisprudence of the ECtHR on the freedom of the press. Section III then considers the contours of press freedom under stress in Slovenia, firstly by analysing public media outlets, especially the role of RTV Slovenia in Slovenian constitutional democracy, and secondly by providing an overview of private media outlets and their role and impact on the exercise of the rule of law in practice. Overall, this chapter argues that the constitutional and institutional frameworks underpinning the functioning of the press in Slovenia are comparable in nature and quality to those in more established constitutional democracies, but cannot by themselves guarantee the functioning of a free, independent and pluralistic press. The existence of such a press is severely hampered by influential informal political, economic and other networks which rely on the media to preserve and maintain their influence.

II. THE CONSTITUTIONAL AND INSTITUTIONAL FRAMEWORKS OF PRESS FREEDOM IN SLOVENIA

A. The Press as a Fourth Branch of Government

The press and media in the broader meaning of the terms in Slovenia have been able to rely on wide and broad constitutional protections complemented by regional protections ensured by the ECtHR. In this way, the formal constitutional protections of the freedom of the press in Slovenia are essentially

[19] Freedom House, Slovenia, 2015, https://freedomhouse.org/report/freedom-press/2015/slovenia (accessed 23 April 2019).

[20] Reporters without Borders, World Press Freedom Index, https://rsf.org/en/ranking (accessed 23 April 2019).

[21] See eg Eric Barendt who noted that 'traditionally the state has posed the greatest threat to this freedom [of press], but arguably similar dangers are created by both private censorship and concentrations of power'. Eric Barendt, 'Introduction' in Eric Barendt (ed), *Media Law* (Aldershot, Dartmouth Publishing, 1993) xi–xx, xi.

comparable to Western European standards. Freedom of the press as a fourth branch of the government derives from the principle of the rule of law. Primary protections for a free press are located in several foundational provisions of the Constitution of the Republic of Slovenia. Freedom of the press indirectly derives from Article 1, which states that 'Slovenia is a democratic republic'; Article 2, stating that 'Slovenia is a state governed by the rule of law'; and Article 3, stating that 'In Slovenia power is vested in the people. Citizens exercise this power directly and through elections, consistent with the principle of the separation of legislative, executive, and judicial powers.'[22] The freedom of the press derives indirectly from all these provisions and ensures the media's public interest function of controlling the three branches of government. In so doing, the media has also been fostering the rule of law and democracy.

Not all the press, however, has been able or willing to adapt to its 'fourth estate' role of public watchdog. It has lacked independence from the formal and informal political, economic and social networks due to the specific model of media ownership as well as due to internal and external political pressures. The supervisory role of the media is best ensured if it can operate financially independently from government subsidies, corporate interests and informal networks. Norris has argued that 'the independent media functions as another check and balance on government although it remains unclear which of the roles of the free press – as watch-dog, as civic forum or as agenda-setter – is most important in this relationship'.[23] The supervisory role of a free press is theoretically divided into two categories: firstly, exercising checks on power; and secondly, providing balances. It is, of course, informal in nature, but as such no less important as that of the main branches of government. Norris concedes that 'the effectiveness of the press as watch-dogs should have the greatest impact upon stamping out corruption and promoting transparency and freedom of information'.[24] By insisting on transparency and meritocracy, and by opposing corruption, the free press can therefore provide a useful tool for moving from a mere formal normative democracy to a fully fledged constitutional democracy based on the rule of law. It can positively affect state institutions and the quality of a constitutional democracy. However, those tools will only work if a society has already sociologically developed a critical stance towards arbitrary and corrupt practices. If the press does not internalise the values of constitutional democracy and considers only the interests of institutional, economic, political and other elites, as is often the case with the media in Slovenia, its impact on strengthening the rule of law will be negligible.

[22] Constitution of the Republic of Slovenia, Official Gazette of the Republic of Slovenia No 33/91-I, 42/97, 66/2000, 24/03, 69/04, 68/06 and 47/13.

[23] Pippa Norris, *Driving Democracy: Do Power-Sharing Institutions Work?* (Cambridge, Cambridge University Press, 2008) chapter 8, 16.

[24] ibid.

A direct legal basis for the protection of the freedom of the press is Article 39 of the Constitution. Paragraph 1 provides that that 'freedom of expression of thought, freedom of speech and public appearance, freedom of the press, and other forms of public communication and expression shall be guaranteed. Everyone may freely collect, receive, and disseminate information and opinions.'[25] Relying on this legal basis, the Slovenian Constitutional Court has developed an extensive jurisprudence strengthening further the freedom of the press. It noted, for instance, in its Decision No U-I-172/94 that: '[I]t is the necessary condition for the ability of the [free press] to control all branches of power, and ensures efficient operation of political opposition to those in power at each particular time.'[26] It added that all branches of government are obliged

> to specially ensure freedom of the press and of each individual journalist. For this purpose it is necessary to ensure freedom of expression of individual persons, as well as the protection of freedom of the press as an institution. The responsibility of the State in ensuring and developing freedom of the press, including of radio and television, is especially important at the time of rebuilding of democratic institutions in the new Slovenian State, which has inherited numerous and strong elements of non-democratic political culture, which formed the constitutional and actual basis for the single-party authorities in the area of former Yugoslavia. This is why feelings of anxiety and fear with regard to authorities may still exist and may in the case of journalists find their expression in (self-)censorship, and in the case of the public in political apathy and alienation.[27]

One can concur with these observations and add that not only is freedom of the press essential to the workings of constitutional democracy, but that such a press has to be pluralistic in nature to provide for the plurality of opinions in a democratic society, which is, inter alia, constitutive of the efficient exercise of the rule of law. In a recent case, the Constitutional Court reaffirmed its position and noted that it 'attributes special significance to the freedom of the press and journalistic reporting ... they contribute to the establishment and formation of an impartially informed public'.[28] The Court further held that 'the finding of the special importance of the freedom of expression when journalistic reporting is concerned entails that when balancing interests and values in a conflict of human

[25] Constitution of the Republic of Slovenia, Official Gazette of the Republic of Slovenia Nos 33/91-I, 42/97, 66/2000, 24/03, 69/04, 68/06, and 47/13 Article 39, s. 1.

[26] Constitutional Court of Slovenia, Decision No U-I-172/94, 9 November 1994, para 1.

[27] ibid.

[28] Constitutional Court of Slovenia, Decision Up-407/14, 14 December 2016, para 12 (footnote omitted). See also decision Up-2940/07, 5 February 2009, where the Constitutional Court noted that 'freedom of speech bears a particular significance in cases concerning expression within the framework of journalistic profession as the broad boundaries of freedom of the press is one of the foundations of modern democratic societies', para 7.

rights the freedom of expression must be attributed greater weight'.[29] However, those protections afforded to the freedom of the press are, of course, not absolute and need to be carefully balanced with other state interests.[30] Constitutional protections have been particularly advanced in guaranteeing individual rights to freedom of expression and the press, even though the Constitutional Court in the case *Mladina v Slovenia* failed to strike the correct balance between the protection of reputation of a politician and the press freedom of journalists.[31] Those normative protections have therefore been exemplary and in line with the standards of modern constitutional democracies; however, as the next sections show, they have not been fully translated into the daily working of Slovenian constitutional democracy.

Beyond the individual protections of the freedom of the press, there has been a lack of further systemic protections to ensure a pluralistic media landscape and to prevent monopolies in media ownership or to ensure a pluralistic media with equal representation of different partisan views. The state has both negative and positive obligations to ensure that media outlets respect the basic values of constitutional democracy such as human dignity, pluralism, tolerance and broadmindedness. This obligation is accentuated with regard to public media outlets and state-owned media, As a result, states ought to ensure that public broadcasters represent pluralistic views on public matters, and not advance any particular ideological perspective, typically favouring the government or informal networks. A free press manifests itself in different, often intertwined and interdependent, forms. In what follows, we will examine protection in audiovisual media as well in print and online media, respectively.

B. The Press as a Guarantor and a Protector of Pluralistic Public Debate

Freedom of the press in audiovisual, print, internet and social media derives from similar premises, namely pluralism, tolerance and broadmindedness, with some particularities developed for each form of media.[32] Those postulates have been enhanced at the normative level by the pronouncements and guidance of

[29] ibid, para 12 (footnote omitted).

[30] Jernej Letnar Černič, 'Democracy as a Trump Card? Combating Hate Speech in Pluralistic Societies' in Dorota Anna Gozdecka and Magdalena Kmak (eds), *Europe at the Edge of Pluralism*, Ius Commune Europeaum no 134 (Cambridge, Intersentia, 2015) 163–76.

[31] Constitutional Court of Slovenia, Decision Up-1391/07-13, 10 September 2009. For a overview of the jurisprudence of the Constitutional Court of Slovenia, see Andraž Teršek, 'Commentary of Article 39 of the Slovenian Constitution' in Matej Avbelj (ed), *Commentary of the Constitution of the Republic of Slovenia* (Nova Gorica, Nova univerza, 2019) 384–89.

[32] Jernej Letnar Černič, 'Freedom of Press in the European context: Klein v Slovakia' (2007) 11(3) *Edinburgh Law Review* 444.

the ECtHR. The ECtHR has repeatedly argued that freedom of expression 'is a prerequisite for the functioning of democracy'.[33] States carry negative and positive obligations to guarantee freedom of expression, thereby enabling pluralism and broadmindedness.[34] Media 'unless it is grounded in the principle of pluralism, of which the State is the ultimate guarantor … which the public is moreover entitled to receive … such an undertaking cannot be successfully accomplished'.[35]

Freedom of the press also plays a role in the right of individuals to receive objective and impartial information. More specifically, 'the public has a right to receive information as a corollary of the specific function of journalists, which is to impart information and ideas on matters of public interest'.[36] Therefore, freedom of the press has at least two dimensions: first, the right of the press to publish information; and second, the right of individuals to receive this information. Only both of these dimensions taken together guarantee a proper functioning of constitutional democracy. Freedom of the press also includes protection of whistleblowers, particularly 'where the employee or civil servant concerned is the only person … aware of what is happening at work and is thus best placed to act in the public interest by alerting the employer or the public at large'.[37] It is therefore important that constitutional democracies also protect the press in order for whistleblowers to function properly. States carry positive obligations to ensure conditions and protections for the exercise of press freedoms. Nonetheless, those protections are not without limits; they only apply to 'journalists in relation to reporting on issues of general interest' if 'they are acting in good faith and on an accurate factual basis … in accordance with the ethics of journalism'.[38] As a result, freedom of the press does not protect fabricated and fake information.[39]

[33] *Özgür Gündem v Turkey* no 23144/93 (ECtHR, 16 March 2000) para 43. See also seminal quote from *Handyside v the United Kingdom* no 5493/72 EHRR 737 (ECtHR, 7 December 1978) para 49, where the ECtHR extended freedom of expression 'to information or ideas that are favourably received or regarded as inoffensive or as a matter of indifference, but also to those that offend shock or disturb the state or any sector of the population. Such are the demands of that pluralism, tolerance and broadmindedness without which there can be no democratic society'.

[34] Jean-François Flauss, 'The European Court of Human Rights and Freedom of Expression' (2009) 84(3) *Indiana Law Journal* 810.

[35] *Informationsverein Lentia and others v Austria* no 13914/88, 15041/89, 15779/89 and 17207/90 17 EHRR 93 (ECtHR 1 December 1993) para 38 (footnotes omitted).

[36] *Sirbu and Others v Moldova* no 73562/01, 73565/01, 73712/01, 73744/01, 73972/01, 73973/01 (ECtHR 15 June 2014) para 17; *Ligens v Austria* no 9815/82 8 EHRR 407 (ECtHR 8 July 1986) para 41.

[37] *Guja v Moldova* no 14277/04 (ECtHR 12 February 2008) para 72. See also *Guja v Moldova* no 1085/10 (ECtHR 27 February 2018).

[38] *Stoll v Switzerland* no 69698/01 (ECtHR 10 December 2007) para 103.

[39] European Commission, Final Report of the High Level Expert Group on Fake News and Online Disinformation, 12 March 2018, https://ec.europa.eu/digital-single-market/en/news/final-report-high-level-expert-group-fake-news-and-online-disinformation (accessed 23 April 2019).

Limiting political pluralism or not guaranteeing its full exercise can result in the erosion of constitutional democracy.[40] Freedom of expression, and of the press accordingly, can be curtailed only if it promotes and incites hate, intolerance and violence.[41] The ECtHR traditionally combats the most radical expression of hate speech by employing Article 17 of the ECHR. The European Commission thus held in *Glimmerveen and Hagenbeek v the Netherlands* that 'the general purpose of Article 17 (abuse of rights) is to prevent totalitarian groups from exploiting in their own interests principles enunciated by the Convention'.[42] Similarly, the ECtHR argued that 'the applicant attempts to deflect Article 10 of the Convention from its real purpose by using his right to freedom of expression for ends which are contrary to the text and spirit of the Convention'.[43] Freedom of expression and freedom of the press therefore do not protect speech that denies historical facts about genocide and crimes against humanity and that incites and promotes intolerance, violence and hate. Democratic states are justified in suppressing speech only where there exists a pressing social need to do so.

A state has a positive obligation to ensure plural, tolerant and broad-minded freedom of the press relating to operations of public broadcasters and an obligation of conduct relating to privately owned media corporations. The ECtHR noted in *Centro Europa 7 SRL and Di Stefano v Italy* that states are obliged to ensure 'effective access to the market so as to guarantee diversity of overall programme content, reflecting as far as possible the variety of opinions encountered'.[44] It added that 'a licensing regime which allows the public broadcaster a monopoly over the available frequencies cannot be justified unless it can be demonstrated that there is a pressing need for it'.[45] More importantly, the Court has submitted 'that in such a sensitive sector as the audio-visual media, in addition to its negative duty of non-interference the State has a positive obligation to put in place an appropriate legislative and administrative framework

[40] Jernej Letnar Černič, 'National Security – A Trump Card? The European Court of Human Rights Decision in *Herri Batasuna and Batasuna v Spain*, *Etxeberria and others v Spain* and *Herritarren Zerrenda v Spain*', EUI working papers, MWP 2010/12, http://cadmus.eui.eu/bitstream/handle/1814/13343/MWP_2010_02.pdf?sequence=1 (accessed 23 April 2019).

[41] See specifically David Keane, 'Attacking Hate Speech under Article 17 of the European Convention on Human Rights' (2007) 25(4) *Netherlands Quarterly of Human Rights* 641. James Weinstein, 'Extreme Speech, Public order, and Democracy: Lessons from The Masses' in Ivan Hare and James Weinstein (eds), *Extreme Speech and Democracy* (Oxford, Oxford University Press, 2009) 23–61.

[42] *Glimmerveen and Hagenbeek v the Netherlands* no 8348/78 and 8406/78 (ECtHR 11 October 1979) point 11, 195. See in detail Hannes Cannie and Dirk Voorhoof, 'The Abuse Clause and Freedom of Expression under the European Human Rights Convention: an Added Value for Democracy and Human Rights Protection?' (2011) 29(1) *Netherlands Quarterly for Human Rights* 54.

[43] *Garaudy v France* no 65831/01 (ECtHR, 24 June 2003) 2–12.

[44] *Centro Europa 7 SRL and Di Stefano v Italy*, no 38433/09 (ECtHR 7 June 2012) para 130.

[45] ibid para 133.

to guarantee effective pluralism'.[46] The Court has clearly explained that states carry positive obligations to ensure a pluralistic media landscape; however, this is quite difficult to engineer in those national contexts where editors and journalists working for public broadcasters advance their partisan views as the only possible version. Additionally, states have obligations to ensure a pluralistic public media. The Court has further stipulated that it is necessary 'to ensure, first, that the public has access through television and radio to impartial and accurate information and a range of opinion and comment'[47] and that 'journalists and other professionals working in the audio-visual media are not prevented from imparting this information and comment'.[48] It further construed pillars for pluralistic debate, which all public broadcasters in the system of the Council of Europe have to follow, namely:

> Where a State does decide to create a public broadcasting system, it follows from the principles outlined above that domestic law and practice must guarantee that the system provides a pluralistic service. Particularly where private stations are still too weak to offer a genuine alternative and the public or State organisation is therefore the sole or the dominant broadcaster within a country or region, it is indispensable for the proper functioning of democracy that it transmits impartial, independent and balanced news, information and comment and in addition provides a forum for public discussion in which as broad a spectrum as possible of views and opinions can be expressed.[49]

It therefore found that Moldova failed to discharge its positive obligations to provide a pluralistic public broadcaster 'in the light in particular of the virtual monopoly enjoyed by TRM over audio-visual broadcasting in Moldova'.[50] Guaranteeing pluralism is therefore of the utmost importance not only for maintaining free public debate, but also for the execution of constitutional democracy and, in particular, for carrying out fair electoral processes as these are dependent on free, pluralistic and objective media. The ECtHR also held that: 'The legislative framework … did not provide sufficient safeguards against the control of TRM's senior management, and thus its editorial policy, by the political organ of the Government.'[51] Public audiovisual broadcasters are to provide pluralistic reporting, which should stimulate public debate in national environments, thereby guaranteeing foundations for the workings of the rule of law and constitutional democracy. As for online media, the ECtHR noted in *Delfi AS v Estonia* (no 64669/09) that 'the rights and interests of others and of society as a whole may entitle Contracting States to impose liability on Internet

[46] ibid para 134.
[47] *Manole and Others v Moldova* no 13936/02 (ECtHR,17 December 2009) para 100.
[48] ibid.
[49] ibid para 101.
[50] ibid para 111.
[51] ibid para 111.

news portals, without contravening Article 10 of the Convention, if they fail to take measures to remove clearly unlawful comments without delay'.[52] States and online media portals therefore have positive obligations to protect individuals from incitement to and promotion of violence.[53]

As for private media, Baker has argued for the widest and most pluralistic dispersal of media ownership. He noted that 'democracy implies as wide as practical a dispersal of power within public discourse',[54] which requires dispersed media ownership. He explained that 'in any local, state, or national community, concentrated media ownership creates the possibility of an individual decision maker exercising enormous, unequal and hence undemocratic, largely unchecked, potentially irresponsible power'.[55] Such and similar unrestricted powers in Central and Eastern Europe have often affected the daily functioning of constitutional democracies thanks to the ruling political parties and parallel realities created by tycoons and oligarchs. The latter have often used media propaganda to advance political candidates loyal to them, who have subsequently taken over the control of the state and its public media. The ECtHR has noted that 'the audio-visual media … have a particularly important role in this respect. Because of their power to convey messages through sound and images, such media have a more immediate and powerful effect than print.'[56] It further observed that 'the function of television and radio as familiar sources of entertainment in the intimacy of the listener's or viewer's home further reinforces their impact'.[57] In this respect, states are obliged to ensure a conducive environment for the coexistence of pluralistic media conveying various worldviews. The existing practices of transitional societies additionally call for even more diligent and efficient oversight over public and private media outlets.

III. FREEDOM OF THE PRESS UNDER STRESS IN SLOVENIA

The rights of television and radio broadcasters have been well protected in the Slovenian normative order. Nonetheless, challenges have arisen concerning plurality in the ownership and functioning of audiovisual, print and online media. The media landscape has been under stress in Slovenia since democratisation and independence. Plurality and freedom of the press have suffered

[52] *Delfi AS v Estonia* no 64669/09 (ECtHR, 16 June 2015) para 159. See also *Magyar Tartalomszolgáltatók Egyesülete and Index hu Zrt v Hungary* no 22947/13 (ECtHR, 2 February 2016).

[53] Ian Cram, 'Constitutional Responses to Extremist Political Associations – ETA, Batasuna and Democratic Norms' (2008) 28(1) *Legal Studies* 68.

[54] C Edwin Baker, *Media Concentration and Democracy: Why Ownership Matters* (Cambridge, Cambridge University Press, 2006) 7.

[55] ibid 16.

[56] *Centro Europa 7 SRL and Di Stefano v Italy* no 38433/09 (ECtHR 7 June 2012) para 132.

[57] ibid.

from non-transparent networks of political and economic forces, which have over the decades instigated systematic deficiencies in the freedom of the press. The lack of media pluralism appears to have affected the (non-)functioning of constitutional democracy and the rule of law in Slovenia by creating parallel realities. The state-owned and privately owned companies have distorted the media landscape in Slovenia to advance their parochial interests and have created their own media reality which has on a daily basis affected Slovenia's constitutional democracy.[58] Furthermore, this media concentration in the hands of non-transparent informal networks has resulted in there being hardly any investigative journalists in Slovenia, with few exceptions. Some commentators have even submitted that some journalists are even supplied with information by these non-transparent informal networks. Another feature of the media landscape, as pointed out below, has been the cross-sectorial ownership of media outlets by members of the Slovenian post-communist economic and political elites. Representatives of those elites have usually been active in other economic sectors, such as the production of semi-finished industrial products, or in construction, agriculture and other businesses, and it appears that they purchased media outlets to protect their public image or those of their informal networks. Similar patterns of media ownership can be seen across Central and Eastern Europe.[59] The Association of Journalists and Commentators noted in its 2015 Annual Report that 'non-plurality remains one of the main issues in the Slovenian media space'.[60] They added that: 'Both our largest public media companies … are controlled by the incumbent Government's majority in the National Assembly, which appoints most members of the highest bodies of these two media companies, and this is often reflected in their reporting.'[61] A recent study confirms the constant challenges to freedom of the press elsewhere in Central and Eastern Europe.[62] As a result, this section will briefly address challenges to the fully fledged exercise of

[58] Daniel Smilov and Jurij Toplak (eds), *Political Finance and Corruption in Eastern Europe: The Transition Period* (Farnham, Ashgate, 2007); Robert W McChesney, *Rich Media, Poor Democracy: Communication Politics in Dubious Times* (Champaign, University of Illinois Press, 1999); Denis McQuail, *Mass Communication Theory*, 4th edn (London, Sage, 2000); Jan Van Cuilenburg, 'Media Diversity, Competition and Concentration: Concepts and Theories' in Els de Bens (ed), *Media between Culture and Commerce* (Bristol, Intellect Books, 2007).

[59] Karol Jakubowicz and Miklós Sükösd, 'Twelve Concepts Regarding Media System Evolution and Democratization in Post-Communist Countries' in Karol Jakubowicz and Miklós Sükösd (eds), *Finding the Right Place on the Map: Central and Eastern European Media Change in a Global Perspective* (Bristol, Intellect Books, 2008), 9; Bajomi-Lázár (n 13); Peter Bajomi-Lázár, *Reinventing Media: Media Policy Reform in East–Central Europe* (Budapest, Central European University Press, 2003).

[60] Annual Report of the Association of Journalists and Commentators (ZNP) on the Situation in the Media Field in Slovenia in 2015, http://www.znp.si/english-texts-mainmenu-27/431-annual-report-of-the-association-of-journalists-and-commentators-znp-on-the-situation-in-the-media-field-in-slovenia-in-2015 (accessed 23 April 2019).

[61] ibid.

[62] Petra Bard and Judit Bayer, 'A Comparative Analysis of Media Freedom and Pluralism in the EU Member States', European Parliament, 15 September 2016.

freedom of the press in Slovenia, by examining, first, public media outlets, and second, private media outlets.

A. Public Media Outlets[63]

RTV Slovenia has since independence performed the role of public broadcaster in Slovenia. It is publically financed through an obligatory monthly contribution from taxpayers.[64] It is the largest media outlet in Slovenia, with 2192 employees[65] and an annual budget of over €100 million.[66] Given its size, the public broadcaster has been a major player in the Slovenian broadcasting and larger media market, thereby attracting the attention of, and attempts at control by, governing political parties and powerful informal networks.[67] The Radio and Television Corporation of Slovenia Act states that the Radio and Television Corporation of Slovenia 'shall perform a public service in the area of radio and television activities … for the purpose of providing for the democratic, social and cultural needs of citizens' and minorities.[68] The Act clearly sets out the obligations of the editors and journalists of RTV Slovenia, which are inter alia to 'adhere to the principle of truthfulness, impartiality and integrity of information'; 'respect human individuality and dignity'; 'adhere to the principle of political balance and pluralism of world views'; 'ensure impartial and integral provision of information, such that citizens have the possibility to freely form their opinions'; and 'adhere to the principle of political independence and autonomy of journalists'.[69] In reality, however, it has been difficult for RTV Slovenia to comply with such principles in practice. RTV Slovenia has often been reproached by different sides of Slovenian society that it only provides partial information to the public, thereby assisting the incumbent government and its networks in the creation parallel media reality approved by the financial and political benefits of economic and political elites.[70]

Anecdotally, RTV Slovenia is often described as an extension of the post-communist transitional and governing institutional elites. Commentators, including civil society organisations, have maintained that the large majority of

[63] This section draws on the author's experience as member of the Programme Board of RTV Slovenia (May 2012–May 2016).

[64] Radio and Television Corporation of Slovenia Act (ZRTVS-1), Art 32.

[65] RTV Slovenia, Financial Plan 2018, 25 January 2018, www.rtvslo.si/files/letno_porocilo/financni_nacrt_2018.pdf, 26 (accessed 23 April 2019).

[66] ibid 37–43.

[67] Klemen Jaklič, 'Ustavni vidik svobode izražanja in javna RTV' (2005) 25 *Dignitas* 104.

[68] Radio and Television Corporation of Slovenia Act (ZRTVS-1), Art 1.

[69] ibid Art 5.

[70] See eg Association of Journalists and Commentators (ZNP), 'V ZNP ostro obsojamo zlorabo RTVS v politične namene!', 26 October 2018, http://www.znp.si/arhiv/484-v-znp-ostro-obsojamo-zlorabo-rtvs-v-politicne-namene (accessed 23 April 2019); Stane Granda (president of Združenje za Slovensko Besedo), 'Je odziv enak pri Dumančičevi in Možini?', 12 August 2018.

editors and journalists of RTV Slovenia have directly violated the principle of political balance and pluralism of worldviews by presenting their own views as objective truth. They have also argued that most of the editors and journalists lack the professionalism and integrity required to perform their duties, because they are allegedly connected to governing elites and powerful informal economic networks.[71] Moreover, it appears that RTV Slovenia, despite being the largest media institution in Slovenia, has so far produced only a handful of examples of high-quality investigative journalism.

Such concerns have culminated, first, in constant and repeated calls by parts of civil society and some political parties for the abolition of the compulsory licence fee, the main source of RTV Slovenia's income.[72] Second, some civil society organisations and political parties have demanded the dissolution of RTV Slovenia (citing a lack of political pluralism) and termination of the employment contracts of all of its permanent and contractual employees. On the other hand, RTV Slovenia and its associated organisations have not done much to defend themselves against these accusations.[73] It does not help that the incumbent ombudsman of viewers and listeners' rights has often taken a biased and partial approach to various complaints and programmes.[74] However, the complex political and economic conflicts taking place within RTV Slovenia and in its programmes can be partially explained by the station's complex governance structure.

The main organs in the governance structure of RTV Slovenia are the Programme Board and the Supervisory Board. The Programme Board consists of 29 members, which are individuals allegedly capable of 'contribut(ing) to the good functioning and enhancement of the reputation of the public radio and television corporation, both in Slovenia and abroad'.[75] They are to perform their duties 'independently and impartially, and shall be bound to fulfil only the interests of RTV Slovenia as a public radio and television corporation'.[76] The Programme Board is inter alia obliged to 'regularly address the fulfilment of the adopted programme plan and production plan, and provide the director-general with instructions related to eliminating deficiencies in these areas',

[71] See eg Association of Journalists and Commentators (ZNP), 'V ZNP ostro obsojamo zlorabo RTVS v politične namene!', 26 October 2018, http://www.znp.si/arhiv/484-v-znp-ostro-obsojamo-zlorabo-rtvs-v-politicne-namene (accessed 23 April 2019).

[72] See Radio and Television Corporation of Slovenia Act (ZRTVS-1), Art 31.

[73] Gibanje Osveščeni Prebivalci Slovenije, 3 March 2014, www.gibanje-ops.com/dejavnosti-gibanja-ops/drugacna-politika/604-mnoino-vlaganje-reklamacije-za-zavrailo-plaila-rtv-prispevka (accessed 23 April 2019).

[74] Zadeva Intervju/Dežman – Poročilo varuhinje z mnenjem in priporočili, 2 August 2018, http://img.rtvslo.si/_up/drown/files/2018/08/03/1570547_dezman-2018_8_3.pdf (accessed 23 April 2019).

[75] Radio and Television Corporation of Slovenia Act (ZRTVS-1), Art 17, s 1.

[76] ibid Art 17, s 2.

'address fulfilment of the adopted programme plan', and 'address the comments and suggestions of viewers and listeners of RTV Slovenia channels and indicate its position in this regard'.[77] The National Assembly of Slovenia appoints 16 members of the Programme Board on the proposal of viewers and listeners of RTV Slovenia and five members as proposed by the political parties; the rest are appointed or elected by different stakeholders (two members as representatives of registered religious communities; one member from the Slovenian Academy of Sciences and Arts, three members who are employees of RTV Slovenia, one member from the Hungarian national minority, and one member from the Italian national minority).[78] However, in the practice the vast majority, with few rare exceptions, of the Programme Board appear to struggle with ensuring independence and impartiality. Some of the members have in the past run on the lists of political parties for the National Assembly and local elections or have held high political office. As a result, the governing political parties have in the past decades exercised influence on the political direction of RTV Slovenia. Such influence has been felt mostly indirectly through the role of the Programme Board in the election of directors of RTV Slovenia.

The Programme Board elects the Director of RTV Slovenia and gives consent to the appointments of directors of Radio Slovenia and Television Slovenia.[79] These directors are therefore responsible for the appointment of editors of news, culture and entertainment programmes, thereby directly influencing the shape, scope and content of broadcast material. Through the Programme Board, the governing elites thereby exert immense pressure on the editorial policies of individual programmes, subjecting RTV Slovenia directors, editors and individual journalists to the direct influence of the political masters who engineered their appointments in first places. Such policies work directly against the principles of pluralism, independence and impartiality coined in the normative and constitutional frameworks regulating the freedom of the press. As a result, a sector of Slovenian society has come to view RTV Slovenia as a politically biased institution. The regular and extraordinary sessions of the Programme Board have often been reminiscent of the ideological debates taking place in the National Assembly, thereby going against the objectives of public institutions such as RTV Slovenia. Moreover, representatives of RTV Slovenia employees, in most cases well-known journalists, have not shied away from taking an ideological stance at some sessions of the Programme Board, directly violating the prohibition of actual or apparent conflicts of interest demanded of journalists working for the public broadcaster. In so doing, the Programme Board and RTV Slovenia have lost the appearance of delivering professional, independent and impartial programming and reporting.

[77] ibid Art 16, s 1.
[78] ibid Art 17, s 6.
[79] ibid Art 21, ss 1 and 2.

Moreover, the Supervisory Board is even more directly under the influence of the governing political parties. It has 11 members. The political parties within the National Assembly elect five members, the government appoints four members, and the employees appoint two members, thereby leaving RTV Slovenia even deeper under the daily influence of political parties and governing elites.[80] The Supervisory Board inter alia adopts 'the financial plan and annual report of the public institution and decide[s] on the use of possible surplus income over expenditure', supervises 'the operations of RTV Slovenia' and 'the management of accounts books and the legality of operations, and review[s] periodic accounts'.[81]

Given the actual and perceived lack of credibility, independence and legitimacy, the Programme Board and the Supervisory Board of RTV Slovenia have not fulfilled their constitutional and statutory obligations to ensure that RTV Slovenia functions as an independent, impartial and pluralistic broadcaster. In contrast, the direct and indirect involvement of politics has turned RTV Slovenia into untrustworthy institution representing the interests of political parties and informal networks, and feeding information on their behalf. Given the above-described societal, political and economic contexts, calls for the abolition of the compulsory licence fee and even the dissolution of RTV Slovenia may not appear as straightforwardly unfounded and unjustified. Political and informal networks would always be eager to take control over RTV Slovenia – a major player in the limited Slovenian media market – in order to create parallel media realties that can advance their financial and political agendas. RTV Slovenia has in this way also affected the current functioning of constitutional democracy in Slovenia by constructing parallel realities. For these reasons, the normative framework of RTV Slovenia is in need of a major overhaul in order to introduce safeguards that will eliminate the direct influence of daily politics and current governments. In the end, however, it falls upon the Directors, editors, journalists and other staff of RTV Slovenia to discharge their responsibilities compliant with constitutional values, principles and rules. Such reforms will thereby engender more qualitative, independent, credible and professional reporting and will allow for pluralistic reporting, creating more space for investigative journalism.

B. Private Media Outlets

Many forms and types of private media outlets are presently active in Slovenia, but only a handful of these are major ones. As it stands, the major players in the media market appear to be connected with the post-communist political and

[80] ibid Art 26, s 1.
[81] ibid Art 27, s 1.

economic networks. Media ownership has been one of the central problems of media freedom in Slovenia. Scholars have argued that pluralist and dispersed media ownership is essential to achieving genuine freedom of press.[82] Slovenia, like most CEE countries,[83] has significant media concentration, preventing a mature press plurality that would allow the equal presence of different views. Four out of five major dailies (*Delo*, *Večer*, *Dnevnik* and *Slovenske novice*) in Slovenia are owned by representatives of post-communist elites, who have been active in various cross-sectoral business activities. The Media Act on paper prohibits concentrations of ownerships 'of twenty percent or more',[84] but has been toothless in curtailing informal behind-the-scenes connections. The Kolektor Group owns both *Delo* and *Slovenske novice* through shadow companies, thereby exercising influence on the daily functioning of Slovenia's constitutional democracy.[85] *Dnevnik* is owned by Bojan Petan through a web of connected companies,[86] whereas the *Večer* from Štajerska region is under the control of three families, Polanič – owners of the construction corporation Pomgrad and the largest Slovenian agriculture corporation – Panvita and Hakl, through complicated and non-transparent ownership structures.[87] The financial daily, *Finance*, is the only exception, owned by the Swedish media corporation Bonnier Business Press AB.[88] The largest print media in Slovenia, the Delo group and the soon to be merged Večer-Dnevnik, all are therefore through ownership controlled by two construction/agriculture corporations, testifying to one of the features of transitional medial landscape in CEE Europe, namely the cross-sectoral ownership of media structures by informal economic and political networks.

[82] Baker (n 54); Ben H Bagdikian, *The New Media Monopoly* (Boston, MA, Beacon Press, 2014); McChesney (n 58).

[83] Auksė Balčytienė, Peter Bajomi-Lázár, Václav Štětka and Miklós Sükösd, 'Oligarchization, De-Westernization and Vulnerability: Media between Democracy and Authoritarianism in Central and Eastern Europe' (2015) 3(1) *Tidsskrift for Medier, Erkendelse og Formidling* 119.

[84] The Mass Media Act, Official Gazette of the Republic of Slovenia No 35/01, Art 58(1), www.rtvslo.si/files/razno/mass_media_act.pdf (accessed 23 April 2019). See eg Polona Božičko and Peter Gorše, 'Merger Control in Slovenia: Overview', *Thomson Reuters Practical Law* (1 October 2018) https://uk.practicallaw.thomsonreuters.com/w-017-1948?transitionType=Default&contextData=(sc.Default)&firstPage=true&comp=pluk&bhcp=1 (accessed 23 April 2019). See also Helena Motoh, 'Slovenia Economy Briefing: The Attempt to Sale Pro Plus to United Group', *China-CEE Institute* (30 November 2018) https://china-cee.eu/2018/11/30/slovenia-economy-briefing-the-attempt-to-sale-pro-plus-to-united-group/ (accessed 23 April 2019).

[85] Bizi profile of Delo Časopisno založniško podjetje doo shows only one owner, FMR Financiranje in upravljanje naložb dd, 23 September 2018.

[86] School of Advanced Social Studies (FUDŠ), 'Analiza medijskega prostora v Republiki Sloveniji', Final Report (2015) 6, www.mk.gov.si/fileadmin/mk.gov.si/pageuploads/Ministrstvo/raziskave-analize/mediji/2015_Analiza_medijskega_prostora_v_RS.pdf (accessed 23 April 2019).

[87] J G, 'Prekmurska hobotnica Hakl-Židan-Polanič izčrpava davkoplačevalske milijone, ki jih uporabijo za prevzeme medijev v službi Židanove SD' *Demokracija* (29 May 2018) www.demokracija.si/slovenija/prekmurska-hobotnica-hakl-zidan-polanic-izcrpava-davkoplacevalske-milijone-ki-jih-uporabijo-za-prevzeme-medijev-v-sluzbi-zidanove-sd.html (accessed 23 April 2019).

[88] Bonnier Business Press AB, www.bonnierb2b.com (accessed 23 April 2019).

The informal and formal economic, political and institutional networks have thereby created a spider's web of powerful corporations, which only serve the preservation and advancement of their private interests, for instance, through their influence on the state-owned corporations, and on the recruitment and promotion of officials and ministers within state institutions and public administration. Those companies have, through loyal editors and journalists, recreated the reality of Slovenian constitutional democracy as a perceived parallel reality, which appears even more real and credible than the actual reality. The most widely read weekly magazines are *Mladina* and *Reporter*, with the former being representative of opinions of the post-communist elites and radical left, whereas the latter appears to represent more centre-right views. The ownership of *Mladina* is transparent, as it is majority owned by Transmedia spa (13.0667%) and Distriest doo (57.3%), which was formerly owned by the bank KB1909 Societa Finanziaria per Vega Finanz sa.[89] These are allegedly connected with resources close to the former post-communist elites.[90] On the other hand, the weekly *Reporter* is owned by the publicly unknown individual Tara Milikić, apparently indirectly connected with networks of another media tycoon, Martin Odlazek.[91]

The printed press in Slovenia has in recent decades experienced losses in advertising income due to the rise of online media and a decrease in the number of copies sold. It has attempted to modify its business model by partially moving its content to online platforms, although this has failed to replace lost advertising revenue.[92] However, even though some of the largest media corporations are privately and foreign owned, their marketing revenue depends on the Slovenian market, where largest and even majoritarian share belongs to fully or semi state-owned companies. State advertisements therefore play an influential role in the marketing revenues of Slovenian media corporations. State and institutional, economic and political elites can therefore also exercise influence on private corporations by awarding marketing contracts based on how critical these media corporations are of the incumbent government and its informal networks. If they behave sympathetically towards the government, their marketing revenue from those state-owned corporations will increase; if not, it will decrease. In this light, one should carefully read the statement of the Slovenian Prime Minister in November 2018, which discouraged corporations fully or partially owned by the state from contracting marketing space in those media that promote hate speech, with his government and connected informal networks deciding on the

[89] Kizo, 'Grega Repovž in prijatelji, sluge davčnih oaz ali kako kazino kapitalizem hrani Mladino' *Portal Plus* (1 February 2015) www.portalplus.si/686/kapitalizem-hrani-mladino/ (accessed 23 April 2019).

[90] ibid.

[91] Bizi profile of Reporter Media doo.

[92] Project SOZ (Slovenska oglaševalska zbornica), Revidiranje prodanih naklad, July–December 2018, www.soz.si/projekti_soz/rpn_revidiranje_prodanih_naklad (accessed 23 April 2019).

definition of hate speech.[93] This statement had a chilling effect across the Slovenian media and public space, but especially in those media outlets that are more or less close to the opposition. Such practices therefore attest that most media outlets in Slovenia have not fulfilled their role as public watchdog as they are not willing to understand their role in a constitutional democracy. The press outlets in Slovenia therefore fulfil the interests of their masters by protecting the privileges of informal political, economic and other networks.

Similar traits can be observed in the audiovisual media market, which is dominated by two commercial channels, Pop TV and Kanal A, run by the Produkcija Plus storitveno podjetje doo Ljubljana (Pro Plus). These are the most watched television stations due to their light entertainment nature of their programme content. They are owned by Central European Media Enterprises, which is a media corporation registered in Bermuda that owns several media outlets across Central and Eastern Europe. However, the ownership structure of the parent Bermudian corporation is unclear and non-transparent,[94] despite statutory obligations, although the company is listed under the name CETV on the NASDAQ Global Select Market and on the Prague Stock Exchange. But this ownership structure does not convey who are the majority shareholders. As a result, such listings have not been transparent and are highly problematic in the low-level rule-of-law environments often encountered in CEE countries. Pop TV, Kanal A and other channels of the same group have in recent decades exercised over-reaching control over the functioning of Slovenian democracy by choosing topics of public concerns and by the manner of reporting. Their impact has been such that some commentators have suggested that they can, through their programmes, single-handedly promote a candidate to win parliamentary elections or even propel her to the position of prime minister. They have in this way contributed to the creation of parallel realities compliant to the interests of their leadership, editors and/or owners. Therefore, is a major risk of the media being subjected to interference by political parties and/or informal networks.[95]

As a result, these two commercial channels have attracted the largest share of marketing revenues in Slovenia, dwarfing in this respect RTV Slovenia, Planet TV, TV 3 and some other minor stations.[96] Other major players on the

[93] A L, 'Premierju predlagamo, da z držo in delovanjem, izkazanim v pozivu, ravna bolj previdno' *Večer* (24 November 2018) www.vecer.com/premierju-predlagamo-da-z-drzo-in-delovanjem-izkazanim-v-pozivu-ravna-bolj-previdno-6618574 (accessed 23 April 2019).

[94] CME, company overview, www.cetv-net.com/about-cme/company-overview/default.aspx (accessed 23 April 2019).

[95] Marko Milosavljevic, 'Media Pluralism Monitor 2016 Monitoring Risks for Media Pluralism in the EU and Beyond. Country Report: Slovenia', European University Institute – Centre for Media Pluralism and Media Freedom, http://cadmus.eui.eu/bitstream/handle/1814/46811/Slovenia_EN.pdf?sequence=1&isAllowed=y, p (accessed 23 April 2019).

[96] Agency for Communication Networks and Services of the Republic of Slovenia, 'Poročilo o trgu elektronskih medijev in delu agencije za četrto četrtletje 2017' (26 March 2018) 8–9.

audiovisual market are Planet TV, owned by a Greek corporation, Antenna Slovenia BV, and Telekom, the largest Slovenian telecommunications company, which is state owned. In the light of this monopoly or oligopoly, the centre-right political parties have over several years attempted to establish their own television channels in order to counter partial and biased media reporting in the dominant media outlets. For instance, the television station Nova24 was established in 2016. However, concerns have arisen due to its financing as most its financial resources, as well as its ownership, stem from a network of corporations associated with Peter Schatz, a Hungarian businessmen, who has close links to Hungary's ultra-right Fidesz party of Prime Minister Viktor Orbán.[97] Mr Schaltz's companies are also majority shareholders in the company New Horizon, which owns the weekly *Demokracija*.[98] This level of foreign ownership has created the impression that foreign politicians are attempting to influence constitutional democracy in Slovenia. All of the above therefore created the appearance of potential and actual conflicts of interest between media owners and the editorial policies of those media. This risk for pluralism also derives from 2016 research by the Centre for Media Pluralism and Media Freedom highlighted in Figure 8.1.

Figure 8.1 Risks to media plurality in Slovenia[99]

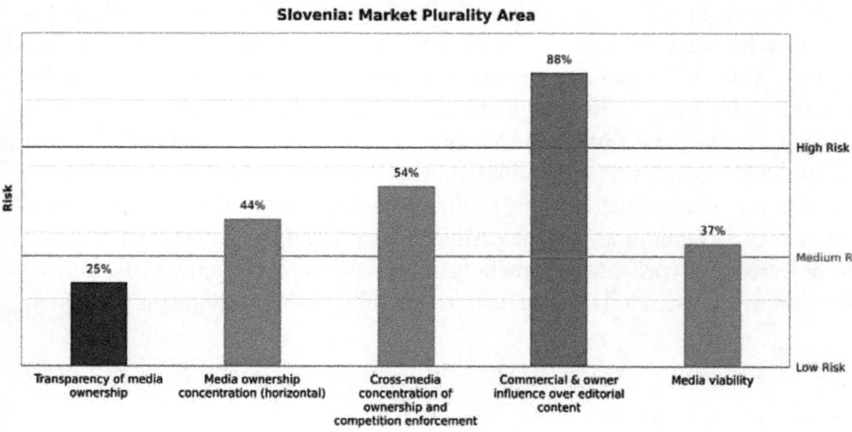

Additionally, there exist several minor news outlets, some of them capable of producing quality investigative journalism, which largely finance themselves

[97] Patrick Kingsley, 'Safe in Hungary, Viktor Orban Pushes His Message Across Europe' *New York Times* (Ljubljana, 4 June 2018) www.nytimes.com/2018/06/04/world/europe/viktor-orban-media-slovenia.html (accessed 23 April 2019).
[98] ibid.
[99] Milosavljevic (n 95), p 5.

through private funding, mostly through donations.[100] Nonetheless, their influence has been minor as they do not have an overwhelming presence in the Slovenian public space. Nonetheless, the media market has been partially democratised by the rise of online and social media, which has prevented the traditional media from having a monopoly over news delivery as there now exists a plethora of small outlets – albeit of limited reach – which have been challenging the predominant post-communist left-leaning media.

C. The Media and the (Re-)Construction of Societal (Parallel) Realities in Slovenia

Given the above societal, economic and political contexts, almost all Slovenian press outlets, from both public and private sectors, have been involved in the creation of parallel realities benefiting one or more dominant interest groups in order to advance their different private, economic and political interests.[101] They choose whether or not to publish articles or air programmes on specific topics or on specific public personalities.[102] In so doing, they protect the interests of those informal political and economic networks.[103] The mass media have been described as mediators between what occurs on the ground and their viewers, listeners and readers.[104] As a result, it is almost impossible to check if what they report as news is accurate as reports are often modified before they are delivered to final consumer.[105] The institutional, economic and political elites have in this way employed the press as an engine to advance their agenda in contradiction of the real facts. The press outlets in Slovenia therefore sometimes publish or chose not to publish information depending on whether it is favourable to the interests of informal networks. Further, due to the precarious financial situation of most journalists in Slovenia, they can be easily subjected to pressure and intimidation from powerful networks. Media owners are often reported to pressurise editors to hire or fire (un)friendly journalists or to publish or withhold a particular

[100] See eg casnik.si, pozareport.si and podcrto.si.

[101] Michael Parenti, 'Inventing Reality: The Politics of the Mass Media' (1987) 51(1) *Science and Society* 97; Gabriel Weimann, *Communicating Unreality: Modern Media and the Reconstruction of Reality* (London, Sage, 2000).

[102] William A Gamson, David Croteau, William Hoynes and Theodore Sasson, 'Media Images and the Social Construction of Reality' (1992) 18(1) *Annual Review of Sociology* 373; James W Chesebro 'The Media Reality: Epistemological Functions of Media in Cultural Systems' (1984) 1(2) *Critical Studies in Mass Communication* 111.

[103] ibid.

[104] See also Michael A Stefanone, Derek Lackaff and Devan Rosen, 'The Relationship between Traditional Mass Media and "Social Media": Reality Television as a Model for Social Network Site Behavior' (2010) 54(3) *Journal of Broadcasting & Electronic Media* 508.

[105] cf Morten Skovsgaard, Erik Albæk, Peter Bro and Claes de Vreese, 'A Reality Check: How Journalists' Role Perceptions Impact their Implementation of the Objectivity Norm' (2013) 14(1) *Journalism* 22.

news story. As a result, they have been creating a perceived reality, which has directly and indirectly impacted the functioning of constitutional democracy and the rule of law. The press in Slovenia has, for these reasons, run into difficulties about ensuring plural, independent and impartial reporting. They have been used to manipulate reality and/or create a parallel reality of the Slovenian constitutional democracy in order to preserve and advance the interests of the privileged few. It has been accepted that the media can in theory recreate a reality that does not correspond with real events.[106] The creation of a parallel reality can include fabrication of events, false news, character assassination, partial representation of facts, and the purchase of individual articles and journalists.

Similar to other institutions of Slovenian society, media outlets have been very weak and therefore subject to the influence of powerful actors. Müller has argued that 'countries with a higher degree of media performance show higher levels of political participation and less corruption'.[107] She added 'that media performance is clearly related to at least some aspects of the functioning of a democratic regime'.[108] The media therefore have through the creation of public reality affected the formation of the free will of viewers, readers and listeners, thereby affecting their decisions to make informed decisions when electing their representatives. In a constitutional democracy making informed decisions is essential to its functioning. It concerns all branches of government and all levels of state and public administration. The creation by the media of a parallel reality therefore affects the functioning of the rule of law, from police enforcement to administrative and judicial decision-making.

IV. OVERALL ASSESSMENT

The press outlets in Slovenia have in recent decades suffered from a lack of pluralism and the concentration of ownership of the major media outlets in the hands of various informal networks of political, economic and other origins. The Slovenian market has therefore been an example of the typical post-socialist and post-communist media market found elsewhere in Central and Eastern Europe, where grabbing power is all important. Milosavljević argues that: 'Media pluralism is in general, in quantitative terms, in a good state in Slovenia. Regulations for

[106] Michael A Shapiro and Tamara Makana Chock, 'Media Dependency and Perceived Reality of Fiction and News' (2004) 48 *Journal of Broadcasting & Electronic Media* 675. See also S Senyo Ofori-Parku, 'Reality effect or Media Effect? Television's Moulding of the Environmental Sanitation Agenda in Ghana' (2014) 35(2) *Ecquid Novi: African Journalism Studies* 40.

[107] Lisa Müller, 'The Impact of the Mass Media on the Quality of Democracy within a State Remains a Much Overlooked Area of Study' (London School of Economics and Political Science, 10 December 2014) http://blogs.lse.ac.uk/eurocrisispress/2014/12/10/the-impact-of-the-mass-media-on-the-quality-of-democracy-within-a-state-remains-a-much-overlooked-area-of-study/ (accessed 23 April 2019).

[108] ibid.

ensuring media pluralism are mostly clearly defined by laws and legal acts, and there are authorities that monitor compliance with the rules.'[109] We can concur with the last sentence. Normative safeguards for the freedom of the press have been introduced and entrenched since democratisation. However, we cannot agree with his first sentence. The pluralistic dimension of the freedom of the press has been extremely deficient both in private, but also public aspects of the markets.

The majority of the media landscape in Slovenia has therefore become politically monopolised and biased. As a result, different and contradictory opinions have not been adequately and proportionately represented in all major media, thereby leaning more strongly to monism than to pluralism. Connections between political, economic and other formal and informal elites derive from cross-sectoral ownership of media, where members of the informal networks from other industrial sectors (eg the construction industry, agriculture and tourism) own the media outlets. Connections between informal networks and incumbent governments are widespread in the Slovenian public space (see Figure 8.2).

Figure 8.2 Political influence on media plurality in Slovenia[110]

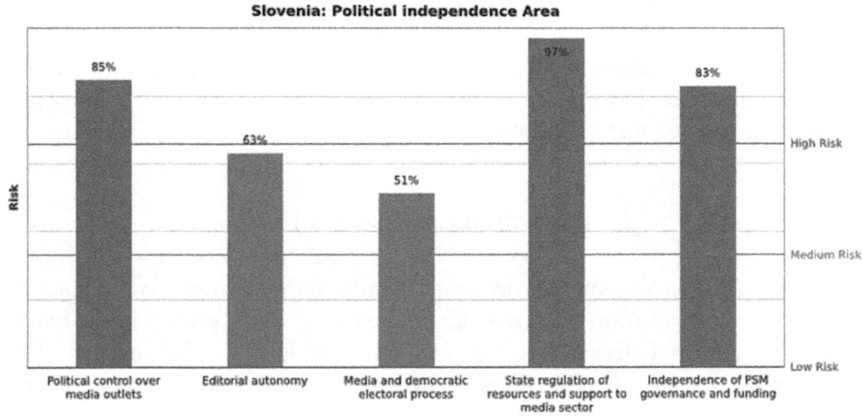

As a result, issues concerning transparency of ownership and financing of the media in the private sector suggest the need for external oversight as it is not clear who the actual owners are of the some of the largest print and audiovisual media, or how are they connected to informal political and economic networks. Even more troubling is the fact that the public media institution, RTV Slovenia, has been unable and unwilling to provide pluralist, independent and impartial reporting. Both its normative foundations and ensuring

[109] Milosavljevic (n 95) 3.
[110] ibid 7.

plurality in its programmes have been deficient, thereby directly violating its constitutional, international and statutory obligations to guarantee pluralistic, independent and objective reporting. What is more, the normative framework has allowed for the direct external and internal pressures of daily politics through political parties and informal political networks. For those reasons, RTV Slovenia's main supervisory bodies have not been able to conduct proper and effective supervisions. On the other hand, editors, journalists and other staff within RTV Slovenia have, with some few exceptions committed to ideological reporting, advanced the interests of informal economic and political networks. Such lack of perceived and actual political impartiality has not contributed to the realisation of the constitutional requirements for a public broadcaster to function plurally and impartially.

Media outlets that should have been objective, according to the constitution and legislation, performing the function of public 'watchdog', have favoured a particular ideological stance close to post-communist economic and political networks. Moreover, the majority of private media has been even more directly linked to political and economic informal networks often characterised by tycoons and oligarchs.[111] For instance, the owners of the dailies *Delo* and *Slovenske novice* appear to have been indirectly part of 'Forum 21', an interest group composed of businessmen and elites of the former Communist Party of Slovenia. This combination of media concentration, cross-sectoral ownership, informal networks and the monistic nature of Slovenian press has in recent decades to a large extent manipulated Slovenian public space.[112] These groupings have employed and argued for the monistic expression of freedom of press, which goes against the doctrine developed by the ECtHR that insists on pluralism and tolerance. The ECtHR has often argued, as in *Batasuna and Herri Batasuna v Spain*, that 'there is no democracy without pluralism. … Democracy thrives because of the freedom of expression.'[113] Institutional, political and economic elites appear to have employed the press as a tool for preserving and advancing their parochial interests. By creating parallel realities, the media outlets have directly affected the creation of the free will of individuals, thereby distorting their right to vote freely and independently in electoral processes. As a result, they have contributed to the creation of a constitutional democracy that is not based on meritocracy, fairness, transparency and impartiality. For those reasons, the functioning of the press in Slovenia can be described as only partially free, impartial and plural. Media outlets have in this way negatively affected the functioning of state institutions and society at large as

[111] cf with media freedom in the Czech Republic: Tim Gosling, 'How an Internet Impostor Exposed the Underbelly of the Czech Media, When Politicians Own the Press, Trolls have the Last Laugh' *Foreign Policy* (3 December 2018) https://foreignpolicy.com/2018/12/03/how-an-internet-impostor-exposed-the-underbelly-of-the-czech-media/# (accessed 23 April 2019).

[112] cf Henrik Örnebring, 'Clientelism, Elites, and the Media in Central and Eastern Europe' (2012) 17(4) *International Journal of Press/Politics* 497.

[113] *Herri Batasuna and Batasuna v Spain* no 25803/04 and 25817/04 (ECtHR, 30 June 2009) para 76.

they have shied away from reporting or supported arbitrary practices. Due to the lack of supervisory oversight by the 'fourth estate' Slovenia's constitutional democracy has also been crippled and has not been functioning as it should have been (see Figure 8.3).

Figure 8.3 The vicious circle of the role of the media in Slovenia's constitutional democracy, Source: author's own.

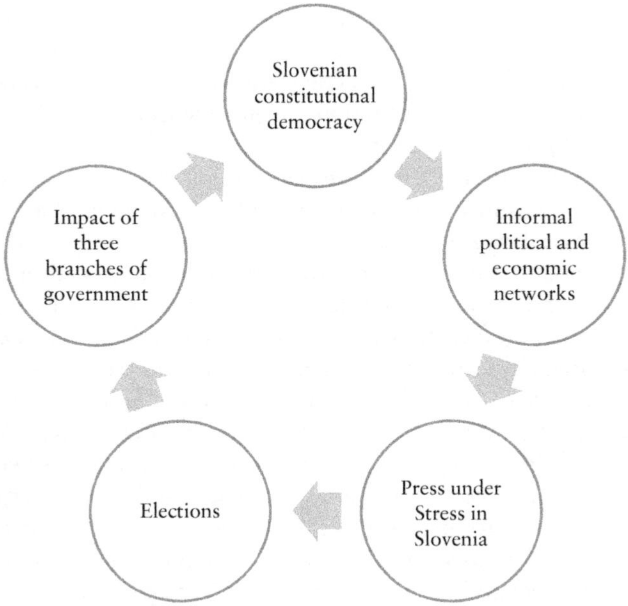

Such deficiencies have in recent years been partially remedied with the rise of public journalism, social media and independent investigative portals. However, much more has to be remedied in order for media outlets in Slovenia to function properly. First, the normative framework of the public broadcaster should be reformed in order to exclude external political influence, and it should also be reformed internally in order for its editors and journalists to provide for pluralist, independent, impartial and fair programming. We have argued previously that '[i]ndividuals also bear a key responsibility in creating a tolerant, open-minded and pluralistic public sphere in the respective European societies',[114] including editors, journalists and others working in the media industry. In doing so, the education of future journalists has to undergo drastic structural reform. Secondly, state regulations should insist on transparency of media ownership in order for them to disfranchise media companies from

[114] Letnar Černič (n 30) 176.

political and economic networks. Thirdly, civil society should work towards improving funding of independent individual and group investigative journalists by individual donors and crowd-funding, and establish new and reform existing supervisory bodies. Fourthly, the reform of freedom of press in Slovenia depends greatly on the reform of constitutional democracy and the rule of law in Slovenia.

V. CONCLUSION

George Orwell observed in 1945 that 'the British press is extremely centralised, and most of it is owned by wealthy men who have every motive to be dishonest on certain important topics'.[115] The Slovenian press has in the three decades since democratisation suffered from similar issues, notably non-transparent and cross-sectoral ownership, as well as a lack of investigative journalism pluralism, professionalism and integrity. The impact of the press on the functioning of Slovenia's constitutional democracy and the rule of law has been in the prevailing sense weak or even negative. The Slovenian media has been, with few exceptions, one of the actors most responsible for the deficient workings of the country's constitutional democracy as it has at different levels directly and indirectly affected electoral processes, thereby interfering with the proper functioning of all three primary branches of government. Even more conspicuous has been the role of RTV Slovenia, which has in recent decades failed to provide independent and pluralist news reporting.

Rather than exercising a supervisory role as the fourth branch of government, the Slovenian press has in most cases served as an apologist for the power and privileges of institutional, governmental and societal (in)formal elites and has advanced their private interests. It has therefore aided in the preservation of the power of these elites throughout Slovenian society by allowing for kleptokratic, nepotistic, clientelistic and corrupt practices. Moreover, where the rise of social media has allowed for the creation of the small independent media, the mainstream media has attempted to delegitimize and disqualify these new outlets. Those informal networks have used journalists to discredit individuals who have threatened their privileges and interests. As a result, the press has therefore been one of the actors most responsible for the failure to fully internalise the values of constitutional democracy, the rule of law, pluralism and tolerance in Slovenia. It therefore bears much responsibility for state institutions still being run by informal political and economic networks with origins in the unresolved totalitarian past. For those reasons, freedom of the press in Slovenia calls for reform of the rule of law and constitutional democracy in order to ensure pluralist media environments where all in the society have equal access and space to present and argue their views and opinions.

[115] Orwell (n 1).

9

Welfare State and Solidarity in Slovenia

I. INTRODUCTION

SLOVENIA IS ONE of the most developed countries in Central and Eastern Europe. It prides itself as having one of Europe's highest levels and scope of socioeconomic rights protections, with solidarity forming one of the centrepieces of its constitutional and welfare systems. As a result, Slovenia has been regarded as a (relative) success story concerning its welfare state and social policies; its income equality level is among the highest in the world. It grants its residents certain generous socioeconomic rights such as a combined 365 days maternity and parental leave.[1] It has also been traditionally ranked among the top ten countries globally concerning children's rights[2] and has topped the global ranking of Save the Children's End of Childhood Index, which measures the quality of childhood.[3] It also fares relatively well in terms of access to health care,[4] and its public pension system has been functioning quite well, despite shortcomings and future challenges.[5] Slovenia has, for instance, provided every resident with access to free education up to the end of university education.[6] Additionally, the OECD Better Life Index indicates that Slovenia scores above average in the areas such as 'housing, health status, social connections, education and skills, work–life balance, environmental quality, and personal security'.[7] Guardiancich therefore notes that 'Slovenia's achievements

[1] Republic of Slovenia, Ministry of Labour, Family, Social Affairs and Equal Opportunities, 'Rights under Insurance for Parental Protection', www.mddsz.gov.si/en/areas_of_work/family/rights_under_insurance_for_parental_protection/ (accessed 24 April 2019).

[2] Kidsrights, 'KidsIndex Ranking 2018', 10, www.kidsrightsindex.org/Portals/5/The%20KidsRights%20Index%202018.pdf?ver=2018-06-01-112649-877 (accessed 24 April 2019).

[3] Save the Children, 'End of Childhood 2018 Report: The Many Faces of Exclusion', 3, https://resourcecentre.savethechildren.net/node/13429/pdf/endofchildhood_report_2018_english_0.pdf (accessed 24 April 2019).

[4] See eg Igor Guardiancich, 'Slovenia: The End of a Success Story? When a Partial Reform Equilibrium Turns Bad' (2016) 68(2) *Europe-Asia Studies* 205.

[5] See eg Igor Guardiancich, *Pension Reforms in Central, Eastern and South-Eastern Europe: From Post-Socialist Transition to the Global Financial Crisis* (London, Routledge, 2013).

[6] OECD, 'Education Policy Outlook: Slovenia' (April 2016) www.oecd.org/slovenia/Education-Policy-Outlook-Country-Profile-Slovenia.pdf (accessed 24 April 2019).

[7] OECD, 'Better Life Index', Slovenia, www.oecdbetterlifeindex.org/countries/slovenia/ (accessed 24 April 2019).

were supported by … gradualism underpinned by a consensual political system, developed neocorporativist institutions and the partly inherited technologically intensive industrial production'.[8] The Slovenian welfare state has therefore guaranteed individuals have a broad safety net to cover potential events that can occur over the course of an individual's lifetime. Given the above data, it could appear that Slovenia is a fairytale story not only in Central and Eastern Europe but also globally. However, the relatively generous scope of the welfare state has taken a large toll on public finances: social security expenditures amount to staggering 16.7 per cent of the annual budgets for 2018 and 2019.[9] Moreover, the generous levels of the welfare state and socioeconomic rights have been subjected to substantial decreases during the economic crises, which have affected the ability of the Slovenian state to provide socioeconomic rights.[10]

Nonetheless, Slovenia ranks as below average in terms of income and wealth and subjective well-being.[11] For instance, the gross domestic product per capita in purchasing power standards was in 2017 only 85 per cent of the average of 28 EU Member states.[12] As this chapter will show, Slovenia has, despite its high rankings on the various global socioeconomic indices, increasingly struggled to maintain its welfare and equality standards. Moreover, a substantial number of 345,500 persons out of an overall population of just over two million are currently at risk of poverty.[13] Moreover, the public health system has been for decades described as being under the control of various influential, secretive and corrupt 'old boys' networks that have undermined its function to their private financial gain.[14] Overall, Slovenians submitted a score of 5.8 on average when asked about their general satisfaction with life on a scale from 0 to 10, which is below the OECD average.[15] Hence, these

[8] Guardiancich (n 4) 208. See also Igor Guardiancich (ed), *Recovering from the Crisis through Social Dialogue in the New EU Member States: The Case of Bulgaria, the Czech Republic, Poland and Slovenia* (Budapest, International Labour Organization, 2012); and Jože P Damijan, 'Reentering the Markets of the Former Yugoslavia' in Mojmir Mrak, Matija Rojec and Carlos Silva-Jáuregui (eds), *Slovenia: From Yugoslavia to the European Union* (Washington, DC, World Bank, 2004) 336.

[9] Government of the Republic of Slovenia, 'Draft Budgetary Plan 2018–2019', 15, www.mf.gov.si/fileadmin/mf.gov.si/pageuploads/EU_semester/SI_DBP19_-_no_policy.pdf (accessed 24 April 2019). See also Špela Lovšin, 'Bolniški stalež – delitev bremen med delodajalci in javnimi blagajnimi po Evropi' (2019) 14 *Pravna praksa* 10.

[10] See eg Igor Guardiancich and Oscar Molina (eds), *Talking through the Crisis: Social Dialogue and Industrial Relations Trends in Selected EU Countries* (Geneva, International Labour Organization, 2017).

[11] Guardiancich (n 4).

[12] Statistical Office of the Republic of Slovenia, Simona Krže, 'Actual Individual Consumption Per Capita in Slovenia in 2017 23% Lower than the EU-28 Average', www.stat.si/StatWeb/en/News/Index/7839 (accessed 24 April 2019).

[13] Statistical Office of the Republic of Slovenia, Stanka Intihar, 'In 2017 at-Risk-of-Poverty Rate Slightly Lower (13.3%), At-Risk-of-Poverty Threshold Higher than in 2016', www.stat.si/StatWeb/en/News/Index/7464 (accessed 24 April 2019).

[14] See eg Krištof Zevnik, 'Govor na javni tribuni ZZZS' (26 March 2019) www.youtube.com/watch?v=9E-JrPd0kDU&feature=youtu.be (accessed 24 April 2019).

[15] OECD (n 7).

and other statistical indicators have therefore indicated that not all appears to be as perfect in Slovenia as certain measures of international socioeconomic success seem to portray.

The broad scope of socioeconomic rights does not come for free; it depends on state budgetary resources. Slovenia spends a large portion of its annual budget on social transfers. In spite of its frontrunner position among CEE countries, it still lags behind countries in northern Europe, triggering one commentator to observe that 'all are equal in poverty in Slovenia'.[16] Why does Slovenia, for example, trail northern European countries in socio-economic development?[17] This chapter studies the normative and policy safeguards of the welfare state in Slovenia and explores the impact of the current state of constitutional democracy and the rule of law on the welfare state and solidarity in Slovenia. Several studies have in the past decade illustrated that the quality of living depends greatly on the quality of democratic institutions and the level of the rule of law.[18] It will be argued that crises of constitutional democracy connected to the abuse of the rule of law and denial of fundamental rights, as described in the preceding chapters of this book, have meant that ensuring and maintaining equal levels of solidarity and welfare provision has been increasingly costly. Moreover, guaranteeing solidarity and maintaining equal levels of socioeconomic rights in Slovenia has come at the expense of needed reforms in the exercise of the rule of law, namely in fairness, independence and impartiality of the judiciary, and the functioning of the rule of law. In this respect, higher levels of socioeconomic rights have been more difficult to achieve given the lower standards of quality of living and reduced capacity of the state's budgetary resources.

This chapter is divided into five subsequent sections. Section II aims to explain the interplay between (in)equality, equal capabilities and socioeconomic livelihoods in Slovenia. Section III thereafter takes a normative turn and analyses normative protections of welfare state and socioeconomic rights. The following section IV analyses the reasons behind regional inequality in Slovenia, whereas section V is dedicated to examining the impact of the weak rule of law and constitutional democracy on the level of welfare state and socioeconomic rights

[16] Aleš Žužek, 'Urban Vehovar: V Sloveniji smo enaki v revščini' *Siol.net* (7 November 2013) https://siol.net/novice/siol/urban-vehovar-v-sloveniji-smo-enaki-v-revscini-211055 (accessed 24 April 2019).

[17] See eg UNDP, 'Human Development Reports – Germany', http://hdr.undp.org/en/countries/profiles/DEU (accessed 24 April 2019); UNDP, 'Human Development Reports – Slovenia' http://hdr.undp.org/en/countries/profiles/SVN (accessed 24 April 2019).

[18] See eg John Luke Gallop, Jeffrey D Sachs and Andrew D Mellinger, 'Geography and Economic Development' (1999) 22(2) *International Regional Science Review* 179; See also Stanley L Engerman and Kenneth L Sokoloff, 'Factor Endowments, Inequality, and Paths of Development Among New World Economies' (October 2002) NBER Working Paper no 9259; Daron Acemoglu, Simon Johnson and James Robinson, 'Institutions as the Fundamental Cause of Long-Run Growth' (May 2004) NBER Working Paper no 10481. Transparency International, 'Corruption Perception Index 2017' (21 February 2018) www.transparency.org/news/feature/corruption_perceptions_index_2017#table (accessed 24 April 2019).

provisions in Slovenia. Finally, section VI examines the future of welfare state and human development in Slovenia.

II. (IN)EQUALITY, EQUAL CAPABILITIES AND SOCIOECONOMIC LIVEHOODS IN SLOVENIA

Slovenia has been described as one of the most equal countries worldwide. It has traditionally ranked among the top ten countries according to the Gini index, which measures income inequality. More specifically, the annual UN Human Development Index score of 0.896 also places Slovenia relatively high, at 25th place, concerning its capabilities to guarantee human development.[19] It is hence placed in the 'very high human development category'.[20] The UNDP notes that 'Slovenia's 2017 HDI of 0.896 is above the average of 0.894 for countries in the very high human development group and above the average of 0.895 for countries in OECD.'[21] Slovenia has in its transition from a totalitarian system to a constitutional democracy employed state-centred policies of gradualism, which have maintained the scope and role of the welfare state.[22] Whereas governments were able to maintain those policies during periods of economic growth, the scope of the welfare state decreased during the economic crises of 2008–14, where GDP per capita measured was cut to 83 per cent of the average of the 28 EU Member States.[23] Slovenia currently ranks second worldwide on the Gini index with a score of 25.70.[24] More specifically it has been ranked second or third on Gini index depending on which survey is considered.[25] However, the Gini coefficient has in recent years increased, indicating increased income inequality.[26] Such high rankings can be explained by Slovenia's historical transitional context: the former communist regime, although disregarding civil and political rights, placed much emphasis on the provision of socioeconomic rights, high levels of income equality and a reasonable quality of public services; in other words, 'a state-socialist welfare system in which the state played a dominant role'.[27] The state-centred welfare system and normative recognition of socioeconomic

[19] UNDP, Slovenia (n 17).

[20] UNDP, 'Human Development Indices and Indicators: 2018 Statistical Update', Briefing note for countries on the 2018 Statistical Update, Slovenia, 2.

[21] ibid, 3.

[22] Guardiancich (n 4) 208–09.

[23] ibid, 212.

[24] Index Mundi, 'GINI index (World Bank estimate) – Country Ranking', www.indexmundi.com/facts/indicators/SI.POV.GINI/rankings (accessed 24 April 2019).

[25] Caelainn Barr, 'Inequality Index: Where Are the World's Most Unequal Countries?', *The Guardian* (26 April 2017) www.theguardian.com/inequality/datablog/2017/apr/26/inequality-index-where-are-the-worlds-most-unequal-countries (accessed 24 April 2019).

[26] Index Mundi (n 24).

[27] Maša Filipovič Hrast and Tatjana Rakar, 'The Future of the Slovenian Welfare State and Challenges to Solidarity', Paper prepared for the Annual ESPAnet Conference: The Lost and the New Worlds of Welfare (3-5 September, 2015, Odense, Denmark) 2, https://blogs.kent.ac.uk/welfsoc/files/2015/05/Draft_Paper_FilipovicHrastRakar.pdf (accessed 24 April 2019).

rights have also been translated into independent and democratic Slovenia, where the welfare state appears to have been turned into a bureaucratic, positivistic and formalistic unequal overreach of public power. Liberalisation and privatisation, as Justinek explains in Chapter 4 have been limited.[28] For those reasons, the low Gini coefficient has been maintained since independence and democratisation. In contrast, many CEE countries now have higher Gini coefficients, and therefore Slovenia appears to display many anomalies compared to the rest of the CEE panorama. Its Gini coefficient after taxes and transfers is substantially higher than before taxes and transfers, thereby illustrating that the impact of the Slovenian welfare state on income equality has been substantial.[29] Figure 9.1 illustrates that Slovenia has been traditionally placed among those EU Member

Figure 9.1 Income inequality in Slovenia

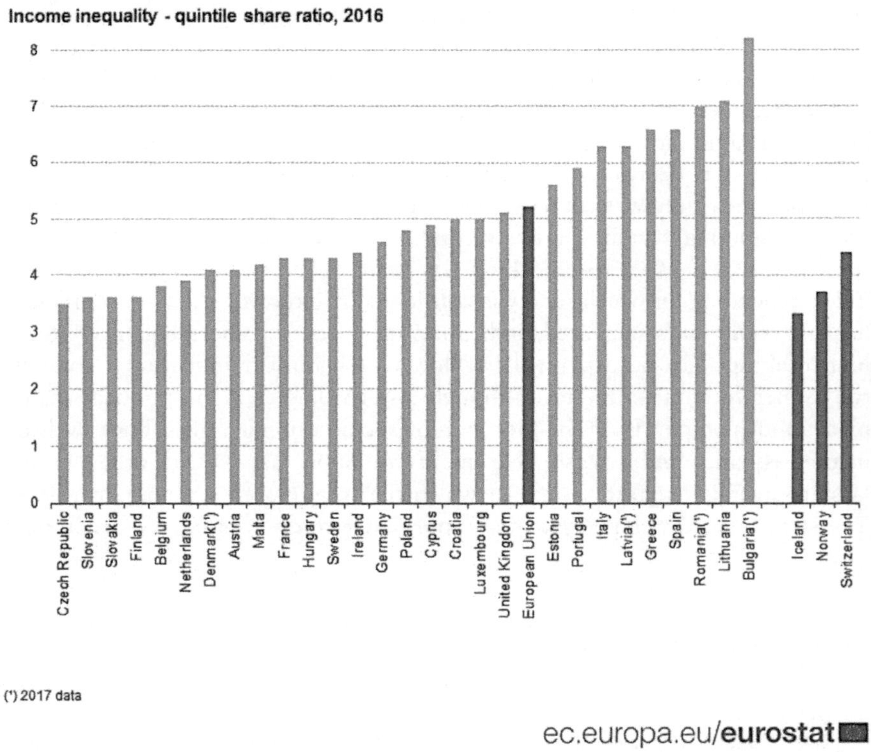

Source: Eurostat, 'Quality of Life Indicators – Material Living Conditions', https://ec.europa.eu/eurostat/statistics-explained/index.php/Quality_of_life_indicators_-_material_living_conditions (accessed 24 April 2019).

[28] See Chap 4 above. See also Janez Šušteršič, 'Political Economy of Slovenia's Transition' in Mrak et al (n 8) 402.

[29] Lisa Charlotte Rost, 'Equality, Before & After Taxes, The Gini Index, Explained', *Chartable* (8 April 2018) https://blog.datawrapper.de/weekly-chart-gini/ (accessed 24 April 2019).

States with the lowest levels of income inequality. One of the reasons for the generous scope of the welfare state has also been that normative protections of welfare state and socioeconomic rights in Slovenia have been broad and have generated a positive impact on ensuring the right to dignity to vulnerable individuals and groups.

In order to obtain an objective picture, it is necessary to combine levels of income inequality with levels of GDP per capita and household wealth. In this respect, Figure 9.2 shows the poverty rate and the proportion of the population having a relatively high income, illustrating the relatively low levels of risk of poverty in Slovenia. Nonetheless, over 345,500 persons live at risk of poverty.[30]

Even though Slovenia has enjoyed the low levels of income inequality, available data show increasing inequalities in household wealth.[31] The statistical data on income and wealth equality testifies that Slovenia may have low levels of income inequality, but that the rate of change in the inequality of wealth has been increasing in recent decades, indicating that inequality will increase in

Figure 9.2 At-risk-of-poverty rate and proportion of the population having a relatively high income

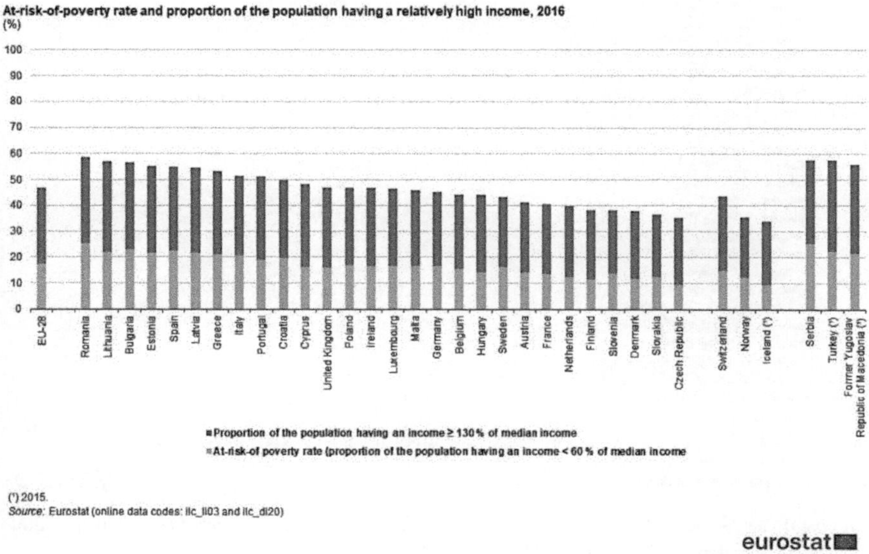

Source: Eurostat, 'At-risk-of-poverty rate and proportion of the population having a relatively high income, 2016', https://ec.europa.eu/eurostat/statistics-explained/index.php?title=File:At-risk-of-poverty_rate_and_proportion_of_the_population_having_a_relatively_high_income,_2016_(%25)_QoL18.png#filelinks (accessed 24 April 2019).

[30] Statistical Office of the Republic of Slovenia (n 13).

[31] Carlotta Balestra and Richard Tonkin, 'Inequalities in Household Wealth Across OECD Countries: Evidence from the OECD Wealth Distribution Database', OECD Statistics Working Papers no 2018/01, https://doi.org/10.1787/7e1bf673-en (accessed 24 April 2019).

Slovenia. These findings are corroborated by recent data on the concentration of wealth and income in OECD states.

Figure 9.3 clearly illustrates that the richest 10 per cent in Slovenia own 49 per cent of the wealth, whereas the richest 10 per cent earn only 20 per cent of the income. Wealth is therefore much more concentrated at the top than salaries, which is somehow contradictory in a country with a history of generous welfare state provision such as Slovenia. This raises the question as to how the richest 10 per cent accumulated more than 49 per cent of all wealth in Slovenia in less than three decades after democratization.

Figure 9.3 The concentration of wealth in OECD states

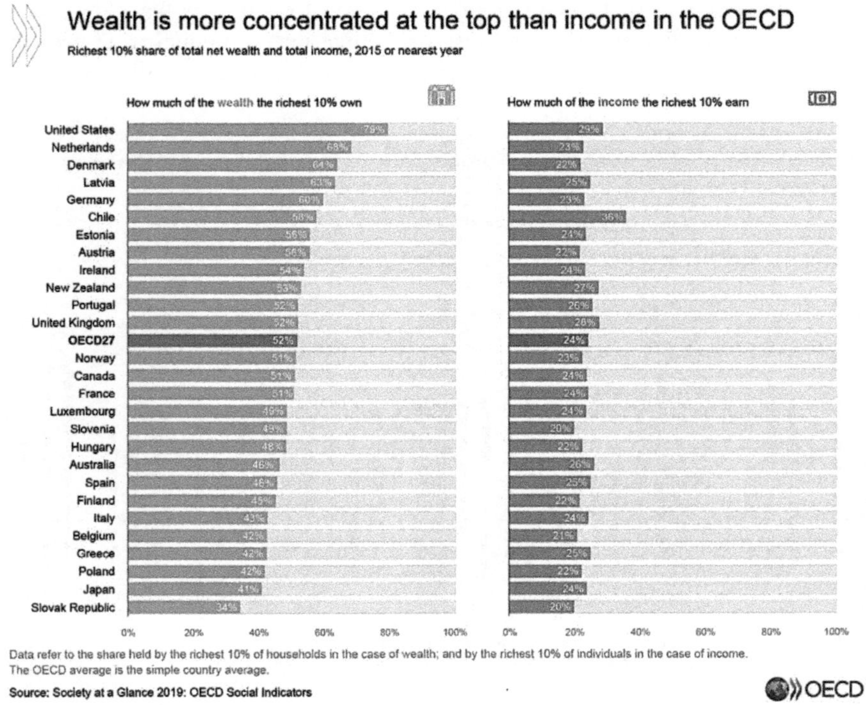

Source: OECD, 'Society at a Glance 2019, OECD Social Indicators', 27 March 2019, 99, https://doi.org/10.1787/soc_glance-2019-en (accessed 24 April 2019).

III. THE NORMATIVE PROTECTIONS OF WELFARE STATE AND SOCIOECONOMIC RIGHTS IN SLOVENIA

The welfare state is categorized as one of the primary fundamental constitutional values and principles of Slovenia. The Constitution of the Republic of Slovenia states in Article 2 that: 'Slovenia is a state governed by the rule of law and a social state.'[32] The principle of a welfare state has been widely introduced and internalised through the different layers of Slovenian society and the country's constitutional systems.

The Slovenian Constitution includes in its second and third chapters several provisions on socioeconomic rights. For instance, the second chapter of the Constitution on human rights and fundamental freedoms includes rights such as freedom of work,[33] the right to social security,[34] the right to health care,[35] the rights of disabled persons,[36] and provisions on education and schooling.[37] Those provisions are quite general as they mostly refer to the statutory legal basis. For instance, Article 50 states in paragraph 1 that 'Citizens have the right to social security, including the right to a pension, under conditions provided by law',[38] whereas paragraph 2 provides that: 'The state shall regulate compulsory health, pension, disability, and other social insurance, and shall ensure its proper functioning.'[39] Another set of socioeconomic rights can be found in the third chapter of the Constitution on social and economic relations. This chapter inter alia consists of rights such the right to drinking water,[40] a healthy living environment[41] and provisions on proper housing.[42] All in all, the Constitution therefore establishes solid protections for individuals against vulnerable socioeconomic conditions such as poverty. One can agree with Teršek that: '[T]he constitution already implicitly contains points for the concretization of the individual's right to protection against life in poverty.'[43] Socioeconomic rights traditionally create state obligations of conduct and not of result as they are dependent on state budgetary resources. States are at most bound by the reasonable core of socio-economic rights, which signifies the minimum level of socioeconomic rights obligations that they have to meet. As a result, most of the socioeconomic provisions found in the Constitution have a programmatic and general nature. However, the legislative and judiciary branches of government have in the past recognised that socioeconomic rights have a justiciable nature

[32] Constitution of the Republic of Slovenia, Official Gazette of the Republic of Slovenia No 33/91-I, 42/97, 66/2000, 24/03, 69/04, 68/06 and 47/13.
[33] ibid Art 49.
[34] ibid Art 50.
[35] ibid Art 51.
[36] ibid Art 52.
[37] ibid Art 57.
[38] ibid Art 50(1).
[39] ibid Art 50(2).
[40] ibid Art 70a.
[41] ibid, Art 72.
[42] ibid, Art 78.
[43] Andraž Teršek, 'Komentar 2. člena ustave (načelo socialne države)' in Matej Avbelj (ed), *Komentar Ustave Republike Slovenija* (Nova Gorica, Nova Univerza–Evropska Pravna Fakulteta, 2019). See more in detail Andraž Teršek, *Socialna ustavna demokracija* (Koper, Zložba Univerze na Primorskem, 2017).

in the Slovenian constitutional system. They have been further strengthened by the executing legislation.

Beyond constitutional protections, the statutory basis makes socioeconomic rights not only directly applicable, but also directly enforceable before specialised labour and social security courts.[44] Relevant statutes include the Social Assistance Benefits Act,[45] the Social Assistance Act,[46] the Health Care and Health Insurance Act,[47] the Pension and Disability Insurance Act[48] and the Equalisation of Opportunities for Persons with Disabilities Act.[49] Additionally, the labour courts are competent to decide both individual and collective labour disputes,[50] whereas social courts decide cases arising from pension and disability insurance, health insurance, unemployment and employment insurance, parental protection and family benefits, and social benefits.[51] These courts have throughout recent decades established a doctrine of enforceable socioeconomic rights ranging from the right to social security to the freedom to work. Most of the Slovenian welfare subsystems, such as the public health and pension systems, function through the contributions of employees and employers, with the state stepping in cases of the most vulnerable individuals.

The Constitutional Court of the Republic Slovenia has in its case-law on the principle of the welfare state developed the principle of the protection of human dignity of individuals who find themselves in the most vulnerable situations in order to ensure them an equal capacity for self-fulfilment throughout their lifetime. Although quite unknown in comparative law practice, the Constitutional Court has in several decisions confirmed the justiciability of socioeconomic rights. In this way, it has aimed to protect the decent life of individuals at risk of poverty and social exclusion, and to ensure a reasonable distribution of burdens between state and private sector. For instance, the Constitutional Court developed the doctrine of a 'subsistence minimum' in

[44] Labour and Social Courts Act, Official Gazette of the Republic of Slovenia No 2/04, 10/04 – popr, 45/08 – ZArbit, 45/08 – ZPP-D, 47/10 – odl US, 43/12 – odl US and 10/17 – ZPP-E.

[45] Social Assistance Benefits Act, Official Gazette of the Republic of Slovenia No 61/10, 40/11, 14/13, 99/13, 90/15, 88/16, 31/18 and 73/18.

[46] Social Assistance Act, Official Gazette of the Republic of Slovenia No 3/07 – official consolidated text, 23/07 – popr, 41/07 – popr, 61/10 – ZSVarPre, 62/10 – ZUPJS, 57/12, 39/16, 52/16 – ZPPreb-1, 15/17 – DZ, 29/17, 54/17, 21/18 – ZNOrg and 31/18 – ZOA-A.

[47] Health Care and Health Insurance Act, Official Gazette of the Republic of Slovenia No 72/06 – official consolidated text, 114/06 – ZUTPG, 91/07, 76/08, 62/10 – ZUPJS, 87/11, 40/12 – ZUJF, 21/13 – ZUTD-A, 91/13, 99/13 – ZUPJS-C, 99/13 – ZSVarPre-C, 111/13 – ZMEPIZ-1, 95/14 – ZUJF-C, 47/15 – ZZSDT, 61/17 – ZUPŠ and 64/17 – ZZDej-K.

[48] Pension and Disability Insurance Act, Official Gazette of the Republic of Slovenia No 96/12, 39/13, 99/13 – ZSVarPre-C, 101/13 – ZIPRS1415, 44/14 – ORZPIZ206, 85/14 – ZUJF-B, 95/14 – ZUJF-C, 90/15 – ZIUPTD, 102/15, 23/17, 40/17 and 65/17.

[49] Equalisation of Opportunities for Persons with Disabilities Act, Official Gazette of the Republic of Slovenia No 94/10, 50/14 and 32/17.

[50] ibid s 5.

[51] ibid s 6.

the case -I-166/03, where it noted that 'enforcement must not be affected by the enforcement of the debtor's salary to the extent that his subsistence minimum is compromised'.[52] In an another case, it emphasised that the burden of welfare state should be carried equally by the state and employers. It observed that 'the legislator, deriving from the principle of the welfare state ... distributed the burden of redundant workers between employers and the state'.[53]

The Constitutional Court further noted in the case U-I-66/98 that 'the legislator ... has the duty to establish an effective social policy and to regulate, establish and maintain a social security system which will also provide social net and and enable them to live a decent life'.[54] It added that 'in shaping the social security system, the legislator has a wide margin of discretion in which it draws up various measures that it considers best suited for achieving the defined social policy objectives'.[55] The Constitutional Court has therefore strongly reinforced the principle of welfare state through various provisions of the Slovenian Constitution. As a result, socioeconomic rights have been well protected by the Slovenian courts. Moreover, the Constitutional Court has in the past developed the doctrine of a core of socioeconomic rights. It observed in its decision that: 'The essence or the core of the right to a pension entails an individual's right to obtain and enjoy a pension that provides social security, on the basis of paid pension insurance contributions.'[56] It added in another decision Up-195/13 and U-I-67/16-20 that:

> In the decisions of the Constitutional Court, with regard to the right to a pension, the views were formulated that this right constitutes a constitutionally guaranteed core, that is the very essence of this right, to which the legislator can not inadvertently interfere, that the right to a pension must primarily be based on the insurance principle in this sense, the pension is a property right because it depends mainly on the duration and the amount of contributions paid, and that as a property right it enjoys double constitutional protection – according to the first paragraph of Article 50 and Article 33 of the Constitution. Since the Constitution defines pension insurance as a type of social insurance, the elements of reciprocity or solidarity in this system are constitutionally admissible. However, the pension must, to a certain extent, ensure the continuity of the standard of living that the insured person had in the active period (income security), since the pension, in proportion (proportional), is compensated for by the income from which contributions for the pension insurance were paid.[57]

[52] Constitutional Court of the Republic Slovenia, Decision U-I-166/03, 11 November 2004, para 8.
[53] Constitutional Court of the Republic Slovenia, Decision Up-63/04, 27 January 2005, para 10.
[54] Constitutional Court of the Republic Slovenia, Decision U-I-66/98, 18 April 2002, para 5.
[55] ibid.
[56] Constitutional Court of the Republic Slovenia, Decision Up-360/05, 2 October 2008, para 6. See also Constitutional Court of the Republic Slovenia, Decision U-I-159/07, 10 June 2010, para 16.
[57] Constitutional Court of the Republic Slovenia, Decision Up-195/13 and U-I-67/16-20, 26 January 2017, para 10 (footnotes omitted).

It further expanded its doctrine of the core of constitutional rights in its decision on the rights of disabled persons. It noted that '[e]very human right has its constitutionally guaranteed core, in which the legislator must not intervene',[58] and continued: 'The purpose of such a special arrangement can only be to ensure that disabled persons, in addition to their general rights, have additional, special rights.'[59] It added that:

> The specific constitutional provision for the protection of people with disabilities is due to the recognition that active measures are needed to ensure equal opportunities and equal treatment for them to eliminate, overcome or at least reduce obstacles to their independent life, and to equally integrate into society and work.[60]

The Constitutional Court extended its doctrine of the core of constitutional rights also to other constitutional provisions. It held in decision U-I-20/96, for example, that: 'The obligation of the state to create opportunities for citizens to acquire adequate housing … means the obligation of the state to enable the acquisition of a suitable dwelling by any citizen concerned.'[61] In an another decision, U-I-144/14-6, the Constitutional Court noted that:

> Acquisition of non-profit apartments and renting them through public tenders is one of the measures for implementing the state's commitment under Art 78 of the Constitution, according to which the state creates the possibility for citizens to obtain adequate housing.[62]

It added that '[r]enting non-profit apartments … is thus a form of social assistance to eligible individuals to provide adequate housing',[63] and concluded that 'a non-profit rent paid for the renting of a non-profit apartment is, in substance, a social right'.[64] Additionally, socioeconomic rights are sometimes also protected, similarly to how the ECtHR acts, through civil and political rights.[65]

The protection of socioeconomic rights has therefore been well developed in the case-law of the Constitutional Court deriving from the constitutional principles of the welfare state.[66] The Court has emphasised that socioeconomic rights not only create state obligations of conduct, but also of result, particularly in relation to the core of socioeconomic rights, which covers the provision

[58] Constitutional Court of the Republic Slovenia, Decision U-I-11/07-45, 13 December 2007, para 18.

[59] ibid.

[60] ibid (footnotes omitted).

[61] Constitutional Court of the Republic Slovenia, Decision U-I-20/96, 17 December 1998, para 3 (footnotes omitted).

[62] Constitutional Court of the Republic Slovenia, Decision U-I-144/14-6, 9 March 2017, para 15.

[63] ibid.

[64] ibid.

[65] See eg Jernej Letnar Černič, 'The European Court of Human Rights, Rule of Law and Socio-Economic Rights in Times of Crises' (2016) 8(2) *Hague Journal on the Rule of Law* 227.

[66] See generally eg Wojciech Sadurski, 'Constitutional Courts in the Process of Articulating Constitutional Rights in the Post-Communist States of Central and Eastern Europe, Part I: Social and Economic Rights', EUI LAW Working Paper no 2002/14.

of minimum subsistence of every individual. It has also recognised that not only the state institutions, but also non-state actors, such as employers, are to reasonably share the burden of guaranteeing socioeconomic rights. The doctrine of the Constitutional Court is therefore quite advanced in comparison with other domestic constitutional systems. Although not much has been written internationally on its doctrine on socioeconomic rights, its decisions concerning the principle of the welfare state, the right to social security and the rights of disabled persons place the Constitutional Court of Slovenia, among those constitutional courts, such as the South African and the Colombian constitutional courts,[67] that pay most attention to the socioeconomic capabilities of individuals to fulfil themselves. Individuals have therefore benefited not only from strong constitutional guarantees, but also strong labour and social justice, which regularly upholds socioeconomic rights both against public bodies, but also against private corporations.

IV. REGIONAL INEQUALITY IN SLOVENIA

The state of constitutional democracy and the rule of law appear to have had the greatest impact on regional equality in Slovenia. Their exercise has so far been concentrated and centralised in the Osrednjeslovenska region, with only marginal parts of public administration located elsewhere in the country. This has in past created the multilayered patterns of inequality in Slovenia and there exist huge discrepancies between the rate of human development among the various regions of Slovenia.[68] As a result, persons in different regions of

[67] See eg Avinash Govindjee, 'Adjudication of Socio-Economic Rights by the Constitutional Court of South Africa: Walking the Tightrope between Activism and Deference?' (2013) 25(1) *National Law School of India Review* 62; Eric C Christiansen, 'Adjudicating Non-Justiciable Rights: Socio-Economic Rights and the South African Constitutional Court' (2007) 38(2) *Columbia Human Rights Law Review* 321; Tom Ginsburg and Rosalind Dixon, 'The South African Constitutional Court and Socio-Economic Rights as "Insurance Swaps"' (August 2013) University of Chicago, Public Law and Legal Theory Working Paper no 436; Magdalena Correa Henao and Andrés Mauricio Gutiérrez Beltrán, 'Introduction to I-CONnect Symposium – Contemporary Discussions in Constitutional Law' (31 October 2018) blog of the International Journal of Constitutional Law, www.iconnectblog.com/2018/10/introduction-to-i-connect-symposium-contemporary-discussions-in-constitutional-law (accessed 24 April 2019); Jorge González Jácome, 'The Promise and Peril of "Transformative Constitutionalism" – A Reply to Justice Carlos Bernal' (27 December 2018) blog of the International Journal of Constitutional Law, www.iconnectblog.com/2018/12/the-promise-and-peril-of-transformative-constitutionalism-a-reply-to-justice-carlos-bernal/ (accessed 24 April 2019); Carlos Bernal, 'The Challenges of Transformative Constitutionalism – A Reply to Jorge González Jácome' (1 January 2019) blog of the International Journal of Constitutional Law, www.iconnectblog.com/2019/01/the-challenges-of-transformative-constitutionalism-a-reply-to-jorge-gonzalez-jacome/ (accessed 24 April 2019); Liliana Lizarazo-Rodríguez, 'Constitutional Adjudication In Colombia: Avant-garde or Case Law Transplant? A Literature Review' (2011) 13(1) *Estudios Socio-Jurídicos* 145.

[68] See eg UMAR, Janja Pečar, 'Delovni zvezek 1/2017, let XXVI: Kako živimo v regijah' (September 2017) Republic of Slovenia, Institute of Macroeconomic Analysis and Development Ljubljana,

Slovenia have unequal access to, or access to unequal qualities of, basic goods such as social services and health care, education, transportation, decent housing, and essential supplies such as food and water.[69] Slovenia is divided for statistical purposes into 12 regions: Gorenjska, Goriška, Koroška, Osrednjeslovenska, Obalno-kraška, Jugovzhodna Slovenija, Podravska, Posavska, Pomurska, Primorsko-notranjska, Savinjska and Zasavska. The central and western parts of Slovenia have traditionally been more developed than the regions in the east. The statistical data in Figure 9.4 on quality of life, for instance, inidicate that regions where the percentage of the persons at risk of poverty is higher are Jugovzhodna Slovenia, Podravska, Pomurska and Posavska in eastern Slovenia. Those regions are also those where children will enjoy unequal opportunities to fulfil themselves in comparison to more developed regions.[70]

Figure 9.4 At-risk-of-poverty rate, statistical regions, Slovenia, 2014

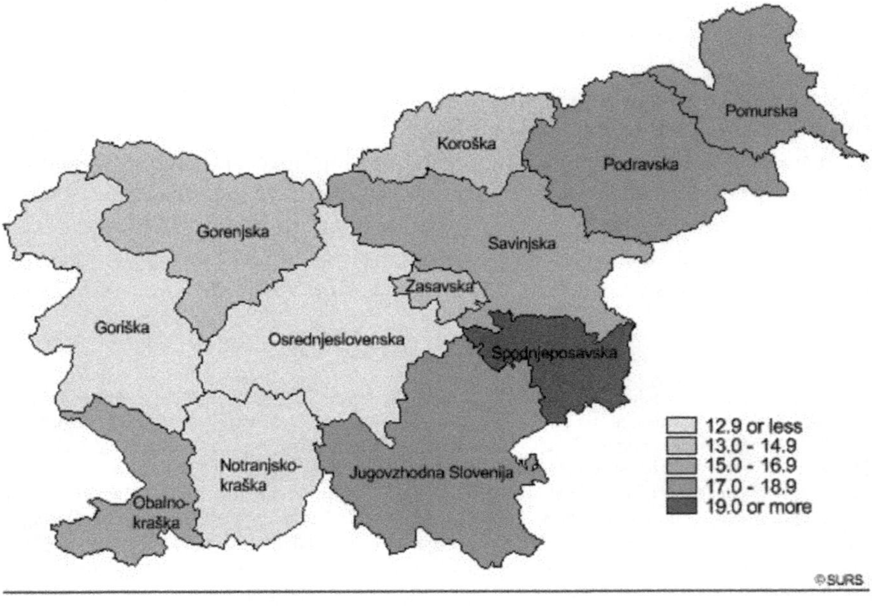

Source: Statistical Office of the Republic of Slovenia, Stranka intihar, 'Unchanged At-Risk-of-Poverty Rate in 2014 (14.5%); Household Income Slightly Higher', www.stat.si/StatWeb/en/News/Index/5426 (accessed 24 April 2019).

www.umar.gov.si/fileadmin/user_upload/publikacije/dz/2017/DZ-Kako_zivimo_v_regijah.pdf (accessed 24 April 2019).

[69] ibid.

[70] See eg Jernej Letnar Černič, 'Ali imajo vsi otroci v Sloveniji enake začetne možnosti za samouresničitev?' *IUS-info* (16 November 2018).

Therefore, the share of households receiving social assistance and financial help is also highest in the regions of eastern Slovenia.[71] Moreover, the GDP per capita in purchasing power standards was only 52.4 % in Zasavska region and 67.2 % in Pomurska region with the respect to the EU average.[72]

Figure 9.5 Gross domestic product per capita and per employee, statistical regions, Slovenia, 2017

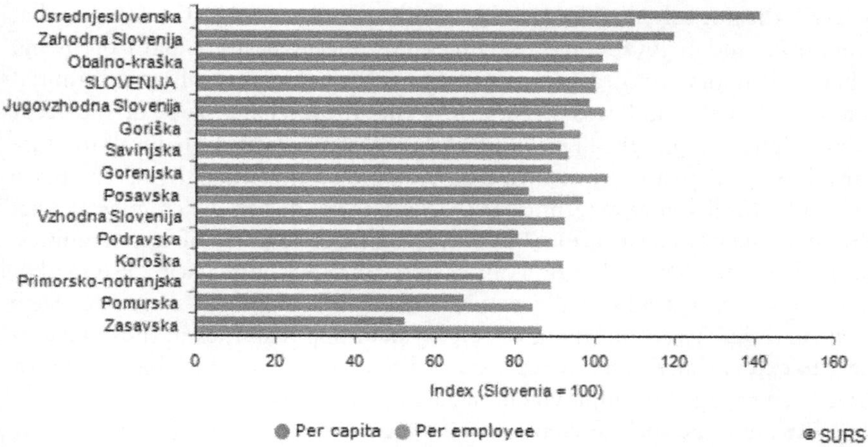

Source: Statistical Office of the Republic of Slovenia, Milen Jankovič, 'In 2017 the GDP Growth Was 6.5% in Slovenia; The Highest Was in the Jugovzhodna Slovenija Region (by 10.4%)', www.stat.si/StatWeb/en/news/Index/7820 (accessed 24 April 2019).

It is therefore no wonder that inhabitants with the highest overall life satisfaction are found in the regions of western Slovenia such as Osrednjeslovenska and Gorenjska.[73] Moreover, the statistical data illustrate that 'almost half of the households from the Koroška statistical region had difficulties making ends meet'.[74] The highest percentage of persons living under the risk of poverty threshold can be found in the statistical regions of Posavska, Podravska, Savinjska, Zasavska and Pomurska.[75] The eastern or north-eastern statistical regions are therefore those with the highest rate of the development

[71] Statistical Office of the Republic of Slovenia, 'Regions in Figures – Statistical Portrait of Slovene Regions 2018', www.stat.si/StatWeb/File/DocSysFile/9960/regions_in%20_Figures_2018.pdf, 8 (accessed 24 April 2019).

[72] Statistical Office of the Republic of Slovenia, Milen Jankovič, 'In 2017 the GDP Growth Was 6.5% in Slovenia; The Highest Was in the Jugovzhodna Slovenija Region (by 10.4%)', www.stat.si/StatWeb/en/news/Index/7820 (accessed 24 April 2019).

[73] Statistical Office of the Republic of Slovenia, Stranka intihar, 'Unchanged At-Risk-of-Poverty Rate in 2014 (14.5%); Household Income Slightly Higher', 8, www.stat.si/StatWeb/en/News/Index/5426 (accessed 24 April 2019).

[74] ibid.

[75] ibid.

risk indices.[76] Such differences also arise from the statistics concerning GDP per capita, which has traditionally been highest in Osrednjeslovenska and Obalno-kraška and lowest in Zasavska and Pomurska regions.[77] In 2016 Osrednjeslovenska region had, along with Jugovzhodna Slovenija, enjoyed the highest average net earnings, whereas Primorsko-notranjska, Zasavska and Pomurska had the lowest.[78] Furthermore, people have poorer health and die earlier in the eastern parts of Slovenia than in its western parts.[79] These indicators show quite clearly that Osrednjeslovenska, Obalno-Kraška, Gorenjska and Jugovzhodna Slovenija enjoy the highest standard of living, whereas Primorsko-notranjska, Zasavska and Pomurska trail by substantial margins in various indicators. They show that the level and scope of socioeconomic rights, despite the high-flying promises of a constitutional welfare state for all, differ depending in which part Slovenia an individual lives. The place of residence therefore determines the levels of solidarity, which goes against the fundamental constitutional principles such as equality of opportunities. Individuals in statistical regions in eastern Slovenia, along with Primorsko-notranjska, have traditionally experienced lower standards of living. Such traits and the lack of meaningful employment opportunities in those regions help to explain why so many individuals from those regions are looking for or have been engaged in employment in Austria and Germany.

Why are there such discrepancies between different parts of Slovenia? Do, for instance, children have equal opportunities for self-fulfilment in different parts of Slovenia?[80] One of the answers is that respective governments have not developed the fully fledged human and economic policies for under- and less-developed regions. Most of the decision-making in Slovenia has been centralized, with other regions excluded from the process. Therefore, the central government has, under the Ministry of Public Administration, only drafted a set of incoherent policies, which seem unlikely to reduce differences in economic and human development. It has been struggling under pressure from different interest groups to put more focus on regional differences. State authorities should not turn a blind eye to regional inequalities in Slovenia and should design a set of normative and policy measures in order to tackle those challenges.

[76] IMAD, 'Development Report 2018' (Ljubljana, June 2018) 16, www.umar.si/fileadmin/user_upload/razvoj_slovenije/2018/aPOR2018_splet_novo.pdf (accessed 24 April 2019).

[77] Statistical Office of the Republic of Slovenia (n 71) 14. See also study by monthly Magazine *Moje Finance*: Marja Milič, 'Kje v Sloveniji se najbolje živi v letu 2018? Razkrivamo lestvico 212 občin!' *Moje Finance* (15 October 2018) https://mojefinance.finance.si/8939584 (accessed 24 April 2019).

[78] Statistical Office of the Republic of Slovenia (n 71) 12.

[79] Tanja Pirnat, 'Razsekana na pol: Zakaj je vzhod Slovenije bolj bolan kot zahod?' *Pod črto* (10 June 2017) https://podcrto.si/zdravje-v-obcinah-revnejsi-kot-so-prebivalci-slabse-je-zdravje/ (accessed 24 April 2019). See also Tanja Pirnat, 'Zdravje na Koroškem: veliko bolezni, malo zdravljenja', *Pod črto* (17 June 2017) https://podcrto.si/zdravje-na-koroskem-veliko-bolezni-malo-zdravljenja/ (accessed 24 April 2019).

[80] See eg Letnar Černič (n 70).

V. THE IMPACT OF WEAK RULE OF LAW AND CONSTITUTIONAL DEMOCRACY ON THE LEVEL OF WELFARE STATE AND SOCIOECONOMIC RIGHTS IN SLOVENIA

The previous sections have testified that the scope and nature of the welfare state and provision of socioeconomic rights in Slovenia are quite generous, particularly in comparison with other parts of Central and Eastern Europe.[81] However, this section will attempt to argue that the weak rule of law and state institutions, combined with a consistent, general and systemic failure in the exercise of constitutional democracy, have consistently affected the levels and scope of the Slovenian welfare state and socioeconomic rights. The welfare state and socioeconomic rights traditionally depend on the financial resources of a state, which are often connected to the standard of living, which depends particularly on the openness and competitiveness of country's economy, which generates tax revenues. The strength of a country's economy and investment environment often parallels the quality and strength of its state institutions. The stronger the institutions, the stronger is the economy and investment environment, and the higher the standard of living and consequently also the level of socioeconomic rights. The greater the budget of a particular state, the more generous will be the scope of socioeconomic rights. The provision of rights that are basic for the development of human capabilities, such as the right to education, food, health care, housing, water, but also rights to social security, rights for disabled persons and the right to work, hinge on available budgetary resources. The welfare state therefore barely exists in countries of the Global South as most of these are struggling even to provide their citizens with basic goods.

Several explanations have been advanced as to why some countries are more developed than the others.[82] Some researchers have highlighted the importance of culture,[83] others geography[84] and access to natural resources, and some the importance of strong, independent, impartial and fair institutions

[81] See generally János Mátyás Kovács and Violetta Zentai (eds), *Capitalism from Outside? Economic Cultures in Eastern Europe after 1989* (Budapest, Central European University Press, 2012).

[82] See eg Adam Smith, *Inquiry into the Nature and Causes of the Wealth of Nations* (Oxford, Clarendon Press, 1976).

[83] David S Landes, *The Wealth and Poverty of Nations: Why Some Are so Rich and Others so Poor* (New York, WW Norton, 1998); Max Weber, *The Protestant Ethic and the Spirit of Capitalism* (London: Unwin University Books 1930). See also Douglass C North, William Summerhill and Barry Weingast, 'Order, Disorder, and Economic Change: Latin America Versus North America' in Bruce Bueno de Mesquita and Hilton L Root (eds), *Governing for Prosperity* (New Haven, CT, Yale University Press, 2000).

[84] John Luke Gallup, Jeffrey D Sachs and Andrew D Mellinger, 'Geography and Economic Development' (1999) 22(2) *International Regional Science Review* 179. See also Douglas A Hibbs and Ola Olsson, 'Geography, Biogeography, and Why Some Countries Are Rich and Others Are Poor" (2004) 101(10) *Proceedings of the National Academy of Sciences of the United States of America* 3715; Andrew Mellinger, Jeffrey D Sachs and John Luke Gallup, 'Climate, Water Navigability, and Economic Development' (1999) CID Working Papers 24A.

to explain why some countries are more developed or richer than the others. Some have argued that one reason alone cannot explain why some states are more developed than others, and it is likely that a combination of factors helps explain differences in economic and human development. Sokoloff and Engerman attempted to explain the rapid economic growth of the United States and Canada by 'substantial differences in the degree of inequality in wealth, human capital, and political power, which were initially rooted in the factor endowments'.[85] Wolla observes that 'many economists suggest that institutions such as property rights, free and open markets, and the rule of law … provide the best incentives and opportunities for individuals to produce goods and services'.[86] Low levels of economic development also contribute to low levels and a narrow scope of socioeconomic rights. Acemoglu, Johnson and Robinson have argued that 'the available evidence is consistent with the view that whether or not a society grows depends on how its economy is organized – on its economic institutions'.[87] They have submitted that: 'Political institutions and the distribution of economic resources are, themselves, endogenous, determined by political power and economic institutions.'[88] Even though critical of their account, Sachs notes that: 'Acemoglu and Robinson's story is sometimes right: politics matters, and bad governments can indeed kill development.'[89] Whereas culture, geography and access to natural resources have been quite favourable in Slovenia, the independence, impartiality and fairness of institutions has been often described as deficient, which explains why the country's welfare state has not been able to draw upon richer financial resources. The quality of free-market institutions and of the rule of law often depends on the levels and scope of the welfare state, socioeconomic rights and human development. Therefore, it is not surprising that the most economically developed states are also those with the highest rates of human development. They are mostly found, with some exceptions, in the Global North; therefore geography may be seminal, along with the quality of government institutions, in determining why some countries are more developed than the others.

Constitutional democracy and the welfare state are intrinsically and internally connected.[90] They mutually depend on, and reinforce, each other.

[85] Kenneth L Sokoloff and Stanley L Engerman, 'Institutions, Factor Endowments, and Paths of Development in the New World' (2000) 14(3) *Journal of Economic Perspectives* 217.

[86] Scott A Wolla, 'Why Are Some Countries Rich and Others Poor?' *Page One Economics* (September 2017).

[87] Daron Acemoglu, Simon Johnson and James Robinson, 'Institutions as a Fundamental Cause of Long-Run Growth' in Philippe Aghion and Steven Durlauf (eds), *Handbook of Economic Growth*, vol 1A (Amsterdam, Elsevier, 2005) 463. See also Stanley L Engerman and Kenneth L Sokoloff, 'Institutional and Non-Institutional Explanations of Economic Differences' in Claude Ménard and Mary M Shirley (eds), *Handbook of New Institutional Economics* (Berlin, Springer, 2008).

[88] ibid 457.

[89] Jeffrey D Sachs, 'Government, Geography, and Growth: The True Drivers of Economic Development' *Foreign Affairs* (September/October 2012) 142.

[90] Dennis C Mueller, 'Constitutional Democracy and Social Welfare' (1973) 87(1) *Quarterly Journal of Economics* 60.

Forbath notes that: 'Constitutional democracy is impossible without some limits on social and economic inequality.'[91] On the other hand, a properly functioning constitutional democracy engenders a generous welfare state where socioeconomic rights are not only guaranteed but also judicially enforced. Other authors have submitted that the rule of law requires respect for socioeconomic rights too.[92] And perhaps we can agree with the observation that mature constitutional democracy and the rule of law also require high levels of welfare state provision and socioeconomic rights. Some authors agree that the rule of law and constitutional democracy have a transformative impact on the functioning of the welfare state. Kovac, for instance, argues that civil and political rights provide incentives for social rights.[93] The effective protections against the arbitrary exercise of state power eventually generate equal capabilities and opportunities of individuals to fulfil themselves through and on the basis of socioeconomic rights. The failings of the rule of law and constitutional democracy have therefore affected the levels of the Slovenian welfare state. Many of the problems of the welfare state therefore have their roots in challenges to the rule of law involving conflicts of interest, corruption and nepotism, which have created the culture of 'dirty togetherness', thereby stimulating arbitrary and corrupt practices in decision-making concerning public tenders and managing public finances and budgetary spending at all levels of public administration. The rule of law and constitutional democracy proceeds from the basis of human dignity, which requires that every individual has access to a reasonable core of basic socio-economic rights to fulfil him/herself in society. However, as argued by Hayek, 'while an equality of rights under a limited government is possible and an essential condition of individual freedom, a claim for equality of material position can be met only by a government with totalitarian powers'.[94] Socioeconomic rights generally create state obligations of conduct and only to a limited extent state obligations of result concerning the core of socioeconomic rights. In this way, the state of the rule of law and constitutional democracy affects also the state and conditions of the welfare state. The Slovenian welfare state requires a proper and effective functioning of constitutional democracy and the rule of law in order to advance and close the gap with countries in Northern Europe.

[91] 'Social Rights, Courts and Constitutional Democracy – Poverty and Welfare Rights in the United States' (2005) University of Texas School of Law, Public Law and Legal Theory Research Paper no 81, 1-40, 1.

[92] Paul Gowder, *The Rule of Law in the Real World* (Cambridge, Cambridge University Press, 2016).

[93] Janos Matyas Kovacs, 'Approaching the EU and Reaching the US? Rival Narratives on Transforming Welfare Regimes in East-Central Europe' in Peter Mair and Jan Zielonka (eds), *The Enlarged European Union: Diversity and Adaptation* (London, Frank Cass, 2002).

[94] Friedrich A von Hayek, *Law, Legislation and Liberty*, vol 2: *The Mirage of Social Justice*, 1st edn (Chicago, University of Chicago Press, 1978) 83.

VI. THE FUTURE OF THE WELFARE STATE AND HUMAN DEVELOPMENT IN SLOVENIA

Slovenia is, as noted in the introduction, ranked quite high in terms of its level of human development, ahead of countries such as the Czech Republic, Italy and Spain. It has also been the leading CEE country concerning socioeconomic and human development. Ordinary citizens in the region are used to, and therefore also expect that their governments should carry the greatest burden for maintaining and advancing the welfare state.[95] Much of developments in the rise of the welfare state can be ascribed to the state-centred welfare system of the past.[96] Individuals justifiably expect that the Slovenian state will maintain the level and scope of the welfare state and socioeconomic rights.[97] Questions at the core of the future of human and economic development in Slovenia are how to maintain and advance the scope of the welfare state and at the same time generate high economic growth, high incomes and high living standards?

Nonetheless, much is at stake for the future of welfare state and human development in Slovenia. Andersen has highlighted 'a strong legacy ingrained in institutions and policies constituting a social and political capital … making it possible to implement far reaching reforms in due time'[98] as one of the advantages of the Nordic welfare mode. Much of the Swedish welfare state and its benefits are subject to an individual's employment.[99] Similar safeguards are to lesser extent found in the normative and policy structures of the Slovenian welfare state. Structural reforms of many systems and subsystems will soon be urgently needed to maintain the current levels of welfare state provision or even more so to increase these. Partial and piecemeal reforms, as done so far, are no longer acceptable.[100] The continuation of the status quo seems unlikely. There is not much scope in the area of taxation as the incomes and profits of taxpayers are already some of the highest taxed among the 28 EU Member States. Slovenia's population has been also ageing very fast, thereby making the current levels of welfare state provision very difficult to sustain. One of few alternatives is to

[95] Stefan Svallfors, 'Public Attitudes' in Francis G Castles, Stephan Leibfried, Jane Lewis, Herbert Obinger and Christopher Pierson (eds), *The Oxford Handbook of the Welfare State* (Oxford, Oxford University Press, 2010).

[96] Rado Pezdir and Janez Šušteršič, 'Yugoslav Companies in Zone A of the Free Territory of Trieste: The Formation of an Institutionalized Parallel Economy Controlled by the State Security Service' (2018) 176(2) *Archivio storico italiano* 313.

[97] Tatjana Rakar and Maša Filipovič Hrast, 'The Future of the Slovenian Welfare State: A View from Deliberative Forums' (2018) 25(2) *Revija za socijalnu politiku* 157.

[98] Torben M Andersen, 'The Welfare State and Economic Performance: Bilaga 4 Långtidsutredningen', 104–05 (2015) Statens Offentliga Utredningar, Sverige, www.regeringen.se/contentassets/c3cd2706e07b-4fc7860533f1ae8ad5d8/sou-201553-the-welfare-state-and-economic-performance.pdf (accessed 24 April 2019).

[99] Ann-Sofie Kolm and Mirco Tonin, 'Benefits Conditional on Work and the Nordic Model' (2015) 127 *Journal of Public Economics* 115.

[100] Guardiancich (n 4).

increase the productivity and competitiveness[101] of the country's economy,[102] thereby a producing business environment that is more investment friendly.[103] This could lead to Slovenia recovering some lost ground in comparison with other CEE countries such the Czech Republic and Poland.[104] To be fair, the Slovenian economy has in the last few years been one of the highest performing among the EU Member States. Another alternative is to provide incentives for immigration, but also to encourage the educated younger generation to stay in Slovenia instead of looking for better employment and living opportunities in Northern Europe.[105] However, in order for Slovenia to be placed along the globally most developed countries in Northern Europe, substantial reforms need to be undertaken, which should aim to ensure high levels of economic growth, high incomes and wider socioeconomic rights.

In order for the levels and scope of the welfare state and human development to improve in Slovenia, more concrete efforts are required to create a free economic environment conducive to development which would stimulate economic growth, address regional increasing inequalities and in turn lead to more generous levels and scope of the welfare state and socioeconomic rights. Both the welfare state and socioeconomic rights are dependent on the available budgetary resources of the government, which condition even the basic features of socioeconomic rights such as their core values and the principle of non-retrogression. The government of Slovenia allocates a high percentage of its annual budget to maintaining the welfare state, which along with its post-communist legacy explains the country's high level of socioeconomic rights.[106] For those reasons, the future of human development in Slovenia may not be so positive as the past and present, and will be dependent on the success of the Slovenian economy and its openness to foreign investment. The challenges, therefore, are how to increase both national and individual wealth in order to maintain and expand the welfare state and socioeconomic rights.

Three points should be considered for improving the Slovenian welfare state in the future. First, it seems indispensable to consider the future nature and scope of the welfare state. Serious decisions have to be made about budgetary control

[101] Gorazd Justinek and Katja Lautar, 'Slovensko gospodarstvo med preteklostjo in prihodnostjo', in Matej Avbelj Gašper Dovžan, Jernej Letnar Černič and Miha Movrin (eds), *Evropska Slovenija* (Ljubljana, Inštitut Nove revije, 2013).

[102] Marjan Sternad, Tina Cvahte Ojsteršek, Darja Topolšek and Gorazd Justinek, 'The Influence of Logistics Barriers on Lead Times and Service Levels in Slovenia' (2016) 23(4) *International Journal of Logistics Systems and Management* 519.

[103] Gorazd Justinek, 'Izvozniki uspešni na ključnih evropskih trgih' *Kojunktura Gibanja* (March 2015). See also Government of Republic of Slovenia, 'Slovenska industrijska politika – SIP' (6 February 2013) www.mgrt.gov.si/fileadmin/mgrt.gov.si/pageuploads/DPK/SIP/SIP_-_vladni_dokument.pdf (accessed 24 April 2019).

[104] Gorazd Justinek. 'Is Central Europe an Economic Entity? Special Focus on Slovenia' (2015) 7(2) *Journal on European Perspectives of the Western Balkans* 119.

[105] Jernej Letnar Černič, 'Eksodus', *IUS-info* (12 January 2018).

[106] Government of the Republic of Slovenia (n 9) 15.

over expenditure on the welfare state as the current levels of expenditure may not be sustainable over the long term. Another proposal that could be worth exploring is taxing the wealth of the richest individuals more. Secondly, it is time to recognise that weak institutions of the rule of law and democracy have affected the nature and scope of the Slovenian welfare state. State institutions should be reformed in order to create a more competitive economy and an investment-friendly environment, which would in turn engender higher economic growth and broaden the scope of the welfare state. It is necessary to move away from gradualism and state capitalism in order to create a proper market environment, which will be conducive for socioeconomic rights in order to maintain and increase the levels of welfare state provision. Thirdly, for the welfare state to be maintained, the obligations of duty-bearers should be redrawn so that individuals and corporations take over a greater burden of its costs. Therefore, we can concur with Guardianchich that 'if the current and future governments will bow down to demands to maintain the status quo … the transformative needs of Slovenian society will be jeopardised'.[107] Undoubtedly, the future of the welfare state in Slovenia should be based on the principle of non-retrogression from the current levels of socioeconomic rights and with human dignity, as an individual and collective value, being placed at the centre of the Slovenian welfare state. Every individual in Slovenia should be afforded basic and equal capabilities to fulfil himself in society.

VII. CONCLUSION

The welfare state and socioeconomic rights have in the past been well protected in Slovenia, resulting in low levels of income inequality. This situation appears to stem from the state-centric welfare system inherited from the previous communist regime. This chapter has attempted to analyse the current situation with the welfare state and socioeconomic rights in Slovenia by describing and explaining reasons behind the current state of affairs. It has noted that Slovenia is placed relatively high in most rankings of human development, and particularly with respect to protection of children's rights. The scope and levels of the welfare state and socioeconomic rights have been relatively high, thereby consuming a high percentage of Slovenia's budgetary resources. Although socioeconomic rights have been well protected, both normatively and judicially, their scope ultimately depends on available budgetary resources. The available budgetary resources, in turn, hinge on national and individual wealth. On the other hand, it is striking that individual wealth is disproportionately unequally concentrated among the richest members of society. By contrast, individual and national wealth often

[107] Guardiancich (n 4) 228.

depend on the state of the rule of law and constitutional democracy. The levels of the Slovenian welfare state have very much dependend on the state of the rule of law and constitutional democracy. It is beyond doubt that arbitrary practices in the exercise of government have in the past affected, and continue to affect, the capability of the Slovenian authorities to maintain welfare state levels in Slovenia. The challenges facing welfare state in Slovenia are therefore immanent and will also largely depend how constitutional democracy and the rule of law develop, and most importantly whether their values can be fully internalised by people within and outside democratic institutions. The higher the compliance with the rule of law, the friendlier the environment for the exercise of business and investment activities. As a rule, stronger institutions and the rule of law can in turn bring about not only higher standards of living for the population, but also increase the levels of the welfare state and the scope of socioeconomic rights, thereby realising human dignity as a collective and individual value.

10

The Influence of the Council of Europe on the Rule of Law in Slovenia

> What's there to remember? I live the same way as everyone else. Perestroika … Gorbachev … The postmistress opened the gate: 'Did you hear? The Communists are out' 'What do you mean?' 'They shut down the Party' No shots fired, nothing. These days they say we used to have a mighty fortress and then we lost it all. But what have I really lost?[1]

I. INTRODUCTORY REMARKS

THE COUNCIL OF Europe has been since its inception in 1949 the principal European institution working for the promotion and strengthening of constitutional democracy, human rights protection and the rule of law in Europe.[2] These principles have since the World War II been transformed into the quintessential pillars of free, pluralistic and democratic societies based on the rule of law. After the fall of the iron curtain, the Council of Europe has engineered formal constitutional reforms across Central and Eastern Europe.[3] As the result, the Council of Europe has in the past three decades, through its headquarters and specialised institutions, aimed to strengthen constitutional democracy, the rule of law and human rights protections in CEE countries.[4]

[1] Svetlana Alexievich, *Second-Hand Time* (London, Fitzcarraldo Editions, 2017) 693.

[2] Statute of the Council of Europe, London, 5 May 1949. For a detailed examination, see Stefanie Schmahl and Marten Breuer (eds), *The Council of Europe: Its Law and Policies* (Oxford, Oxford University Press, 2017). For a critical account, see Marco Duranti, *The Conservative Human Rights Revolution: European Identity, Transnational Politics and the Origin of the European Convention* (Oxford, Oxford University Press, 2017).

[3] Florence Benoit-Rohmer and Heinrich Klebes, *Council of Europe Law: Towards a Pan-European Legal Area* (Strasbourg, Council of Europe Publishing, 2005).

[4] See generally Iulia Motoc and Ineta Ziemele (eds), *The Impact of the ECHR on Democratic Change in Central and Eastern Europe: Judicial Perspectives* (Cambridge, Cambridge University Press, 2017). See also Jernej Letnar Černič, 'Impact of the European Court of Human Rights on the Rule of Law in Central and Eastern Europe' (2018) 10(1) *Hague Journal on the Rule of Law* 111; Ivan T Berend and Bojan Bugarič, 'Unfinished Europe: Transition from Communism to Democracy in Central and Eastern Europe' (2015) 50(4) *Journal of Contemporary History* 768–85;

The seven founding Member States coined the aims of the Council of Europe as fostering 'a greater unity between its members for the purpose of safeguarding and realising the ideals and principles which are their common heritage and facilitating their economic and social progress'.[5] The primary institutions of the Council of Europe are the Parliamentary Assembly, the Committee of Ministers, the ECtHR, the Congress of Local and Regional Authorities and the Conference of International Non-governmental Organisations, whereas the European Commission for Democracy through Law (the 'Venice Commission') is only the consultative body of the Council of Europe. The Parliamentary Assembly and the Committee of Ministers have also acted as the two main decision-making bodies, whereas the others have dealt with complaints and provided remedies and recommendations to individuals and states.

Have the Council of Europe and its institutions had any measurable impact on the rule of law in Slovenia and elsewhere in Central and Eastern Europe? How successful have been those measures to convert the domestic legal systems of CEE countries from authoritarian and totalitarian regimes to those based on constitutional democracy? This chapter therefore attempts to describe and analyse the influence of the Council of Europe on the rule of law in Slovenia by examining the impact of the Venice Commission, the Commissioner for Human Rights of the Council of Europe, and the ECtHR. These institutions and bodies have introduced the formal de jure standards of constitutional democracy and the rule of law in the nascent liberal democracies of Central and Eastern Europe. The rule of law is defined in this chapter as the concept that aims to curtail the arbitrary application of power by ruling institutional and informal elites and affords effective human rights protection to everyone.[6]

Divided into five parts, this chapter studies the normative influence of the Council of Europe on the rule of law and human rights protections in Slovenia and draws insights from similar developments elsewhere in Central and Eastern Europe. It investigates its impacts on the ground in Slovenia and compares them with similar challenges elsewhere. The second section delves into the workings of the Venice Commission by describing its role and analysing its impact in Slovenia and elsewhere in Central and Eastern Europe. The third section deals with the work of the Office of Commissioner for Human Rights of the Council

Gentian Zyberi and Jernej Letnar Černič, 'Transitional Justice Processes and Reconciliation in the former Yugoslavia: Challenges and Prospects' (2015) 33(2) *Nordic Journal of Human Rights* 132; Bojan Bugarič and Alenka Kuhelj, 'Slovenia in Crisis: A Tale of Unfinished Democratization in East-Central Europe', (2015) 48(4) *Communist and Post-Communist Studies* 273.

[5] Statute of the Council of Europe, London, 5 May 1949, Art 1(a).

[6] Martin Krygier, 'The Rule of Law' in Michel Rosenfeld and András Sajó (eds) *Oxford Handbook of Comparative Constitutional Law* (Oxford, Oxford University Press, 2012) 233–49. See also Martin Krygier, 'The Rule of Law: Pasts, Presents, and Two Possible Futures' (2016) 12 *Annual Review of Law and Social Science* 199; Giovanni Palombella, 'The Rule of Law and its Core' in Giovanni Palombella and Niel Walker (eds), *Re-locating the Rule of Law* (Oxford, Hart Publishers, 2009) 17–42; Michael Rosenfeld, 'The Rule of Law and the Legitimacy of Constitutional Democracy' (2001) 74 *Southern California Law Review* 1307.

of Europe. Finally, the fourth section examines the role and workings of the ECtHR and its potential influence on the rule of law and human rights protections in Slovenia and beyond. Overall, this chapter studies what the impact of the Council of Europe has been on the rule of law in Slovenia by drawing general parallels with elsewhere in Central and Eastern Europe.

II. THE EUROPEAN COMMISSION FOR DEMOCRACY THROUGH LAW

A. Institutional Settings

The European Commission for Democracy through Law (or the 'Venice Commission') was initially established in the early 1990s within the Council of Europe. It was part of the momentous project in the early 1990s to introduce standards of constitutional democracy and the rule of law in Central and Eastern Europe. Various advisers have collected air miles from Tallinn to Zagreb and from Warsaw to Tbilisi while discovering the 'new' Europe and teaching the 'ignorant' and 'uncivilised' Easterners how to exercise and safeguard the rule of law. The Venice Commission has been tasked with assisting newly created democracies in Central and Eastern Europe in their transition to constitutional democracy based on the rule of law by advising them how to design reforms of their newly formed constitutional systems. In general, the Venice Commission does not belong to the formal institutions of the Council of Europe.

The statute of the Venice Commission notes that 'the Commission is an independent consultative body', which provides expert support to the Member States of the Council of Europe and beyond.[7] It lists among its objectives: 'strengthening the understanding of the legal systems of the participating states', 'promoting the rule of law and democracy' and 'examining the problems raised by the working of democratic institutions and their reinforcement and development'.[8] The Commission's role is clarified in the section 2 of Article 1 of its Statute, which provides that it concentrates on 'the constitutional, legislative and administrative principles and techniques which serve the efficiency of democratic institutions and their strengthening, as well as the principle of the rule of law', 'fundamental rights and freedoms, notably those that involve the participation of citizens in public life', and 'the contribution of local and regional self-government to the enhancement of democracy'.[9] The Commission currently

[7] Revised Statute of the European Commission for Democracy through Law, Art 1, s 1, Resolution (2002)3, adopted by Committee of Ministers of the Council of Europe, 21 February 2002.

[8] ibid. See generally, Gianni Buquicchio and Pierre Garrone, 'L'harmonisation du droit constitutionnel européen: Lacontribution de la Commission européenne pour la démocratie par le droit' (1998) 3(2–3) *Uniform Law Review* 323; Sergio Bartole, 'Final Remarks: The Role of the Venice Commission' (2000) 26(3) *Review of Central and Eastern European Law* 351; Steffen Rülke, *Venedig-Kommission und Verfassungsgerichtsbarkeit* (Köln, Heymanns, 2003).

[9] Revised Statute of the European Commission for Democracy through Law (n 7) Art 1, s 2.

has 61 members, 47 Member States of the Council of Europe, and 14 countries beyond this geographical area.[10] The website of the Venice Commission refers to 'the European constitutional heritage', which it defines as including 'democracy, human rights and the rule of law'.[11] Therefore, its current activities are concentrated on the three areas: 'democratic institutions and fundamental rights', 'constitutional justice and ordinary justice', and 'elections, referendums and political parties'.[12] The Venice Commission has often pointed in its opinions to the common constitutional heritage of all Member States, which can at times be difficult to pin down given the diversity of its membership.[13] However, 'the European constitutional heritage' has been interpreted as the lowest common denominator and often goes beyond the above-mentioned principles. De Visser aptly argues in this respect that 'it should maintain a clear distinction between common constitutional standards and constitutional best practices or guidelines. Only the former should be regarded as constituent elements of the shared heritage that the Venice Commission seeks to safeguard and realize.'[14] Jowell accordingly notes that 'the Commission possessed the self-assurance to insist that democracy contains a set of absolute standards from which there is limited scope for deviation'.[15] All in all, these constitutional standards include constitutional democracy, the rule of law and state obligations as to the procedural and substantive protections of human dignity.

As it stands, the Venice Commission accordingly does not deal with individual cases or complaints submitted by individual applicants, but it provides expert opinions and recommendations on specific constitutional law and the rule-of-law questions either upon the request of state authorities or on its own initiative. Its opinions are generally legally non-binding or at best quasi-binding. However, the Venice Commission has in the past gradually increased its reputation whereby it has also amplified the authority of its opinions despite these having formally only soft-law power. Soft-law documents and opinions can through their argumentation, persuasiveness, and reasoning attain binding powers, particularly if they are used in sources that are clearly of a binding

[10] European Commission for Democracy through Law (Venice Commission) www.venice.coe.int/WebForms/pages/?p=01_Presentation&lang=EN (accessed 24 April 2019).

[11] Venice Commission (ibid), The Commission's activities www.venice.coe.int/WebForms/pages/?p=01_activities&lang=EN (accessed 24 April 2019). According to Bartole: '[T]he European constitutional heritage is made up not only by the European treaties and conventions in the field of the human rights and rule of law, but also by those principles which have been at the basis of the historical process of gradual growth of the legal orders of the European States.' Sergio Bartole, 'Standards of Europe's Constitutional Heritage' (2015) 30(2) *Giornale di Storia Costituzionale* 17, 18.

[12] Venice Commission (n 10).

[13] ibid.

[14] Maartje De Visser, 'A Critical Assessment of the Role of the Venice Commission in Processes of Domestic Constitutional Reform' (2015) 63(4) *American Journal of Comparative Law* 963, 1001.

[15] Jeffrey Jowell, 'The Venice Commission: Disseminating Democracy through Law' (2001) 4 *Public Law* 675, 682. See also Sergio Bartole, 'International Constitutionalism and Conditionality: The Experience of the Venice Commission' (2014) 4 *Rivista Associazione Italiana dei Costituzionalisti*.

nature such as judicial decisions of the ECtHR. The content of the soft-law documents drafted and published by the Venice Commission derives from hard-law standards, particularly, those produced by the ECHR. Hoffman-Riem argues that the Venice Commission relies on the 'interpretation and application by the ECtHR as "hard law"', which 'constitutes the absolute minimum standard'.[16] As a result, if soft law includes hard-law norms, it also itself takes up their binding nature. Apart from this, the rule of law, constitutional democracy and human rights protection form the essential pillars of constitutional traditions of every domestic system of Member States of the Council of Europe.

As for the composition of the Commission, the Statute provides that 'the Commission shall be composed of independent experts who have achieved eminence through their experience in democratic institutions or by their contribution to the enhancement of law and political science'.[17] However, the selection procedures cast doubt on the independence and impartiality of members as they are nominated by respective governments. The Rules of Procedure of the Venice Commission provide that: 'Members shall notify the President through the Secretary of any potential conflict of interest, ie any circumstance which might appear to influence their impartial and objective consideration of any issue examined by the Commission."[18] Obviously, its members have to excuse themselves in a case of any actual or perceived conflict of interests. De Visser notes that 'individual Commission members should be persons of high standing as a result of their involvement with democratic institutions or through their contribution to the fields of law or political science'.[19] However, its selection process has been quite controversial as its members have often been nominated by the governments, thereby casting doubts as to their formal connections with the incumbent governments or arbitrary non-formal networks of a different nature. Therefore, several former and current members of the Venice Commission have political backgrounds, including some from previous communist totalitarian regimes.[20] To be clear, the selection procedures have been far from being as rigorous and independent as the selection of judges for the ECtHR.

B. The Venice Commission and Slovenia

The Venice Commission has so far produced only one opinion on the constitutional system of the Republic of Slovenia, more specifically in 2000 on

[16] Wolfgang Hoffmann-Riem, 'The Venice Commission of the Council of Europe: Standards and Impact' (2014) 25(2) *European Journal of International Law* 579, 582.

[17] Revised Statute of the European Commission for Democracy through Law (n 7) Art 2, s 1.

[18] Venice Commission, Revised Rules of Procedures, Art 3a(3), www.venice.coe.int/webforms/documents/default.aspx?pdffile=CDL-AD(2015)044-e (accessed 24 April 2019).

[19] De Visser (n 14) 968.

[20] For instance, the current Slovenian member of the Venice Commission, Ciril Ribičič, was in the previous totalitarian regime a high-ranking member of the Communist Party and was first president of its successor political party in the newly formed democratic state.

constitutional amendments concerning legislative elections in the Republic of Slovenia, following opposing referendum results and two judgments of the Constitutional Court of Slovenia.[21] The then Slovenian Prime Minister, Andrej Bajuk, asked the Venice Commission the following:

> Is it consistent with the European constitutional standards and tradition to amend the constitutional provision on parliamentary elections in order to allow a new electoral law which would be, however, inconsistent with the one chosen by referendum whose results were upheld on two occasions by the Slovenian Constitutional Court?[22]

The case was at that time extremely controversial as the National Assembly of Slovenia sidestepped the affirmative referendum decision concerning approval of the majoritarian electoral system and confirmed by judgments of the Slovenian Constitutional Court. The opinion was delivered on the basis of the opinion prepared by rapporteurs, namely Antonio La Pergola, Pieter van Dijk and Sergio Bartole.[23] The Commission thereafter observed that

> [T]here is no common European standard according to which the results of any referendum of whatever nature are binding upon the constituent power even in the absence of a constitutional provision. Consequently, the results of the referendum of 8 December 1996 should not prevent the National Assembly from exercising its constitution making powers under the Constitution.[24]

It added that:

> [I]f after the referendum the legislator fails to introduce new legislation to fill the legal vacuum or amend the electoral provisions, there would be no effective remedy to oblige the Parliament to enact a law and the situation amounts to a crisis in the functioning of representative democracy. To avoid this, a referendum affecting the rules of functioning of constitutional bodies should only be admitted if the rules that remain in force after the referendum allow the constitutional body concerned to function without any further legislative action being required.[25]

The Venice Commission therefore explained that the National Assembly is not obliged to follow the referendum results if it is not constitutionally bound to do so. Its opinion was not well received by the Slovenian government or by the Slovenian members of the Venice Commission. The Slovenian member of the Venice Commission at that time, Peter Jambrek, and his alternate member, Klemen Jaklič, argued that 'the Constitutional Amendment which has been enacted solely out of arbitrary intent and reasons – to supersede the referendum results and to override the two final judgments of the Constitutional

[21] Venice Commission, 'Opinion on the Constitutional Amendments Concerning Legislative Elections in the Republic of Slovenia, CDL-INF(2000)013', 16 October 2000.

[22] ibid 8.

[23] Venice Commission, 'Opinion of the Rapporteurs on the Constitutional Amendments concerning Legislative Elections in Slovenia, CDL(2000)077', Strasbourg, 29 September 2000.

[24] ibid 4.

[25] ibid 5.

Court – could be declared as unconstitutional'.[26] They added that 'the arbitrary preclusion of judicial review … can similarly be characterized as infringement of the rule of law (Rechtsstaat) principle in connection with the principle of democracy and thus judged unconstitutional'.[27] They concluded that: 'We do no hide our disappointment that the discussed Opinion of the Venice Commission remained largely uninformed of the respective developments in the evolving trans-national and the domestic constitutional law.'[28] The Opinion of the Venice Commission was not well reasoned as it did not fully and deeply explain why it took the view that the constitutional amendment was not contrary to established standards in spite of the contradicting referendum results and even more importantly contravening two judgments of the Constitutional Court. By contrast, the Venice Commission has in its opinion on Romania emphasised the importance of constitutional democracy by noting that 'democracy cannot be reduced to the principle of the majority, or, particularly, to the rule that the majority may do whatever it wishes to do simply because of the fact that it is the majority'.[29] It is particularly peculiar that the Slovenian opinion of the Commission went in this respect against the most basic understanding of constitutional democracy, one of the principles that the Commission promotes across Europe and beyond. Its approach is difficult to reconcile with the values of constitutional democracy, which have been the core pillars of the work of the Venice Commission and the Council of Europe. It seems that the Venice Commission could have reasoned its opinion in more persuasive manner. In so doing it has turned a blind eye to the core of a modern constitutional democracy.

C. The Impact of the Venice Commission in Slovenia and Beyond

Has the Venice Commission generated a positive impact on the rule-of-law reforms in the constitutional systems of the newly formed constitutional democracies in Central and Eastern Europe? The impact of the Venice Commission on the rule of law and constitutional democracy in CEE countries has been mixed.[30]

[26] Venice Commission, 'Contribution to the Opinion of the Venice Commission on the Constitutional Amendments Concerning Legislative Elections in Slovenia, CDL-INF(2000)013', Peter Jambrek and Klemen Jaklič, Appendix I, para 20.

[27] ibid.

[28] ibid para 24.

[29] Venice Commission, 'Opinion on the Compatibility with Constitutional Principles and the Rule of Law of Actions taken by the Government and the Parliament of Romania in respect of other State Institutions and on the Government Emergency Ordinance on Amendment to the Law no 47/1992 Regarding the Organisation and Functioning of the Constitutional Court and on the Government Emergency Ordinance on Amending and Completing the Law no 3/2000 Regarding the Organisation of a Referendum of Romania, Strasbourg, 17 December 2012, para 74.

[30] Hoffmann-Riem (n 16) 590–95. See also Venice Commission, 'Opinion on Amendments to the Act of 25 June 2015 on the Constitutional Tribunal of Poland, CDL-AD(2016)001', Venice, 11 March 2016.

Its influence can be distinguished in de jure and de facto form.[31] The Venice Commission and its experts, however, certainly do not possess a magic wand to change 'business as usual' in the institutional life of CEE states, which have for decades suffered under the arbitrary practices of their former totalitarian regimes. In this respect, de jure impact refers to the introduction of normative reforms. The Venice Commission's influence has been in this respect quite substantial. Its de jure impact has therefore mainly concentrated on the introduction of laws based on good legislative and normative practices derived from the already established democracies. The de facto impacts measured have been limited as the new democracies have yet to substantially internalise the values of modern constitutional democracy. Their introduction has faced challenges due to the persistence of 'dirty togetherness' and 'old practices' often omnipresent in the state institutions and public administrations of CEE countries.[32]

The normative influence of the Venice Commission has been greater in those CEE countries that have attempted to tear apart the remnants of their previous totalitarian regimes.[33] Such developments have been almost completely missing in countries of the former Soviet Union.[34] These countries have therefore encountered difficulties in breaking away from the practices of their former totalitarian regimes and their elites. For those reasons, these countries seem to have experienced far greater problems in formally introducing the principles and rules of the Venice Commission and the Council of Europe. As a result, Hoffman Ries submitted that the Venice Commission 'has no direct influence on the basic conditions that drive practical application of norms in the state concerned'.[35] In contrast, the impact of the opinions of the Venice Commission can even generate negative impacts, as we have seen from an example of one opinion concerning the electoral law in Slovenia, where the Venice Commission endorsed the view that can be prima facie deemed contrary to the fundamental principles of constitutional democracy. As a result, its impact on Slovenian constitutional democracy has been reserved. The influence of the Venice Commission certainly rests on the fact of whether a request for an opinion came directly from the current government of the Member States, from the previous government or from institutions of the Council of Europe. If the request came from the current government, it might be more eager to comply with it, even though such an approach has not always been the case. Accordingly, Hoffman-Riem argued that

[31] See similarly as to the impact of the European Court of Human Rights, Letnar Černič (n 4).

[32] Hoffmann-Riem (n 16). See also Venice Commission, 'Republic of Moldova, Joint Opinion on the Legal Framework Governing the Funding of Political Parties and Electoral Campaigns, CDL-AD(2017)027', Strasbourg, Warsaw, 11 December 2017.

[33] ibid.

[34] See eg complaince with opinions concerning Russia: Venice Commission, 'Russian Federation, Opinion on Federal Law no 129-fz on Amending certain Legislative Acts (Federal Law on Undesirable Activities of Foreign and International Non-Governmental Organisations), CDL-AD(2016)020', Strasbourg, 13 June 2016.

[35] Hoffmann-Riem (n 16) 590.

'the willingness of the state concerned to accept an opinion correlates closely with whether the opinion was requested by it or instead imposed upon it'.[36] In general, the Venice Commission has been less successful when addressing the systematic and general problems of the rule of law in countries such as the Russian Federation[37] and Ukraine.[38] The Venice Commission explained its approach in its opinion on Ukraine by noting that: 'New democracies, however, did not yet have a chance to develop these traditions, which can prevent abuse and therefore … explicit constitutional and legal provisions are needed as a safeguard to prevent political abuse in the appointment of judges.'[39]

The Commission has been much more successful when its proposals for constitutional reforms have been taken up by international financial institutions and other international actors. The World Bank and/or the International Monetary Fund have often made their financial assistance conditional on the introduction of the rule of law and constitutional reform proposed by the Venice Commission. For instance, the Venice Commission,[40] the World Bank[41] and the International Monetary Fund have joined to forces to exert pressure on the government of Ukraine concerning the creation of an anti-corruption court.[42] Governments under such pressure are unlikely not to conduct constitutional reforms proposed by the Venice Commission.[43] The country director for

[36] ibid 592.

[37] Venice Commission, 'Opinion on the Federal Law on the Election of the Deputies of the State Duma of the Russian Federation, CDL-AD(2012)002', Strasbourg, 19 March 2012; Venice Commission, 'Opinion on the Law on Political Parties of the Russian Federation, CDL-AD(2012)003', Strasbourg, 20 March 2012; Venice Commission, 'Opinion on the Federal Law no 54-fz of 19 June 2004 on Assemblies, Meetings, Demonstrations, Marches and Picketing of the Russian Federation, CDL-AD(2012)007', Strasbourg, 20 March 2012; Venice Commission, 'Opinion on the Federal Law on Combating Extremist Activity of the Russian Federation, CDL-AD(2012)016', Strasbourg, 20 June 2012; Venice Commission, 'Opinion on the Federal Law on the Federal Security Service (FSB) of the Russian Federation, CDL-AD(2012)015', Strasbourg, 20 June 2012.

[38] See generally, Lauri Mälksoo and Wolfgang Benedek (eds), *Russia and the European Court of Human Rights: The Strasbourg Effect* (Cambridge, Cambridge University Press, 2018) 188.

[39] Venice Commission, 'Joint Opinion on the Law Amending certain Legislative Acts of Ukraine in relation to the Prevention of Abuse of the Right to Appeal, CDL-AD(2010)029', Strasbourg, 18 October 2010, para 29, quoting Venice Commission, Report adopted by the Venice Commission at its 82nd Plenary Session (Venice, 12–13 March 2010) on the independence of the judicial system part I: the independence of judges, 16 March 2010, CDL-AD(2010)004 Or Engl, study no 494/2008, para 31.

[40] See Venice Commission, 'Draft Opinion on the Draft Law on Anti-Corruption Courts and on the Draft Law on Amendments to the Law on the Judicial System and the Status of Judges (Concerning the Introduction of Mandatory Specialisation of Judges on the Consideration of Corruption and Corruption-Related Offences), CDL(2017)020', Strasbourg, 21 September 2017; see also Venice Commission, 'Opinion on the Amendments to the Rules of Procedure of the Verkhovna Rada of Ukraine, CDL-AD(2017)026', Strasbourg, 9 October 2017.

[41] 'World Bank Joins IMF in Criticism of Ukraine's Anti-Corruption Draft Law' *Reuters* (Kiev, 16 January 2018) www.reuters.com/article/us-ukraine-corruption-worldbank/world-bank-joins-imf-in-criticism-of-ukraines-anti-corruption-draft-law-idUSKBN1F5236 (accessed 24 April 2019).

[42] 'IMF, Venice Commission to Meet over Anti-Corruption Court in Ukraine' *112. International* (21 May 2018) https://112.international/ukraine-top-news/imf-venice-commission-to-meet-over-anti-corruption-court-in-ukraine-28668.html (accessed 24 April 2019). See also Bartole (n 15).

[43] For more detail, see: Hoffmann-Riem (n 16); Maartje De Visser (n 14).

World Bank even observed concerning Ukraine that 'the draft law requires the following revisions to bring it into alignment with the recommendations of the Venice Commission and satisfy the requirements of the World Bank's estimated $800 million Policy-Based Guarantee to support key reforms in Ukraine'.[44] The opinions of the Venice Commission serve in such cases as tools of financial conditionality in the form of constitutional reforms in exchange for financial loans.

The Venice Commission has in the past influenced the workings of the ECtHR, which has to date referred to its opinions and documents on several hundred occasions.[45] The ECtHR has relied on the opinions and documents of the Venice Commission as legal authorities sustaining the arguments of their decisions or in the description of the state of the art of a particular area in human rights law.[46] The influence of the Venice Commission, however, goes beyond individual request opinions. The Venice Commission has been involved in educational programmes and training in the countries with the weak formal standards of the rule of law.[47] Its experts have trained public officials, judges and civil societies across Central and Eastern Europe.[48]

Overall, the influence of the Venice Commission has been in the past piecemeal and often dependent on various factors, from the political weight of a state in the European continent to procedural and technical aspects. The Venice Commission has yet to introduce a formal supervision system, which could oversee whether their opinions have been implemented in practice. The Secretariat of the Venice Commission currently has so far only informally supervised if the Commission's recommendations have been implemented in practice. Such an approach may be appropriate given the legal and advisory nature of its work. Nonetheless the introduction of some formal supervision system connected with the Committee of Ministers of the Council of Europe would contribute to the completion of domestic reforms. Hoffman-Riem argued in this context that: '[A]t a minimum, those states that initiate requests to the VC on their own could be obligated to report … about the implementation of recommendations in a systematic, comprehensive, and reliable manner.'[49] The current domestic

[44] *Reuters* (n 41).

[45] European Court of Human Rights, Hudoc database, https://hudoc.echr.coe.int/eng#{"documentcollectionid2":["GRANDCHAMBER","CHAMBER"]} (accessed 1 July 2019).

[46] Hoffmann-Riem (n 16) 587. See also Pieter Van Dijk, 'The Venice Commission on Certain Aspects of the European Convention of Human Rights Ratione Personae' in Stephan Breitenmoser, Bernhard Ehrenzeller, Marco Sassòli, Walter Stoffel and Beatrice Wagner Pfeifer (eds), *Human Rights, Democracy and the Rule of Law: Liber Amicorum Luzius Wildhaber* (Zurich/Baden-Baden, Dike/Nomos, 2007).

[47] Paul Craig, 'Transnational Constitution-Making: The Contribution of the Venice Commission on Law and Democracy', (2017) 2 *UC Irvine Journal of International, Transnational, and Comparative Law* 57, 83.

[48] ibid 83–85.

[49] Hoffmann-Riem (n 16) 589, n 44.

practices of some CEE countries certainly call for more external oversight. On the other hand, such improved supervision would turn generally the informal and advisory procedure of the Venice Commission into at least a quasi-binding or even a quasi-judicial procedure, which may not have been the wish of the Member States. After all, the current non-binding nature of its decision-making equips the Venice Commission with privileged soft-law diplomatic tools, which often have a wider and deeper impact than often toothless and limited binding mechanisms.

III. THE COMMISSIONER FOR HUMAN RIGHTS OF THE COUNCIL OF EUROPE

The Commissioner for Human Rights of the Council of Europe is a fairly new body, which was created in 1999 to foster human rights protections in the Member States of the Council of Europe. It does not officially have individual institutional status as it operates within the General Secretariat of the Council of Europe.[50] A person holding the position of Commissioner is expected to be 'of a high moral character having recognised expertise in the field of human rights, a public record of attachment to the values of the Council of Europe and the personal authority necessary to discharge the mission of the Commissioner effectively'.[51]

The founding resolution on the Council of Europe Commissioner for Human Rights provides in Article 10 that 'the Commissioner shall … promote education in, awareness of and respect for human rights, as embodied in the human rights instruments of the Council of Europe'.[52] Its mandate is clearly separated from the mandates of other human rights institutions of the Council of Europe; however, the Office of the Commissioner is encouraged to work and cooperate with similar bodies in order to avoid duplication and fragmentation of the mandate.[53] Article 1 provides that the Commissioner cannot accept individual complaints, but works as a policy organ. It provides that the Commissioner is to 'respect the competence of, and perform functions other than those fulfilled by, the supervisory bodies set up under the European Convention of Human Rights or under other human rights instruments of the Council of Europe'.[54] As for the competences of the Commissioner, the Resolution states that the Commissioner is inter alia asked to: 'promote education in and awareness

[50] Council of Europe, Committee of Ministers, 'Resolution (99) 50 on the Council of Europe Commissioner for Human Rights', 104th Session, 7 May 1999, Art 12, https://search.coe.int/cm/Pages/result_details.aspx?ObjectID=09000016805e305a (accessed 24 April 2019).

[51] ibid Art 11.

[52] ibid Art 1, para 1.

[53] ibid Art 3, para i.

[54] ibid Art 1, para 2.

of human rights in the member States';[55] 'contribute to the promotion of the effective observance and full enjoyment of human rights in the member States';[56] and 'provide advice and information on the protection of human rights and prevention of human rights violations'.[57] His role is therefore principally focused on advising national authorities, human rights bodies and civil society on how to improve human rights, in particular in the national setting.[58] Further, he is asked to 'identify possible shortcomings … promote the effective implementation of these standards … and assist them … in their efforts to remedy such shortcomings'.[59] He can decide to prepare a report on a specific issue for the Committee of Ministers and for the Parliamentary Assembly of the Council of Europe,[60] and is to annually present a report to both institutions on the Commission's activities.[61] Both these institutions can also submit a request to the Commissioner to respond as he sees fit on the specific issue of respect for human rights standards to the Council of Europe.[62]

The Commissioner has in practice mainly operated through educational and advisory activities, preparation of thematic reports and visits to Member States of the Council of Europe.[63] The Commissioner has to perform its mandate impartially and independently. When conducting a country visit, the Commissioner has to strive to conduct pluralistic conversations with relevant actors among national authorities and civil society, and not to resort to only one side of the civil society spectrum. Should Commissioner only meet with only one part of civil society when on a country visit, she would run the risk that her final report will be perceived as unconvincing, partial and not independent. One example of such danger can be seen from the 2017 mission report of the Commissioner for Human Rights of the Council of Europe on Slovenia. Nils Muižnieks, the former Commissioner, on 11 July 2017 published a country report on the basis to his visit to Slovenia between 20 and 23 March 2017.[64] It appears that the former Commissioner was not given sufficient information to create a full, independent and impartial picture of the human rights protection landscape in Slovenia. On the contrary, his report addresses only a few of the

[55] ibid Art 3, para a.
[56] ibid Art 3, para b.
[57] ibid Art 3, para c.
[58] ibid Art 3, para d.
[59] ibid Art 3, para e.
[60] ibid Art 3, para f.
[61] ibid Art 3, para h.
[62] ibid Art 3, para g.
[63] Council of Europe, Commissioner for Human Rights, The Mandate, www.coe.int/en/web/commissioner/mandate (accessed 24 April 2019).
[64] Council of Europe, Report by Nils Muižnieks, Commissioner for Human Rights of the Council of Europe, following his visit to Slovenia from 20 to 23 March 2017, CommDH(2017)21, Strasbourg, 17 July 2018, https://rm.coe.int/report-on-the-visit-to-slovenia-from-20-to-23-march-2017-by-nils-muizn/1680730405 (accessed 24 April 2019).

problems of human rights protection in Slovenia, such as the rights of migrants, asylum seekers and refugees, Roma and 'erased' persons.[65] These certainly constitute some the gravest human rights concerns in Slovenia, but are far from being the only issues as the report appears to suggest. As a result, the report therefore turned a blind eye to the long list of further human rights issues such the right to a fair trial before Slovenian courts (in particular, the doubts about the independence and impartiality of the Slovenian judiciary); the lack of effective investigation and prosecution of post-World War II crimes against humanity and the failure to preserve the memory and perform proper burial of the victims; violations of freedom of expression and press freedom; and others.[66] All in all, the report failed to provide a full and objective picture about the human rights situation in Slovenia. It rather reflected partial and biased opinions of certain NGOs.[67] Therefore, one queries the influence of a Commissioner who does not attempt to provide an objective picture of human rights problems, but rather appears to take sides in domestic ideological skirmishes.

The impact of the Commissioner on the rule of law and human rights in CEE countries has been therefore limited. Nonetheless, the Commissioner can underscore systematic and general problems with human rights protections in domestic systems. However, the Commissioner only has limited options at his disposal, and even those are of a soft legal nature. Perhaps the widest-reaching power of the Commissioner is to underline sensitive issues to the Committee of Ministers and to the Parliamentary Assembly of the Council of Europe, thereby pressuring them to adopt resolutions or employ binding measures. As it stands, his powers are only of a non-binding character. As a result, the legitimacy, credibility and persuasiveness of his actions hinges on the honesty and credibility of individual who occupies the post. Therefore, any person holding the position of the Commissioner has to strive to provide a full picture of the human rights situation in domestic systems. In the absence of a full picture, partial reports may bias the legitimacy and credibility of his actions.

IV. THE EUROPEAN COURT OF HUMAN RIGHTS

The ECtHR serves as the main judicial organ of the Council of Europe, and is mainly tasked with resolving applications concerning alleged domestic failures to respect and protect the ECHR. It proceeds under its Article 19, which stipulates that 'to ensure the observance of the engagements undertaken by the High Contracting Parties in the Convention and the Protocols thereto, there shall be

[65] ibid.

[66] See in detail, Jernej Letnar Černič, 'Čigave človekove pravice?' *IUS-info* (14 July 2018).

[67] See also, for a detailed analysis, Jernej Letnar Černič, *Slovenija na Razpotju: Geneza Varstva Človekovih Pravic v Slovenski Družbi* (Kranj, Nova Univerza–Fakulteta za Državne in Evropske Študije, 2018).

set up a European Court of Human Rights'.[68] The ECHR grants individuals and legal persons the right to individual application to the Court for any alleged violation of Convention rights occurring on the territory or under the control of any of the 47 Member States of the Council of Europe.[69] As it stands, the ECtHR is today still the only regional human rights court that affords victims the direct right to an individual application.[70] The ECHR was initially envisaged as the guardian of individual rights against the arbitrary conduct of state authorities. However, it has also overseen positive obligations of states to control private actors.[71] The ECtHR has protected the lowest common denominator of mostly civil and political human rights, but also of socioeconomic rights, some of them included in the additional protocols to the ECHR.[72]

The ECtHR has been the principal harbinger and advocate of constitutional transition and reform in CEE countries, which were in the early 1990s and onwards emerging from totalitarian and authoritarian regimes, which have in the past systematically and generally violated human rights and curtailed fundamental freedoms. The past decades have shown that this has been formidable task as it is one thing to introduce formal standards of the rule of law and effective protections in newly established liberal democracies, but it has been far more challenging to internalise the constitutional values of human rights protections. Under the totalitarian regimes the societies of most CEE countries were characterised by an authoritarian mentality, the abuse of powers, conflicts of interests, the lack of separation of powers between branches of government, and serious human rights violations.[73] It is impossible, in a short space of time for any transitional society to break away from arbitrary practices, 'dirty togetherness', nepotism, clientalism and the culture of impunity. For those reasons, the main challenges facing those societies have been how to incorporate the formal standards of constitutional democracy into decision-making within state institutions, public administration and the private sector. The ECtHR has through

[68] Council of Europe, European Convention for the Protection of Human Rights and Fundamental Freedoms, as amended by Protocols nos 11 and 14, supplemented by Protocols nos 1, 4, 6, 7, 12, 13 and 16, 4 November 1950, Art 19.

[69] ibid, Art 34.

[70] Thomas Buergenthal, 'Keynote Lecture: International Human Rights: Need for Further Institutional Development' (2018) 50(1) *Case Western Reserve Journal of International Law* 9, 13 and 14.

[71] Jernej Letnar Černič and Tara Van Ho (eds), *Human Rights and Business: Direct Corporate Accountability for Human Rights* (Oisterwijk, Wolf Legal Publishers, 2015).

[72] See Philip Leach, *Taking a Case to the European Court of Human Rights* (Oxford, Oxford University Press, 2011) 6.

[73] See eg Adam Czarnota, Martin Krygier and Wojciech Sadurski, 'Introduction' in Adam Czarnota, Martin Krygier and Wojciech Sadurski (eds), *Rethinking the Rule of Law after Communism* (Budapest, Central European University, 2005). See also Bojan Bugarič, 'The Rule of Law Derailed: Lessons from the Post-Communist World' (2015) 7(2) *Hague Journal on the Rule of Law* 175; Alenka Kuhelj and Bojan Bugarič, 'A Day in the Life of Post-Communist Europe' (2016) 8(1) *Hague Journal on the Rule of Law* 183; Paul Blokker, *New Democracies in Crisis: A Comparative Constitutional Study of the Czech Republic, Hungary, Poland, Romania and Slovakia* (New York, Routledge, 2014); Bugarič and Kuhelj (n 4) 274.

its case-law indirectly argued for the introduction of normative standards of the rule of law, effective human rights protection and constitutional democracy. Yet it cannot adopt public policies as it is *only* competent to resolve individual complaints concerning alleged violations of the ECHR. However, the real dilemma has been whether the ECtHR has also generated any positive impacts on the rule of law and human rights protection in practice?

A. Slovenia and the European Court of Human Rights

The ECtHR has so far decided that Slovenia violated the ECHR in 337 out of 363 judgments delivered up to June 2019.[74] The Court has also delivered two proper pilot judgments[75] and one semi-pilot judgment against Slovenia.[76] These numbers are relatively high, particularly when taking into account the country's population. Most judgments against Slovenia have dealt with failures to comply with procedural state obligations under the right to life and the prohibition of torture, inhuman and degrading treatment, as well as violations of the right to a fair trial (mostly concerning the duration of proceedings); to privacy and family life; to freedom of expression; to effective remedy; and to property.[77] These judgments illustrate that the Slovenian domestic system has not functioned as well as it could have done. As a rule, domestic authorities have not invested sufficient efforts into strengthening the system internally by concentrating on the internalisation of the ECHR's values within state institutions and public administration. Therefore, challenges have arisen also in the execution of some of the judgments. Slovenia has encountered resistance in the execution of the ECtHR's judgments in some branches of government. As a rule, judicial authorities seem to show particular resistance against internalisation of Convention values.[78] Nonetheless, Slovenia has fared quite well in translating the formal standards of the Council of Europe and the ECtHR into its domestic constitutional system. In contrast, it has so far only partially

[74] European Court of Human Rights, 'Violations by Article and by States (1959–2018)', www.echr.coe.int/Documents/Stats_violation_1959_2018_ENG.pdf (accessed 24 April 2019); European Court of Human Rights, 'Annual Report 2018', www.echr.coe.int/Documents/Annual_report_2018_ENG.pdf (accessed 24 April 2019). See also European Court of Human Rights, Hudoc database, https://hudoc.echr.coe.int/eng#{"documentcollectionid2":["GRANDCHAMBER","CHAMBER"]} (accessed 1 July 2019).

[75] *Kurić and others v Slovenia* no 26828/06 (ECtHR, 26 June 2012); *Ališić and others v Bosnia and Herzegovina, Croatia, Serbia, Slovenia and The Former Yugoslav Republic Of Macedonia* no 60642/08 (ECtHR, 16 July 2014).

[76] *Lukenda v Slovenia* no 23032/02 (ECtHR, 6 October 2005).

[77] Jernej Letnar Černič et al, *Slovenija pred Evropskim Sodiščem za Človekove Pravice: (1994–2016)* (Ljubljana, Fakulteta za Državne in Evropske Študije, 2017).

[78] Jan Zobec, 'Slovenia: Just a Glass Bead Game?' in Iulia Motoc and Ineta Ziemele (eds), *The Impact of the ECHR on Democratic Change in Central and Eastern Europe: Judicial Perspectives* (Cambridge: Cambridge University Press, 2015) 425–56.

translated the formal standards into practice as the Convention values have not been fully internalised.[79] Nonetheless, the judgments of the ECtHR have so far contributed to formal improvements in state institutions, public administration, the judicial system and prison conditions.

The two pilot judgments have, in particular, positively influenced the normative reforms and practice of Slovenian institutions and public administration. For instance, after the Court's judgment in *Kurić and others v Slovenia*[80] the National Assembly adopted a new Act granting the right to compensation for damage to everyone who was erased from the permanent population register after Slovenia gained independence.[81] Similarly, the National Assembly adopted a new Act to execute a judgment in the case of *Ališić and Others*[82] giving individuals the right to claim back their savings.[83] The National Assembly had previously adopted a law on the right to a fair trial without undue delay[84] after the ECtHR's judgment in *Lukenda v Slovenia*.[85] By contrast, the situation has been for al long time far from ideal concerning the execution of other ECtHR judgments against Slovenia.[86]

In this respect, the domestic legal system only partially provides for the direct execution of ECtHR judgments as it lacks a fully fledged statutory legal basis for their implementation. The Criminal Procedure Act[87] provides the only basis for the execution of the judgments, whereas neither the Civil Procedure Act[88] nor the Administrative Procedure Act[89] provide a legal basis for direct execution of the ECtHR's judgments, thereby preventing individuals from requesting

[79] Matej Avbelj and Jernej Letnar Černič, 'Slovenia', in Leonard Hammer and Frank Emmert (eds), *The European Convention on Human Rights and Fundamental Freedoms in Central and Eastern Europe* (The Hague: Eleven International Publishing, 2012) 527–56.

[80] *Kurić and others v Slovenia* no 26828/06 (ECtHR, 26 June 2012).

[81] Act Regulating Compensation for Damage to Persons Erased from the Permanent Population Register, Official Gazette of the Republic of Slovenia No 99/13.

[82] *Ališić and others v Bosnia and Herzegovina, Croatia, Serbia, Slovenia and the Former Yugoslav Republic of Macedonia* no 60642/08 (ECtHR, 16 July 2014). Government of the Republic of Slovenia, 'Report of the Republic of Slovenia on the Execution of the Judgment of the European Court of Human Rights of 16 July 2014, Action Plan, 11 December 2014', www.vlada.si/fileadmin/dokumenti/si/projekti/2015/Varcevalci/Akcijski_nacrt_za_implementacijo_sodbe.pdf (accessed 24 April 2019); Government of the Republic of Slovenia, 'Implementation of the Ališić and Others judgments against the successor states of the SFRY', www.vlada.si/teme_in_projekti/implementacija_sodbe_alisic_in_drugi_proti_drzavam_naslednicam_sfrj/ (accessed 24 April 2019).

[83] Act on the Implementation of the judgment of the European Court of Human Rights in the case 60642/08, Official Gazette of the Republic of Slovenia No 48/2015.

[84] Act on the Protection of the Right to a Trial without Undue Delay, Official Gazette of the Republic of Slovenia No 67/12.

[85] *Lukenda v Slovenia* no 23032/02 (ECtHR, 6 October 2005).

[86] Letnar Černič et al (n 77). See also Jernej Letnar Černič, 'The European Court of Human Rights in the States of the Former Yugoslavia' (2018) 1 *East European Yearbook on Human Rights* 32.

[87] Criminal Procedure Act, Official Gazette of the Republic of Slovenia No 32/12, official consolidated text 47/13, 87/14 and 8/16.

[88] Civil Procedure Act, Official Gazette of the Republic of Slovenia No 73/07, official consolidated text 45/08 – ZArbit, 45/08, 111/08.

[89] Administrative Dispute Act, Official Gazette of the Republic of Slovenia No 105/06, 107/09.

reinitiation of procedures. Nonetheless, the state institutions are obliged to execute them directly under Article 8 of the Constitution of the Republic of Slovenia.[90] Moreover, there is strong resistance from the judicial elites at the highest levels of the domestic judiciary, particularly at the Supreme Court of Slovenia, towards executing the ECtHR's judgments.[91] In spite of the majority of judgments having now been executed in the Slovenian domestic system, the number of complaints from Slovenia and the rest of Central and Eastern Europe has not ceased, which appears to illustrate that the values of the European Convention have not been entirely internalised. In general, some CEE countries, eg Estonia, the Czech Republic and Slovenia have made substantial normative progress in recent years, whereas others have not fared so well.[92] This observation testifies to the fact that the normative changes have not been significantly taken into consideration in the institutional lives of the newly formed democracies.[93]

B. Influence of the Court on the Rule of Law and Human Rights Protection in Slovenia and Beyond

What has been the most substantial impact of the ECtHR on the rule of law and human rights protection? Even though the ECtHR functions on the basis of individual applications, there can be no doubt that its influence stretches beyond individual cases. Such indirect but binding influence has been seen not only in the Member States from Western Europe, but also in CEE states.[94] The ECtHR has through and with the assistance of the Committee of Ministers of the Council of Europe pressured individual governments to adopt individual and general measures in order to comply with its judgments, thereby generating and designing legislative and constitutional reforms in various domestic systems.[95] It

[90] Constitution of the Republic of Slovenia, Official Gazette of the Republic of Slovenia No 33/91-I, 42/97, 66/2000, 24/03, 69/04, 68/06, 47/13, and 75/16, Art 8.

[91] See eg Jernej Kosec, 'How Communist Is the Judiciary in Slovenia? A Survey' (July 2018) CRCE Briefing Paper. See also judgment of the Supreme Court of Slovenia, Decision I Ips 58203/2011, 7 June 2018, failing to execute the judgment in the case *Koprivnikar v Slovenia* no 67503/13 (ECtHR 24 January 2017).

[92] See Hubert Smekal, Katarína Šipulová, Ivo Pospíšil, Jozef Janovský and Petr Kilian, Making Sense of Human Rights Commitments: A Study of Two Emerging European Democracies (Brno, Scientia edn, MUNI Press, 2016); Letnar Černič (n 4); Letnar Černič (n 86).

[93] Adam Czarnota, 'Rule of Law as an Outcome of Crisis. Central-Eastern European Experiences 27 Years after the Breakthrough' (2016) 8(2) *Hague Journal on the Rule of Law* 311.

[94] See eg Motoc and Ziemele (n 4); András Baka, 'The European Court of Human Rights and the Central and Eastern European States', (2018) 1 *East European Yearbook on Human Rights* 79; Letnar Černič (n 4); Letnar Černič (n 86).

[95] See generally on compliance with the judgments of the EctHR: Courtney Hillebrecht, 'The Power of Human Rights Tribunals: Compliance with the European Court of Human Rights and Domestic Policy Change' (2014) 20(4) *European Journal of International Relations* 1100; Janneke H Gerards and Joseph Fleuren (eds), *Implementation of the European Convention on Human Rights and of the Judgments of the ECtHR in National Case Law* (Cambridge, Intersentia, 2014);

has triggered reforms of domestic systems by advocating for the most appropriate design to structure the functioning of the judiciary, executive and legislative branches. In doing so it has inspired changes in public policy and has pressured parliaments to adopt new statutes and/or change old frameworks in order to execute its judgments and provide standards for national judiciary that could prove useful and be included in the case-law of the ordinary and constitutional courts. As a result, its normative influence on the core structure of domestic legal systems has been substantial and has instigated positive impacts in drafting and designing national policies and legislation to protect the rule of law and human rights.[96]

The ECtHR has as a rule triggered structural reforms to introduce or to improve the rule of law de jure in the daily functioning of state institutions in Slovenia and in other CEE countries by applying pressuring and requiring normative reforms based on the values of human dignity, pluralism, tolerance and accountability in order to place them in line with developed democracies. As a result, fundamental normative standards have been basically translated from already developed constitutional democracies to new democracies. These developments have been entirely straightforward as CEE countries forsaking totalitarian regimes were not familiar with constitutional democracy and its primary features such the rule of law, separation of powers and human rights protections. Most of these countries have now accepted such reforms, often with the assistance of foreign advisers such as the Venice Commission, and have accordingly reformed their constitutions and engineered domestic legal reforms. More specifically, the actual influence has been observed in several areas concerning absolute rights, particularly negative and positive substantive and procedural state obligations concerning the right to life and the prohibition of torture,[97] the right to liberty[98] and the right to a

Janneke H Gerards, 'The Transformative Power of the European Court of Human Rights' Treaties of Nijmegen Medal 2006' (November 2016) 2; Helen Keller and Alice Stone Sweet, *A Europe of Rights: The Impact of the ECHR on National Legal Systems* (Oxford, Oxford University Press, 2008); David Kosař and Lucas Lixinski, 'Domestic Judicial Design by International Human Rights Courts. (2015) 109(4) *American Journal of International Law* 713.

[96] David Kosař, 'Nudging Domestic Judicial Reforms from Strasbourg: How the European Court of Human Rights Shapes Domestic Judicial Design' (2017) 13(1) *Utrecht Law Review* 120.

[97] *Šilih v Slovenia* no 71463/01 (ECtHR 9 April 2009); *Y v Slovenia* no 41107/10 (ECtHR, 28 May 2015); *L M v Slovenia* no 32863/05 (ECtHR, 12 June 2014); *Mučibabić v Serbia* no 34661/07(ECtHR, 12 July 2016); *Mladenović v Serbia* no 1099/08 (ECtHR, 22 May 2012); *M and others v Croatia* no 50175/12 (ECtHR, 2 May 2017); *Bilbija and Blažević v Croatia* no 62870/13(ECtHR, 12 January 2016); *B and others v Croatia* no 71593/11 (ECtHR, 18 June 2015); *Starčević v Croatia* no 80909/12 (ECtHR, 13 November 2014); *Bljakaj and others v Croatia* no 74448/12 (ECtHR, 18 September 2014); *Jelić v Croatia* no 57856/11 (ECtHR, 12 June 2014); *Kudra v Croatia* no 13904/07 (ECtHR, 18 December 2012); *Bajić v Croatia* no 41108/10 (ECtHR, 13 November 2012); *Jularić v Croatia* no 20106/06 (ECtHR, 20 January 2012); *Skendžić and Krznarić v Croatia* no 16212/08 (ECtHR, 20 January 2011); *Branko Tomašič and others v Croatia* no 71463/01 (ECtHR, 15 January 2009).

[98] See eg *Mandić and Jovič v Slovenia* no 5774/10 and 5985/10 (ECtHR, 20 October 2011); *Vitkovsky v Ukraine* no 24938 (ECtHR, 26 September 2013); *Rezmives and others v Romania* no 61467/12, 39516/13, 48231/13, and 68191/13 (ECtHR, 25 April 2017); *Neshkov and others v Bulgaria*

fair trial.[99] The ECtHR has also assisted transitional societies to break away from the past, particularly dealing with cases concerning individual responsibility for past crimes,[100] restitution of property,[101] amnesties,[102] lustration[103] and access to archives.[104] It has instigated reforms of the normative underpinnings of a pluralistic society, which guarantees freedom of expression, assembly, association and religion.[105] On the other hand, the ECtHR has on various occasions emphasised the importance of the impartiality and independence of judiciary to realise constitutional democracy in the newly formed democracies.[106] It requires that states ensure both external and internal independence. The Court emphasised in *Parlov Taklčič v Croatia* that 'judicial independence demands that individual judges be free not only from undue influences outside the judiciary, but also from within'.[107] It added that 'the internal judicial independence

no 36925/10, 21487/12, 72893/12, 73196/12, 77718/12 and 9717/13 (ECtHR, 27 January 2015); *Varga and others v Hungary* no 14097/12, 45135/12, 73712/12, 34001/13, 44055/13, and 64586/13 (ECtHR, 10 March 2015).

[99] *Lukenda v Slovenia (no 2)* no 16492/02 (ECtHR, 13 April 2006); *Dimitrov and Hamanov v Bulgaria* no 48059/06 and 2708/09 (ECtHR, 10 May 2011); *Rutkowski and Others v Poland* no 72287/10, 13927/11 and 46187/11 (ECtHR, 7 July 2015).

[100] *Kononov v Latvia* no 36376/04 (ECtHR, 24 July 2008); *Kolk and Kislyiy v Estonia* no 24018/04 (ECtHR, 17 January 2006); *Streletz, Kessler and Krenz v Germany* (Grand Chamber) no 34044/96, 35532/97 and 44801/98 (ECtHR, 22 March 2001); *Ecaterina Mirea and others v Romania* no 43626/13 (ECtHR, 12 April 2016); *Association '21 December 1989' and other v Romania* no 33810/07 and 18817/08 (ECtHR, 24 May 2011).

[101] *Preda and others v Romania* no 9584/02, 33514/02, 38052/02, 25821/03, 29652/03, 3736/03, 17750/03 and 28688/04 (ECtHR, 29 April 2014); *Broniowski v Poland* (Grand Chamber) no 31443/96 (ECtHR, 22 June 2004).

[102] *Fatullayev v Azerbaijan* no 40984/07 (ECtHR, 22 April 2010); *Uzeyir Jafarov v Azerbaijan*, no 54204/08 (ECtHR, 29 January 2015); *Klein v Slovakia* no 72208/01 (ECtHR, 31 October 2006); *Ziembinski v Poland* (no 2) no 1799/07 (ECtHR, 5 July 2016); *Wizerkaniuk v Poland* no 18990/05 (ECtHR, 5 July 2011) para 65; *Kaperzynski v Poland* no 43206/07 (ECtHR, 3 April 2012) para 74; *Malone and others v Moldova* no 13936/02 (ECtHR, 17 September 2009) para 111; *Partidul Comunistilor (Nepeceristi) and Ungureanu v Romania* no 44626/99 (ECtHR, 3 February 2005) para 44; *United Communist Party and others v Turkey* no 19392/92 26 EHRR 1211 (ECtHR, 30 January 1998) para 45; *Veniamin Tymoshenko and others v Ukraine* no 48408/12 (ECtHR, 2 October 2014); *Promo Lex and others v Moldova* no 42757/09 (ECtHR, 24 February 2015); *Navalnyy and Yashin v Russia* no 76204/11 (ECtHR, 4 December 2014); *Kasparov and others v Russia* (no 1) no 21613/07 (ECtHR, 3 October 2013); *Kasparov and others v Russia* (no 2) no 51988/07 (ECtHR, 13 December 2016).

[103] *Naidin v Romania* no 38162/07 (ECtHR, 21 October 2014), para 49. See also *Turek v Slovakia* no 57986/00 (ECtHR, 14 February 2006); *Matyjek v Poland* no 38184/03 (ECtHR, 30 May 2006); *Luboch v Poland* no 37469/05 (ECtHR, 15 January 2008); *Bobek v Poland* no 68761/01 (ECtHR, 17 July 2007); *Schulz v Poland* no 43932/08 (ECtHR, 13 November 2012); *Sidabras and Džiautas v Lithuania* no 55480/00 and 59330/00 (ECtHR, 27 July 2004); *Rainys and Gasparavicius v Lithuania* no 70665/01 and 74345/01 (ECtHR, 7 April 2005).

[104] *Janowiec and others v* 55508/07 and 29520/09 (ECtHR, 16 April 2012); *Janowiec and others v Russia* (Grand Chamber) no 55508/07 in 29529/09 (ECtHR, 21 October 2013).

[105] See eg the following cases: Savva *Terentyev v Russia* no 10692/09 (ECtHR, 28 August 2018); *Mladina v Slovenia* no 20981/10 (ECtHR, 17 April 2014).

[106] *Baka v Hungary* (Grand Chamber) no 20261/12 (ECtHR, 23 June 2016); *Kudeshkina v Russia* no 29492/05, (ECtHR, 26 February 2009); *Harabin v Slovakia* no 58688/11 (ECtHR, 20 November 2012).

[107] *Parlov Taklčič v Croatia* no 24810/06 (ECtHR, 22 December 2009) para 84.

requires that they are free from both directives or pressures from the fellow judges or those who have administrative responsibilities in the court'.[108] The ECtHR's impact has been particularly felt through the form of pilot judgments, which have addressed systematic and general violations of Convention rights.[109] The impact of the pilot judgments has been quite substantial in the area of property rights,[110] the length of proceedings,[111] the lack of effective remedies and non-enforcement of domestic judicial decisions[112] and degrading conditions in prisons.[113] The ECtHR's influence has been felt in all branches of state authorities, which have been pressured to implement legislative, judicial and executive changes. States have in most cases executed the judgments, although in some cases they refused to do so despite pressure from the ECtHR and the Committee of Ministers. The ECtHR has in one recent case – *Burmych and others v Ukraine* concerning non-enforcement of a domestic judicial decision – controversially decided to strike out 12,143 similar applications arising from the non-execution of the pilot judgment in *Yuriy Nikolayevich Ivanov v Ukraine*, claiming that it is a matter for the Committee of Ministers to ensure execution of general measures.[114] It observed that 'the resolution of the present applications ... is more properly part of the process of execution of the Ivanov pilot judgment ... within the framework of the execution procedure, under the supervision of the Committee of Ministers'.[115] Seven judges noted in their dissenting opinion that: 'The present solution follows a trend whereby the Court discontinues the award of just satisfaction in repetitive cases where the State has failed to comply with

[108] ibid.

[109] See eg *Olaru and others v Moldova* no 476/07, 22539/05, 17911/08 and 13136/07 (ECtHR, 28 July 2009). See in detail on pilot judgments, Lize Glas, 'The Functioning of the Pilot-Judgment Procedure of the European Court of Human Rights in Practice' (2016) 34(1) *Netherlands Quarterly of Human Rights* 41; Tatiana Sainati, 'Human Rights Class Actions: Rethinking the Pilot-Judgment Procedure at the European Court of Human Rights' (2015) 56 *Harvard International Law Journal* 147.

[110] See eg *Atišić and others v Bosnia And Herzegovina, Croatia, Serbia, Slovenia and the Former Yugoslav Republic of Macedonia* no 60642/08 (ECtHR, 16 July 2014).

[111] *Rumpf v Germany* no 46344/06 (ECtHR, 2 September 2010); *Athanasiou and Others v Greece* no 50973/08 (ECtHR, 21 December 2010); *v Turkey* no 24240/07 (ECtHR, 20 March 2012); *Michelioudakis v Greece* no 54447/10 (ECtHR, 3 April 2012); *Glykantzi v Greece* no 40150/09 (ECtHR, 30 October 2012).

[112] See eg *Yuriy Nikolayevich Ivanov v Ukraine* no 40450/04 (ECtHR, 15 October 2009); *Burmych and others v Ukraine* no 46852/13, 47786/13, 54125/13, 56605/13 and 3653/14 (ECtHR 12 October 2017); *Burdov v Russia* (no 2) no 33509/04 (ECtHR, 15 January 2009); *Olaru and others v Moldova* no 476/07, 22539/05, 17911/08 and 13136/07 (ECtHR, 28 July 2009); *Gerasimov and others v Russia* no 29920/05, 3553/06, 18876/10, 61186/10, 21176/11, 36112/11, 36426/11, 40841/11, 45381/11, 55929/11 and 60822/11 (ECtHR, 1 July 2014).

[113] *Ananyev and others v Russia* nos 42525/07 and 60800/08 (ECtHR, 10 January 2012); *Torreggiani and others v Italy* no 43517/09, 46882/09, 55400/09, 57875/09, 61535/09, 35315/10 and 37818/10 (ECtHR, 8 January 2013).

[114] *Ivanov v Ukraine* no 40450/04 (ECtHR, 15 October 2009).

[115] *Burmych and others v Ukraine* no 46852/13, 47786/13, 54125/13, 56605/13 and 3653/14 (ECtHR 12 October 2017), para 215.

the Court's judgment.'[116] They added that: 'The Court was set up specifically to respond to these violations as an independent judicial body, and not to concentrate on statistics. … By failing to address this issue the Court is shooting itself in the foot.'[117] One can agree with the dissenting judges as the majority accepted that non-compliance is an acceptable manner to execute the ECtHR's judgments, particularly in those CEE countries where subsidiarity has not worked well as the values of the ECHR have not been fully internalised. As a result, the ECtHR can even undermine the fragile state of the rule of law in domestic systems.[118] In this aspect, Helfer and Slaughter observed that 'a State government lagging behind in the protection of a certain rights is allowed to maintain its national policy but is forced to bear a heavier burden of proof before the ECHR'.[119] All in all, the Court has contributed to the construction of normative standards and values in CEE countries. Contrary to expectations, their internalisation has not been fully seen through in the light of the erosion of the rule of law and overall human rights protections across the region. In this way, the CEE countries still top the rankings of the highest numbers of applications and of judgments finding at least one violation. Therefore, the influence of the Court on the rule of law has in practice been only indirect and piecemeal.

Firstly, one contestation that can be made is that the accession of CEE countries to the Council of Europe improved domestic legal frameworks that have enabled individuals to invoke their rights before the regional human rights court in Strasbourg. If not for any other effect, the accession of Slovenia to the ECHR was certainly a positive step. As a result, it equipped ordinary and vulnerable individuals with an avenue to protect their rights outside national judiciaries, which have often been subjected to the parochial interests of powerful governmental or corporate elites. However, the primary objective of the Strasbourg human rights system is not only to provide individuals with the right to individual application, but to improve the rule of law in domestic systems and to incorporate into domestic systems the values and tools that individuals will be able to resort to primarily protect their human and fundamental rights.

Secondly, even the normative influence of the Strasbourg court has found its constraints. Kosař has, for instance, observed that 'the ECtHR has been increasingly intervening in domestic judicial design and, ultimately, in the separation of powers within CoE Member States'.[120] He emphasised that the ECtHR prioritised the judicial model of a national judicial council, which as recent studies

[116] ibid, joint dissenting opinion of Judges Yudkivska, Sajó, Bianku, Karakaş, DeGaetano, Laffranque and Motoc, para 32 (footnote omitted).

[117] ibid para 39.

[118] Jernej Letnar Černič, 'Korak nazaj', *IUS-info*, 7 September 2018.

[119] Laurence R Helfer and Anne-Marie Slaughter, 'Toward a Theory of Effective Supranational Adjudication' (1997) 107 *Yale Law Journal* 273, 317.

[120] Kosař (n 96) 123. See also David Kosař, 'Politics of Judicial Independence and Judicial Accountability in Czechia: Bargaining in the Shadow of the Law between Court Presidents and the Ministry of Justice' (2017) 13(1) *European Constitutional Law Review* 96.

suggest may not be the best to ensure judicial independence and impartiality of judiciaries in CEE countries.[121] To be clear, this model of national judicial councils prioritises judicial self-governance, which may be appropriate in established constitutional democracies, but has not functioned properly in most CEE countries, where doubts have been cast as to the internal independence of the highest branches of the judiciary.

Thirdly, we have on the other hand previously argued that 'the Court's impact in CEE cannot be underestimated. It has contributed to forming of normative orders based on the rule of law and protection of human rights.'[122] We added that: 'On the other hand, its influence has been limited, since it has not been possible to convince the domestic elites to internalize the values of the Convention and to fully establish the rule of law de facto.'[123] We have further observed that 'the Court has contributed to the rule of law *de iure* frameworks, whereas such normative structures have not been translated into practice and translated in the rule of law de facto'.[124] In spite of the substantial – normative – impacts of the ECtHR the number of new applications from CEE countries does not seem to be decreasing. The impact has been substantial in overseeing constitutional reforms on paper, but not in practice.[125] It seems that there has been resistance among institutional elites in Slovenia and beyond to internalise the most fundamental values of constitutional democracy, which in essence attempt to curtail the power of the governing elites and networks.[126] This current situation calls for reform of institutional and societal mentality to internalise the values of constitutional democracy and the rule of law, thereby strengthening state institutions and public administration in Slovenia and across Central and Eastern Europe. The ECtHR has to rethink and re-evaluate its approach even to normative reforms in the Member States in order to heed particular and specific national contexts and attempt to reform not only juridically but also the rule of law in practice. In doing so the reforms from one country may not be appropriate

[121] ibid. See in detail David Kosař, *Perils of Judicial Self-Government in Transitional Societies* (Cambridge, Cambridge University Press, 2016).

[122] Letnar Černič (n 4) 133.

[123] ibid.

[124] ibid.

[125] See eg Michal Bobek and David Kosař, 'Global Solutions, Local Damages: A Critical Study in Judicial Councils in Central and Eastern Europe' (2014) 15 *German Law Journal* 1257. See also Wojciech Sadurski, 'Postcommunist Constitutional Courts in Search of Political Legitimacy', EUI LAW Working Paper no 2001/11; Wojciech Sadurski, *Rights before Courts: A Study of Constitutional Courts in Postcommunist States of Central and Eastern Europe*, 2nd edn (Heidelberg, Springer, 2014).

[126] See Maria Popova, 'Why Doesn't the Bulgarian Judiciary Prosecute Corruption?' (2012) 59(5) *Problems of Post Communism* 35. See also Maria Popova, *Politicized Justice in Emerging Democracies: A Study of Courts in Russia and Ukraine* (Cambridge, Cambridge University Press, 2012); Alexei Trochev, 'Meddling with Justice: Competitive Politics, Impunity, and Distrusted Courts in Post-Orange Ukraine' (2010) 18(2) *Demokratizatsiya* 122; see also Diana Bozhilova, 'Measuring Success and Failure of EU-Europeanization in the Eastern Enlargement: Judicial Reform in Bulgaria' (2007) (9)2 *European Journal of Law Reform* 285.

in other national contexts. The deficiencies in the domestic systems of CEE countries call for the eradication of the old practices and customs of nepotism, clientelism and corruption from the institutional and public lives of the CEE countries. In order to maintain its credibility and legitimacy, the ECtHR should not turn a blind eye to systematic and structural human rights violations in the domestic legal systems of Central and Eastern Europe.

V. CONCLUSION

This chapter has attempted to describe and analyse the influence of the primary institutions of the Council of Europe on the rule of law in Slovenia by drawing parallels with similar developments elsewhere in Central and Eastern Europe. It has first explored the work of the European Commission for Democracy through Law and its influence on the rule of law in Slovenia by contextualising it with some developments elsewhere in Central and Eastern Europe. Thereafter, it examined the role of the Commissioner for Human Rights of the Council of Europe in reforming the rule of law, and particularly in designing more effective human rights protections in Slovenia. Finally, it has studied the work of the ECtHR and its impact on the rule of law in Slovenia, and compared its impact with developments elsewhere in Central and Eastern Europe. Overall, it has found out that these institutions, particularly the Venice Commission and the ECtHR, have positively contributed to the normative change of the rule of law in domestic frameworks, although their normative influence has not been always positive and in some cases even detrimental to the rule of law. Where they have failed is in the incorporation of the proper application of the rule of law in practice. As a result, Slovenia and some other CEE states have not fully internalised the values of the rule of law in their state institutions and public administration. The overall impact of the institutions of the Council of Europe in Slovenia and beyond has therefore been mixed. They have initiated several positive changes in the normative rule of law in Slovenia and beyond. On the other hand, it appears that their political and institutional elites have taken up the values of the institutions of the Council of Europe only when they have served their agendas and their parochial interests, particularly in the power struggles to protect and advance their private – financial – objectives. Nonetheless, the influence of the Council of Europe on the rule of law in Slovenia and beyond has been substantial, particularly in the normative field, whereas it has struggled to change daily arbitrary and corrupt exercises of the rule of law in practice. Overall, the positive impacts of the institutions of the Council of Europe are a light on the horizon in realising a paradigm shift in the daily practice of Slovenian institutions and public administration.

11

The Impact of the European Union on Constitutional Democracy in Slovenia

Europe will not be made all at once, or according to a single plan. It will be built through concrete achievements which first create a de facto solidarity.
The Schuman Declaration, 9 May 1950

THE PRECEDING CHAPTERS have examined the state of constitutional democracy in Slovenia. Several significant shortcomings with regard to its constitutive elements were identified, most notably in the fields of rule of law, the building blocks of democracy, the functioning of economy, the welfare state and human rights protection. This chapter will examine the influence of the European Union in these fields. Has the European Union contributed in any meaningful way to the improvement of the rule of law, democracy, the functioning of economy and human rights protection in Slovenia? This question is situated in a broader debate on the Europeanisation of candidate countries and later Member States of the European Union.[1] As is true of European studies in general, the study of the process of Europeanisation has been event-driven too, and hence shaped by sentiments attached to specific events in a respective historical period.[2] The chronological focus has traditionally distinguished between the pre-accession phase and the membership phase.[3] The former was presented as a learning period, a period of catching up, returning to Europe, in which the candidate countries tried to do their best to meet the conditions of the club. The membership phase, on the other hand, has been predominantly

[1] The process of Europeanisation has also been studied independently of the accession procedure, as a general phenomenon of the EU's impact on its Member States' policies, politics and polity; see eg Tanja A Börzel and Thomas Risse, 'When Europe Hits Home: Europeanization and Domestic Change' (2000) 4(15) *European Integration Online Papers*, https://papers.ssrn.com/sol3/papers.cfm?abstract_id=302768 (accessed 16 February 2019); Tanja A Börzel and Thomas Risse, 'Conceptualizing the Domestic Impact of Europe' in Kevin Featherstone and Claudio M Radaelli (eds), *The Politics of Europeanization* (Oxford, Oxford University Press, 2003).

[2] Neil Walker, 'Legal Theory and the European Union: A 25th Anniversary Essay' (2005) 25(4) *OJLS* 581.

[3] K Featherstone and C M Radaelli, *The Politics of Europeanization* (Oxford, Oxford University Press, 2003); M Baun and D Marek, *The New Member States and the European Union: Foreign Policy and Europeanization* (Abingdon, Routledge, 2013).

understood as a period of consolidation. The achievements of the successful pre-accession accommodation should have now come to fruition.

The assessment of the process of Europeanisation by politicians, the general public and scholars alike has been positive and optimistic, indeed overly so according to a few, isolated and more sceptical voices.[4] However, this mood suddenly changed after 2008, with the eruption of the global financial crisis. Under economic constraints and subject to political upheavals across the European Union, it became clear that the process of Europeanisation has been largely limited to only meeting the formal conditions, merely touching on the surface of new EU Member States' realities without penetrating deeper in the substructure to cause real and lasting differences to the sociopolitical and economic models of these states.[5] The practices and narratives of backsliding post-2010 have since been well known and need no repetition here.[6]

The impact of Europeanisation on Slovenia has not received much research attention, neither domestically[7] and even less in the international scholarly community. The existing literature has, however, similarly been strongly event-driven. Most of the expert and academic writing took place during or immediately after the country's accession to the European Union. These works, discussing Europeanisation lato sensu,[8] as well as with regard to particular fields such as public administration,[9] foreign policy[10] and law,[11] have, however, remained scattered, undertheorised and do not present a systematic analysis of the process of Europeanisation. Moreover, most of these works have been forward-looking, anticipating the probable effects of Europeanisation in Slovenia. They thus stop

[4] Dimitry Kochenov, *EU Enlargement and the Failure of Conditionality: Pre-accession Conditionality in the Fields of Democracy and the Rule of Law* (The Hague, Kluwer Law International 2008).

[5] Jacques Rupnik and Jan Zielonka, 'The State of Democracy 20 Years On: Domestic and External Factors' (2013) 27(1) *East European Politics and Societies* 3, 13, https://journals.sagepub.com/doi/abs/10.1177/0888325412465110 (accessed 16 February 2019).

[6] For an overview, see A Jakab and D Kochenov, *The Enforcement of EU Law and Values, Ensuring Member States' Compliance* (Oxford, Oxford University Press, 2017).

[7] However, see Bojan Bugarič, 'A Crisis of Constitutional Democracy in Post-Communist Europe: "Lands in-Between" Democracy and Authoritarianism' [2015] *International Journal of Constitutional Law* 219.

[8] Drago Zajc (ed), 'Evropeizacija slovenske politike: zbornik referatov' [1998] *Politološki dnevi, Portorož*; Aldo Bibič, 'Evropeizacija politične družbe in civilne družbe: nekateri aspekti slovenskega primera' [1997] *Teorija in praksa: družboslovna revija* 56.

[9] Bojan Bugarič, 'Evropeizacija državne uprave: vpliv evropskega prava na strukturo nacionalnih državnih uprav' [2004] 64 *Zbornik znanstvenih razprav* 101.

[10] Bojko Bučar, 'Evropeizacija slovenske zunanje varnostne politike: (ne)prepričljivost interesa za vstop v NATO' in Drago Zajc (ed.), *Evropeizacija slovenske politike: zbornik referatov*, (Ljubljana, Slovensko politološko društvo 1998) 51–60; and more recently: Sabina Kajnč Lange, 'Evropeizacija slovenske zunanje politike: od pridružitvenega procesa do predsedovanja Svetu EU' [2011] *Teorija in praksa: družboslovna revija* 668.

[11] Damjan Možina, 'Evropeizacija in modernizacija obligacijskega prava' [2008] *Dnevni slovenskih pravnikov* 1270; Viktorija Žnidaršič Skubic, 'Evropeizacija družinskega prava' in Franjo Štiblar, Janez Kranjc (eds.), *Pravni vidiki slovenske samobitnosti leto po vstopu v EU* (Ljubljana, Pravna fakulteta 2005) 153–164.

before the economic crisis sets in.[12] This chapter will therefore try to fill this void, although without making any attempt at a comprehensive assessment of Europeanisation. Instead, we will only illuminate – by way of highlighting – the main influences of the European Union on four studied fields: the rule of law, democracy, economy, and human rights protection, across three different historical periods: the accession phase (1995–2004), the poster-child membership phase (2004–09) and the (post)-crisis phase (2009–present).

I. PRE-ACCESSION PHASE

Slovenia was the last of the EU member states that joined in 2004 to sign the Association Agreement with the European Union. The country entered into the so-called Europe Agreement on 10 June 1996 and simultaneously applied for full EU membership.[13] Slovenia was thus a latecomer. The then Czechoslovakia, Hungary and Poland had already signed the Europe Agreement in 1992, while Bulgaria and Romania followed suit in 1993. The reason for this delay was not of a domestic character. To the contrary, still in socialist times, in 1990, the then socialist government adopted the so-called 'Europe 1992' programme requiring that all newly adopted laws were streamlined with the *acquis communautaire*.[14] The aspiration toward independence was hence inextricably linked with the desire to participate in European integration. The narrative of a return to Europe, to escape the Balkans, was absolutely dominant, part of national-identity building,[15] which was eventually confirmed in the EU accession referendum in 2003, in which 89.64% of those casting their vote supported accession.[16] As observed by the then chief negotiator on behalf of Slovenia, Janez Potočnik: [T]he determination to become an EU member was on overriding argument that helped Slovenian citizens support and accept the difficult and sometimes unpopular decisions made by the authorities.'[17] This sentiment was only reinforced by the external obstacles faced on the way to Europe.

The highest foreign policy hurdle was erected by Italy, which effectively sought immediate and non-discriminatory access of its citizens to the real-estate

[12] See also Sabina Kajnč Lange, 'Effects of EU Enlargement: Slovenia' [2009] http://tepsa.be/Enlarging%20the%20European%20Union.pdf (accessed 9 September 2019) 41, who notes that 'following the accession to the EU, systemic research into the effects of the EU has faded'.

[13] Janez Potočnik and Jaime Garcia Lombardero, 'Slovenia's Road to Membership in the European Union' in Mojmir Mrak, Matija Rojec and Carlos Silva-Jáuregui (eds), *Slovenia: From Yugoslavia to the European Union* (Washington, DC, World Bank 2004) 369.

[14] A Bojinović Fenko and M Svetličič, 'Slovenia and the European Union' in *Oxford Research Encyclopedia of Politics* (Oxford, Oxford University Press, 2017) 6.

[15] ibid 10.

[16] The turnout was 60.44 per cent. See 'Poročilo o izidu glasovanja in o izidu referenduma o pristopu Republike Slovenije k EU', 23 March 2003.

[17] Janez Potočnik and Jaime Garcia Lombardero, 'Slovenia's Road to Membership in the European Union' in Mrak et al (n 13) 372.

market in Slovenia, even prior to the latter's accession to the EU. Although apparently a straightforward single-market issue, this policy in fact had much deeper historical roots and was motivated, at least to a certain extent, by Italy's desire for compensation from Yugoslavia for losses of territory and, above all, people and property after World War II.[18] The protracted and politically painful negotiation with Italy eventually resulted in the so-called Spanish compromise,[19] which even required an amendment to the Slovenian Constitution,[20] but which eventually and simultaneously cleared the path for Slovenia's ratification of the Europe Agreement.[21] The formal accession negotiations began only two years later in December 1997. Slovenia took part in the so-called Luxembourg group of candidate countries and was soon, despite its initial delay, considered as a front-runner in the group of states, consisting of Cyprus, the Czech Republic, Estonia, Hungary and Poland. All of this fed the sentiment of an 'Euro-euphoria',[22] marked by a relatively uncritical popular acceptance of EU accession conditions, which in institutional and overall political terms also functioned as an outside pressure for faster reform[23] despite resistance, sometimes not insignificant, from the established system of political and economic power.[24]

In the context of this overwhelming political and civic consensus about EU membership being Slovenia's main strategic goal,[25] part of which was also Slovenia's desire to be seen as a 'flexible, constructive and well-organized' country,[26] a process of adjustment in which significant reform of judiciary and other state institutions, responsible for a solid functioning of a market-based economy, took place.[27] In 1995 a reorganisation and modernisation of

[18] Andrew Geddes and Andrew Taylor, 'Those Who Knock on Europe's Door Must Repent? Bilateral Border Disputes and EU Enlargement' (November 2013) KFG Working Paper no 54, http://userpage.fu-berlin.de/kfgeu/kfgwp/wpseries/WorkingPaperKFG_54.pdf (accessed 16 February 2019).

[19] See Vlada Republike Slovenije, 'What Is Spanish Compromise', available at www.ukom.gov.si/en/media_room/background_information/foreign_affairs/what_is_spanish_compromise/ (accessed 15 May 2019).

[20] The text of Art 68 as amended in 1997 reads as follows: 'Aliens may acquire ownership rights to real estate under conditions provided by law or if so provided by a treaty ratified by the National Assembly, under the condition of reciprocity. Such law and treaty from the preceding paragraph shall be adopted by the National Assembly by a two-thirds majority vote of all deputies.'

[21] Austria too introduced its objections and conditions for Slovenian EU membership, raising concerns related to the safety of the Krško nuclear plant and the protection of the German national minority. However, these concerns were resolved much more quickly on a diplomatic, bilateral expert level. For a more in-depth discussion, see Ana Bojinović Fenko and Ana Urlić, 'Political Criteria v Political Conditionality: Comparative Analysis of Slovenian and Croatian European Union Accession Processes' (2015) 21(72) *Croatian International Relations Review* 121.

[22] Bojinović Fenko and Svetličič (n 14) 6.

[23] Janez Šušteršič, 'Political Economy of Slovenia's Transition' in Mrak et al (n 13) 407.

[24] Janez Potočnik and Jaime Garcia Lombardero, 'Slovenia's Road to Membership in the European Union' in Mrak et al (n 13) 375.

[25] Matej Makarovič, Lea Prijon, Mateja Rek and Matevž Tomšič, 'The Strength of Pro-European Consensus Among Slovenian Political Elites' [2016] *Historical Social Research* 197.

[26] Potočnik and Garcia Lombardero (n 24) 375.

[27] ibid 372.

the Slovenian judiciary was implemented. In 1997 a new administrative court was established. These reforms were destined to adapt the Slovenian socialist judiciary to the challenges of a capitalist economy. They consisted mainly of legislative amendments, judicial training and organisational attempts at cutting the duration of trials and consequently reducing judicial delays. Their success was, however, ambiguous. Several authors, including representatives of judiciary themselves, argued that the reform, as prepared and carried out, deteriorated rather than improved the efficiency of the Slovenian judiciary.[28] The ECtHR *Lukenda* ruling, which found judicial delays to be a systemic problem in Slovenia,[29] confirmed that impression.

Nevertheless, the prospect of joining the EU and acting under the shadow of conditionality created an impetus, sometimes also pressure, for judicial reform. This resulted in an institutional culture in which the need for reform, for progress beyond the existing status quo, was shared widely. It stretched beyond the judiciary into the organisation of the executive branch. It effectuated the reform of public administration, which was 'at the beginning of the transition … characterized by bureaucratic lethargy, dependence on orders, lack of creativity, and lack of professional knowledge',[30] but should soon be capable of autonomous and efficient implementation of EU law.[31] The impact of the EU accession process was felt in the economy as well, where the state started retreating, albeit reluctantly, gradually and mostly partially, from the country's financial and broader economic sector, both in terms of ownership and control.[32] The business environment continued to face many legal, administrative and judicial obstacles as well, typically informal, discriminatory practices, but these were counterbalanced with an ambition of gradually liberalising the economy.[33] Nevertheless, political pressure, across the party spectrum, to defend the national economy, the so-called national interest, to preserve state or at least Slovenian ownership in the leading companies (eg Slovenian economic champions) was extremely strong.[34] This economic nationalism, which was in fact about preserving control over the economy, media and hence society in the hands of the post-communist left and its allies, was made explicit in the field of banking privatisation, which was progressing with significant difficulties, and even more so in the so-called

[28] See eg Katarina Zajc, 'Independence of Judiciary in Slovenia: Economic and Historic Perspective' (2014) 22(3) *Acta Histriae* 741.

[29] See *Lukenda v Slovenia* App no 23032/02 (ECHR, 6 October 2005).

[30] See Rasto Ovin and Boštjan Kramberger, 'Building an Institutional Framework for a Full-Fledged Market Economy' (Washington, DC, World Bank 2004) 219, referring to France Bučar, *Demokracija in kriza naših ustavnih institucij* (Nova Revija, 1998).

[31] Ovin and Kramberger (n 30).

[32] ibid.

[33] ibid 216–19.

[34] For a more in-depth discussion, see Rok Spruk, *The Failure of Economic Nationalism in Slovenia's Transition: Political Economy Behind the Calamity of Kleptocratic Institutions and Economic Performance* (Lambert Academic Publishing, 2012).

brewery war between Belgian and the Slovenian competitors.[35] The latter prevailed and hence cleared their path to control not just the retail of beverages in Slovenia, but indirectly also the biggest Slovenian newspaper company.

In macroeconomic terms, the state tailored its fiscal and monetary policies to meet the Maastricht criteria and to adopt the euro. For this purpose an agreement was concluded between the partners in the social dialogue, ie employers, employees and the government, to join forces, most importantly to limit the pressure on public expenses, to facilitate the adoption of the single currency.[36] All these reform initiatives were made possible in light of an overarching societal and political consensus about the pre-eminent importance of acceding to the EU, as well as, and perhaps even more importantly, due to the external oversight by the EU institutions guaranteeing that the declared political commitment to Europeanisation was also met in practice. Nevertheless, influential civil society groups warned even at the very outset of the accession process that this commitment was largely declaratory, superficial and limited to the formal level of legislative and organisational change, while in reality the status quo, resting on and shielding informal networks of power stemming from the old communist regime, was being preserved under the newly tailored clothes of the EU emperor.[37] This civic anxiety was, unfortunately, corroborated by actual practice over the next decade.

II. POSTER-CHILD MEMBERSHIP PHASE

However, before 'the hour of [European] truth for Slovenia'[38] struck, Slovenia indulged in five glory years of EU membership. Not only was the country presented as a poster child of enlargement among the 10 post-communist states, but in many respects this was indeed true. It was the first among the new Member States to adopt the euro, bringing thus a difficult economic transition from communism to an open market economy to a successful conclusion. It was also the first post-communist country to become a full member of the Schengen region. This was a recognition that the country was a consolidated democracy, based on the rule of law, robust judiciary and credible security forces, and therefore able partake as a reliable and trustworthy partner in the EU's area of freedom, security and justice. Slovenia was also the first new Member State to hold the presidency of the European Council. In a difficult period of exiting from the post-constitutional *Denkpause* (period of reflection) Slovenia executed

[35] Nicole Lindstrom and Dora Piroska, 'The Politics of Privatization and Europeanization in Europe's Periphery: Slovenian Banks and Breweries for Sale?' [2007] *Competition and Change* 117.

[36] Igor Guardiancich, 'Slovenia: The End of a Success Story? When a Partial Reform Equilibrium Turns Bad' [2016] *Europe-Asia Studies* 205, 211.

[37] Drago Jančar et al, *The Hour of European Truth for Slovenia* (Nova Revija, 1997).

[38] ibid.

its task of an honest broker beyond the expectation of its EU partners.[39] Several Slovenian politicians developed good reputations in the EU. They were increasingly integrated into influential policy-making circles[40] and were awarded international prizes for their contribution to the process of Europeanisation in Slovenia.[41] Not only has Slovenia thus achieved its main foreign policy goals, in particular winning full EU and NATO membership, it has also established itself as an example of regional stability, as a respected member of the international community, a forum for the world superpowers,[42] as well as, admittedly proportionate to its size and influence, an international policy-maker.

These foreign policy achievements translated also into the state of Slovenian democracy. After 12 years of a basically uninterrupted reign by the post-communist left, the 2004 elections brought a change in government. A switch in the political and governing elite testified to the fact that in Slovenia too political pluralism is possible and that a veritable system of checks and balances in lieu of a unified rule under a single dominant political power was emerging. This signalled a break away from the political status quo, whose roots still dated back to the times of the old communist regime. The actual materialisation of EU membership proved, in a way, that the reformist culture, the belief in progress beyond the status quo, was not only possible, but also bore fruit. This popular sentiment, encouraged by the process of Europeanisation, translated into a democratic political life where, for the first time since independence, it appeared that a genuine readiness for change, for breaking the old political and economic monopolies, did actually exist. This optimism was also fuelled by the exceptional economic growth which was helping Slovenia to close its developmental gap to the average of developed EU Member States.[43]

However, the stimulus for change evaporated quickly. The government's attempts at reform to liberalise the economy encountered opposition from influential trade unions as well as from coalition partners, in particular the

[39] Sabina Kajnč, 'Channels of Cooperation: A Case Study of Slovenia's Presidency of the EU' (2009) European Policy Institutes Network Working Paper no 21.

[40] Lojze Peterle was, for example, Member of the Praesidium of the Convention on the Future of Europe (2002–03); Žiga Turk was Secretary General of Felipe Gonzalez's Reflection Group on the Future of Europe (2008–10).

[41] See eg 'Peterle Gets MEP Award for the Third Time' (13 March 2015) EPP Group, www.eppgroup.eu/how-we-make-it-happen/with-eu-countries/slovenia/news/peterle-gets-mep-award-for-the-third-time (accessed 16 February 2019); 'Bajuk Receives European Finance Minister of the Year Award (3 March 2006) STA, english.sta.si/1030257/bajuk-receives-european-finance-minister-of-the-year-award (accessed 16 February 2019); 'Minister Mramor the Top Finance Minister in Europe in 2016' (8 January 2016) www.vlada.si/en/media_room/news_from_slovenia/news_from_slovenia/article/minister_mramor_the_top_finance_minister_in_europe_in_2016_57322/.

[42] Jaka Bartolj, 'Bush Saw Putin's Soul in Slovenia' (*RTVSLO*, 3 April 2015) www.rtvslo.si/news-in-english/slovenia-revealed/bush-saw-putin-s-soul-in-slovenia/361776.

[43] Hermine Vidovic, 'Slovenia: Rapid Growth with Accelerating Inflation' [2008] *Current Analyses and Forecasts* 1, 1–4, https://wiiw.ac.at/slovenia-rapid-gdp-growth-with-accelerating-inflation-dlp-51.pdf.

Pensioners' Party.[44] Economic reforms were thus stalled. Economic prosperity driven by the high economic growth was also seized as an opportunity to compensate for the conservative economic policy in the pre-accession era with its limit on the growth of salaries and other state expenses in order to fulfil the Maastricht criteria. The grip on public expenditure was now loosened. This provided an additional boost to economic growth, particularly in the construction sector, which was, with the benefit of hindsight, in fact fuelling the economic bubble.[45] Moreover, the new political elite, realising that it could not push through the anticipated reforms to make economy more liberal and competitive, and in so doing, contribute to a more open Slovenian society and better functioning democracy, apparently decided to keep the various monopolies in place, but replace the allies of the preceding political establishment with their own loyalists.[46]

In political life this reinvigorated the old *Kulturkampf* from the 1990s,[47] which again poisoned the democratic discourse with intense fights between competing lobbying groups, and led to massive disillusionment on the part of the electorate, which again learned the lesson, repeated time and again in the communist regime, that all politicians are essentially the same, that no reform is actually possible and that the most rational reaction is to stick to the status quo. The positive effects of EU membership on the state of Slovenian democracy thus did not last long. They appeared to be precarious and at best temporary. As research shows, there has been no decisive impact of Europeanisation on the political culture of the Slovenian civil society and its constitutive interest groups.[48] Furthermore, EU membership and the invitation for Slovenian political parties to join the family of European political parties has influenced certain policy priorities of the major Slovenian parties, but this impact has remained limited and has been almost absent as far as the functioning and organisational structure of the political parties are concerned.[49] In fact, 2008 was the last time an electoral battle was held between two established and well-organised political parties. Since then, as we shall see in the analysis of the post-crisis phase, a process of political implosion has taken place.

In the fields of rule of law and human rights protection the three branches of power in Slovenia acted under the impact of the *Lukenda* ruling by the ECtHR.[50] In this case, which was discussed thoroughly in Chapter 6, the Strasbourg court

[44] See Chap 4 above.

[45] For an excellent analysis, see Guardiancich (n 36) 221.

[46] ibid 219.

[47] Makarovič (n 25).

[48] Danica Fink-Hafner, Mitja Hafner-Fink and Meta Novak, 'Europeanisation as a Factor of National Interest Group Political-Cultural Change: The Case of Interest Groups in Slovenia' [2015] *East European Politics and Societies and Cultures* 287, 301. See also Chap 5 above.

[49] Makarovič (n 25).

[50] See *Lukenda v Slovenia* App no 23032/02 (ECHR, 6 October 2005).

observed that a violation of the right to a trial within a reasonable time is 'a systemic problem that has resulted from inadequate legislation and inefficiency in the administration of justice'.[51] In a response to this pilot judgment the government launched an ambitious 'Lukenda project' consisting of legislative, administrative, personnel, organisational and financial measures aimed at a systemic resolution of the problems identified by the ECtHR by 2010.[52] This, again externally introduced stimulus, created a constructive atmosphere inside the judicial branch which took an active part in the project until disagreements regarding judicial remuneration started; these reached their peak in 2008 with a judicial strike. This, and the political developments that followed, stalled the potential for reform in the Slovenian judiciary.

The latter was also relatively unaffected by EU membership.[53] In the first five years since accession there were only a few cases before the ordinary courts relating to EU law. Moreover, in the same period of time there was not a single case of a preliminary ruling procedure launched by a Slovenian court. The Slovenian judiciary was hence the least interested in judicial cooperation with the CJEU among all the new Member States.[54] EU law thus remained mainly a theoretical issue. The Slovenian legal order, including the Constitution, which has for the purpose of acceding to the EU been amended four times,[55] has been formally brought in compliance with EU law, but the latter's practical relevance remained limited.[56] The reception of EU law in judicial and administrative practice was thus very slow. The professional careers of institutional actors in a completely different political system, eg communism, with no training in EU law was the main reason for this.[57] This low level of knowledge of EU law in general still persists,[58] but the institutional attachment to a statutory-based legal positivism is even more sticky. A reductionist conception of law, centred on statutes to the detriment of courts' case-law, which is considered as a mere persuasive authority and therefore still relatively rarely taken into account, prevented Slovenian courts and legal practitioners, unused to an inductive, case-based approach to

[51] Ibid para 93.

[52] 'The Elimination of Court Backlogs: The Lukenda Project: Operational Action Plan' (12 December 2005) www.mp.gov.si/fileadmin/mp.gov.si/pageuploads/mp.gov.si/zakonodaja/angleski_prevodi_zakonov/The_Lukenda_Project_angl.pdf (accessed 16 February 2019).

[53] Matej Avbelj, 'Report on the Role and Status of the ECHR and EU Law in Slovenia' in Giuseppe Martinico and Oreste Pollicino (eds), *The National Judicial Treatment of the ECHR and EU Laws* (Europa Law Publishing, 2010) 441–53, https://ssrn.com/abstract=1645822.

[54] http://curia.europa.eu/jcms/upload/docs/application/pdf/2015-04/en_ecj_annual_report_2014_pr1.pdf.

[55] Art 3a; Art 47; Art 68 (twice).

[56] Matej Avbelj, 'Slovenia: The Case of a Maturing Relationship' in Stefan Griller, Monica Claes, and Lina Papadopoulou (eds), *Member States' Constitutions and EU Integration* (Oxford, Hart Publishing, 2019).

[57] ibid.

[58] The lack of EU knowledge was openly admitted even by the group of experts charged with drafting the above-mentioned Slovenian EU constitutional clause; 'Ustavne razprave 2001–2003, Izbor gradiv Državnega zbora' [2004] (3).

the law, from timely and correct application of EU law. The latter has also been understood as foreign law that is, in principle, less habitually obeyed in any case.[59] However, this negative predisposition towards foreign law is perhaps in Slovenia accentuated further due to the specific mind-set there, characterised by a lack of self-confidence and consequent unfounded aggrandisement of foreign authorities.[60] This also explains the reason for a total initial lack of preliminary references from Slovenian judges. They were simply embarrassed at asking a question of the foreign court, as they believed that sending a preliminary reference would demonstrate their ignorance and would thus be ridiculed by the CJEU judges. Finally, the very slow emergence of EU law in Slovenia can be also ascribed to the country's economic isolationism. Unlike the other CEE countries, Slovenia has received very little direct foreign investment. There were thus fewer cross-border transactions involving influential transnational investors, which also explains the lower share of EU-law-related cases in Slovenia in comparison to other CEE states.[61]

The poster-child membership phase, which lasted only five short years between 2004 and the onset of the economic crisis in 2009, was thus marked by two characteristics: the incremental waning of reformist enthusiasm for Europeanisation and the existence of two parallel realities – one, declaratory and formal, which was expressed through a legalist and nominal compliance with EU law on paper;[62] and the other reflected in actual practice, which exhibited ignorance of and disregard for EU law as well as widespread *praeter legem* actions, ie following the letter of the law, but defying its spirit, object and purpose.[63] The success associated with accession and its immediate aftermath increasingly bred complacency in officials of all three branches, as well as in the economy at large. When Slovenia achieved full EU membership it became clear that the previous external oversight had came to an end, which in practical terms invited a return to business as usual. With the EU mission accomplished, the judiciary again concentrated foremost on its status, thus lending credence to the view of a German judge Norman Manfred Doukoff, who observed after his pre-accession twinning process with his Slovenian counterparts that they made no shift in their mind-set and were occupied mainly by themselves and their salaries.[64] The offended, solipsistic response of the Slovenian judge's association corroborated their German colleague's point.[65] Beyond the judiciary, the

[59] JHH Weiler, 'Transformation of Europe' [1991] *Yale Law Journal* 2403.

[60] See similarly Chap 10 above.

[61] Avbelj (n 56).

[62] See also Makarovič et al (n 25) 196 who query whether the Slovenian dedication to Europeanisation was more about paying lip-service than an actual willingness to change.

[63] Bugarič (n 7) 229.

[64] 'Slovenia's Judges Appalled at Doukoff's Criticism' *STA* (2003) english.sta.si/779193/slovenias-judges-appalled-at-doukoffs-criticism (accessed 16 February 2019).

[65] ibid.

executive branch, in whose ministries the impact of Europeanisation was quite limited,[66] was preoccupied with organising and conducting the EU presidency, while the parliament already braced for the new election, at which the post-communist left was desperately looking for a comeback.

Finally, following the adoption of euro, interest rates on Slovenian bonds dropped to a historic low. The Europeanisation of the Slovenian economy thus resulted in a surplus of cheap and easily obtainable loans that fuelled economic complacency[67] and provided a new, indeed unprecedented boost to the practices of Slovenian crony capitalism.[68] Guardiancich probably captures this paradox of economic Europeanisation of Slovenia best:

> The euphoria following good economic results is a poisoned apple, as it triggered calls for slowing down privatisation – in the name of the often-invoked national interest – as well as growing demands for windfall benefits. Protracted gradualism, which entrenched the most distorting practices of state-managerial capitalism … has thrived precisely due to the conniving complacency of Slovenian elites during the boom years.[69]

III. POST-CRISIS PHASE

All these developments where taking placing on the eve of an unexpected global financial crisis, for which Slovenia was ill prepared, both economically and politically. Immediately at the onset of the economic crisis, in 2008, Slovenian GDP contracted by 7.8 per cent. Slovenia was thus the fifth most crisis-affected EU Member State.[70] The general government debt in GDP almost quadrupled in just six years, rising from 22 per cent in 2008 to 81 per cent in 2014.[71] Most of those funds were spent to save the ailing banking sector, which received €5 billion of tax-payers' money.[72] Unlike in Ireland or Spain, the banking crisis was not caused by a housing bubble, but by a uniquely Slovenian post-socialist economic-political model founded on an intricate web of relationships 'between politicians, state-owned bank directors and state-owned enterprise managers, which locked the country in a partial reform equilibrium'.[73] In this condition, the state-owned banks offered massive loans to corporations (to be) owned or

[66] Radoslaw Zubek and Katarina Staronova, 'Organizing for EU Implementation: The Europeanization of Government Ministries in Estonia, Poland and Slovenia' (2012) 90(4) *Public Administration* 937.

[67] Guardiancich (n 36) 228.

[68] ibid; also Bugarič (n 7) 219.

[69] Guardiancich (n 36) 228.

[70] Statistični urad Republike Slovenije, *National Accounts on the Economic Crisis in Slovenia* (2016) 16. See Chap 4 above for a detailed overview.

[71] Statistični urad Republike Slovenije, ibid 13.

[72] Guardiancich (n 36) 215.

[73] ibid.

managed by (politically) loyal managers with little or even no risk assessment.[74] The competent authorities, independent economic and financial agencies as well as the Central Bank failed to fulfil their supervisory roles. Politicians, on all sides of the political spectrum, defending their economic fiefdoms, took part and encouraged this process, which eventually resulted in an acute banking – sovereign debt spiral, creating a complete economic meltdown.[75] In 2011 the country ended up in a bad equilibrium.[76]

Since then a process of political implosion has been in full swing in the Slovenian political space. In a 2011 snap election the political party of the mayor of Ljubljana, Zoran Janković, a notorious businessman without any political experience, won by a landslide. As he failed to build a coalition, the established political parties of the center-right, led by Janez Janša, were in power for a year, before this government lost support due to a corruption scandal and consequent popular protests and was taken over by a new prime minister, Alenka Bratušek, a previously publicly unknown bureaucrat from the Ministry of Finance. Under pressure because of the economic crisis, and because this coalition was politically extremely weak, her government failed as well and a new snap election was called in 2013. This time around a party initiated by a media-supported law professor, Miro Cerar, a political novice, won a landslide only to see his government collapse prematurely in 2018. Again, as in the two preceding elections, a new political party was formed only weeks before the 2018 election. Chaired by a comedian and a former mayor of a small town, Marjan Šarec, it failed to obtain a majority of votes, but nevertheless managed to form a coalition with the center-left and radical-left political parties only to prevent the center-right political party, the Slovenian Democrats, which had the highest share of the vote in the 2018 election, from seizing the power. In short, since 2008 elections in Slovenia have been conducted against a particular political party rather than to promote a particular constructive political programme. In so doing, as described in Chapter 7, the country has witnessed a complete implosion of its political space.

This has deprived Slovenia of any capacity actually to govern its domestic affairs.[77] For an entire decade now elections have failed to result in a meaningful political coalition that could move the country out of the tyranny of the status quo.[78] In fact, in Slovenia the influence of institutional and economic insiders actively working to preserve the status quo is so strong that electing a

[74] ibid.

[75] ibid.

[76] ibid.

[77] See also Matevž Tomšič, 'Crisis and (Re)Structuring of the Slovenian Political Space' in Frane Adam (ed), *Slovenia: Social, Economic and Environmental Issues* (Nova Science Publishers, 2017).

[78] Milton Friedman and Rose Friedman, *The Tyranny of the Status Quo*, 1st edn (Boston, MA, Houghton Mifflin Harcourt, 1984).

government that can introduce any meaningful reforms has proven impossible.[79] These strong factions have worked hand in hand with the populace at large that is also opposed to any relevant change due to the deception that the Slovenian welfare state works in its favour. This weakness in domestic affairs has gradually also eroded the country's foreign policy social capital. One of the most embarrassing Slovenian foreign policy missteps in the EU was the self-nomination of the then Slovenian prime minister, Alenka Bratušek, as an EU Commissioner. Her presentation in front of the European Parliament displayed a glaring lack of competence to act as the Commission's vice-president for the energy union and led the responsible EU parliament committees to reject her candidacy by an overwhelming majority.[80] Slovenia's difficulties in finding a qualified candidate almost threatened a timely confirmation of Juncker Commission and significantly undermined the political reputation and credibility that the country had initially enjoyed.[81] Unsurprisingly, and as a consequence of these developments too, recent studies have shown that Slovenia is, contrary to its status in the pre-accession and poster-child membership phase, among the countries least sought-after as a 'coalition partner' and simultaneously one of the least influential EU Member States.[82]

If Slovenia's capacity to influence the European Union was therefore small, the opposite was true of the EU's impact during the economic crisis. The rising interest rates on Slovenian bonds significantly limited the country's access to the global financial markets. The yawning budget deficit and the deep crisis in the state banking sector brought the country to its knees, inches away from an EU troika intervention. However, Slovenia narrowly escaped the EU bailout mechanism and its accompanying strict institutional oversight through self-imposed austerity measures and a reform agenda approved by the European Commission.[83] The latter, inter alia, included privatisation measures in 15 state-owned companies, most importantly in Slovenia's two biggest state-owned banks.[84] In fact, the privatisation of Nova Ljubljanska Banka had been

[79] See Tomšič (n 77) 53, who argues: 'However, the changes and events connected with financial crisis and economic crisis after 2008 may indicate that [the] entire architecture of Slovenian social corporatism in the framework of state (national) type of capitalism generated a sort of immobilismo and inability to execute the necessary reforms.'

[80] Dave Keating, 'MEPs Reject Bratušek and Force Juncker Rethink' *Politico* (10 August 2014) www.politico.eu/article/meps-reject-bratusek-and-force-juncker-rethink (accessed 16 February 2019).

[81] Žiga Turk, 'If Bulc Is Nominated, the Next Dan Brown Novel Should Be about the Brussels Bubble' *Euractiv* (14 October 2014) www.euractiv.com/section/eu-priorities-2020/opinion/if-bulc-is-nominated-the-next-dan-brown-novel-should-be-about-the-brussels-bubble (accessed 16 February 2019).

[82] European Council on Foreign Relations, EU Coalition Explorer, www.ecfr.eu/page/ECFR269_EU_COALITION_EXPLORER_2018_V1.10.pdf.

[83] Alex Barker, 'Slovenia Struggles to Avoid EU Bailout' (*Financial Times*) www.ft.com/content/1d17fdd6-5053-11e3-9f0d-00144feabdc0 (accessed 16 February 2019).

[84] '15 State Companies Listed for Privatisation' *Slovenia Times* (9 May 2013) www.sloveniatimes.com/15-state-companies-listed-for-privatisation (accessed 16 February 2019).

mandated by the European Commission as a condition of legality of the state-aid mechanism implemented by Slovenia in the course of reconstruction of the bankrupt banking sector. Only in this way, under the external shock mechanism, as the literature predicted,[85] and the threat of EU sanctions, has it been possible to start breaking the above-described clientelistic, deeply politicised system of rent extraction from the state-owned economy, in particular from the biggest Slovenian bank. Hence, in 2018, after significant delay and at a relatively low price, the Nova Ljubljanska Banka, which has, like its predecessor Ljubljanska Banka, for three decades served as a backbone of the regime, parasitic on taxpayers' money and the common good in general, was finally privatised.[86]

However, this formal and informal pressure by the EU, in particular in the form of economic conditionality during the crisis, has taken its toll. Slovenia, always known as a good disciple and one of the most pro-EU Member States, in the midst of the crisis changed its attitude toward the EU. As Makarovič et al noted:

> Till the beginning of the crisis EU-related issues were very rarely a matter of political disputes. However, when a package of anti-crisis measures entailing cuts in public spending and a reduction of the public sector, the privatisation of state-owned companies and reform of the banking sector was launched, not insignificantly due to the pressure of international political and financial circles and following a significant downgrade of Slovenian government bond ratings, this 'outside' intervention triggered anti-capitalist and anti-EU sentiments.[87]

The narrative, dictated by the media and influential political circles, suddenly changed so that Slovenia was represented as a 'victim' of international financial circles and European policy-makers,[88] irrespective of the fact that, as we have seen above, the crisis and its consequences have been politically and economically self-inflicted. As a result, for the first time in 10 years of EU membership elements of the process of de-Europeanisation could be identified in internal and external relations.

Domestically the relics of the deceased Yugoslavia were unearthed and revived by the post-communist left, their leaders and connected NGOs. The municipality of Ljubljana again dedicated a street to the Josip Broz Tito;[89] communist commemorations were attended by the political leadership and state prizes awarded;[90] 'Yugonostalgia' has been promoted and a former flag of the

[85] Matija Rojec, Janez Šušteršič, Boštjan Vasle, Marijana Bednaš and Slavica Jurančič, 'The Rise and Decline of Gradualism in Slovenia' [2004] *Post-Communist Economies* 62.

[86] 'First Phase of NLB Privatization Completed' *Slovenia Times* (12 November 2018) www.sloveniatimes.com/first-phase-of-nlb-privatisation-completed accessed (16 February 2019).

[87] Makarovič et al (n 25) 209–10.

[88] ibid.

[89] 'Naming Street After Tito Unconstitutional' *Slovenia Times* (5 October 2011) www.sloveniatimes.com/naming-street-after-tito-unconstitutional (accessed 16 February 2019).

[90] Georgi Gotev, '"Sexist" Spanish Commissioner under Parliamentary Spotlight' *Euractiv* (10 September 2014) www.euractiv.com/section/eu-priorities-2020/news/sexist-spanish-commissioner-under-parliamentary-spotlight (accessed 16 February 2019).

socialist Republic of Slovenia boasting a red star has become a frequent sight in public manifestations. Twenty years after independence a sentiment started to emerge that the EU is turning Slovenia into an outback province, creating a situation which trails even that of the former Yugoslavia.[91] Rather than a genuine change in the popular attitude toward the EU, this domestic switch in favour of the anti-EU narrative could be better understood as a compensatory and retaliatory reaction of the elites partaking in the practices of crony-capitalism,[92] whose status came under attack from Brussels oversight, recommendations and regulations. In short, this domestic process of de-Europeanisation was in defence of vested interests. This is, perhaps, even better seen through the de-Europeanization in external affairs. Not only has Slovenia become disengaged from the EU foreign policy, but it has even substantially departed from its normative framework, for example, by protecting Belorussian oligarchs with close economic ties to Slovenian companies,[93] and, in particular, by a general turn towards Russia at the expense of transatlantic relationships.[94]

Although the EU has traditionally enjoyed broad and almost unanimous cross-party support in Slovenia, the situation has gradually been changing. In 2016 research demonstrated what was already clearly visible in the events that unfolded during the crisis, namely that EU-scepticism had started to grow in the centre-left corner of the Slovenian political spectrum, in particular with regard to the EU's interventions in the economy and democracy.[95] While this did not come as a great surprise, given that for influential members of the post-communist elite the West, the EU included, has never been their first choice of partner, it was much more interesting to observe a decisive anti-EU turn by the centre-right political parties. This occurred in the aftermath of the migration crisis; its massive scope and apparently uncontrollable character instilled fear in the population at large. The centre-right political parties, having exhausted all other avenues of policy-making, as well as to conceal their own domestic and international enfeeblement, decided to exploit this crisis, by putting anti-migration, and hence also anti-Brussels rhetoric, at the centre of their political agenda. Moreover, the main opposition party also departed from its previous centre-right political course and, by striking a close political as well as economic relationship with the Hungarian party of Viktor Orbán, has moved decisively to the right, taking sides with the Visegrad countries against the allegedly politically

[91] Boris Vasev, Gregor Cerar and Saša Banjanac Lubej, 'Bruseljske zahteve: "Gre za neke vrste kapitalistični fundamentalizem"' *RTVSLO* (30 May 2013) www.rtvslo.si/slovenija/bruseljske-zahteve-gre-za-neke-vrste-kapitalisticni-fundamentalizem/309959 (accessed 16 February 2019).

[92] Tomšič (n 77).

[93] Bojinović Fenko and Svetličič (n 14) 20; Ana Bojinović Fenko and Marko Lovec, 'From a Good to a Poor Student: The De-Europeanization of Slovenian Foreign Policy in the Light of (European) Economic and Financial Crisis' [2015] *Etudes helléniques = Hellenic studies* 111.

[94] Andrej Benedejčič, 'Slovenia and its Relations with Russia in the Euro-Atlantic Context' [2016] *Teorija in praksa* 1143.

[95] Makarovič et al (n 25) 208.

motivated and discriminatory political treatment by Brussels-based as well as other Western European political elites.[96] Finally, the EU Commission's lukewarm reaction[97] to the Croatian rejection of the arbitral award on the border delimitation between Slovenia, which was part of Croatia's EU accession conditions overseen by the Commission, fuelled opposition to the EU across the political spectrum as well as in Slovenian society as a whole. In so doing, for the first time since independence the pro-European narrative finds itself under pressure both from the political right and the political left, leaving the viability and success of the process of Europeanisation facing an unprecedented challenge.

This finding might be less concerning when it is considered that mainstream support for European integration among Slovenian elites has always been much more declaratory than genuine.[98] In line with the *homo sovieticus* modus operandi, prevalent during socialist times,[99] in which, as Havel famously observed, appearances were passed as a reality,[100] compliance with EU (law) imperatives was mainly nominal during the crisis. The example of a long-delayed actual implementation of the golden fiscal rule in the Slovenian constitution is a case at hand. In order to fulfil the requirements stemming from the Treaty on Stability, Coordination and Governance in the Economic and Monetary Union (the 'Fiscal Compact')[101] and to constitutionalise the so-called golden fiscal rule, in May 2013 the Slovenian parliament amended Article 148 of the Constitution concerning the budget. However, the actual implementation of the golden fiscal rule, as laid down in the Constitution, was left to the Fiscal Rules Act[102] (an implementing act) which was to be adopted by the National Assembly by a two-thirds majority vote of all deputies.[103] This Act was for tactical political reasons adopted only two years later in June 2015. By so doing Slovenia formally complied with the requirements of EU law, but in practice the fiscal rule was simply not operational, in clear violation of the Constitution and EU law requirements. Finally, when the Act was eventually adopted, the Fiscal Council,[104] which was conceived of and declared as an independent and autonomous state authority vested with powers to supervise and monitor compliance

[96] Patrick Kingsley, 'Safe in Hungary, Viktor Orban Pushes His Message Across Europe' *New York Times* (4 June 2018) www.nytimes.com/2018/06/04/world/europe/viktor-orban-media-slovenia.html (accessed 16 February 2019).

[97] Peter Müller, 'Fueling the Populists, Why Did EU Commission Chief Go Silent in Border Dispute?', https://www.spiegel.de/international/europe/eu-commission-chief-silent-in-slovenia-croatia-dispute-a-1228169.html (accessed 15 May 2019).

[98] Makarovič et al (n 25) 196.

[99] Matej Avbelj, 'Sociology of (Slovenian) Constitutional Democracy' [2017] *Hague Journal on the Rule of Law* 35.

[100] Václav Havel, 'The Power of Powerless' in Vaclav Havel (ed), *Living in Truth* (London, Faber & Faber, 1989) 44.

[101] Treaty on Stability, Coordination and Governance in the Economic and Monetary Union 2012 (also known as the fiscal compact).

[102] Official Gazette of the Republic of Slovenia no 55/15 [2015].

[103] Constitution of the Republic of Slovenia 1991, 2016, Art 148/3.

[104] Fiscal Council of the Republic of Slovenia, www.fs-rs.si/news/ (accessed 8 June 2018).

with fiscal rules, as well as monitoring the implementation of EU legislation regulating economic governance in Member States,[105] was set up in practice as an organisationally extremely weak institution, being de facto deprived of effective means to achieve its statutory mandated objectives.[106]

It should be noted, however, that the European Union, in particular the Commission as its guardian of the treaties, appears to be satisfied with mere formal compliance with EU law, and pays insufficient attention to the extent to which EU law translates into actual practice. This is also confirmed by the number of violations of EU law by Slovenia that have been found by the CJEU. Over the last 15 years of EU membership Slovenia has been convicted of EU law violation altogether in seven cases. All of these, but two,[107] concerned a lack of compliance with EU environmental laws and standards.[108] This confirms that the Commission, and the EU law compliance mechanism ensured by the CJEU in general, is not well suited even to detect, let alone to remedy, systemic rule-of-law or democracy problems in a Member State.[109] The Commission is good at identifying and pursuing single-issue-related cases, but lacks the capacity, as well as the political will, to dig deeper into the actual functioning of Member States until this reaches the level of gravity that threatens to cause serious negative externalities to the EU as a whole.[110]

Admittedly, this is as unsurprising as it is understandable. The EU institutions, the Commission and the Court, have not been set up to police the status and quality of the rule of law and democracy in EU Member States, for it is part and parcel of their membership status that they exist and function as well-ordered societies, acting both as a source of and as a role model for the EU institutions and the countries still aspiring to join the Union. The Commission-instigated procedures on the basis of Article 258 TFEU and consequent rulings of the CJEU have so far, therefore, not had a major impact on the status of

[105] Pursuant to Art 7 of the Fiscal Rules Act [2015].

[106] According to Art 10 of the Fiscal Rules Act ([2015] OJ 55/15) the President of the Fiscal Council shall be employed with the Fiscal Council for at least 50 per cent of full-time employment. The members of the Fiscal Council shall be employed with the Fiscal Council for not more than 50 per cent of full-time employment. Not more than four public employees may be employed by the Fiscal Council, performing expert support for members of the Fiscal Council. Administrative and technical tasks for the Fiscal Council shall be performed by the services of the Court of Audit of the Republic of Slovenia.

[107] C-185/11, *European Commission v Republic of Slovenia* [2012]; C-627/10 *European Commission v Republic of Slovenia* [2013].

[108] See cases C-153/16 *European Commission v Republic of Slovenia* [2017]; C-140/14 *European Commission v Republic of Slovenia* [2015]; C-365/10 *European Commission v Republic of Slovenia* [2011]; C-49/10 *European Commission v Republic of Slovenia* [2010]; C-402/08 *European Commission v Republic of Slovenia* [2009].

[109] Matej Avbelj, 'Pluralism and Systemic Defiance in the European Union' in András Jakab and Dimitry Kochenov (eds), *The Enforcement of EU Law and Values: Ensuring Member States' Compliance* (Oxford, Oxford University Press, 2015).

[110] See *Celmer* case and the Commission's disparate reaction to the Hungarian and Polish attacks on the judiciary.

constitutional democracy in Slovenia. In fact, the soft powers exercised by the European Commission, such as the EU Justice scoreboard,[111] in which Slovenia has continuously scored very low in terms of perceived independence of the judiciary among the general public, business and the judges themselves,[112] might be more efficient by putting informal blame-and-shame pressure on the government to overcome its complacency and adopt the necessary measures.

On the other hand, it should be noted that EU law has made headway, in some respects considerable, in the practices of the Slovenian judiciary. Since 2010 the ordinary courts have been applying EU law much more often. The administrative courts have decided the highest number of EU-law-related cases, concerning matters of international protection (asylum) or protection of constitutional rights. EU law is also widely present in the decisions of civil courts in the field of mutual recognition of judgments in civil matters. Other EU-law-relevant cases have concerned restitution of property confiscated after World War II, where Slovenian courts have consistently ruled that these cases fall ratione temporis outside the scope of EU law.[113] Cases related to value-added tax, customs, European Arrest Warrants in criminal cases, and the determination of citizenship have also increasingly raised EU-law issues, however, without major controversies or potential case-law developments. In addition, the number of preliminary ruling procedures initiated by the Slovenian courts rose from zero in 2009 to 20 in 2018,[114] which also reflects the Slovenian courts' gradual habituation to EU law. This might be particularly true of the Slovenian Constitutional Court.

As has been described in more detail elsewhere,[115] the Constitutional Court has acted as a path-breaker in the judicial implementation of EU law in Slovenia. Despite the small number of EU-law-related cases that has so far reached it, the Court has managed to lay down, albeit in a more implicit and sometimes very modest and abstract manner, the basic principles governing the relationship between national and EU law,[116] although a fully fledged doctrine of the relationship between national and EU law is still lacking. Nevertheless, the Constitutional Court has adopted an explicitly EU-law-friendly attitude. It has often insisted on the centrality of the respect of the principle of loyalty.[117]

[111] EU Justice Scoreboard, https://ec.europa.eu/info/policies/justice-and-fundamental-rights/effective-justice/eu-justice-scoreboard_en (accessed 16 February 2019).

[112] EU Justice Scoreboard (2018) https://ec.europa.eu/info/sites/info/files/justice_scoreboard_2018_en.pdf, 41–42 (accessed 16 February 2019).

[113] Matej Avbelj, 'Slovenska sodišča in postopek za predhodno odločanje' [2009] *Pravna praksa* 9.

[114] https://curia.europa.eu/jcms/upload/docs/application/pdf/2018-04/_ra_2017_en.pdf, 122 (accessed 16 February 2019).

[115] Avbelj (n 56).

[116] Constitutional Court Case U-I-65/13 [2013]; Constitutional Court Case U-II-1/12, U-II-2/12 [2012].

[117] Constitutional Court Case Up-2012/08 [2009]; Constitutional Court Case U-II-1/12, U-II-2/12 [2012].

The Court has, thus, not only declaratorily subscribed to all the structural principles of EU law, including its primacy, but has also applied them in its own practice and mandated the same in the practice of ordinary courts. The gist of this case-law is that the central role in the correct application of EU law in Slovenia has to be played by the ordinary courts and the Supreme Court as the highest judicial authority in Slovenia.[118] On this basis the Constitutional Court has also devised a special division of labour with the ordinary courts that plays a very important role in particular in the protection of rights stemming from the EU Charter of Fundamental Rights (the 'Charter'). By now the Constitutional Court has referred to the Charter several times, but only in passing,[119] without developing any significant case-law on it.

Furthermore, the Constitutional Court has not just explicitly declared itself to be bound by EU law,[120] but it has also proven this in practice by actively engaging in a judicial dialogue with the CJEU. In Decision U-I-295/13 the Constitutional Court for the first time made a reference for a preliminary ruling to the CJEU. That case concerned the constitutionality of a banking law that was adopted as a crisis-management mechanism implementing the instructions (soft law) of the European Commission on the bailing-out of previously private banks and consequent deletion of the shares and subordinate bonds. The CJEU found the applicable EU provisions valid and the Slovenian Constitutional Court, consequently, also approved the national implementing measures.[121] Probably the most far-reaching EU-law-related decision handed down by the Constitutional Court was made at the peak of the economic crisis in December 2012. The Constitutional Court banned a referendum on a statute, which was also indirectly intended to give full effect to the Fiscal Compact.[122] In so doing, the Constitutional Court overrode the constitutional right to a referendum and gave precedence to a financial instrument of EU law. While for some this was just another sign of the Constitutional Court's commitment to EU law, others criticized the case as a token of the Court's bending to the demands of EU institutions and to the neoliberal forces cornering Slovenia during a period of financial duress.[123]

[118] Constitutional Court Case Up-1056/11 [2013]; which was later confirmed in Constitutional Court Case Up-797/14 [2015]; see also Constitutional Court Case Up-150/13 [2014].

[119] Constitutional Court Case U-I-146/07 [2008].

[120] Constitutional Court Case U-I-146/12 [2013].

[121] Constitutional Court Case Case U-I-295/13 [2014]; C-526/14 *Kotnik and Others v National Assembly of Republic of Slovenia* [2016].

[122] Constitutional Court Case U-II-1/12, U-II-2/12 [2012].

[123] Bojan Bugarič, 'Problem v Evropi so socialni demokrati, ki so neoliberalci s 50-odstotnim popustom. Tudi oni verjamejo v neoliberalizem, le še par drobtinic zraven ponujajo ljudem' *Mladina* (15 March 2013) www.mladina.si/141981/dr-bojan-bugaric-problem-v-evropi-so-socialni-demokrati-ki-so-neoliberalci-s-50-odstotnim (accessed 16 February 2019).

IV. CONCLUSION

In light of the above discussion, how can we answer the question if the EU has in any meaningful way contributed to the improvement of the rule of law, democracy, the functioning of economy and human rights protection in Slovenia? The answer can be only multifaceted and certainly not completely unequivocal. It is clear that the process of accession and actual membership of the European Union entailed a formal streamlining of the Slovenian legal order to align it with the rules and principles of EU law. The legal framework within which practices in the four key domains of Slovenia's constitutional democracy can be carried out is thus fully compliant with European standards, certainly on paper. These legal benchmarks have not been disputed, but their relevance and impact in practice have varied. In the pre-accession period these legal benchmarks were indeed taken as the standards of official behaviour. The biggest progress, indeed a breakthrough, under the influence of EU law was thus engendered at the pre-accession stage. Later on, with the celebratory mood setting in, pervaded by a growing complacency of being the best pupil in the class, these formal legal benchmarks started losing their influence. The discrepancy between formal requirements and actual practice started to grow, but EU membership has continued to force the stakeholders in Slovenia to stick to their practice of organised hypocrisy.[124] Even if EU-law-mandated standards have been increasingly losing their grip in practice, the subjects of EU law in Slovenia have had to pretend as if they were still playing by the book, and in so doing they have, both intentionally and unintententionally, continued to entrench EU law, not infrequently even contrary to their genuine intentions.

In this way the European Union has played a double role in Slovenia. On the one hand, it has provided a safety net, preventing practices eroding the rule of law and democracy to fall below the minimum standards agreed on paper. On the other hand and at the same time, EU membership has legitimated those social and political forces that have remained genuinely committed to the pursuit of the rule of law and democracy. In this context, it remains quintessential that the EU institutions execute their competences, and especially those which relate to the fundamental values of the Union, stipulated in Article 2 TEU, with the highest degree of institutional coherence and professional integrity. Every misstep or act of omission by EU institutions kills the hopes of forces supporting the rule of law and democracy, and strengthens those who are intent on undermining these values and who can, by their less than virtuous behaviour, point to the same kind of conduct by EU institutions. In this way, the Commission's discretionary decision not to press the case against Croatia in its border dispute with Slovenia,

[124] To paraphrase Stephen D Krasner, *Sovereignty: Organized Hypocrisy* (Princeton, NJ, Princeton University Press, 1999).

despite an unobjectionable arbitral award under international law, is perceived as an example of an arbitrary application of rule-of-law standards in the Union.

Another clear lesson that trickles from the above discussion of the impact of the Europeanisation on Slovenian constitutional democracy is that the degree and intensity of external oversight by the European Union, especially by the Commission, matters. In the economic domain it is safe to argue that the Slovenian political establishment would never have parted from statist control of the major banks were it not for pressure exerted by the European Commission in the state-aid procedure. Here the European Union has played a role that John Ely described in the context of US constitutional law as a representation-reinforcing approach.[125] It has enabled the at least partial breaking up of the state economic monopoly, in particular in the banking sector, that the majoritarian political process and the mainstream media had had no interest in doing away with it. In that sense the EU has acted as an emancipatory power in a country in which the increasingly fragile, indeed imploded, political spectrum has been much more in the service of a variety of influential factions than of a general interest.

Nevertheless, the fact remains that the systemic problems of Slovenia's constitutional democracy described in this book remain, and are to a certain extent even deteriorating, despite the country's membership of the European Union. While the latter certainly, formally and informally, acts, and is perceived, as a constraint on the most deviant national legal, political and economic practices, many practices remain at the discretion of the political process and have gone largely unaffected by EU membership. More importantly, in the case of Slovenia the EU has several times turned a blind eye to practices that clearly called for more external criticism and oversight. This was, in particular, true during the economic crisis and in its aftermath. Slovenia has long been dragging its feet in terms of making its economy more open, limiting inefficient state ownership and even in complying with the explicit privatisation commitments it gave to the European Commission. However, the latter has practised an extremely lenient approach, tolerating limited or merely formal compliance in a clear desire not to be exposed too much in yet another crisis-ridden country.

This ambition of silencing, rather than assisting in resolving the crisis, has also been combined with ideological political alliances. There has been a lot of misunderstanding, as well as deliberate disregard, by Western political parties and European political families of what their eponymous political parties in Eastern Europe, including in Slovenia, actually stand for. As we have argued in more detail elsewhere, due to Eastern Europe's totalitarian communist experience, the post-communist Member States present not just different epistemic, but indeed profoundly different social sites. This has gone unnoticed by the old Member States' political elites, who have also deliberately, in order to secure the

[125] John Hart Ely, *Democracy and Distrust: A Theory of Judicial Review* (Cambridge, MA, Harvard University Press 1981) 101–04.

necessary supranational political majorities, played along on with the presupposition that the political labels of liberalism, socialism and conservativism come with the same substance and practices on both sides of the former iron curtain.[126]

In the case of Slovenia this has created a situation in which the capture of the state by the post-communist left and their economic allies has gone uncriticised, unsanctioned and has been taken as part of the new normal of the slightly peculiar Slovenian capitalist model. In this way it has gone unrecognised that exactly due to this economic model the state of constitutional democracy, the remaining space for pluralism and non-arbitrariness, ie two of the constitutive elements of democracy and the rule of law, might be even narrower than in a polity such as Orbán's Hungary. There a particular party has taken over all the institutions of the state, but it has failed to seize the economy, as this still remains dispersed in private hands. In Hungary, and in Poland too, the economic pluralism created post-1990 acts as a guarantee of societal and political pluralism, whereas the latter is considerably more constrained in Slovenia in the conditions of pervasive economic state-owned monism.

Finally, especially since the outbreak of the economic crisis and a parallel derailment of the Slovenian political process, which has provoked a general sentiment of social dispiritment, the EU has provided an escape route to all those who have failed to secure their living in Slovenia or simply could no longer stand the pervasive practices of dirty-togetherness. The number of people leaving Slovenia in 2017 is double the number in 2004.[127] However, these figures alone do not reveal that among those leaving the country, the highest proportion are the young and the most qualified, which means that Slovenia is losing its most productive and qualified generations. This is, however, yet another guarantee that the politics of the status quo, even when subject to the conditions of EU membership, and sometimes thanks to it, is unlikely to change even in the longer run. The prospects for Slovenia's constitutional democracy therefore remain relatively dim, making it most probable that the country will remain a flawed democracy.[128] It might not be the worst performing Member State in the European Union, but it will certainly not be a poster-child either.

[126] Matej Avbelj, 'Transformation in the Eye of the Beholder' in Michal Bobek (ed), *Central European Judges under the European Influence: The Transformative Power of the EU Revisited* (Oxford, Hart Publishing, 2015) 278.

[127] Statistical Office of the Republic of Slovenia, https://pxweb.stat.si/pxweb/Dialog/Saveshow.asp.

[128] 'Democracy Index 2018: Me Too? Political Participation, Protest and Democracy' *The Economist* (2019) 17.

12

The Case for a Resilient Constitutional Democracy

Freedom should be social life itself, should be the reality of our life.[1]

I. THE CONCENTRIC CIRCLES OF WESTERN DEMOCRATIC DECAY

This book has asked a question about the particularities of constitutional backsliding in Slovenia. More specifically, the question has been posed with two overall objectives in mind. First, to expose the specificity of the Slovenian decline in the rule of law and democracy. Second, to learn some lessons from the less researched Slovenian case and to extrapolate these to the broader region of Central and Eastern Europe. In the final chapter we shall draw some conclusions from this extrapolating exercise, not just for Central and Eastern Europe, but for the European Union and the Council of Europe as a whole, which have in recent years come under significant economic and political strain.

The Slovenian case can neither be analyzed nor understood in isolation from its broader environment. Slovenia is just one concentric circle, embraced by the outer circles of Central and Eastern Europe, the European Union and what has traditionally been known in post-World War II vernacular as the West. These concentric circles stand for distinctive epistemic and political sites, which requires a context-specific and hence analytically nuanced approach to them. Hasty generalisations should be thus avoided, including, and in particular, falling prey to a belief that eponymous phenomena, ie those that carry the same names, also contain the same substantive content across all the countries of the EU, let alone of the West.[2] A lot can be, and indeed has been, lost in translation in analysing the recent process of constitutional democratic decline across Europe.[3] At the same time this is not to argue that the crisis of constitutional democracy across all

[1] Jože Pučnik, *Članki in spomini 1957–1985* (Maribor, Obzorja, 1986) 29, quoted in Dean Komel, 'Jože Pučnik: Personal Freedom, Culture, and Politics' (2014) 43(1) *Traditiones* 125, 126.

[2] See Matej Avbelj, 'Transformation in the Eye of the Beholder' in Michal Bobek (ed), *Central European Judges Under the European Influence* (Oxford, Hart Publishing, 2015) 275.

[3] ibid 290.

the concentric circles of the Western democratic world does not exhibit some shared, universal features, common to the West as a whole.

The most universal feature, the common factor that has triggered the crisis of constitutional democracy in the West, was the financial crisis starting in 2008 with the collapse of the Lehman Brothers, which spread across the West, hitting the European Union particularly hard between 2009 and 2013. The outbreak of the financial crisis soon resulted in a notable decline in the output legitimacy of Western democracies. The democratic processes and the democratically elected governments on the top of them could no longer ensure or deliver the economic and social prosperity anticipated by their constituents. If unfulfilled expectations are just another name for a crisis, the financial crisis soon mutated into a crisis of constitutional democracy.

The stagnation, or even decline, in living standards, reduced welfare rights and rising unemployment, in particular among the youth, spurred two natural political reactions in the constituencies of Western democracies. First, 'the people' started to look for culprits. Who has done this to us? Second, 'the people' demanded solutions. Who is going to dig us out of this economic despair, and how? Or, in those countries less severely hit by the crisis, who is going to deliver for us the prosperity we have been promised, and how? As is well known, history teaches us that the greatest political success in answering these questions is reaped by those politicians who offer the simplest answers to the hardest questions, simultaneously putting the blame for the crisis on internal and external political enemies. In so doing, populism has been born.

The central element of populism is its fixation on the people.[4] Populism is from the people for the people, where 'people' is understood in specific way. What is at stake is not the entire demos, a people, but only the part of it that is culturally homogeneous[5] and morally sound: the right people.[6] Hence, populists need to create their people first, by carving their own people from the people as a whole.[7] This is done through the social construction of reality, in which the media play a decisive role by fostering a moralist account of politics.[8] This distinguishes neatly between the morally impeccable, our people, and all the others, who in the populists' own judgement do not live up to those unilaterally imposed moral expectations.[9] In so doing, populism invests heavily in an emotional way of doing politics, breeding, in particular, negative emotions that are capable of creating and deepening the schism in the population, between us

[4] Jan-Werner Müller, *What Is Populism?* (Philadelphia, University of Pennsylvania Press, 2016).
[5] Ernesto Laclau, *On Populist Reason* (London, Verso, 2005) 11.
[6] Jan-Werner Müller, 'The People Must Be Extracted from Within the People: Reflections on Populism' (2014) 21(4) *Constellations* 483, referring to Claude Lefort and David Macey, *Democracy and Political Theory* (Cambridge, Polity, 1988) 88.
[7] ibid.
[8] ibid 11.
[9] ibid 12.

and them;[10] between common or normal people and various deviant, in one way or another, elites. These corrupt elites have corrupted society which therefore requires purification. Populism is therefore about the fight against corruption,[11] imposing a single and exclusively right moral code on the population as a whole. If there is any ideological essence to populism – which many deny, and the alleged almost perfect ideological malleability of populism may also explain its great success[12] – this is, as Müller has argued, monism or principled anti-pluralism.[13] Diversity is thus considered as bad, something that takes away from the purity of the people and is a threat to our singular moral code, which in turn can and must be defended by all means, whatever it takes.

The most important means for fighting corruption relentlessly is replacing the corrupt people, as widely as possible, with our own, loyal, morally pure people. This clientelism with a clean moral conscience, as Müller again has labelled it,[14] does not eradicate corruption; at best, it only supplants the corruption of other people with that of our kind. In this way, the political project of populism ultimately and plainly fails to achieve its proclaimed objectives. This is not a tragedy for populism, a sign of its theoretical incoherence, since these proclaimed objectives are not more than just proclaimed. The gist of populism, as of any other anti-democratic movement, is namely power for power's own sake.

To make this less than vulgar objective appear (more) legitimate, populism desperately looks for justification. Historically we have distinguished between different kinds of populism: socio-economic, xenophobic and nationalist.[15] The latter is justified in the name of the overall good of the people, the people's very identity. This is its trump card; but Christian values, protection of the family and marriage might be useful to strengthen nationalist populist appeal too. Fear against the other, strangers and the threats they bring, in particular security threats, fuels xenophobic populism, which often, but not always, works hand in hand with nationalism and is sometimes even indistinguishable from it. Socioeconomic populism, on the other hand, defends the values and the interests of the unprivileged classes (typically labour, but historically also the agrarian class) promising their redemption and emancipation. However, almost unexceptionally, the values advocated by different populist movements are not relied upon due to a sincere commitment to

[10] Nicolas Demertzis, 'Emotions and Populism' in Simon Clarke, Paul Hoggett and Simon Thompson (eds), *Emotions, Politics and Society* (London, Palgrave Macmillan, 2006).

[11] Müller (n 6) 11.

[12] Cas Mudde and Cristóbal Rovira Kaltwasser, *Populism* (Oxford, Oxford University Press, 2013) 498–499.

[13] Müller (n 6) 17.

[14] ibid 22.

[15] On historically different kind of populisms, see Mudde and Kaltwasser (n 12) 495–97; see also Cristóbal Rovira Kaltwasser, *Populism vs Constitutionalism? Comparative Perspectives on Contemporary Western Europe, Latin America, and the United States* (Oxford, Foundation for Law, Justice and Society, 2013).

them; rather they are used instrumentally, in open self-contradiction and self-denial, just to pay lip-service, to window-dress and to create a smokescreen concealing the concentration of power in the hands of the few in the name of the many.

II. IN PURSUIT OF A RESILIENT CONSTITUTIONAL DEMOCRACY

To what an extent a constitutional democracy is able to resist internal and external political shocks provoked by a decline in its output legitimacy and not bend to the rise of populism depends on its resilience. The resilience of a constitutional democracy is, however, in turn dependent on at least three factors.

First, any constitutional democracy hinges to a degree on its actual institutionalization. A country that features robust, meritocratic, independent and professional legislative and executive institutions, which are guaranteed by professional political parties and a corresponding viable political class; a country that boasts of a qualified, professional, well-remunerated, and hence independent judiciary with integrity; a country which has a vibrant, diverse, pluralist and relatively affluent civil society that essentially is also served by pluralist media committed to a high level of journalistic professionalism, will be, as a rule, far less affected by the political shocks of a declining output legitimacy than a country whose political, administrative, judicial, civil society and media institutions are weak. In short, a constitutional democracy which is better institutionalised across the political, administrative, judicial, civil society and media spheres is less likely to quickly and/or extensively succumb to the disintegrative forces of populism.

Second, the resilience of a constitutional democracy is determined also by the degree of civic awareness and active citizenship supporting a democratic constituency. This is itself dependent on the existence of a large middle class, which is in economic terms affluent enough to care not just about its imminent economic survival and quotidian private affairs, but can and is interested in devoting some of its time, energy and financial resources to the pursuit of public affairs too. The presence of such a middle class is a social source of stability of the above-mentioned institutions of constitutional democracy.[16] The members of the middle (as well as upper-middle class) are the driving force behind civil society; they are the primary audience and a financial resource supporting serious journalism; and through their civic and political engagement contribute to

[16] OECD, 'Under Pressure: The Squeezed Middle Class' (2019) www.oecd.org/social/under-pressure-the-squeezed-middle-class-689afed1-en.htm (accessed 24 April 2019): 'The middle class has shrunk in most OECD countries as it has become more difficult for younger generations to make it to the middle class, defined as earning between 75% and 200% of the median national income. While almost 70% of baby boomers were part of middle-income households in their twenties, only 60% of millennials are today.'

the existence of professional, moderate, centrist political parties and ensure their long-term institutional viability. The weakening of the middle class translates into a weaker civil society, a decline in serious journalism and enfeeblement of center-gravitating political parties.

Third, the resilience, indeed existence, of a constitutional democracy is finally dependent on the presence of a vibrant economy based on dispersed private ownership. The latter is a guarantee of economic pluralism, which is at the base of a social and consequently also political pluralism, in whose absence a constitutional democracy cannot exist. As this book has argued, constitutional democracy derives from and protects equal human dignity. Its essence is a right to self-actualisation, self-fulfilment within the scope of equal rights of others that is, in our inevitably imperfect material world, dependent on economic resources. The more monopolised these are, the fewer individuals are able to pursue their right to self-fulfilment, the less actually pluralist, in civil and political terms, and also the less democratic such a society will be. Economic monopoly translates into civil society, media and political monopoly, which gradually removes the system of checks and balances and eventually dismantles constitutional democracy altogether.

III. WHY IS THE EAST MORE FRAGILE THAN THE WEST?

The disparate impact of populism and constitutional backsliding in Europe can thus be generally explained with the help of three constitutive variables of a constitutional democracy: institutionalisation; civic awareness and active citizenship; and finally economic pluralism. While all across Europe a trend of destabilisation of constitutional democracy and the rise of populism can be observed, the CEE countries have been affected by it much more than their Western European counterparts. Due to their shorter democratic tradition, which began only after the fall of the Berlin wall and was also prior to the World War II very weak or even non-existent, the degree of institutionalisation of constitutional democracy in Central and Eastern Europe is generally lower than in Western Europe. The same applies to civic awareness and active citizenship, where in CEE countries the traits of *homo sovieticus* clearly continue to persist.[17] Also economic pluralism, the dispersal of wealth and with it the existence of several centres of economic and political power, which are necessary for the checks and balances in society, are in general still better ensured in the West than in Central and Eastern Europe. The same can be said of the presence or relative absence of the middle class. All of this explains why Western European countries, even when some of them, such as Greece, Portugal and

[17] Lev Dmitrievich Gudkov, '"Soviet Man" in the Sociology of Iurii Levada' (2008) 47(6) *Sociological Research* 6.

even Ireland, suffered severely from the global financial crisis, have not upended their constitutional democracies to the same extent as has been happening in Hungary or Poland.

Nevertheless, this is not to argue that Hungary and Poland are constitutionally the worst performing countries in Europe. They have, admittedly, attracted the most international media and supranational political as well as judicial and academic attention,[18] but the latter fact alone does not necessarily tell us much about the actual state of constitutionally democratic affairs in other CEE Member States. For example, the state of constitutional democracy in Romania and Bulgaria might be even more fragile than in Hungary and Poland, given that the two countries, while full members of the EU, still operate under the auspices of a verification mechanism. Similarly, to distinguish other CEE countries, such as Croatia, Czechia and the Slovak Republic, from the most criticised cases of Hungary and Poland would require a close sociological case study of all these countries.

With regard to Slovenia, this book has argued that the country is set apart from all other CEE countries by its specific model of state-owned capitalism. This has resulted in the absence of economic pluralism, which hence stands in the way of all other forms of social pluralism, including the existence of a vibrant pluralist civil society and professional pluralist media, all of which consequently translates into the decline of citizens' civic engagement. The relatively small size of the country and the increasing weakness of the state's formal institutional infrastructure have enabled strong factional groups in the context of the growing passivity of the electorate to create a parallel infrastructure of decision-making which uses the formal institutions of the state as an instrument for their ongoing economic enrichment and further entrenchment of their de facto political power. In Slovenia, unlike in Hungary and Poland where we can still observe incessant political attempts to conquer the formal institutions of the state, control over and the occupancy of the formal institutions are much less important since power lurks in the economic monopoly of the state and private companies attached to it. In this way, the state of constitutional democracy in Slovenia is in a worse condition than in Hungary and Poland.

The rulers in these two countries apparently still strive for the formal capture of the state in order to gain access and control over the privatised and hence

[18] See eg Jan-Werner Müller, 'Should the EU Protect Democracy and the Rule of Law Inside Member States?' (2015) 21(2) *European Law Journal* 141; Bojan Bugarič and Alenka Kuhelj, 'Varieties of Populism in Europe: Is the Rule of Law in Danger?' (2018) 10(1) *Hague Journal on the Rule of Law* 21; Dimitry Kochenov and Laurent Pech, 'Better Late than Never: On the European Commission's Rule of Law Framework and its First Activation' (2016) 54(5) *Journal of Common Market Studies* 1062; Bojan Bugarič, 'The Rule of Law Derailed: Lessons from the Post-Communist World' (2015) 7(2) *Hague Journal on the Rule of Law* 175; Bojan Bugarič, 'A Crisis of Constitutional Democracy in Post-Communist Europe: "Lands in-between" Democracy and Authoritarianism' (2015) 13(1) *International Journal of Constitutional Law* 219; R Daniel Kelemen and Mitchell A Orenstein, 'Europe's Autocracy Problem: Polish Democracy Final Days?' *Foreign Affairs* (7 January 2016).

presently still pluralist economy. Alas, in Slovenia control over the monopolised economy has been ensured from the very beginning. All 'political' efforts in Slovenia are hence directed at preserving this control in order to hamper the development of social pluralism, which could eventually bring about a political change resulting in winning over of the formal institutions by individuals, who might actually end up constraining and eventually even ending the decisive influence of the informal infrastructure on Slovenia's constitutional democracy. The state capture in Slovenia has thus progressed much further than in Hungary and Poland. The regimes in these two states have still so much to do, especially with regard to subordinating the formal institutions of the state, which explains their more explicit authoritarian mode of governing. By contrast, in the more 'progressive' Slovenia, where formal institutions have long been in the service of informal interests closely connected to the state-run economy, there is simply no need for authoritarian pushes. The mission has been accomplished and all that it takes now is to preserve and entrench its achievements. While the regimes in Hungary and Poland first need to turn the two countries into autocracies, Slovenia only needs to continue performing as a kleptocracy. Hence, due to the softness of its kleptocratic approach, Slovenia is, not unexpectedly, attracting far less international attention than the rogue Hungarian and Polish rulers do. However, to conclude on the basis of the appearance of hardness or softness of their constitutional decline that Hungary and Poland are therefore worse off than Slovenia could not be further from the truth.

Generally, Slovenia has been in this respect a particular example as it does not fall directly into the category of populist erosion of constitutional democracy. On a declarative level, it has introduced normative standards of constitutional democracy and the rule of law. Nonetheless, its institutional and informal elites have turned a blind eye to questionable – old – practices such as corruption, nepotism and 'dirty togetherness'. As a rule, they have protected their status quo, privileges and interests, thereby simultaneously undermining the values and principles of constitutional democracy. In contrast to other CEE countries, as previously pointed out, the post-transitional elites have together with the nouveau riche elites maintained control of democratic institutions in Slovenia ever since its democratisation and independence. As the preceding chapters have explained, those elites have successfully sought to subordinate to themselves almost every institution in the Slovenian state and public administration. As a result, they have only declaratively followed the Weberian bureaucracy model, whereas they have behind the scenes protected and advanced their parochial interests. The Slovenian constitutional democracy is therefore an example of formal and informal networks of vested interests resulting in cronyism and business as usual. Nonetheless, populism has in recent years emerged in the Slovenian public space, where it has been taken up by some political parties which have, not unsurprisingly, also often preached and practised loyalty over meritocracy. They have eagerly embraced the questionable rhetoric of illiberal democracies, so often employed by the governmental elites in Hungary and Poland, and have even allowed for their direct interference in the Slovenian media space.[19] As a result, all of those traits of Slovenia's constitutional democracy have rendered state institutions and public administration weak, vulnerable and dependent, and thereby ready to please respective incumbent governments. As a rule, persons in those institutions have hardly been able to fully protect the values of constitutional democracy such as human dignity, freedom, equality, solidarity and pluralism. The judiciary has, in particular, turned a blind eye to ensuring the right to fair, impartial and independent trial.[20] By contrast, public employees and public officials have not been able or willing to entirely embrace the values of constitutional democracy in the light of a dominant presence of old habits and old ways of doing business. All in all, they have failed to fully advance the rule of law and human rights protections in order to realise the common good over furthering their private interests. As a result, Slovenia could be therefore described as a formal constitutional democracy caught somewhere in between the old corrupt practices and the recent populist movements in Hungary and Poland.

IV. DEMOCRATIC AND ACADEMIC DECAY

Some of the rogue CEE regimes have now been in power for quite a long time; Orbán has now governed for a whole decade. In Slovenia there has never been a meaningful change, and the same could be said of Romania, Bulgaria, Slovakia or CEE countries emerging from the former Soviet Union. Such a long existence of a regime deviating quite strongly from an ideal of constitutional democracy causes systemic and structural changes in the society that are not easy to undo rapidly. This conclusion is exacerbated further when a country in question has never actually scored high on a scale measuring the quality of democracy. In these countries the regimes not only take over all the institutions of the state, but start monopolising economic power, with the help of which they conquer the media, win over civil society and gradually contribute to the transformation of the civic identity of people living under such a deformed democratic regime. In short, the longer an anti-democracy movement lasts, the more institutionalized it becomes.

[19] See eg Bálint Magyar, *Post-Communist Mafia State: The Case of Hungary* (Budapest, New York, Central European University and Noran Libro, 2016). See also Frane Adam, 'The Relevance of Social Capital and Intermediary Structures for the Creation of Systemic Competitiveness: Some Lessons from Southern and Eastern-Central Europe' (1998) 14(26) *Družboslovne Razprave* 48.

[20] Jan Zobec and Jernej Letnar Černič, 'The Remains of the Authoritarian Mentality within the Slovene Judiciary' in Michal Bobek (ed), *Central European Judges Under the European Influence: The Transformative Power of the EU Revisited* (Oxford, Hart Publishing, 2015); Jan Zobec, 'Slovenia: Just a Glass Bead Game?' in Iulia Motoc and Ineta Ziemele (eds), *The Impact of the ECHR on Democratic Change in Central and Eastern Europe: Judicial Perspectives* (Cambridge, Cambridge University Press, 2016).

The exact scope of the actual depth of the anti-democratic transformation of societies in these states will become apparent only in due course and ex post facto. As the process is under way, we can only have a patchy understanding of it. Nevertheless, in recent years a new trend, previously nonexistent, has started to emerge in the scholarship addressing the problem of democratic backsliding. There is a growing number of scholars from the affected countries, who either because they are benefiting (economically) from the regimes in these states or for ideological reasons, are increasingly willing to justify these non-democratic processes and abuses of the rule of law. However, this is not being done by advancing an alternative paradigm of 'democracy', such as illiberal or Christian democracy, but by relativising the allegedly contested concepts of democracy and the rule of law altogether and applying them, in this relativised manner, to the disputed facts on the ground. The outcome is theoretically and practically perverse. If we cannot settle on a single meaning of democracy and the rule of law, and history and constitutional mores prove that there are many ways to do democracy and exercise the rule of law, then we do not have an objective criterion against which we measure the political facts of an actual democratic and rule-of-law decline. In this manner, we simply cannot say whether, or to what an extent, the allegedly anti-democratic countries are actually anti-democratic. In this case, academic fairness and political correctness require deference to the disputed regimes, essentially saying the each country can have it its own way, so that, eventually, anything goes. This can go even so far as claiming that the contested CEE regimes have simply developed their own version of constitutionalism, which, in turn essentially not only legitimises them in their political pursuits, but makes these, despite objections from the EU and Western states, which practice their own Western constitutionalism, also legal and constitutional.[21]

V. MAKING THE CASE FOR A RESILIENT CONSTITUTIONAL DEMOCRACY

The crisis of constitutional democracy, with its many faces across the European Union and the West, should be addressed by adopting both short-term and long-term measures, acting simultaneously on national and supranational planes. The measures remedying the short-term crisis are most directly related to stimulating economic growth, which is the source of prosperity that is the ultimate measure of output democratic legitimacy. Political systems across the European Union should again deliver greater economic welfare for the greatest number,

[21] For a critique, see Matej Avbelj, 'There Is No Such Thing as a Particular "Center and Eastern European Constitutionalism"' *Verfassungsblog* (18 May 2018) https://verfassungsblog.de/there-is-no-such-thing-as-a-particular-center-and-eastern-european-constitutionalism/ (accessed 24 April 2019).

rather than only for the few at the expense of the middle class. This requires the implementation of economic reforms on supranational and national levels. Ever since the outbreak of the global financial crisis the EU has been on a reforming path.[22] This was first paved by ad hoc measures, which were later replaced by more systemic measures. In this regard, the deepening of the monetary union with the banking union, and launching of the fiscal union and investing, admittedly very cautiously, in the social union are important steps that could ensure sustainable EU-wide economic growth and, perhaps even more importantly, prevent the kind of economic cataclysm experienced between 2009 and 2013. Simultaneously, the Member States should, within the framework of supranational economic governance, follow suit by increasing their competitiveness and simultaneously building welfare nets for those who are worse off. In so doing, the democratic output legitimacy could be preserved at a level that is sufficiently high to take the wind from the political sails of the populists, deprive the radical political parties on both sides of the extreme of their appeal, and strengthen the centre.

However, economic utility is just one layer of output legitimacy. The practice and feeling of security is important too. It is here that the EU, with its reinforced external border control and overall enhancement of the functioning of the area of freedom, security and justice, could contribute a lot to the actual and perceived loss of security among the people across the Union, and by so doing remove another potent and inflammatory political issue from the populists' agenda.

Nevertheless, economic and security reforms tailored to increasing output legitimacy in the shorter term should be complemented by structural reforms of a more lasting character too. These should address the three building blocks of constitutional democracy: the institutions, civic awareness and engagement, and economic pluralism. As in case of economic, short-term reforms, here too the actions should take place on both the supranational and national planes.

The EU could have much to offer in all three dimensions of the national institutional functioning. In political terms the EU political parties and its leaders, in particular within the European Council as the EU's foremost and strongest political institution, should lead by example and stimulate good political practices across the EU's federal laboratory. In case of violations of the fundamental values of the Union, the European political parties would be obliged to apply peer pressure to members from countries in which they have engaged in activities detrimental to constitutional democracy. If necessary, political sanctions could be imposed too, in terms of either suspension or expulsion of the rogue political party. Only recently has a major European political party decided to take such a sanctioning step; in general, the attitude of appeasement or explicit defence of

[22] For an overview, see Matej Avbelj, 'What Future for the European Union', WZB Discussion Paper SP IV 2017-802.

rogue national politicians has prevailed. In so doing, an opportunity of exercising political checks and balances has been missed to act earlier, constraining national political parties from engaging in policies that would systematically undermine the fundamental values of constitutional democracy.

The EU also has important leverage in contributing to the viability of constitutional democracy through its administrative branch. The European Commission, as the guardian of the treaties, should be committed to a principled approach in tackling the alleged cases of departure from the values of Article 2 TFEU. Its approach must be systematic, irrespective of the size of the country as well as of transnational political alliances, which are of course also reflected in the composition and internal functioning of the more democratic, but hence also far more political, Commission. The Commission has at its disposal both informal and diplomatic means for stimulating good practices and dissuading bad ones. However, the formal measures, such as the use of Article 258 as well triggering of Article 7 procedures should not be shied away from either. Perhaps the utilization of Article 258, which is less explicit in political terms, could despite its case-by-case focus generate better outcomes, than the far more politicised, notorious and hence controversial Article 7 procedure. Furthermore, the European Commission is just one part of the EU's expanding administrative branch. An important role in it is also played by the system of comitology. This administrative, expert-based deliberative framework, while hidden away from the public eyes, probably does not have huge potential for a wide democratisation of the EU,[23] but does play an influential role in transnational socialisation of national bureaucrats. Through involvement in the creation of EU executive legal acts and other bylaws, the administrators from all Member States are engaged into deliberative practices, which could again provide an avenue for stimulating good and constraining bad practices in the field of constitutional democracy by raising awareness among national administrators and exercising peer pressure on the representatives of less well performing Member States.

In judicial terms, there again is room for informal stimulation of good practices, constitutional democracy-enhancing attitudes through transnational judicial cooperation, conferences, meetings and symposia. However, the CJEU notably plays an important role in formally adjudicating cases and controversies in infringement and preliminary ruling procedures. The Court admittedly cannot select its cases, as these are brought by the litigants; but its jurisprudence nevertheless should be aware of the systemic importance (or potential) of the individual cases and should hence be conducted with the utmost care, coherence, persuasiveness and highest quality of reasoning, expressing a commitment to the fundamental values of constitutional democracy, rather than, in a somewhat

[23] Christian Joerges and Jürgen Neyer, 'From Intergovernmental Bargaining to Deliberative Political Processes: The Constitutionalisation of Comitology' (2002) 3(3) *European Law Journal* 273.

politically circumscribed manner, showing deference to national authorities. Nevertheless, the courts are not omnipotent institutions. We ought to be aware of their institutional limitations and curb our expectations from them accordingly, lest we risk disappointment, or even worse a judicial overreach that would be grossly corrosive of the Court's legitimacy. The courts can, at best, constrain populism in a piecemeal fashion, reasserting fundamental constitutional values, but their wholesale defence and institutionalization is in the hands of political and broader social processes, taking place in particular, if not exclusively, on the national level.

The European Union can help contributing to pro-constitutional democracy forces in the national political and civic environment both through the use of soft power mechanisms and by spending its, admittedly limited, financial resources. Soft power mechanisms are coordination initiatives which involve national governments and NGOs alike in a model of a federal laboratory in which via peer pressure they stimulate good democratic and rule-of-law practices. This kind of supranational approach requires the national stakeholders, including those from disobedient Member States, to engage in a supranational debate, in a process of public justification of their respective national measures, which can help smoke out illegitimate interests, creating pressure on corrosive national democratic practices and, indirectly, helping those political and civic groups that fight for the reinforcement of constitutional democracy. In terms of EU financial stimulus, the approach of carrot and stick can be used. Within the framework of the EU cohesion policy, programmes for the enhancement of rule of law and democracy on the national level could be financed by the EU and run by the national civil society groups. On the other hand, any receipt of EU funds should be subject to compliance with fundamental rule-of-law and democracy standards, as has indeed been proposed in the forthcoming EU financial framework. Last but not least, within the scope of its economic governance competences the EU could also stimulate those national policies that favour privatisation, and dispersed economic ownership as opposed to economic monopolies; as well as encouraging those reforms, including with some supranational economic stimulus, that foster the preservation of the middle class, while simultaneously creating welfare safety nets for the most economically deprived.

VI. WHAT CAN THE COUNCIL OF EUROPE ADD TO ITS EXISTING ACTIVITIES TO STRENGTHEN THE RESILIENCE OF CONSTITUTIONAL DEMOCRACY IN CEE COUNTRIES?

The Council of Europe has been, as pointed out in Chapter 10, one of the pillars of constitutional democracy, the rule of law and human rights protection in Europe. As a rule, it has contributed to normative reforms in CEE countries. The ECtHR and the Venice Commission have in particular generated positive change in the normative frameworks of constitutional democracy, the rule of law and the human rights protection.[24] Nonetheless, the recent normative influence of the ECtHR has not always been positive as, for example, Kosař observes in respect of the functioning of the Judiciary Councils in CEE countries.[25] In some respects, the external actors can undermine the rule of law given the particularities of environments in CEE countries. Interestingly, the ECtHR has increasingly encountered several hurdles in the execution of its judgments and has in some cases even held that it cannot be responsible for the proper implementation of its judgments in domestic legal systems.[26] Although such case-law is inconclusive, the way forward for the ECtHR lies in its proactive role and applying pressure on domestic authorities to execute its judgments.

On the other hand, the positive impact has been less apparent in the application of the values and principles of constitutional democracy on the daily functioning of domestic institutions and public administrations, particularly in CEE countries. As a result, normative reforms have not been translated into daily practices of the majority of state institutions and public administration in most CEE countries.[27] As a rule, the impact of the Council of Europe on constitutional democracy and rule of law has not been as transformative as expected, since it has not properly addressed the major deficiencies in their exercise in the daily practice of public and private spheres.

The normative reforms have encountered strong resistance from the existing authoritarian mentality, old practices and the status quo. The values of their various constitutional democracies have not been fully internalised in the mindsets of people living and working in CEE societies. As a result, the Council of Europe could enhance its existing activities to strengthen the resilience of constitutional democracy in CEE countries, in particular by strengthening efforts to proceed with practical reforms of the performance, fairness and transparency of state institutions and public administration. In so doing, it can augment and enhance its efforts to supervise the execution of ECtHR judgments in the domestic constitutional systems of CEE countries. Some efforts have been recently already made in this direction particularly after the adoption of protocol 14 to the ECHR.[28] Additionally, the ECtHR confirmed in a recent judgment its

[24] See eg Jernej Letnar Černič, 'Impact of the European Court of Human Rights on the Rule of Law in Central and Eastern Europe' (2018) 10(1) *Hague Journal on the Rule of Law* 111.

[25] David Kosař, 'Nudging Domestic Judicial Reforms from Strasbourg: How the European Court of Human Rights Shapes Domestic Judicial Design' (2017) 13(1) *Utrecht Law Review* 112; David Kosař, 'Beyond Judicial Councils: Forms, Rationales and Impact of Judicial Self Governance in Europe' (2018) 19(7) *German Law Journal* 1567.

[26] *Burmych and others v Ukraine* no 46852/13, 47786/13, 54125/13, 56605/13 and 3653/14 (ECtHR 12 October 2017). See also Helen Keller and Cedric Marti, 'Reconceptualizing Implementation: The Judicialization of the Execution of the European Court of Human Rights' Judgments' (2015) 26(4) *European Journal of International Law* 829.

[27] See eg Letnar Černič (n 24); Martin Mendelski, 'Europeanization of Good Governance in Romania: Where and Why Does it Fail, and What Can Be Done About it?' (1 March 2017), https://ssrn.com/abstract=2926871.

[28] See also recent efforts by the European Implementation Network, www.einnetwork.org/implementation-activities (accessed 24 April 2019). See also eg Elisabeth Lambert, 'The First

responsibility to oversee implementation of its judgments in domestic systems.[29] It straightforwardly submitted that 'failure to implement a final, binding judicial decision would be likely to lead to situations incompatible with the principle of the rule of law'.[30] Those new developments are a silver lining on the horizon, but need to be translated to the domestic systems. The Venice Commission could also intensify its oversight over the implementation of its recommendations and should increase cooperation with some international financial organisations, eg the World Bank and the International Monetary Fund. In this aspect, these financial institutions could further make their loans and aid conditional on fully fledged normative reforms and their translation into practice.

The Council of Europe as a whole should make more efforts and combat the arbitrary abuses of the rule of law and human rights that are so prevalent in some CEE countries. In general, it should move beyond making general recommendation on the state of the rule of law in Member States. By contrast, it should concentrate on concrete efforts to enhance the levels of constitutional democracy and rule of law in clearly designated Member States. The Parliamentary Assembly of the Council of Europe should take unequivocal stances towards the potential and actual conflicts of interests and alleged arbitrary practices of some of its deputies. For instance, it could cooperate with the European Commission to oversee the fairness, independence and impartiality of the most notorious judicial proceedings in Member States, such as proceedings dealing with corruption and organised crime involving members of formal and informal networks. The Council of Europe could, with the assistance of the European Union, translate its Cooperation and Verification Mechanism for Bulgaria and Romania also to CEE countries beyond EU Member States.[31] Nonetheless, these or similar oversight mechanisms should be strengthened and be granted wide-reaching and binding competences.[32] Similarly, the institutions of the Council of Europe should extend and strengthen their capacity to deliver training and workshops to public employees and officials in state institutions of CEE countries. They should establish a task force that would efficiently address rule-of-law challenges across Central and Eastern Europe.

Infringements Proceedings Within the European System of Human Rights: Using the Court as the Last Bastion for the Credibility of the Council of Europe' (2018) (4) *European Human Rights Law Review* 325; Fiona de Londras and Kanstantsin Dzehtsiarou, 'Mission Impossible? Addressing non-execution through infringement proceedings in the European Court of Human Rights' 66(2) *ICLQ* 467.

[29] See *Ilgar Mammadov v Azerbajdian* no 15172/13 (ECtHR, 29 May 2019).

[30] ibid para 215.

[31] See eg Laurent Pech, Vlad Perju and Sébastien Platon, 'How to Adress Rule of Law Backsliding in Romania: The Case for an Infringement Action Based on Article 325 TFEU' *Verfassungsblog* (29 May 2019) https://verfassungsblog.de/how-to-adress-rule-of-law-backsliding-in-romania/ (accessed 24 April 2019).

[32] Georgi Dimitrov, Kaloyan Haralampiev and Stoycho Stoychev, 'The Adventures of the CVM in Bulgaria and Romania' (August 2016) MaXCaP Project, no 29,; Martin Mendelski, 'The EU's Pathological Power: The Failure of External Rule of Law Promotion in South Eastern Europe' (2015) 39(3) *Southeastern Europe* 318.

As far the EU Member States from Central and Eastern Europe are concerned, the Council of Europe should work closely with the European Commission and the other institutions in order to subject access to the EU cohesion funds to respect for constitutional democracy, the rule of law and human rights. They should coordinate the adoption of measures necessary to combat abuses of the rule of law. Undoubtedly, the Council of Europe should place more emphasis and attention on ensuring pluralistic societies of CEE countries by fostering the existence of pluralist media outlets and civil society. It should not turn a blind eye to the existence of apparently arbitrary and corrupt practices in the constitutional democracies of some of its Member States in Central and Eastern Europe. As a rule, the institutions of the Council of Europe should augment their efforts on the ground and complement the sometimes overly top-down approach with bottom-up initiatives. In doing so they should equally examine all of the rule-of-law challenges in Central and Eastern Europe in order to prevent chilling effects being generated across domestic systems. In order to protect its legitimacy and credibility, the Council of Europe should stand firm in the fight against corruption, abuses of the rule of law and lack of transparency.

VII. BY WAY OF CONCLUSION: CONCRETE PROPOSALS FOR THE REFORM OF SLOVENIA'S CONSTITUTIONAL DEMOCRACY[33]

What concrete proposals can be made for the reform of Slovenia's constitutional democracy? As it stands, it is first necessary to start removing 'dirty togetherness' from the institutional life of the Slovenian state by fully subscribing to standards of professionalism, meritocracy, anti-corruption, independence, integrity and professionalism.[34] As a result, adherence to those values and principles could dissolve the old-boys networks, informal groups and the prevailing post-socialist mentality.[35] How to proceed further is more difficult to answer. The most straightforward answers are to reform the mentality and bet on the education of the younger generation. Only by adopting such measures, will it be possible to eradicate the current abuse of state institutions and public finances. The core values of constitutional democracy, such as human dignity, freedom, equality, solidarity, pluralism, tolerance and broadmindedness, are to be reinforced and their application diligently supervised. In particular, the

[33] This section draws from Jernej Letnar Černič, Matej Avbelj, Marko Novak and Dejan Valentinčič, *Reform of Democracy and the Rule of Law in Slovenia* (Kranj, New University, Faculty of Government and European Studies, 2019).

[34] Carl Dahlström, Victor Lapuente and Jan Teorell, 'The Merit of Meritocratization: Politics, Bureaucracy, and the Institutional Deterrents of Corruption' (2011) 65(3) *Political Research Quarterly* 656. See also Alina Mungiu-Pippidi, *Quest for Good Governance: How Societies Develop Control of Corruption* (Cambridge, Cambridge University Press, 2015).

[35] See generally Michal Bobek, 'The Fortress of Judicial Independence and the Mental Transitions of the Central European Judiciaries' (2008) 14(1) *European Public Law* 99.

effective pluralism – free exchange of various ideas and positions – should be reinforced in order to enable mature debate, and the 'chilling effects' of state censure should be avoided. The definition of public interest should be based and formed on constitutional values and should be again placed at the center of the Slovenian public space, whereas parochial interests should be excluded from state institutions.[36] The survival of state institutions rests on the realisation of these objectives. In this way, the following paragraphs propose concrete measures that are to be employed to reform constitutional democracy in Slovenia. The recommendations for reform could be a silver lining on the horizon if they are realised in practice.

A. Indispensable General Reforms of Constitutional Democracy and the Rule of Law in Slovenia

The Slovenian authorities are to ensure professional, independent and meritocratic public administration modelled on the Weberian bureaucracy model of state institutions and public administration. They should introduce effective normative standards for the supervision of perceived and actual conflicts of interest; lobbying and influence of informal networks; as well the creation of specialised supervisory bodies comprising of foreign experts. As a result, a specialized anti-corruption court should be created and the competences of the existing anti-corruption bodies should be extended. Nonetheless, the normative overhaul of the Slovenian constitutional democracy goes hand in hand with the reform of institutional and societal mentality by internalising the values of human dignity, equality, freedom, solidarity and pluralism. Finally, the values of Slovenia's constitutional democracy and the rule of law should be taught at all levels of education. All in all, the state authorities should intensify their efforts in the fight against state capture.

B. The Proposed Reforms of the Legislative Branch

Reform of the legislative branch should proceed at several levels. First, the National Assembly should reform the constitutional provisions on the composition of the National Council, thereby allowing for direct elections of all of its 40 members. As a result, the legislative powers of the National Council should also be strengthened and its mandate should be shortened from five

[36] Gerhard Hammerschmid, Steven Van de Walle, Rhys Andrews and Philippe Bezes (eds), *Public Administration Reforms in Europe: The View from the Top* (Cheltenham, Edward Elgar Publishing, 2016).

to two years. The National Assembly is obliged to reform the electoral system for elections to the National Assembly by introducing a proportional electoral system with an optional preferential vote and compulsory voting for election to the National Assembly. Additionally, the procedure for government formation should be reformed into the one-phase process. The legislative branch is to enhance the professionalism, transparency, ethical and integrity standards of the deputies of the National Assembly and the members of the National Council; including introducing the possibility of the recall of deputies in the case of criminal convictions. It should generate constitutional reforms and introduce direct normative obligations that the legislative branch be directly bound by the decisions the Constitutional Court of the Republic of Slovenia. Finally, the role and competences of the Parliamentary Inquiry Commissions and of the legislative branch generally in the supervision of the executive and judicial branches should be boosted. As a result, parliamentary oversight should particularly be upgraded towards the judiciary.

C. The Proposed Reforms of the Executive Branch

The executive branch should fully incorporate the values of constitutional democracy and the rule of law in its daily workings. It should pay greater attention to meeting constitutional and international obligations to respect, protect and fulfil human rights and fundamental freedoms. It should introduce the values of the Weberian bureaucracy model of public administration such as professionalism, meritocracy, integrity and transparency into the Slovenian public administration; and ensure independent and meritocratic recruitment. All facets of corruption should be prevented and combated at all levels of state institutions and public administration. As a result, strict rules on the disclosure of any perceived or actual conflict of interest are to be introduced and fully applied in practice. All civil servants, public employees and public officials should be required to annually declare their assets. The application of access to government information needs to be enhanced and new technologies and digitalisation should be introduced into government and public administration. The efficiency, capacity, fairness, transparency and independence of policy-making and as well as monitoring, evaluating and amending public policies should be improved. As a rule, the weekly sessions of the government should be transmitted publically and the number of governmental ministries should be kept reasonable. The territorial powers of the executive branch in the constitution should be reformed by allowing for the decentralisation and deconcentration of executive powers. The executive branch should exercise stricter supervisory constitutional powers over the legislative and judicial branches. The composition of governmental and ministerial commissions and committees should be reformed by including foreign experts in order to ensure their fair, impartial and independent functioning. The accountability mechanisms should be augmented through internal and external oversight bodies, commissions and ombudsmen. The powers of the Human Rights Ombudsman should be extended and made binding relating to the executive and judicial branches of government. The administrative capacity of central and local governments should be increased in order to ensure equitable human and economic development in all regions of Slovenia and to eradicate differences in the levels of socioeconomic development in eastern and western Slovenia. The executive branch should draft the legislative reform of decentralisation by the operationalisation of the second level of local self-government in the form of regions.

D. The Proposed Reform of the Judiciary

The Slovenian judiciary is to reform its traditionally bureaucratic and corporatist judicial organisation and its workings. As a result, the number of judges should be decreased and the number of the courts should be also diminished in order to emphasise quality over quantity. The state authorities should introduce and apply strict rules on the disclosure of any perceived or actual conflicts of interest and require all judges and judicial public employees to annually declare their assets. Comprehensive reform of the Judiciary Council is urgently required, particularly its composition, by including two foreign experts in order to ensure transparency, publicity, independence, impartiality and integrity of its functioning. The procedure for appointing judges should be fully reformed and systemic supervision of judicial decisions should be introduced. The judiciary should introduce a model of judges' offices, whereas legal education and law schools should be reformed and enhanced. The judiciary should work towards increasing its institutional reputation, recognition and professional allure in order to extend trust in courts' procedural and substantive fairness. The accountability mechanism of judges should be enhanced, including introducing civil and criminal liability for judges. Finally, the judiciary should work towards ensuring proper exercise of the right to a fair, independent and impartial trial and of other human rights and fundamental freedoms.

E. The Reform of the 'Fourth Branch' of Government – The Media as Public Watchdog

State authorities should create conditions for supervisory, independent, impartial, fair and unbiased functioning of the media. They should incorporate tax incentives to encourage private support of independent investigative media. Media outlets should be obliged to greatly internalise the values of constitutional democracy such as human dignity and pluralism. As a result, state authorities should augment the protections of freedom of expression as a fundamental value in a constitutional democracy. Overall, the public space in the Slovenian society and increasing oversight role of civil society should be streng pluralised.

F. The Proposed Reforms in the Wider Public and Private Sectors

Slovenian society should strive to eradicate or minimise the old ways and habits of doing business and fully internalise the values of human dignity, pluralism, equality, freedoms and solidarity. The private sector should to the greatest extent possible embrace the values of Slovenia's constitutional democracy. As a result, the state institutions should ensure and guarantee pluralism, meritocracy and transparency in the higher education sector and in research. Oversight over public agencies and bodies in the wider Slovenian public administration should be augmented. The participation of citizens and residents in public affairs should be increased. The public and private sectors should equally and efficiently respect, protect and fulfil human rights and fundamental freedoms in Slovenian society. As a result, the rule of law and human rights in the Slovenian private sector should be fully realised.

Bibliography

'20 let varuha človekovih pravic' www.varuh-rs.si/fileadmin/user_upload/pdf/Razne_publikacije/20let_VCP_a_www.pdf (accessed 24 April 2019).

'A Decade of Measuring Transition', www.ebrd.com/publications/life-in-transition-iii-slovenia.pdf (accessed 24 April 2019).

Abruzzese, Leo, 'Economic Trouble Ahead' *The Economist* https://worldin2019.economist.com/endofthebullrun (accessed 15 February 2019).

Acemoglu Daron, Johnson, Simon and Robinson, James, 'Institutions as the Fundamental Cause of Long-Run Growth' (May 2004) NBER Working Paper no 10481.

Acemoglu, Daron, Johnson, Simon and Robinson, James, 'Institutions as a Fundamental Cause of Long-Run Growth' in Philippe Aghion and Steven Durlauf (eds), *Handbook of Economic Growth*, vol 1A (Amsterdam, Elsevier, 2005).

Act on the Protection of the Right to a Trial without Undue Delay, Official Gazette of the Republic of Slovenia No 67/12.

Act Regulating Compensation for Damage to Persons Erased from the Permanent Population Register, Official Gazette of the Republic of Slovenia No 99/13.

Adam, Frane, 'The Relevance of Social Capital and Intermediary Structures for the Creation of Systemic Competitiveness: Some Lessons from Southern and Eastern-Central Europe' (1998) 14(26) *Družboslovne Razprave* 48.

Adam, Frane, *Na razpotju družbene krize: quo vadis, Slovenija* (Ljubljana, IRSA – Inštitut za razvojne in strateške analize, 2013).

Adam, Frane and Tomšič, Matevž, 'Transition Elites: Catalysts of Social Innovation or Rent Seekers' (2000) *Družboslovne razprave*, http://dk.fdv.uni-lj.si/dr/dr32-33adamtomsic.PDF (accessed 13 September 2019).

Adam, Frane and Tomšič, Matevž, 'Elite (Re)Configuration and Politico-Economic Performance in Post-Socialist Countries' (2002) 54(3) *Europe-Asia Studies* 435.

Adam, Frane and Tomšič, Matevž, 'Elites, Democracy and Development in Post-Socialist Transition' (2002) 31(1) *Österreichische Zeitschrift für Politikwissenschaft* 99.

Adam, Frane and Tomšič, Matevž, 'The Dynamics of Elites and the Type of Capitalism: Slovenian Exceptionalism?' (2012) 37(2) *Historical Social Research* 53.

Administrative Dispute Act, Official Gazette of the Republic of Slovenia No 105/06, 107/09.

Agency for Communication Networks and Services of the Republic of Slovenia, 'Poročilo o trgu elektronskih medijev in delu agencije za četrto četrtletje 2017', 26 March 2018.

Alexievich, Svetlana, *Second-Hand Time* (London, Fitzcarraldo Editions, 2017).

Amnesty International Slovenia, Campaigns, www.amnesty.si (accessed 24 April 2019).

Andersen, Torben M, 'The Welfare State and Economic Performance: Bilaga 4 Långtidsutredningen', Statens Offentliga Utredningar, Sverige, 2015, www.regeringen.se/contentassets/c3cd2706e07b4fc7860533f1ae8ad5d8/sou-201553-the-welfare-state-and-economic-performance.pdf (accessed 24 April 2019).

'Annex to the note verbale dated 16 July 2015 from the Permanent Mission of Slovenia to the United Nations addressed to the President of the General Assembly, Candidacy of Slovenia for the Human Rights Council, 2016–2018', A/70/358, 3 September 2015.

Annual Report 2018 of the European Court of Human Rights, Council of Europe.

Annual Report of the Association of Journalists and Commentators (ZNP) on the Situation in the Media Field in Slovenia in 2015, www.znp.si/english-texts-mainmenu-27/431-annual-report-of-the-association-of-journalists-and-commentators-znp-on-the-situation-in-the-media-field-in-slovenia-in-2015 (accessed 23 April 2019).

Annual Reports of the Human Rights Ombudsman of the Republic of Slovenia 1994–2017.
Association of Journalists and Commentators (ZNP), 'V ZNP ostro obsojamo zlorabo RTVS v politične namene!', 26 October 2018, www.znp.si/arhiv/484-v-znp-ostro-obsojamo-zlorabo-rtvs-v-politicne-namene (accessed 23 April 2019).
Avbelj, Matej, 'Slovenska sodišča in postopek za predhodno odločanje' (2009) *Pravna praksa* Volume 28 Number 40/41, 16 October 2009.
Avbelj, Matej, 'Crises and Perspectives of Building a European Nation – The Case of Slovenia' in Peter Jambrek (ed), *Nation's transitions: Social and Legal Issues of Slovenia's Transitions: 1945–2015 (Slovenia 1945–2015)* (Graduate School of Government and European Studies, European Faculty of Law, 2014).
Avbelj, Matej, 'Failed Democracy: The Slovenian Patria Case – (Non)Law in Context' (2014), originally published in Slovenian as Matej, Avbelj, 'Zadeva Patria – (ne)pravo v kontekstu' [2014] *Pravna praksa*, ssrn.com/abstract=2462613> or <dx.doi.org/10.2139/ssrn.2462613 (accessed 24 April 2019).
Avbelj, Matej, 'Zadeva Patria – (ne)pravo v kontekstu' (2014) 26 *Pravna Praksa* II–VII.
Avbelj, Matej, 'Central Europe as a Legal Phenomenon' (2015) 2(13) *European Perspectives – Slovenia's Role in Visegrad Group* 53.
Avbelj, Matej, *Nepravna država* (GV Založba, 2015).
Avbelj, Matej, 'Slovenia Constitutionally Reloaded but Still Failing' *Verfassungsblog* (25 April 2015) verfassungsblog.de/slovenia-constitutionally-reloaded-but-still-failing/#.VUskk_ntlBc (accessed 24 April 2019).
Avbelj, Matej, 'Pluralism and Systemic Defiance in the European Union' in András Jakab and Dimitry Kochenov (eds), *The Enforcement of EU Law and Values: Ensuring Member States' Compliance* (Oxford, Oxford University Press, 2015).
Avbelj, Matej, 'Mit 10: Politika ni kurba' *Finance* (2 July 2016) www.finance.si/8846859 (accessed 24 April 2019).
Avbelj, Matej, 'Izbiranje predsednika Vrhovnega sodišča – slovenski sodni svet je farsa' *Finance* (19 September 2016) https://www.finance.si/8849193 (accessed 24 April 2019).
Avbelj, Matej, 'Bo sodni svet zdaj odstopil?', *Finance* (17 December 2016) https://www.finance.si/8852458 (accessed 24 April 2019).
Avbelj, Matej, 'Transformation in the Eye of the Beholder' in Michal Bobek (ed), *Central European Judges Under the European Influence: The Transformative Power of the EU Revisited* (Oxford, Hart Publishing 2015) 275.
Avbelj, Matej, 'Transnational Law Between Modernity and Post-modernity' (2016) 7(3) *Transnational Legal Theory* 406.
Avbelj, Matej, 'Naše pravo in pravo ljudstvo: kako braniti ustavno demokracijo pred populizmom' (2016) Dnevi slovenskih pravnikov, Podjetje in delo.
Avbelj, Matej, 'Pravni mit 5: Zakaj slovensko sodstvo ne more biti neodvisno' *Finance* (23. April 2016) https://www.finance.si/8844169 (accessed 24 April 2019).
Avbelj, Matej, 'How to Reform the Rule of Law in Slovenia' in Frane Adam, *Slovenia: Social, Economic and Environmental Issues* (Nova Publishing, 2017).
Avbelj, Matej, 'Pluralism and Systemic Defiance in the European Union' in András Jakab and Dimitry Kochenov (eds), *The Enforcement of EU Law and Values: Ensuring Member States' Compliance* (Oxford, Oxford University Press, 2017).
Avbelj, Matej, 'What Future for the European Union', WZB Discussion Paper SP IV 2017-802.
Avbelj, Matej, 'Slovenia: The Case of a Maturing Relationship' in Stefan Griller, Monica Claes, and Lina Papadopoulou (eds), *Member States' Constitutions and EU Integration* (Oxford, Hart Publishing, 2018).
Avbelj, Matej, 'The Sociology of (Slovenian) Constitutional Democracy' (2018) 10(1) *Hague Journal on the Rule of Law* 35.
Avbelj, Matej, 'Report on the Role and Status of the ECHR and EU Law in Slovenia' in Giuseppe Martinico and Oreste Pollicino (eds), *The National Judicial Treatment of the ECHR and EU Laws* (Europa Law Publishing, 2010) 441–53, available at SSRN: https://ssrn.com/abstract=1645822.

Avbelj, Matej, 'Judicial Self-Government in Slovenia', draft prepared for a workshop organized by David Kosař on 'The Rise of Judicial Self-Government: Changing the Architecture of Separation of Powers without an Architect', Prague, September 2017 (unpublished manuscript on file with author).

Avbelj, Matej, 'There is No Such Thing as a Particular "Center and Eastern European Constitutionalism"', *Verfassungsblog* (18 May 2018) https://verfassungsblog.de/there-is-no-such-thing-as-a-particular-center-and-eastern-european-constitutionalism/ (accessed 24 April 2019).

Avbelj, Matej, 'Contextual Analysis of Judicial Governance in Slovenia' (2018) *German Law Journal* 1901.

Avbelj, Matej, 'Slovenia's Supreme Court Rejects the European Court of Human Rights' *Verfassungsblog* (26 October 2018) verfassungsblog.de/slovenias-supreme-court-rejects-the-european-court-of-human-rights/ (accessed 24 April 2019).

Avbelj, Matej, 'Srhljivke iz slovenskega sodstva' *Finance* (19 January 2019). www.finance.si/8943642 (accessed 24 April 2019).

Avbelj, Matej and Letnar Černič, Jernej, 'Slovenia', in Leonard Hammer and Frank Emmert (eds), *The European Convention on Human Rights and Fundamental Freedoms in Central and Eastern Europe* (The Hague: Eleven International Publishing, 2012).

Avbelj, Matej, Teršek, Andraž, Toplak, Jurij, Trstenjak, Verica, Fikfak, Veronika, Bugarič, Bojan and Letnar Černič, Jernej, 'Dvojna zloraba prava' *Večer* (29 November 2017) www.vecer.com/krsitev-ustavnosti-in-teptanje-ustavne-demokracije-v-drzavnem-zboru-6357244 (accessed 24 April 2019).

Bagdikian, Ben H, *The New Media Monopoly* (Boston, MA, Beacon Press, 2014).

Bairett, Richard L, 'Executive Power and Media Freedom in Central and Eastern Europe' (2015) *48*(10) *Comparative Political Studies* 1260.

Bajomi-Lázár, Peter, *Reinventing Media: Media Policy Reform in East–Central Europe* (Budapest, Central European University Press, 2003).

Bajomi-Lázár, Peter, *Party Colonisation of the Media in Central and Eastern Europe* (Budapest, Central European University Press, 2014).

Bajomi-Lázár, Peter, 'Variations in Media Freedom: Why Some Governments in central and Eastern Europe Respect Media Freedom More than Others' (2015) 8(1) *Central European Journal of Communication* 4.

'Bajuk Receives European Finance Minister of the Year Award (STA, 3 March 2006) english.sta.si/1030257/bajuk-receives-european-finance-minister-of-the-year-award (accessed 24 April 2019).

Baka, András, 'The European Court of Human Rights and the Central and Eastern European States' (2018) 1 *East European Yearbook on Human Rights* 79.

Baker, C Edwin, *Media, Markets and Democracy* (Cambridge, Cambridge University Press, 2002).

Baker, C Edwin, *Media Concentration and Democracy: Why Ownership Matters* (Cambridge, Cambridge University Press, 2006).

Balčytiene, Aukse, 'The Price of Liberalisation and Other Strains on Democracy and Media Freedom in Central and Eastern Europe' in Terry Flew, Petros Iosifidis and Jeanette Steemer (eds), *Global Media and National Policies: The Return of the State* (London, Palgrave Macmillan, 2016).

Balčytiene, Auksė, Bajomi-Lázár, Peter, Štětka, Václav and Sükösd, Miklós 'Oligarchization, De-Westernization and Vulnerability: Media between Democracy and Authoritarianism in Central and Eastern Europe' (2015) 3(1) *Tidsskrift for Medier, Erkendelse og Formidling* 119.

Balestra, Carlotta and Tonkin, Richard, 'Inequalities in Household Wealth Across OECD Countries: Evidence from the OECD Wealth Distribution Database', OECD Statistics Working Papers no 2018/01, https://doi.org/10.1787/7e1bf673-en (accessed 24 April 2019).

Bank of Slovenia, *Full Report on the Comprehensive Review of the Banking System* (Ljubljana, Bank of Slovenia, 2013).

Bard, Petra and Bayer, Judit, 'A Comparative Analysis of Media Freedom and Pluralism in the EU Member States', European Parliament, 15 September 2016.

Barendt, Eric, 'Introduction' in Eric Barendt (eds), *Media Law* (Aldershot, Dartmouth Publishing, 1993).

Barker, Alex, 'Slovenia Struggles to Avoid EU Bailout' *Financial Times* 20 November 2013, www.ft.com/content/1d17fdd6-5053-11e3-9f0d-00144feabdc0 (accessed 24 April 2019).

Barr, Caelainn, 'Inequality Index: Where are the World's Most Unequal Countries?', *The Guardian* (26 April 2017) www.theguardian.com/inequality/datablog/2017/apr/26/inequality-index-where-are-the-worlds-most-unequal-countries (accessed 24 April 2019).

Bartole, Sergio, 'Final Remarks: The Role of the Venice Commission' (2000) 26(3) *Review of Central and Eastern European Law* 351.

Bartole, Sergio, 'International Constitutionalism and Conditionality: The Experience of the Venice Commission' (2014) 4 *Rivista Associazione Italiana dei Costituzionalisti*.

Bartole, Sergio, 'Standards of Europe's Constitutional Heritage' (2015) 30(2) *Giornale di Storia Costituzionale* 17.

Bartolj, Jaka, 'A Slovenian Poster Challenged Yugoslavia's Communist Othodoxy' *RTVSLO* (12 August 2014) www.rtvslo.si/news-in-english/slovenia-revealed/a-slovenian-poster-challenged-yugoslavia-s-communist-orthodoxy/326571 (accessed 24 April 2019).

Bartolj, Jaka, 'Bush Saw Putin's Soul in Slovenia' *RTVSLO* (3 April 2015) www.rtvslo.si/news-in-english/slovenia-revealed/bush-saw-putin-s-soul-in-slovenia/361776 (accessed 24 April 2019).

Baun, M and Marek, D, *The New Member States and the European Union: Foreign Policy and Europeanization* (Abingdon, Routledge 2013).

Bavcon, Ljubo, 'K odločbi Ustavnega sodišča o Titovi cesti' [2011] *Pravna praksa* Vol 30 Nr 41/42, 27 October 2011, p. 16.

Bebler, Anton, 'Slovenia's Smooth Transition' [2002] *Journal of Democracy* 13(1), pp 127–140.

Benoit-Rohmer, Florence and Klebes, Heinrich, *Council of Europe Law: Towards a Pan-European Legal Area* (Strasbourg, Council of Europe Publishing, 2005).

Berend, Ivan T and Bugarič, Bojan, 'Unfinished Europe: Transition from Communism to Democracy in Central and Eastern Europe' (2015) 50(4) *Journal of Contemporary History* 768.

Bernal, Carlos, 'The Challenges of Transformative Constitutionalism – A Reply to Jorge González Jácome', blog of the International Journal of Constitutional Law, 1 January 2019, www.iconnectblog.com/2019/01/the-challenges-of-transformative-constitutionalism-a-reply-to-jorge-gonzalez-jacome/ (accessed 24 April 2019).

Bibič, Aldo, 'Evropeizacija politične družbe in civilne družbe: nekateri aspekti slovenskega primera' [1997] *Teorija in praksa: družboslovna revija* 56.

Blokker, Paul, *New Democracies in Crisis: A Comparative Constitutional Study of the Czech Republic, Hungary, Poland, Romania and Slovakia* (New York, Routledge, 2014).

Bobek, Michal, 'The Fortress of Judicial Independence and the Mental Transitions of the Central European Judiciaries' (2008) 14(1) *European Public Law* 99.

Bobek, Michal (ed), *Central European Judges Under the European Influence: The Transformative Power of the EU Revisited* (Oxford, Hart Publishing, 2015).

Bobek, Michal and Kosař, David, 'Global Solutions, Local Damages: A Critical Study in Judicial Councils in Central and Eastern Europe' (2014) 15 *German Law Journal* 1257.

Boda, Zsolt and Medve-Bálint, Gergő, 'The Politicised Nature of Many Eastern European Institutions Means that They Are Trusted Less than Those in Western Europe' *London School of Economics and Political Science* (21 August 2012) https://blogs.lse.ac.uk/europpblog/2012/08/21/institutional-trust-zsolt-boda/ (accessed 24 April 2019).

Boda, Zsolt and Medve-Bálint, Gergő, 'Does Institutional Trust in East Central Europe Differ from Western Europe?' (2014) 3(2) *European Quarterly of Political Attitudes and Mentalities* 1.

Bogdandy, Armin von and Sonnevend, Pál (eds), *Constitutional Crisis in the European Constitutional Area: Theory, Law and Politics in Hungary and Romania* (Oxford, Hart Publishing, 2014).

Bojinović, Fenko A and Svetličič, M, 'Slovenia and the European Union' in *Oxford Research Encyclopedia of Politics* (Oxford, Oxford University Press, 2017).

Bonnier Business Press AB, www.bonnierb2b.com (accessed 23 April 2019).

Börzel, Tanja A and Risse, Thomas, 'When Europe Hits Home: Europeanization and Domestic Change' (2000) 4(15) *European Integration Online Papers* https://papers.ssrn.com/sol3/papers.cfm?abstract_id=302768 (accessed 24 April 2019).

Börzel, Tanja A and Risse, Thomas, 'Conceptualizing the Domestic Impact of Europe' in Kevin Featherstone and Claudio M Radaelli (eds), *The Politics of Europeanization* (Oxford, Oxford University Press, 2003).

Bozhilova, Diana, 'Measuring Success and Failure of EU-Europeanization in the Eastern Enlargement: Judicial Reform in Bulgaria' (2007) (9)2 *European Journal of Law Reform* 285.

Božicko, Polona and Gorše, Peter, 'Merger Control in Slovenia: Overview', *Thomson Reuters Practical Law*, 1 October 2018, https://uk.practicallaw.thomsonreuters.com/w-017-1948?transitionType=Default&contextData=(sc.Default)&firstPage=true&comp=pluk&bhcp=1 (accessed 23 April 2019).

Bučar, Bojko, 'Evropeizacija slovenske zunanje varnostne politike: (ne)prepričljivost interesa za vstop v NATO' [1998].

Bučar, France, *Demokracija in kriza naših ustavnih institucij* (Ljubljana, Nova revija, 1998).

Bučar, France, '"Pravnik v današnjem času" (uvodno predavanje na 30. Dnevih slovenskih pravnikov) ['"Lawyer in Current Times", The Introductory Lecture at the 30th Day of Slovene Lawyers]' (2004) 36 *Pravna praksa* 4.

Bučar, France, *Slovenci in prihodnost* (Didakta, 2009).

Bučar, France, *Temelji naše državnosti* (Mladinska knjiga, 2012).

Buergenthal, Thomas, 'Keynote Lecture: International Human Rights: Need for Further Institutional Development' (2018) 50(1) *Case Western Reserve Journal of International Law* 9.

Bugarič, Bojan, 'Problem v Evropi so socialni demokrati, ki so neoliberalci s 50-odstotnim popustom. Tudi oni verjamejo v neoliberalizem, le še par drobtinic zraven ponujajo ljudem' (*Mladina*, 15 March 2013) www.mladina.si/141981/dr-bojan-bugaric-problem-v-evropi-so-socialni-demokrati-ki-so-neoliberalci-s-50-odstotnim (accessed 24 April 2019).

Bugarič, Bojan, 'Protecting Democracy and the Rule of Law in the European Union: The Hungarian Challenge', LSE 'Europe in Question' Discussion Paper Series 79/2014.

Bugarič, Bojan, 'A Crisis of Constitutional Democracy in Post-Communist Europe: "Lands in-Between" Democracy and Authoritarianism' (2015) 13(1) *International Journal of Constitutional Law* 219.

Bugarič, Bojan (2015) 'The Rule of Law Derailed: Lessons from the Post-Communist World' (2015) 7(2) *Hague Journal on the Rule of Law* 175.

Bugarič Bojan, 'Administrative Law Developments in Post-Communist Slovenia: Between West European Ideals and East European Reality' (2016) 22(1) *European Public Law* 25.

Bugarič Bojan, 'Evropeizacija državne uprave: vpliv evropskega prava na državno upravo držav članic' (2004) Zbornik znanstvenih razprav 64, pp. 101.

Bugarič Bojan and Kuhelj Alenka, 'Slovenia in Crisis: A Tale of Unfinished Democratization in East-Central Europe' (2015) 48(4) *Communist and Post-Communist Studies* 273.

Bugarič, Bojan and Kuhelj, Alenka, 'Varieties of Populism in Europe: Is the Rule of Law in Danger?' (2018) 10(1) *Hague Journal on the Rule of Law* 21.

Bull, Thomas, 'Rapports: Sweden: The Original Ombudsman: Blueprint in Need of Revision or a Concept with More to Offer?' (2000) 6(3) *European Public Law* 334.

Buquicchio, Gianni and Garrone, Pierre, 'L'harmonisation du droit constitutionnel européen: La contribution de la Commission européenne pour la démocratie par le droit' (1998) 3(2–3) *Uniform Law Review* 323.

Cabada, Ladislav and Tomšič, Matevž, 'The Rise of Person-Based Politics in the New Democracies: The Czech Republic and Slovenia' [2016] *Politics in Central Europe* 12(2).

Cannie, Hannes and Voorhoof, Dirk, 'The Abuse Clause and Freedom of Expression under the European Human Rights Convention: An Added Value for Democracy and Human Rights Protection?' (2011) 29(1) *Netherlands Quarterly for Human Rights* 54.

Carver, Richard, 'National Human Rights Institutions in Central and Eastern Europe: The Ombudsman as Agent of International Law' in Ryan Goodman and Thomas Pegram (eds), *Human Rights, State Compliance, and Social Change: Assessing National Human Rights Institutions* (Cambridge, Cambridge University Press, 2012).

Chesebro, James W, 'The Media Reality: Epistemological Functions of Media in Cultural Systems' (1984) 1(2) *Critical Studies in Mass Communication* 111.

Christiansen, Eric C, 'Adjudicating Non-Justiciable Rights: Socio-Economic Rights and the South African Constitutional Court' (2007) 38(2) *Columbia Human Rights Law Review* 321.

Civil Procedure Act, Official Gazette of the Republic of Slovenia No 73/07, official consolidated text 45/08 – ZArbit, 45/08, 111/08.

CME, company overview, www.cetv-net.com/about-cme/company-overview/default.aspx (accessed 23 April 2019).

Code of Ethics for Public Servants in State Bodies and Local Communities, 11 April 2011, www.mpju.gov.si/fileadmin/mpju.gov.si/pageuploads/Uradniski_svet/Code_of_ethics.pdf (accessed 24 April 2019).

Cogwill, Anthony, *The Repatriation from Austria in 1945: Cowgill Inquiry: The Documentary Evidence Reproduced in Full from British, American, German and Yugoslav Sources* (London, Sinclair Stevenson, 1990).

Commission of Inquiry, Reports to determine the abuses in the Slovenian banking system and to determine the causes and responsibilities for the already second rehabilitation of the banking system in independent Slovenia, Official Gazette of the Republic of Slovenia 30/15, www.dz-rs.si/wps/portal/Home/deloDZ/zakonodaja/izbranZakonAkt?uid=C1257A70003EE749C125826C003D5065&db=kon_akt&mandat=VII (accessed 24 April 2019).

Correa Henao, Magdalena and Gutiérrez Beltrán, Andrés Mauricio, 'Introduction to I-CONnect Symposium – Contemporary Discussions in Constitutional Law', blog of the International Journal of Constitutional Law, 31 October 2018, www.iconnectblog.com/2018/10/introduction-to-i-connect-symposium-contemporary-discussions-in-constitutional-law (accessed 24 April 2019).

Corsellis, John and Ferrar, Marcus, *Slovenia 1945: Memories of Death and Survival after World War II* (London, IB Tauris, 2005).

Council of Europe, Commissioner for Human Rights, The Mandate, www.coe.int/en/web/commissioner/mandate (accessed 24 April 2019).

Council of Europe, Committee of Ministers, 'Resolution (99) 50 on the Council of Europe Commissioner of Europe for Human Rights', 104th Session, 7 May 1999, Art 12, https://search.coe.int/cm/Pages/result_details.aspx?ObjectID=09000016805e305a (accessed 24 April 2019).

Council of Europe, European Convention for the Protection of Human Rights and Fundamental Freedoms, as amended by Protocols nos 11 and 14, supplemented by Protocols nos 1, 4, 6, 7, 12, 13 and 16, 4 November 1950.

Council of Europe, Parliamentary Assembly, 'Need for International Condemnation of Crimes of Totalitarian Communist Regimes', Resolution 1481 (2006), Assembly debate on 25 January 2006.

Council of Europe, Parlimentary Assembly, Resolution 1096 (1996) on Measures to dismantle the heritage of former communist totalitarian systems, 27 June 1996.

Council of Europe, 'Report by Nils Muižnieks, Commissioner for Human Rights of the Council of Europe, following his visit to Slovenia from 20 to 23 March 2017, CommDH(2017)21', Strasbourg, 17 July 2018, https://rm.coe.int/report-on-the-visit-to-slovenia-from-20-to-23-march-2017-by-nils-muizn/1680730405 (accessed 24 April 2019).

Court of Auditors RS, *Revision Report on Judicial Delays* (Ljubljana, 16 March 2011).

Craig, Paul, 'Transnational Constitution-Making: The Contribution of the Venice Commission on Law and Democracy', (2017) 2 *UC Irvine Journal of International, Transnational, and Comparative Law* 57.

Cram, Ian, 'Constitutional Responses to Extremist Political Associations – ETA, Batasuna and Democratic Norms' (2008) 28(1) *Legal Studies* 68.

Criminal Procedure Act, Official Gazette of the Republic of Slovenia No 32/12, official consolidated text 47/13, 87/14 and 8/16.

Cross, Frank, 'Judicial Independence' in Gregory A Caldeira, R Daniel Kelemen and Keith E Whittington (eds), *The Oxford Handbook of Law and Politics* (Oxford, Oxford University Press, 2009).

Cullen, Richard, 'Freedom of the Press and the Rule of Law' in Steve Tsang (ed), *Judicial Independence and the Rule of Law in Hong Kong* (New York, Palgrave, 2001).

Czarnota Adam, 'Rule of Law as an Outcome of Crisis. Central-Eastern European Experiences 27 Years after the Breakthrough' (2016) 8(2) *Hague Journal on the Rule of Law* 311.

Czarnota, Adam, Krygier, Martin and Sadurski, Wojciech, 'Introduction' in Adam Czarnota, Martin Krygier, and Wojciech Sadurski (eds), *Rethinking the Rule of Law after Communism* (Budapest, Central European University, 2005).

Dahlström, Carl, Lapuente, Victor and Teorell, Jan, 'The Merit of Meritocratization: Politics, Bureaucracy, and the Institutional Deterrents of Corruption' (2011) 65(3) *Political Research Quarterly* 656.

Damijan Jože, P, 'Reentering the Markets of the Former Yugoslavia' in Mojmir Mrak, Matija Rojec and Carlos Silva-Jáuregui (eds), *Slovenia: From Yugoslavia to the European Union* (Washington, DC, World Bank, 2004) 334.

Daron, Acemoglu, Robinson, James and Verdier, Thierry, 'Kleptocracy and Divide-and-Rule: A Model of Personal Rule. The Alfred Marshall Lecture' (2004) *Journal of the European Economic Association Papers and Proceedings* 2 (2/3), pp 162.

Dawson, Mark and Muir, Elise, 'Hungary and the Indirect Protection of EU Fundamental Rights and the Rule of Law' (2013) 14(10) *German Law Journal* 1959.

De Visser, Maartje, 'A Critical Assessment of the Role of the Venice Commission in Processes of Domestic Constitutional Reform' (2015) 63(4) *American Journal of Comparative Law* 963.

Demertzis, Nicolas, 'Emotions and Populism' in Simon Clarke, Paul Hoggett and Simon Thompson (eds), *Emotions, Politics and Society* (London, Palgrave Macmillan, 2006).

'Democracy Index 2018: Me Too? Political Participation, Protest and Democracy' *The Economist* (12 January 2019) https://www.prensa.com/politica/democracy-index_LPRFIL20190112_0001.pdf (accessed 14. September 2019).

Demšar, Franci, *Transparentnost in skrb za denar davkoplačevalcev* (Ljubljana, Mladinska knjiga, 2013).

Demšar, Franci and Zatler, Renata, *Javna hiša Slovenija: politično kadrovanje* (Ljubljana, Cankarjeva založba, 2018).

Dežman, Jože, 'Communist Repression and Transitional Justice in Slovenia', in Peter Jambrek (ed), *Crimes Committed by Totalitarian Regimes* (Ljubljana, Slovenian Presidency of the Council of the European Union, 2008).

Dežman, Jože, *Hudo zlo iz Hudih Jam: k ponatisu Poročila Komisije Vlade RS za reševanje vprašanj prikritih grobišč v mandatu 2005–2008* [*Terrible Evil from Caves of Evil: Appendix to the Reprint of the Report of the Committee of the Government of Slovenia for Resolving the Issue of concealed Burial Sites in the 2005–2008 Mandate*] (Družina, 2009).

Dežman, Jože in Jamnik, Pavel, *Slovenija in vojna grobišča: dolga tranzicija* (Komisija Vlade RS za reševanje vprašanja prikritih grobišč, 2017).

Dežman, Jože (ed), *Nemoč laži, Poročilo 4 Komisije Vlade RS za reševanje vprašanj prikritih grobišč* (Ljubljana, Družina, 2019).

Diamond, Larry and Gunther, Richard (eds), *Political Parties and Democracy, A Journal of Democracy Book* (John Hopkins University Press and the National Endowment for Democracy, 2001).

Dimitrov, Georgi, Haralampiev, Kaloyan and Stoychev, Stoycho, 'The Adventures of the CVM in Bulgaria and Romania' (August 2016) MaXCaP Project, No 29.

Djilas, Milovan, *The New Class: An Analysis of the Communist System* (London, Thames & Hudson, 1957).

Dmitrievich Gudkov, Lev, '"Soviet Man" in the Sociology of Iurii Levada' (2008) 47(6) *Sociological Research* 6.

Dobek-Ostrowska, Boguslawa, '25 years after Communism: Four Models of Media and Politics in Central and Eastern Europe' in Boguslawa Dobek-Ostrowska and Michal Glowacki (eds), *Democracy and Media in Central and Eastern Europe 25 Years On* (New York, Peter Lang Edition, 2015).

Dobovšek, Bojan, *Peta veja oblasti* (Ljubljana, eBesede–Dobra država, 2016).

Dovžan, Gašper and Tekavec, Urška, 'Zgodovinski uvod v Komentar slovenske ustave. Temne strani slovenske pravne preteklosti v luči slovenske ustave: Argumenti Ustavnega sodišča Republike Slovenije o hudih množičnih in strukturnih kršitvah človekovih pravic in svoboščin v Sloveniji v času prevlade ideologije in prakse komunizma 1945–1990' (2001) 11/12 *Dignitas* revija za človekove pravice.

Downey, John and Mihelj, Sabina (eds), *Central and Eastern European Media in Comparative Perspective: Politics, Economy and Culture* (Farnham, Ashgate, 2012).

Dunoff, Jeffrey L and Trachtman, Joel P (eds), *Ruling the World? Constitutionalism, International Law, and Global Governance* (Cambridge, Cambridge University Press, 2009).

Duranti, Marco, *The Conservative Human Rights Revolution: European Identity, Transnational Politics and the Origin of the European Convention* (Oxford, Oxford University Press, 2017).

Durão Barroso, José Manuel, 2012 State of the Union Speech, Strasbourg, 12 September 2012, http://europa.eu/rapid/press-release_SPEECH-12-596_en.htm (accessed 24 April 2019).

Dvořáková, Vladimira and Milardović, Anđelko (eds), *Lustration and Consolidation of Democracy and the Rule of Law in Central and Eastern Europe* (Zagreb, Political Science Research Centre, 2007).

ECHR Annual Report 2018 www.echr.coe.int/Documents/Annual_report_2018_ENG.pdf (accessed 24 April 2019).

ECJ Annual Report, curia.europa.eu/jcms/upload/docs/application/pdf/2015-04/en_ecj_annual_report_2014_pr1.pdf (accessed 24 April 2019).

The Economist, Intelligence Unit, 'Democracy Index 2017: Free Speech Under Attack', www.eiu.com/Handlers/WhitepaperHandler.ashx?fi=Democracy_Index_2018.pdf&mode=wp&campaignid=Democracy2018 (accessed 24 June 2019).

Eldon, Glenn, *Country Studies: Former Yugoslavia* (Washington, DC, Library of Congress, 1992).

'The Elimination of Court Backlogs The Lukenda Project: Operational Action Plan' (12 December 2005) www.mp.gov.si/fileadmin/mp.gov.si/pageuploads/mp.gov.si/zakonodaja/angleski_prevodi_zakonov/The_Lukenda_Project_angl.pdf (accessed 24 April 2019).

Eman, Katja, Tine, Furdi, Rok, Hacin and Bojan, Dobovšek, 'Discourse on the Gray Economy, Corruption, and Organized Crime in Slovenia' in Maximilian Edelbacher, Peter C Kratcoski and Bojan Dobovšek (eds) *Corruption, Fraud, Organized Crime, and the Shadow Economy* (Boca Raton, FL, CRC Press, 2015).

Engerman, Stanley L and Sokoloff, Kenneth L, 'Factor Endowments, Inequality, and Paths of Development Among New World Economies' (October 2002) NBER Working Paper no 9259.

Engerman, Stanley L and Sokoloff, Kenneth L, 'Institutional and Non-Institutional Explanations of Economic Differences' in Claude Ménard and Mary M Shirley (eds), *Handbook of New Institutional Economics* (Berlin, Springer, 2008).

European Commission, *European Economy: Macroeconomic Imbalances Slovenia 2014, Occasional Papers 187* (Brussels, European Commission, Directorate General for Economic and Financial Affairs, 2014).

European Commission, 'Communication from the Commission to the European Parliament, the Council, the European Central Bank, the European Economic and Social Committee and the Committee of the Regions–The 2018 EU Justice Scoreboard', COM(2018) 364 final, Brussels, 28 May 2018.

European Commission, 'Cooperation and Verification Mechanism for Bulgaria and Romania', https://ec.europa.eu/info/policies/justice-and-fundamental-rights/effective-justice/rule-law/assistance-bulgaria-and-romania-under-cvm/cooperation-and-verification-mechanism-bulgaria-and-romania_en (accessed 24 April 2019).

European Commission, '2018 European Semester: Assessment of progress on structural reforms, prevention and correction of macroeconomic imbalances, and results of in-depth reviews under Regulation (EU) No 1176/2011, COM(2018) 120 final – Report on Slovenia', ec.europa.eu/info/sites/info/files/2018-european-semester-country-report-slovenia-en.pdf (accessed 16 February 2019).

European Commission, Final report of the High Level Expert Group on Fake News and Online Disinformation, 12 March 2018, https://ec.europa.eu/digital-single-market/en/news/final-report-high-level-expert-group-fake-news-and-online-disinformation (accessed 23 April 2019).

European Commission, *Report on Public Finances in EMU 2017* (Brussels, European Commission, 2018).

European Commission, 'The 2019 EU Justice Scoreboard', https://ec.europa.eu/info/sites/info/files/justice_scoreboard_2019_en.pdf (accessed 24 April 2019).

European Court of Human Rights, 'Annual Report 2018', www.echr.coe.int/Documents/Annual_report_2018_ENG.pdf (accessed 24 April 2019).

European Court of Human Rights, 'Violation by Article and by States (1959–2018)', www.echr.coe.int/Documents/Stats_violation_1959_2018_ENG.pdf (accessed 24 April 2019).

European Court of Human Rights, Hudoc database, https://hudoc.echr.coe.int/eng#{'documentcollectionid2":['GRANDCHAMBER",'CHAMBER']} (accessed 1 July 2019).

European External Action Service, *Compendium of International Standards for Elections* (Luxembourg, Publication Office of the European Union, 2016).

European Implementation Network, www.einnetwork.org/implementation-activities (accessed 24 April 2019).

European Parliament, press release, 'Rule of Law in Hungary: Parliament Calls on the EU to Act' (12 September 2018) www.europarl.europa.eu/news/en/press-room/20180906IPR12104/rule-of-law-in-hungary-parliament-calls-on-the-eu-to-act (accessed 24 April 2019).

European Semester, Country Report: Slovenia, ec.europa.eu/info/sites/info/files/2018-european-semester-country-report-slovenia-en.pdf (accessed 16 February 2019).

Eurostat, 'At-Risk-of-Poverty Rate and Proportion of the Population Having a Relatively high Income, 2016', https://ec.europa.eu/eurostat/statistics-explained/index.php?title=File:At-risk-of-poverty_rate_and_proportion_of_the_population_having_a_relatively_high_income,_2016_(%25)_QoL18.png#filelinks (accessed 24 April 2019).

Eurostat, 'Quality of Life Indicators – Material Living Conditions', https://ec.europa.eu/eurostat/statistics-explained/index.php/Quality_of_life_indicators_-_material_living_conditions (accessed 24 April 2019).

Featherstone, Kevin and Radaelli, CM, *The Politics of Europeanization* (Oxford, Oxford University Press, 2003).

Ferejohn, John, 'Independent Judges, Dependent Judiciary: Explaining Judicial Independence' [2001] *Southern California Law Review* 72.

Ferenc, Mitja, 'Secret World War Two Mass Graves in Slovenia' in Peter Jambrek (ed), *Crimes Committed by Totalitarian Regimes* (Ljubljana, Slovenian Presidency of the Council of the European Union, 2008).

Ferenc, Mitja, *Topografija evidentiranih grobišč: Poročilo Komisije Vlade Republike Slovenije za reševanje vprašanj prikritih grobišč 2005–2008* (Ljubljana, Družina, 2008).

'Fewer Rulings Against Slovenia at European Court of Human Rights' *RTVSLO* (28 January 2017) www.rtvslo.si/news-in-english/fewer-rulings-against-slovenia-at-european-court-of-human-rights/413615 (accessed 16 February 2019).

Fijalkowski, Agata, *From Old Times to New Europe: The Polish Struggle for Democracy and Constitutionalism* (Aldershot, Ashgate, 2010).

Filipovič, Hrast Maša and Rakar, Tatjana, 'The Future of the Slovenian Welfare State and Challenges to Solidarity', paper prepared for the Annual ESPAnet Conference: The Lost and the New Worlds of Welfare (3–5 September, 2015, Odense, Denmark) https://blogs.kent.ac.uk/welfsoc/files/2015/05/Draft_Paper_FilipovicHrastRakar.pdf (accessed 24 April 2019).

Fink-Hafner, Danica, Hafner-Fink, Mitja and Novak, Meta, 'Europeanisation as a Factor of National Interest Group Political-Cultural Change: The Case of Interest Groups in Slovenia' [2015] *East European Politics and Societies and Cultures* Vol 1, Issue 1.

'First Phase of NLB Privatization Completed' *Slovenia Times* (12 November 2018) www.sloveniatimes.com/first-phase-of-nlb-privatisation-completed (accessed 24 April 2019).

Flauss, Jean-François, 'The European Court of Human Rights and Freedom of Expression' (2009) 84(3) *Indiana Law Journal* 810.

Fleck, Zoltán, 'Judicial Independence in its Environment in Hungary' in Jiři Přibáň, Pauline Isobel Roberts and James Young (eds), *Systems of Justice in Transition Central European Experiences since 1989* (Dartmouth, Ashgate, 2003).

Florjančič, Damijan (President of the Supreme Court of the Republic of Slovenia), lecture at University of Maribor, Faculty of Law, 25 October 2018.

Forbath, William E, 'Social Rights, Courts and Constitutional Democracy – Poverty and Welfare Rights in the United States' (2005) The University of Texas School of Law, Public Law and Legal Theory Research Paper No 81.

Freedom House, Slovenia, 2015, https://freedomhouse.org/report/freedom-press/2015/slovenia (accessed 23 April 2019).

Fukuyama, Francis, *The End of History and the Last Man* (New York, Free Press, 1992).

G J, 'Prekmurska hobotnica Hakl-Židan-Polanič izčrpava davkoplačevalske milijone, ki jih uporabijo za prevzeme medijev v službi Židanove SD' *Demokracija* (29 May 2018) www.demokracija.si/slovenija/prekmurska-hobotnica-hakl-zidan-polanic-izcrpava-davkoplacevalske-milijone-ki-jih-uporabijo-za-prevzeme-medijev-v-sluzbi-zidanove-sd.html (accessed 23 April 2019).

Gamson, William A, Croteau, David, Hoynes, William and Sasson, Theodore, 'Media Images and the Social Construction of Reality' (1992) 18(1) *Annual Review of Sociology* 373.

Ganna, Mahmoud Daša, Tawitian, Elissa and Zupančič, Mateja, *Jaz, Midva, Mi* (Ljubljana, Rokus Klett, 2018).

Garlicki, Lech, 'Cooperation of Courts: The Role of Supranational Jurisdictions in Europe' (2008) 6 *International Journal of Constitutional Law* 509.

Georgi, Gotev, ''Sexist' Spanish Commissioner under Parliamentary Spotlight' *Euractiv* (10 September 2014) www.euractiv.com/section/eu-priorities-2020/news/sexist-spanish-commissioner-under-parliamentary-spotlight (accessed 24 April 2019).

Gerald Dalyl, Tom, 'The Judiciary and Constitutional Transitions', International Institute for Democracy and Electoral Assistance, Workshop report, 14–15 November 2014, The Hague.

Gerards, Janneke H and Fleuren, Joseph (eds), *Implementation of the European Convention on Human Rights and of the Judgments of the ECtHR in National Case Law* (Cambridge, Intersentia, 2014).

Gibanje Osveščeni Prebivalci Slovenije, 3 March 2014, www.gibanje-ops.com/dejavnosti-gibanja-ops/drugacna-politika/604-mnoino-vlaganje-reklamacije-za-zavrailo-plaila-rtv-prispevka (accessed 23 April 2019).

Ginsburg, Tom and Dixon, Rosalind, 'The South African Constitutional Court and Socio-Economic Rights as "Insurance Swaps"' (August 2013) University of Chicago-Public Law and Legal Theory Working Paper no 436.

Glas, Lize, 'The Functioning of the Pilot-Judgment Procedure of the European Court of Human Rights in Practice' (2016) 34(1) *Netherlands Quarterly of Human Rights* 41.

González Jácome, Jorge, 'The Promise and Peril of "Transformative Constitutionalism" – A Reply to Justice Carlos Bernal', blog of the International Journal of Constitutional Law, 27 December 2018, www.iconnectblog.com/2018/12/the-promise-and-peril-of-transformative-constitutionalism-a-reply-to-justice-carlos-bernal/ (accessed 24 April 2019).

Good, David F, 'The Economic Lag of Central and Eastern Europe: Income Estimates for the Habsburg Successor States, 1870–1910' (1994) 54(4) *Journal of Economic History* 869.

Gosling, Tim, 'How an Internet Impostor Exposed the Underbelly of the Czech Media, When Politicians Own the Press, Trolls Have the Last Laugh' *Foreign Policy* (3 December 2018) https://foreignpolicy.com/2018/12/03/how-an-internet-impostor-exposed-the-underbelly-of-the-czech-media/# (accessed 23 April 2019).

Govindjee, Avinash, 'Adjudication of Socio-Economic Rights by the Constitutional Court of South Africa: Walking the Tightrope between Activism and Deference?' (2013) 25(1) *National Law School of India Review* 62.

Gowder, Paul, *The Rule of Law in the Real World* (Cambridge, Cambridge University Press, 2016).

Griesser-Pečar, Tamara, *Razdvojeni narod: Slovenija 1941–1945, Okupacija, Kolaboracija, Državljanska Vojna, Revolucija* (Ljubljana, Mladinska knjiga, 2004).

Griesser Pečar, Tamara, 'Generalni register pojavov in žrtev totalitarizma' in *Mateja Čoh, Totalitarizmi- vprašanja in izzivi, Ob dvajsetletnici padca železne zavese v Evropi* (Ljubljana, Študijski center za narodno spravo, 2009).

Griesser Pečar, Tamara, 'Značilnosti revolucionarnega sodstva' [2017] *Dileme: razprave o vprašanjih sodobne slovenske zgodovine* 1(1/2) 119.

Guardiancich, Igor (ed), *Recovering From the Crisis Through Social Dialogue in the New EU Member States: The Case of Bulgaria, the Czech Republic, Poland and Slovenia* (Budapest, International Labour Organization, 2012).

Guardiancich, Igor, *Pension Reforms in Central, Eastern and South-Eastern Europe: From Post-Socialist Transition to the Global Financial Crisis* (London, Routledge, 2013).

Guardiancich, Igor, 'Slovenia: The End of a Success Story? When a Partial Reform Equilibrium Turns Bad' (2016) 68(2) *Europe-Asia Studies* 205.

Guardiancich, Igor and Molina, Oscar (eds), *Talking through the Crisis: Social Dialogue and Industrial Relations Trends in Selected EU Countries* (Geneva, International Labour Organization, 2017).

Habermas, Jürgen, 'Constitutional Democracy: A Paradoxical Union of Contradictory Principles' (2001) 29(6) *Political Theory* 766.

Haček, Miro, '(Dis)trust into the Rule of Law in Slovenia' (2013) *Political Preferences* No 4 (2013).

Halmai, Gabor and Lane Scheppele, Kim (eds), 'Opinion on Hungary's New Constitutional Order: Amicus Brief for the Venice Commission on the Transitional Provisions of the Fundamental Law and the Key Cardinal Laws', February 2012 http://lapa.princeton.edu/hosteddocs/hungary/Amicus_Cardinal_Laws_final.pdf (accessed 24 April 2019).

Halmai, Gabor and Scheppele, Kim, 'Living Well Is the Best Revenge: The Hungarian Approach to Judging the Past' in A James McAdams (ed), *Transitional Justice and the Rule of Law in New Democracies* (Notre Dame, IN, University of Notre Dame Press, 1997).

Halmai, Gabor, 'Second-Grade Constitutionalism? The Case of Hungary and Poland', CSF-SSSUP Working Paper 1/2017.

Halmai, Gabor, 'The Role of Constitutionalism in Central Europe's Transitional Justice Processes' (2005) EUI Working Paper prepared for ICTJ, https://me.eui.eu/gabor-halmai/wp-content/uploads/sites/385/2016/10/constitutions_and_tj_halmai_longacceptedallchanges.pdf (accessed 24 April 2019).

Hammer, Leonard M and Emmert, Frank (eds), *The European Convention on Human Rights and Fundamental Freedoms in Central and Eastern Europe* (The Hague, Eleven International Publishing, 2012).

Hammerschmid, Gerhard, Walle, Steven Van de, Andrews, Rhys and Bezes, Philippe (eds), *Public Administration Reforms in Europe: The View from the Top* (Cheltenham, Edward Elgar Publishing, 2016).

Hančič, Damjan, Kolarič, Boštjan, Letnar Černič, Jernej, Podbersič, Renato and Valič, Andreja, 'National Report of the Crimes of Communism in Slovenia' (2010) www.ustrcr.cz/data/pdf/konference/zlociny-komunismu/COUNTRY%20REPORT%20SLOVENIA.pdf (accessed 24 April 2019).

Hart Ely, John, *Democracy and Distrust: A Theory of Judicial Review* (Cambridge, MA, Harvard University Press 1981).

Hart, HLA, *The Concept of Law* (Oxford, Clarendon Press, 1905).

Havel Václav, 'The Power of Powerless' [letter, October 1978] in Václav Havel (ed) *Living in Truth* (London, Faber & Faber, 1989), https://s3.amazonaws.com/Random_Public_Files/powerless.pdf (accessed 24 April 2019).

Havel, Václav, Speech in the Polish Parliament, 25 January 1990.

Hayek, Friedrich A von, *Law, Legislation and Liberty*, vol 2: *The Mirage of Social Justice*, 1st edn (Chicago, University of Chicago Press, 1978).

Hayo, Bernd and Voigt, Stefan, 'Explaining De Facto Judicial Independence' [2007] *International Review of Law and Economics* vol. 27, issue 3, 269–290.

Helfer, Laurence R and Slaughter, Anne-Marie, 'Toward a Theory of Effective Supranational Adjudication' (1997) 107 *Yale Law Journal* 273.

Hellman, Joel S, 'Winners Take All: The Politics of Partial Reform in Post-Communist Transitions' (1998) 50(2) *World Politics* 203.

Hellman, Joel S., Jones, Geraint and Kaufmann, Daniel, 'Seize the State, Seize the Day: State Capture, Corruption and Influence in Transition' (2000) Policy Research Working Paper Working Paper no 2444.

Hibbs, Douglas A and Olsson, Ola, 'Geography, Biogeography, and Why Some Countries are Rich and Others are Poor" (2004) 101(10) *Proceedings of the National Academy of Sciences of the United States of America* 3715.

Hillebrecht, Courtney, 'The Power of Human Rights Tribunals: Compliance with the European Court of Human Rights and Domestic Policy Change' (2014) 20(4) *European Journal of International Relations* 1100.

Hoffmann-Riem, Wolfgang, 'The Venice Commission of the Council of Europe: Standards and Impact' (2014) 25(2) *European Journal of International Law 579–97*.

'How "New Europe" Has Fared on its Tenth Birthday' *The Economist* (1 May 2014).

IMAD, 'Development Report 2018', Ljubljana, June 2018 www.umar.si/fileadmin/user_upload/razvoj_slovenije/2018/aPOR2018_splet_novo.pdf (accessed 24 April 2019).

IMAD, *Development Report 2014* (Ljubljana, Institute for Macroeconomic Analysis and Development, 2014) 109.

'IMF, Venice Commission to Meet Over Anti-Corruption Court in Ukraine' *112.International* (21 May 2018) https://112.international/ukraine-top-news/imf-venice-commission-to-meet-over-anti-corruption-court-in-ukraine-28668.html (accessed 24 April 2019).

Index Mundi, 'GINI index (World Bank Estimate) – Country Ranking', www.indexmundi.com/facts/indicators/SI.POV.GINI/rankings (accessed 24 April 2019).

International Council on Archives, Principles of Access to Archives www.ica.org/en/principles-access-archives (accessed 24 April 2019).

Jakab, Andras and Kochenov, Dimitry, *The Enforcement of EU Law and Values, Ensuring Member States' Compliance* (Oxford, Oxford University Press, 2017).

Jaklič, Klemen, 'Ustavni vidik svobode izražanja in javna RTV' (2005) 25 *Dignitas* 104.

Jakubowicz, Karol, 'Post-Communist Political Systems and Media Freedom and Independence' in John Downey and Sabina Mihelj (eds), *Central and Eastern European Media in Comparative Perspective: Politics, Economy and Culture* (Farnham, Ashgate, 2012).

Jakubowicz, Karol and Sükösd, Miklós, 'Twelve Concepts Regarding Media System Evolution and Democratization in Post-Communist Countries' in Karol Jakubowicz and Miklós Sükösd (eds), *Finding the Right Place on the Map: Central and Eastern European Media Change in a Global Perspective* (Bristol, Intellect Books, 2008).

Jambrek, Peter, 'Pravice do svobode izobraževanja, do svobode znanosti in umetnosti ter do avtonomije univerze' (2012) 55/56 *Dignitas* 3.

Jambrek, Peter, 'Simbolna sporočila države in jedro slovenske ustavne identitete' *Delo-Sobotna priloga* (3 August 2013).

Jambrek, Peter, *Demokracija in država, Slovenija 1945–2015* (Fakulteta za državne in evropske študije, Evropska pravna fakulteta, 2014).

Jambrek, Peter, *Nation's Transitions: Social and Legal Issues of Slovenia's Transitions 1945–2105* (Graduate School of Government and European Studies, European Faculty of Law 2014).

Jambrek, Peter, 'Slovenska taborišča za prisilno delo – kdaj in zakaj' in Peter Jambrek (ed), *Ženska taborišča: ženska kazenska taborišča za prisilno delo v Sloveniji 1949–50* (Brdo pro Kranju, Fakulteta za državne in evropske študije, 2014).

Jambrek, Peter, *Ustava in svoboda: Ustavna ureditev Slovenije, izvori, temelji in razvoj* (Graduate School of Government and European Studies, European Faculty of Law, 2014).

Jambrek, Peter, Rupel, Dimitrij and Avbelj, Matej, 'Ustavnost in suverenost v razmerju do zunanje oblasti – Slovenija v Jugoslaviji, Natu in Evropski uniji' in Avbelj Matej (ed), *Izzivi moderne države* (Fakulteta za državne in evropske študije, 2012).

Jamnik, Pavel, 'Post-World War Two Crimes on the Territory of Slovenia: Police Investigation and Proof Regarding Criminal Offences that Do Not Fall under the Statute of Limitations' in Peter Jambrek (ed), *Crimes Committed by Totalitarian Regimes* (Ljubljana, Slovenian Presidency of the Council of the European Union, 2008).

Jančar, Drago et al, *The Hour of European Truth for Slovenia* (Nova revija, 1997).

Jančar, Drago (ed), *Temna stran meseca* (Nova revija, 1998).

Jančar, Mateja and Letnar Černič, Jernej (eds), *Poročilo o pobojih: vmesno poročilo o raziskovanju povojnih množičnih pobojev Preiskovalne komisije Državnega zbora Republike Slovenije o raziskovanju povojnih množičnih pobojev, pravno dvomljivih procesov in drugih tovrstnih nepravilnosti, ki jo je vodil dr Jože Pučnik*, (Ljubljana, Inštitut dr Jožeta Pučnika, 2010).

Janneke, H Gerards, 'The Transformative Power of the European Court of Human Rights' Treaties of Nijmegen Medal 2006', November 2016.

Jenne, Erin K and Mudde, Cas, 'Hungary's Illiberal Turn: Can Outsiders Help?' (2012) 23(3) *Journal of Democracy* 147.

Jerovšek, Tone, 'Ustavna ureditev sodstva' (2001) *VII. Dnevi javnega prava Portorož 4.-6. June 2001, pp 47–59.*

Joerges, Christian and Neyer, Jürgen, 'From Intergovernmental Bargaining to Deliberative Political Processes: The Constitutionalisation of Comitology' (2002) 3(3) *European Law Journal* 273.

Jowell, Jeffrey, 'The Venice Commission: Disseminating Democracy through Law' (2001) 4 *Public Law* 675.

Jože, P Damijan, 'Kučan in Janša – botra slovenskih oligarhov' *Razgledi.net* (20 August 2007) http://razgledi.net/2007/08/20/kucan-in-jansa-botra-slovenskih-oligarhov/ (accessed 24 April 2019).

Juhant, Janez, 'Nasilje in sočutje v ideologijah in religijah in slovenska tranzicijska resničnost' (20140 74(2) *Bogoslovni vestnik* 175.

Juhant, Janez, 'Resnica in sočutje se odpirata na bregovih večnosti' (2015) 75(2) *Bogoslovni vestnik* 199.

Justinek, Gorazd, 'Izvoz rešuje slovensko rast' (2015) 23(2) *Ocena konjukturnih gibanj za Slovenijo* 23.

Justinek, Gorazd, 'Izvozniki uspešni na ključnih evropskih trgih' (2015) 23(1) *Ocena konjukturnih gibanj za Slovenijo* 23.

Justinek, Gorazd, 'Is Central Europe an Economic Entity? Special Focus on Slovenia' (2015) 7(2) *Journal on European Perspectives of the Western Balkans* 119.

Justinek, Gorazd, 'The Slovenian Economy: Yesterday and Today' in F Adam (ed), *Slovenia: Social, Economic and Environmental Issues* (New York, Nova Science, 2017) 119.

Justinek, Gorazd and Lautar, Katja, 'Slovensko gospodarstvo med preteklostjo in prihodnostjo', in Matej Avbelj Gašper Dovžan, Jernej Letnar Černič and Miha Movrin (eds), *Evropska Slovenija* (Ljubljana, Inštitut Nove revije, 2013) 265.

Kajnč Lange, Sabina, 'Channels of Cooperation: A Case Study of Slovenia's Presidency of the EU' (2009) European Policy Institutes Network Working Paper no 21.

Kajnč Lange, Sabina, 'Effects of EU Enlargement: Slovenia' [2009] http://tepsa.be/Enlarging%20the%20European%20Union.pdf (accessed 14 September 2019).

Kajnč Lange, Sabina, 'Evropeizacija slovenske zunanje politike: od pridružitvenega procesa do predsedovanja Svetu EU' [2011] *Teorija in praksa: družboslovna revija* Vol 48, Nr 3.

Kaltwasser, Cristóbal Rovira, *Populism vs Constitutionalism? Comparative Perspectives on Contemporary Western Europe, Latin America, and the United States* (Foundation for Law, Justice and Society, 2013).

Kardelj, Edvard, *Smeri razvoja političnega sistema samoupravljanja* (Komunist, 1977).

Kattago, Siobhan, *Memory and Representation in Contemporary Europe: The Persistence of the Past* (Farnham, Ashgate, 2012).

Katzenbach, Christian, Pentzold, Christian, Kannengießer, Sigrid, Adolf, Marian and Taddicken Monika (eds), *Neue Komplexitäten für kommunikationsforschung und Medienanalyse: Analytische Zugänge und empirische Studien* (Berlin, Schriftenreihe Digital Communication Research 4, 2018).

Kaučič, Igor (ed), *Twenty Years of the Constitution of the Republic of Slovenia: Significance of Constitutionality and Constitutional Democracy* (Ljubljana, Faculty of Law – Constitutional Court of the Republic of Slovenia, 2012).

Keane David, 'Attacking Hate Speech under Article 17 of the European Convention on Human Rights', (2007) 25(4) *Netherlands quarterly of human rights* 641.

Keating Dave, 'MEPs Reject Bratušek and Force Juncker Rethink' *Politico* (10 August 2014) www.politico.eu/article/meps-reject-bratusek-and-force-juncker-rethink (accessed 24 April 2019).

Kelemen, R Daniel and Orenstein, Mitchell A, 'Europe's Autocracy Problem: Polish Democracy Final Days?' *Foreign Affairs* (7 January 2016).

Keller, Helen and Marti, Cedric, 'Reconceptualizing Implementation: The Judicialization of the Execution of the European Court of Human Rights' Judgments' (2015) 26(4) *European Journal of International Law* 829.

Keller, Helen and Stone Sweet, Alice, *A Europe of Rights: The Impact of the ECHR on National Legal Systems* (Oxford, Oxford University Press, 2008).

Kidsrights, 'KidsIndex Ranking 2018', www.kidsrightsindex.org/Portals/5/The%20KidsRights%20Index%202018.pdf?ver=2018-06-01-112649-877 (accessed 24 April 2019).

Kingsley, Patrick, 'Safe in Hungary, Viktor Orban Pushes his Message across Europe' *New York Times* (Ljubljana, 4 June 2018) www.nytimes.com/2018/06/04/world/europe/viktor-orban-media-slovenia.html (accessed 23 April 2019).

Kirchheimer, Otto, 'The Transformation of Western European Party Systems' in Joseph La Palombara and Myron Wiener (eds), *Political Parties and Political Development* (Princeton, NJ, Princeton University Press, 1966).

Kizo, 'Grega Repovž in prijatelji, sluge davčnih oaz ali kako kazino kapitalizem hrani Mladino' *Portal Plus* (1 February 2015) www.portalplus.si/686/kapitalizem-hrani-mladino/ (accessed 23 April 2019).

Klemenčič, Manja, Bergan, Sjur and Primožič, Rok, *Student Engagement in Europe: Society, Higher Education and Student Governance* (Strasbourg, Council of Europe Higher Education Series no 20, 2015).

Kochenov, Dimitry, *EU Enlargement and the Failure of Conditionality: Pre-Accession Conditionality in the Fields of Democracy and the Rule of Law* (The Hague: Kluwer Law International 2008).

Kochenov, Dimitry and Pech, Laurent, 'Better Late than Never: On the European Commission's Rule of Law Framework and its First Activation' (2016) 54(5) *Journal of Common Market Studies* 1062.

Kogovšek, Neža and Brankica, Petković (eds), *Brazgotine izbrisa, Prispevek h kritičnemu razumevanju izbrisa iz registra stalnega prebivalstva Republike Slovenije* (Mirovni inštitut, 2010).

Kolm, Ann-Sofie and Tonin, Mirco, 'Benefits Conditional on Work and the Nordic Model', (2015) 127 *Journal of Public Economics* 115.

Komel, Dean, 'Jože Pučnik: Personal Freedom, Culture, and Politics' (2014) 43(1) *Traditiones* 125.

Kosař, David, *Perils of Judicial Self-Government in Transitional Societies* (Cambridge, Cambridge University Press, 2016).

Kosař, David, 'Nudging Domestic Judicial Reforms from Strasbourg: How the European Court of Human Rights Shapes domestic judicial design' (2017) 13(1) *Utrecht Law Review* 112.

Kosař, David, 'Politics of Judicial Independence and Judicial Accountability in Czechia: Bargaining in the Shadow of the Law between Court Presidents and the Ministry of Justice' (2017) 13(1) *European Constitutional Law Review* 96.

Kosař, David, 'Beyond Judicial Councils: Forms, Rationales and Impact of Judicial Self Governance in Europe' (2018) 19(7) *German Law Journal* 1567.

Kosař, David and Lixinski, Lucas, 'Domestic Judicial Design by International Human Rights Courts' (2015) 109(4) *American Journal of International Law* 713.

Kosec, Jernej, 'How Communist Is the Judiciary in Slovenia? A Survey' (July 2018) CRCE Briefing Paper.

Kosovel, Anton and Kavčič, Vladimir (eds), *Zločin brez kazni* (Ljubljana, Slovenska matica, 2003).

Kovač, Polonca, 'Openness and Transparency in (Slovene) Administrative Procedures as Fundamental European Principles' (2016/2017) 9(2) *NISPAcee Journal of Public Administration and Policy* 49.

Krasner, Stephen D, *Sovereignty: Organized Hypocrisy* (Princeton, NJ, Princeton University Press, 1999).

Kristan, Ivan, 'Pravna država in ustavno sodišče: na rob odločbi o referendumu o volilnem sistemu' (1999) *Pravna praksa* 18/17.

Kristan, Ivan, 'Delitev oblasti ob ankaranski zgodbi' [2011] *XVII. dnevi javnega prava in javnega managementa* Portorož 8–9 June 2011, Vol. 47. Nr. 1/2.

Krivic, Matevž, 'Memorandum o ustavnopravnih vprašanjih v zvezi z odločbo US RS št. U-I-12/97 [1999] *Pravna praksa* 17/99, 36–40.

Krygier, Martin, 'Introduction', in Wojciech Sadurski, Adam Czarnota and Martin Krygier (eds), *Spreading Democracy and the Rule of Law? The Impact of EU Enlargement on the Rule of Law, Democracy and Constitutionalism in Post-Communist Legal Orders* (Dordrecht, Springer, 2006).

Krygier, Martin, 'The Rule of Law: Legality, Teleology, Sociology' in Gianluigi Palombella and Neil Walker (eds), *Re-Locating the Rule of Law* (Oxford, Hart Publishing, 2008).

Krygier, Martin, 'The Rule of Law' in Michel Rosenfeld and András Sajó (eds), *Oxford Handbook of Comparative Constitutional Law* (Oxford, Oxford University Press, 2012).

Krygier, Martin, 'The Rule of Law: Pasts, Presents, and Two Possible Futures' (2016) 12 *Annual Review of Law and Social Science* 199.

Kuhelj, Alenka and Bugarič, Bojan, 'A Day in the Life of Post-Communist Europe' (2016) 8(1) *Hague Journal on the Rule of Law* 183.

Kühn, Zdeněk, 'The Authoritarian Legal Culture at Work: The Passivity of Parties and the Interpretational Statements of Supreme Courts' (2006) 2(2) *Croatian Yearbook of European Law and Policy* 19.

Kühn, Zdeněk, *The Judiciary in Central and Eastern Europe: Mechanical Jurisprudence in Transformation?* (Leiden, Brill–Njihoff, 2011).

Kukovič, Simona, '(Dis)trust in Political Institutions: Comparisons Between New Democracies of Central and Eastern Europe' (2013) 6 *Journal of Comparative Politics* 20.

Kuti, Csongor, *Post-Communist Restitution and the Rule of Law* (Budapest, Central European University Press, 2009).

L A, 'Premierju predlagamo, da z držo in delovanjem, izkazanim v pozivu, ravna bolj previdno' *Večer* (24 November 2018) https://www.vecer.com/premierju-predlagamo-da-z-drzo-in-delovanjem-izkazanim-v-pozivu-ravna-bolj-previdno-6618574 (accessed 23 April 2019).

Laclau, Ernesto, *On Populist Reason* (London Verso, 2005).

Lambert, Elisabeth, 'The First Infringements Proceedings Within the European System of Human Rights: Using the Court as the Last Bastion for the Credibility of the Council of Europe' (2018) (4) *European Human Rights Law Review* 325.

Landes, David S,*The Wealth and Poverty of Nations: Why Some Are So Rich and Others So Poor* (New York, WW Norton, 1998).

Lane Scheppele, Kim, 'The Unconstitutional Constitution' *New York Times* (2 January 2012) http://krugman.blogs.nytimes.com/2012/01/02/the-unconstitutional-constitution/ (accessed 24 April 2019).

Lane Scheppele, Kim, 'Romania Unravels the Rule of Law' *New York Times* (5 July 2012) http://krugman.blogs.nytimes.com/2012/07/05/guest-post-romania-unravels-the-rule-of-law/ (accessed 24 April 2019).

Lane Scheppele, Kim, '"Constitutional Revenge" in Hungary' *Eutopia Law* (6 March 2013) https://eutopialaw.com/2013/03/06/constitutional-revenge-in-hungary/ (accessed 24 April 2019).

Lane Scheppele, Kim, 'The End of the End of History', lecture, Berlin, 7 June 2017, www.rewi.hu-berlin.de/de/lf/oe/lsi/termine/prof-dr-kim-lane-scheppele-the-end-of-the-end-of-history (accessed 24 April 2019).

Lane Scheppele, Kim and Perju, Vlad, 'Separating Law and Politics in Romania' *New York Times* (12 July 2012) http://krugman.blogs.nytimes.com/2012/07/12/guest-post-separating-law-and-politics-in-romania/?_php=true&_type=blogs&_r=0 (accessed 24 April 2019).

Leach, Philip, *Taking a Case to the European Court of Human Rights* (Oxford, Oxford University Press, 2011).

Ledeneva, Alena, 'Telephone Justice in Russia' [2008] *Post-Soviet Affairs* 24:4, 324–350.

Lees, Lorraine M., *Keeping Tito Afloat, The United States, Yugoslavia and the Cold War* (Philadephia, Pennsylvania State University Press, 1997).

Lefort, Claude and Macey, David, *Democracy and Political Theory* (Cambridge, Polity, 1988).

Leskovic, Alenka, 'Deset let pozneje' (1999) 18 *Pravna praksa* 33.

Letnar Černič, Jernej, 'Supreme State Prosecutor v Ribičič (Mitja), Order on Whether to Open Pre-Trial Criminal Investigation', Ks 962/2006, *Oxford Reports on International Law in Domestic Courts 523* (SI 2006) (Ljubljana, 27 June 2006) http://opil.ouplaw.com/view/10.1093/law:ildc/523si06.case.1/law-ildc-523si06 (accessed 24 April 2019).

Letnar Černič, Jernej, 'Freedom of Press in the European Context: Klein v Slovakia' (2007) 11(3) *Edinburgh Law Review* 444.

Letnar Černič, Jernej, 'Impact of the European Court of Human Rights on the Rule of Law in Central and Eastern Europe' (2008) 10(1) *Hague Journal on the Rule of Law* 111.

Letnar Černič, Jernej, Svoboda dostopa do arhivov (2011) 9 *Pravna praksa* 20.

Letnar Černič, Jernej, 'Ustavnopravni in mednarodni vidiki svobode do dostopa do arhivov' in Damjan Hančič, Gregor Jenuš and Neža Strajnar (eds), *Odstiranje zamolčanega: Zbornik prispevkov. Zbirka Totalitarizmi – vprašanja in izzivi*, 3 (Ljubljana, Študijski center za narodno spravo, 2013).

Letnar Černič, Jernej, 'Primerjava med slovensko in špansko tranzicijsko izkušnjo' in Mateja Čoh Kladnik and Neža Strajnar (eds), *Represivne metode totalitarnih režimov: Zbornik prispevkov z mednarodnega znanstvenega posveta, Zbirka Totalitarizmi – vprašanja in izzivi*, 2 (Ljubljana, Študijski center za narodno spravo, 2012).

Letnar Černič, Jernej, 'Culture of Fear in Slovenian Society' in Janez Juhant and Bojan Žalec (eds), *From Culture of Fear to Society of Trust* (Zürich, Lit Verlag, 2013).

Letnar Černič, Jernej, 'Nezaupanje' *IUS-info* (25 March 2013).

Letnar Černič, Jernej, 'Vizija učinkovitega varovanja človekovih pravic v slovenski družbi' in Matej Avbelj, Gašper Dovžan, Jernej Letnar Černič and Miha Movrin (eds), *Evropska Slovenija* (Ljubljana, Inštitut Nove revije, 2013).

Letnar Černič, Jernej, 'Kritična ocena dosedanjega delovanja slovenskega varuha človekovih pravic' (2014) 14(4) *Hrvatska i komparativna javna uprava* 921.

Letnar Černič, Jernej, 'Rămăşiţele identităţii comuniste in Slovenia: justiţia de tranziţie – potenţialul, capcanele şi viitorul său' in Cosmin Budeanca and Florentin Olteanu (eds), *Stalinizare şi destalinizare: Evoluţii instituţionale şi impact social* (Bucharest, Polirom, 2014).

Letnar Černič, Jernej, 'Consolidating Democracy through Transitional Justice in Slovenia: Lessons Learnt?' in Agata Fijalkowski and Raluca Grosescu (eds), *Transitional Criminal Justice in Post-Dictatorial and Post-Conflict Societies* (Cambridge, Intersentia, 2015).

Letnar Černič, Jernej, 'Democracy as a Trump Card? Combating Hate Speech in Pluralistic Societies' in Dorota Anna Gozdecka and Magdalena Kmak (eds), *Europe at the Edge of Pluralism* (Cambridge, Intersentia, 2015) 163–76.

Letnar Černič, Jernej, 'Petindvajset let kasneje' in Dean Komel and Tomaž Zalaznik (eds), *Spoprijem z razmerami in razmerji v Sloveniji* (Ljubljana, Inštitut Nove Revije, 2017).

Letnar Černič, Jernej, 'Od Barbarinega rova do rudnika Pečovnik' *IUS-info* (4 November 2016).

Letnar Černič, Jernej, 'The European Court of Human Rights, Rule of Law and Socio-Economic Rights in Times of Crises' (2016) 8(2) *Hague Journal on the Rule of Law* 227.

Letnar Černič, Jernej, et al, *Slovenija pred Evropskim Sodiščem za Človekove Pravice (1994–2016)* (Ljubljana, Fakulteta za Državne in Evropske Študije, 2017).

Letnar Černič, Jernej, 'Eksodus' *IUS-info* (12 January 2018).

Letnar Černič, Jernej, 'Impact of the European Court of Human Rights on the Rule of Law in Central and Eastern Europe' (2018) 10(1) *Hague Journal on the Rule of Law* 111.

Letnar Černič, Jernej, 'The European Court of Human Rights in the States of the Former Yugoslavia' (2018) 1 *East European Yearbook on Human Rights* 32.

Letnar Černič, Jernej, 'Umanjkanje demokracije' *IUS-info* (23 March 2018).

Letnar Černič, Jernej, 'Ali imajo vsi otroci v Sloveniji enake začetne možnosti za samouresničitev?' *IUS-info* (16 November 2018).

Letnar Černič, Jernej, 'Čigave človekove pravice?' *IUS-info* (14 July 2018).

Letnar Černič, Jernej, 'Impact of the European Court of Human Rights on the Rule of Law in Central and Eastern Europe' (2018) 10(1) *Hague Journal on the Rule of Law* 111.

Letnar Černič, Jernej, 'Korak nazaj' *IUS-Info* (7 September 2018).

Letnar Černič, Jernej, 'National Security – A Trump Card? The European Court of Human Rights Decision in *Herri Batasuna and Batasuna v Spain*, *Etxeberria and others v Spain* and *Herritarren Zerrenda v Spain*', EUI working papers, MWP 2010/12, http://cadmus.eui.eu/bitstream/handle/1814/13343/MWP_2010_02.pdf?sequence=1 (accessed 23 April 2019).

Letnar Černič, Jernej, *Slovenija na razpotju: Geneza varstva človekovih pravic v slovenski družbi* (Kranj, Nova Univerza–Fakulteta za Državne in Evropske Študije, 2018).

Letnar Černič Jernej, 'Vzpon "novoreka"', *Slovenski čas-Družina* (30 September 2018).

Letnar Černič, Jernej, 'Človekovo dostojanstvo kot temelj vladavine prava v slovenski družbi' (2018) 78(1) *Bogoslovni vestnik* 147.

Letnar Černič, Jernej, *Slovenija na razpotju: Geneza varstva človekovih pravic v slovenski družbi* (Kranj, Nova Univerza – Fakulteta za Državne in Evropske Študije, 2018).

Letnar Černič, Jernej, 'The European Court of Human Rights in the States of the Former Yugoslavia' (2018) 1 *East European Yearbook on Human Rights* 32.

Letnar Černič, Jernej, 'Komentar 159. člena ustave' in Matej Avbelj (ed), *Komentar Ustave Republike Slovenije* (Nova Gorica, Nova Univerza–Evropska Pravna Fakulteta, 2019).

Letnar Černič, Jernej and Van Ho, Tara (eds), *Human Rights and Business: Direct Corporate Accountability for Human Rights* (Oisterwijk, Wolf Legal Publishers, 2015).

Letnar Černič, Jernej and Avbelj, Matej, 'Introduction to the Special Issue on the Crisis of Constitutional Democracy in Central and Eastern Europe' (2018) 10(1) *Hague Journal on the Rule of Law* 1.

Letnar Černič, Jernej, Nahtigal, Matjaž, Udovič, Boštjan and Mirošič, Iztok, Broadcast 'Future of Europe' *Radio Slovenija-Prvi* (20 september 2018) https://4d.rtvslo.si/arhiv/studio-ob-17h/174563533 (accessed 24 April 2019).

Letnar Černič, Jernej, Avbelj, Matej, Novak, Marko and Valentinčič, Dejan, *Reform of Democracy and the Rule of Law in Slovenia* (Kranj, New University, Faculty of Government and European Studies, 2019).

Lindstrom, Nicole and Piroska, Dora, 'The Politics of privatization and Europeanization in Europe's Periphery: Slovenian Banks and Breweries For sale?' [2007] *Competition and Change 11(2).*

Lipset, Martin Seymour, 'The Social Requisites of Democracy Revisited' [1994] *Am Sociol Review* Vol. 59, No.1.

Lisjak Gabrijelčič, Luka, Conversation with Timothy Snyder, 'Ljudje znamo dobro lagati in dobro znamo ubijati. Zelo težko pa priznamo, da smo ubijali zaradi laži' *Razpotja* (Autumn 2016).

Lizarazo-Rodríguez, Liliana, 'Constitutional Adjudication In Colombia: Avant-garde or Case Law Transplant? A Literature Review' (2011) 13(1) *Estudios Socio-Jurídicos* 145.

Löffler Martin, *Presserecht: Kommentar zu den deutschen Landespressegesetzen mit systematischen Darstellungen zum pressebezogenen Standesrecht, Anzeigenrecht, Werbe- und Wettbewerbsrecht, Urheber- und Verlagsrecht, Arbeitsrecht, Titelschutz, Mediendatenschutz, Jugendmedienschutz und Steuerrecht*, 6th edn (Munich, Beck, 2015).

Londras, Fiona de and Dzehtsiarou, Kanstantsin, 'Mission Impossible? Addressing Non-Execution through Infringement Proceedings in the European Court of Human Rights' 66(2) *ICLQ* 467.

Lovec, Marko, 'Nations in Transit 2018 – Slovenia', Freedom House, https://freedomhouse.org/report/nations-transit/2018/slovenia (accessed 24 April 2019).

Lovšin, Špela, 'Bolniški stalež – delitev bremen med delodajalci in javnimi blagajnimi po Evropi', (2019) 14 *Pravna praksa* 10.

Luke Gallop, John, Sachs, Jeffrey D and Mellinger, Andrew D, 'Geography and Economic Development' (1999) 22(2) *International Regional Science Review* 179.

Madison, Agnus, *The World Economy: A Millennial Perspective*, Historical Statistics vol 2 (Paris, OECD, 2007).

Magyar, Bálint, *Post-Communist Mafia State: The Case of Hungary* (Budapest, Central European University and Noran Libro, 2016).

Makarovič, Matej and Tomšič, Matevž, 'Democrats, Authoritarians and Nostalgics: Slovenian Attitudes Toward Democracy' (2015) 8(3) *Innovative Issues and Approaches in Social Sciences* 8.

Makarovič, Matej, Prijon, Lea, Rek, Mateja and Tomšič, Matevž, 'The Strength of Pro-European Consensus Among Slovenian Political Elites' (2016) 41(4) *Historical Social Research* 195.

Makovec, Urška, 'Sodišča na območju Maribora šestkrat bolj kršijo človekove pravice kot sodišča na Celjskem' *Siol* (28 September 2017) siol.net/novice/slovenija/sodisca-na-obmocju-maribora-sestkrat-bolj-krsijo-clovekove-pravice-kot-sodisca-na-celjskem-447993.

Mälksoo, Lauri and Benedek, Wolfgang (eds), *Russia and the European Court of Human Rights: The Strasbourg Effect* (Cambridge, Cambridge University Press, 2018).

Mátyás Kovács, János, 'Approaching the EU and Reaching the US? Rival Narratives on Transforming Welfare Regimes in East-Central Europe' in Peter Mair and Jan Zielonka (eds), *The Enlarged European Union: Diversity and Adaptation* (London, Frank Cass, 2002).

Mátyás Kovács, János and Zentai, Violetta (eds), *Capitalism from Outside? Economic Cultures in Eastern Europe After 1989* (Budapest, New York, Central European University Press, 2012).

McChesney, Robert W, *Rich Media, Poor Democracy: Communication Politics in Dubious Times* (Champaign, University of Illinois Press, 1999).

McQuail, Denis, *Mass Communication Theory*, 4th edn (London, Sage, 2000).

Mellinger, Andrew, Sachs, Jeffrey D and Luke Gallup, John, 'Climate, Water Navigability, and Economic Development' (1999) CID Working Papers 24A.

Mencinger, Jože, 'Transition to a National and a Market Economy: A Gradualist Approach' in M Mrak et al (ed) *Slovenia: From Yugoslavia to the European Union* (Washington, DC, World Bank, 2004) 67.

Mendelski, Martin, 'The EU's Pathological Power: The Failure of External Rule of Law Promotion in South Eastern Europe' (2015) 39(3) *Southeastern Europe* 318.

Mendelski, Martin, 'Europeanization of Good Governance in Romania: Where and Why Does it Fail, and What Can Be Done About it?', 1 March 2017. https://papers.ssrn.com/sol3/papers.cfm?abstract_id=2926871 (accsessed 14 September 2019).

Mikola, Milko, *Kazenske ustanove in zaporniki v Sloveniji 1945–1951* (Ljubljana, Nova obzorja, 2016).

Milič, Marja, 'Kje v Sloveniji se najbolje živi v letu 2018? Razkrivamo lestvico 212 občin!' *Moje Finance* (15 October 2018) https://mojefinance.finance.si/8939584 (accessed 24 April 2019).

Milosavljevic, Marko, 'Media Pluralism Monitor 2016: Monitoring Risks for Media Pluralism in the EU and Beyond. Country report: Slovenia', *European University Institute-Centre for Media Pluralism and Media Freedom*, http://cadmus.eui.eu/bitstream/handle/1814/46811/Slovenia_EN.pdf?sequence=1&isAllowed=y, p (accessed 23 April 2019).

Mišković, Nataša, Fischer-Tiné, Herald and Boškovska, Nada, *The Non-Aligned Movement and the Cold War: Deli – Bandung – Belgrade* (Abingdon, Routledge, 2014).

Mitchell, Ian David, *The Cost of Reputation: Aldington versus Tolstoy. The Causes, Course and Consequences of a Notorious Libel Case* (Edinburgh, Canongate, 1997).

Mollers, Christopher, *The Three Branches: A Comparative Model of Separation of Powers* (Oxford, Oxford University Press, 2013).

Morlino, Leonardo and Sadurski, Wojciech (eds), *Democratization and the European Union: Comparing Central and Eastern European Post-Communist Countries* (Abingdon, Routledge, 2010).

Motoc, Iulia and Ziemele, Ineta (eds), *The Impact of the ECHR on Democratic Change in Central and Eastern Europe: Judicial Perspectives* (Cambridge, Cambridge University Press, 2017).

Motoh, Helena, 'Slovenia Economy Briefing: The Attempt to Sale Pro Plus to United Group' *China-CEE Institute* (30 November 2018) https://china-cee.eu/2018/11/30/slovenia-economy-briefing-the-attempt-to-sale-pro-plus-to-united-group/ (accessed 23 April 2019).

Možina, Damjan, 'Evropeizacija in modernizacija obligacijskega prava' [2008], dnevi slovenskih pravnikov Portorož 16.-18. October 2008, 1270–1283.

Možina, Damjan, 'Odškodninska odgovornost države' [2013] *Pravni letopis* 2013 http://www.ipp-pf.si/uploads/File/Pravni%20letopis/Pravni%20letopis%202013_v%20tisk.pdf (accessed 14 October 2019).

Mudde, Cas and Kaltwasser, Cristóbal Rovira, *Populism* (Oxford, Oxford University Press, 2013).

Mueller, Dennis C, 'Constitutional Democracy and Social Welfare' (1973) 87(1) *Quarterly Journal of Economics* 60.

Müller, Jan-Werner, 'The Hungarian Tragedy' [Spring 2011] *Dissent* 5.

Müller, Jan-Werner, 'The People Must Be Extracted from Within the People: Reflections on Populism' (2014) 21(4) *Constellations* 483.

Müller, Jan-Werner, 'Eastern Europe Goes South: Disappearing Democracy in the EU's Newest Member States' *Foreign Affairs* (March/April 2014).

Müller, Jan-Werner, 'Should the EU Protect Democracy and the Rule of Law Inside Member States?' (2015) 21(2) *European Law Journal* 141.

Müller Jan-Werner, *What Is Populism?* (Philadelphia, University of Pennsylvania Press, 2016).

Müller, Jan-Werner, 'If You're not a Democracy, You're not European Anymore', *Foreign Policy* (22 December 2017).

Müller, Lisa, 'The Impact of the Mass Media on the Quality of Democracy within a State Remains a Much Overlooked Area Of study' *London School of Economics and Political Science* (10 December 2014) http://blogs.lse.ac.uk/eurocrisispress/2014/12/10/the-impact-of-the-mass-media-on-the-quality-of-democracy-within-a-state-remains-a-much-overlooked-area-of-study/ (accessed 23 April 2019).

Müller, Peter, 'Fueling the Populists, Why Did EU Commission Chief Go Silent in Border Dispute?' *Spiegel Online* (14 September 2018) www.spiegel.de/international/europe/eu-commission-chief-silent-in-slovenia-croatia-dispute-a-1228169.html (accessed 24 April 2019).

Mungiu-Pippidi, Alina, *Quest for Good Governance: How Societies Develop Control of Corruption* (Cambridge, Cambridge University Press, 2015).

N Ž, 'V bran vrhovnemu sodniku Janu Zobcu stopili priznani slovenski pravniki Teršek, Avbelj in Letnar Černič, ki so izrazili zgroženost nad pogromom mainstream medijev!' *Nova 24 TV* (8 June 2018) http://nova24tv.si/slovenija/v-bran-vrhovnemu-sodniku-janu-zobcu-stopili-priznani-slovenski-pravniki-tersek-avbelj-in-letnar-cernic-ki-so-izrazili-zgrozenost-nad-pogromom-mainstream-medijev/ (accessed 24 April 2019).

'Naj odškodnine plačajo tisti, ki so lagali, da jih ne bo' (*Siol*, 2 July 2012) www.siol.net/novice/slovenija/sds-naj-placajo-odskodnine-tisti-ki-so-lagali-da-jih-ne-bo-230950 (accessed 24 April 2019).

Najvišja pokojnina – December 2017, www.seniorji.info/POKOJNINE,_FINANCE_IN_PRAVNI_NASVETI_Najvisja_pokojnina_-_december_2017 archives (accessed 24 April 2019).

'Naming Street After Tito Unconstitutional' *Slovenia Times* (5 October 2011) www.sloveniatimes.com/naming-street-after-tito-unconstitutional (accessed 24 April 2019).

Nicholson, Nigel, *Long Live* (New York, Putnam, 1998).

North, Douglass C, Summerhill, William and Weingast, Barry, 'Order, Disorder, and Economic Change: Latin America versus North America' in Bruce Bueno de Mesquita and Hilton L Root (eds), *Governing for Prosperity* (New Haven, CT, Yale University Press, 2000).

Novak, Marko, 'Kršitve človekovih pravic in zavajanje javnosti' *IUS-info* (7 November 2016) www.iusinfo.si/DnevneVsebine/Kolumna.aspx?id=181814 (accessed 24 April 2019).

Novak, Marko, 'Nevarno razmerje: politika nad Sodnim svetom' (2016) *IUS-info* https://www.iusinfo.si/medijsko-sredisce/kolumne/180818 (accessed 14 September 2019).

Novak, Marko, 'Volitve sodnikov – mora Slovenija ostati evropska izjema?' (2016) *IUS-info* https://www.iusinfo.si/medijsko-sredisce/kolumne/176548 (accessed 14 September 2019).

Novak, Marko, *Delitev oblasti; medigra prava in politike* (Cankarjeva založba, 2003).

OECD, *OECD Income Distribution Database (IDD): Gini, Poverty, Income, Methods and Concepts* (Paris, Organisation for Economic Cooperation and Development, 2015).

OECD, 'Education Policy Outlook: Slovenia' (April 2016) www.oecd.org/slovenia/Education-Policy-Outlook-Country-Profile-Slovenia.pdf (accessed 24 April 2019).

OECD, 'Society at a Glance 2019, OECD Social Indicators', 27 March 2019, https://doi.org/10.1787/soc_glance-2019-en (accessed 24 April 2019).

OECD, 'Under Pressure: The Squeezed Middle Class', 2019, www.oecd.org/social/under-pressure-the-squeezed-middle-class-689afed1-en.htm (accessed 24 April 2019).

OECD, 'Better Life Index', Slovenia, www.oecdbetterlifeindex.org/countries/slovenia/ (accessed 24 April 2019).

Ofori-Parku, S Senyo, 'Reality Effect or Media effect? Television's Moulding of the Environmental Sanitation Agenda in Ghana' (2014) 35(2) *Ecquid Novi: African Journalism Studies* 40.

Omerza, Igor, *Veliki in dolgi pohod Nove revije* (Mohorjeva, 2015).

Opinion on the constitutional amendments concerning legislative elections in the Republic of Slovenia, www.venice.coe.int/webforms/documents/?pdf=CDL-INF(2000)013-e (accessed 24 April 2019).

Orbán, Viktor, 'Speech at the XXV-Bálványos Free Summer University and Youth Camp' in Csaba Tóth, 'Full Text of Viktor Orbán's Speech at Băile Tuşnad (Tusnádfürdő) of 26 July 2014' *Budapest Beacon* (29 July 2014) https://budapestbeacon.com/full-text-of-viktor-orbans-speech-at-baile-tusnad-tusnadfurdo-of-26-july-2014/ (accessed 24 April 2019).

Örnebring, Henrik, 'Clientelism, Elites, and the Media in Central and Eastern Europe' (2012) 17(4) *International Journal of Press/Politics* 497.

Orwell. George, 'The Freedom of the Press', unused preface to *Animal Farm* published in *Times Literary Supplement* (London, 15 September 1972).

Oster, Jan, *Media Freedom as a Fundamental Right* (Cambridge, Cambridge University Press, 2015).

Ovin, Rasto and Kramberger, Boštjan, 'Building an Institutional Framework for a Full-Fledged Market Economy' (Washington, DC, World Bank, 2004).

Ozmec, Martin, 'Zaradi pomanjkanja dokazov je sodišče zadevo ustavilo' *Štajerski tednik* (30 January 2014) https://sterntal.wordpress.com/2014/02/03/zaradi-pomanjkanja-dokazov-je-sodisce-zadevo-ustavilo/ (accessed 24 April 2019).

Palombella, Giovanni 'The Rule of Law and its Core' in Giovanni Palombella and Niel Walker (eds), *Re-locating the Rule of Law* (Oxford, Hart Publishers, 2009).

Parenti, Michael, 'Inventing Reality: The Politics of the Mass Media', (1987) 51(1) *Science and Society* 97.

Pečar, Janja, 'Delovni zvezek 1/2017, let. XXVI: Kako živimo v regijah', Republic of Slovenia, Institute of Macroeconomic Analysis and Development Ljubljana, September 2017, www.umar.gov.si/fileadmin/user_upload/publikacije/dz/2017/DZ-Kako_zivimo_v_regijah.pdf (accessed 24 April 2019).

Pech, Laurent and Scheppele, Kim, 'Illiberalism Within: Rule of Law Backsliding in the EU' (2017) 19 *Cambridge Yearbook of European Legal Studies* 3.

Pech, Laurent, Perju, Vlad and Platon, Sébastien, 'How to Adress Rule of Law Backsliding in Romania: The Case for an Infringement Action Based on Article 325 TFEU' *Verfassungsblog* (29 May 2019) https://verfassungsblog.de/how-to-adress-rule-of-law-backsliding-in-romania/ (accessed 24 April 2019).

Perović, Jeronim, 'The Tito–Stalin Split: A Reassessment in Light of New Evidence' (2007) *Journal of Cold War Studies* 9(2):32–63.

Pesek, Rosvita, *Osamosvojitev Slovenije: ali naj Republika Slovenija postane samostojna in neodvisna država?* (Nova Revija, 2007).

Pesek, Rosvita, *Pučnik* (Mohorjeva, 2013).
Petelinšek, Andrej, 'Sodniško društvo zavrača možnost odškodninskih tožb zoper sodnike' *Večer* (12 April 2018) www.vecer.com/sodnisko-drustvo-zavraca-moznost-odskoninskih-tozb-zopoer-sodnike-6444352 (accessed 24 April 2019).
'Peterle Get MEP Award for the Third Time' *EPP Group* (13 March 2015) www.eppgroup.eu/how-we-make-it-happen/with-eu-countries/slovenia/news/peterle-gets-mep-award-for-the-third-time (accessed 24 April 2019).
Petrovec, Dragan, 'Varuh iztaknjenih oči – Pandorina skrinjica ustavne odločbe' [2011] *Pravna praksa* 41–42/2011.
Pezdir, Rado and Šušteršič, Janez, 'Yugoslav Companies in Zone A of the Free Territory of Trieste: The Formation of an Institutionalized Parallel Economy Controlled by the State Security Service' (2018) 176(2) *Archivio storico italiano* 313.
Pezdir, Rado, Intervju, 4d.rtvslo.si/arhiv/intervju-tv/174479889 (accessed 24 April 2019).
Pezdir, Rado, Slovenska tranzicija od Kardelja do Tajkunov (Časnik Finance, 2008).
Pippa, Norris, *Driving Democracy: Do Power-Sharing Institutions Work?* (Cambridge, Cambridge University Press, 2008).
Pirnat, Tanja, 'Razsekana na pol: Zakaj je vzhod Slovenije bolj bolan kot zahod?' *Pod črto* (10 June 2017) https://podcrto.si/zdravje-v-obcinah-revnejsi-kot-so-prebivalci-slabse-je-zdravje/ (accessed 24 April 2019).
Pirnat, Tanja, 'Zdravje na Koroškem: veliko bolezni, malo zdravljenja', *Pod črto* (17 June 2017) https://podcrto.si/zdravje-na-koroskem-veliko-bolezni-malo-zdravljenja/ (accessed 24 April 2019).
Pjesivac, Ivanka, Spasovska, Katerina and Imre, Iveta, 'The Truth Between the Lines: Conceptualization of Trust in News Media in Serbia, Macedonia, and Croatia' (2016) 19(3) *Mass Communication and Society* 323.
Pjesivac, Ivanka, Spasovska, Katerina and Imre, Iveta, 'Attribution of Global Ethical Norms: Perceptions of Journalistic Independence and Integrity in Serbia, Macedonia, and Croatia' (2017) 13(2) *Global Media and Communication* 157.
Podgorecki, Adam, 'Polish Society: A Sociological Analysis' (1987) 7(1) *Praxis International* 57.
Popova, Maria, 'Why Doesn't the Bulgarian Judiciary Prosecute Corruption?' (2012) 59(5) *Problems of Post Communism* 35.
Popova, Maria, *Politicized Justice in Emerging Democracies: A Study of Courts in Russia and Ukraine* (Cambridge, Cambridge University Press, 2012).
Popović, Dragoljub and Marinković, Tanasije, 'The Emergence of the Human Rights Protection in Serbia under the European Convention on Human Rights: The Experience of the First Ten Years' in Iulia Motoc and Ineta Ziemele (eds), *The Impact of the ECHR on Democratic Change in Central and Eastern Europe: Judicial Perspectives* (Cambridge, Cambridge University Press, 2015).
Potočnik, Janez and Lombardero, Jaime Garcia, 'Slovenia's Road to Membership in the European Union' in Mojmir Mrak, Matija Rojec and Carlos Silva-Jáuregui (ed), *Slovenia: From Yugoslavia to the European Union* (Washington, DC, World Bank, 2004) 367.
Praprotnik, Rok interviewing Marjan Pogačnik, 'Žal mi je, da sodniška toga najboljših študentov ne zanima' *Dnevnik* (1 April 2006) www.dnevnik.si/173264 (accessed 24 April 2019).
'Prikrito in očem zakrito', Public Exhibition, Museum of Contemporary History, Ljubljana, 2005.
Project SOZ (Slovenska oglaševalska zbornica), Revidiranje prodanih naklad, July–December 2018, www.soz.si/projekti_soz/rpn_revidiranje_prodanih_naklad (accessed 23 April 2019).
Pučnik, Jože, *Članki in spomini 1957–1985* (Maribor, Obzorja, 1986).
Pučnik, Jože, *Kultura, družba in tehnologija* (Maribor, Obzorja, 1988).
Przygode, Stefan, *Die deutsche Rechtsprechung zur unmittelbaren Demokratie* (Nomos Verlagsgesellschaft, 1995).
Pučnik, Jože, *Iz arhivov slovenske politične policije* (Ljubljana, Veda, 1996).
Pučnik, Jože, 'Mass Post-War Killings' in Drago Jančar (ed), *The Dark Side of the Moon. A Short History of Totalitarianism in Slovenia 1945–1990* (Ljubljana, Museum of Recent History, 1998).

Pučnik, Jože, 'Kulturna prenova Slovenije', in Niko Grafenauer (ed), *Sproščena Slovenija: Obračun za prihodnost*, (Ljubljana, Nova revija, 1999).

Puddington, Arch, 'Breaking Down Democracy: Goals, Strategies, and Methods of Modern Authoritarians' (June 2017) Freedom House.

Rakar, Tatjana and Filipovič, Hrast Maša, 'The Future of the Slovenian Welfare State: A View from Deliberative Forums' (2018) 25(2) *Revija za socijalnu politiku* 157.

Rakočević, Bergant Vesna, 'Zakaj meni nihče ne piše sodb v Murglah?' [2013] *Pravna praksa* 33.

Rant, Andrej, 'Establishing Monetary Sovereignty' in Mojmir Mrak, Matija Rojec and Carlos Silva-Jáuregui (eds), *Slovenia: From Yugoslavia to the European Union* (Washington, DC, World Bank, 2004).

'Reform of Democratic and Rule-of-law State in Slovenia', Research Project J5-7359 (A) ARRS (1 January 2016–31 December 2018) Slovenian Research Agency, Nova Univerza – Fakulteta za Državne in Evropske Študije, www.fds.si/index.php/en/school/research-and-consulting/raziskovalna-skupina/research-projects/1232-reform-of-democratic-and-rule-of-law-state-in-slovenia (accessed 24 April 2019).

Reporters without Borders, World Press Freedom Index, https://rsf.org/en/ranking (accessed 23 April 2019).

Republic of Slovenia, Ministry of Justice, Implementation of Judgements of the European Court of Human Rights, www.mp.gov.si/si/delovna_podrocja/aktivnosti_na_podrocju_clovekovih_pravic_in_izvrsevanja_sodb_evropskega_sodisca_za_clovekove_pravice/izvrsevanje_sodb_evropskega_sodisca_za_clovekove_pravice/ (accessed 24 April 2019).

Republic of Slovenia, The Ministry of Labour, Family, Social Affairs and Equal Opportunities, 'Rights under Insurance for Parental Protection', www.mddsz.gov.si/en/areas_of_work/family/rights_under_insurance_for_parental_protection/ (accessed 24 April 2019).

Revised Statute of the European Commission for Democracy through Law, Art 1, s 1, Resolution(2002)3, adopted by Committee of Ministers of the Council of Europe, 21 February 2002.

Ribnikar, Ivan and Košak, Tomaž, 'Monetary System and Monetary Policy' in Mojmir Mrak, Matija Rojec and Carlos Silva-Jáuregui (ed) *Slovenia: From Yugoslavia to the European Union* (Washington, DC, World Bank, 2004) 150.

Rodin, Siniša, 'Functions of Judicial Opinion – A View From a Post-Communist European State', www.pravo.unizg.hr/_download/repository/13_Rotterdam.pdf (accessed 24 April 2019).

Rojec Matija, Šušteršič, Janez, Vasle, Boštjan, Bednaš, Maja and Jurančič, Slavica, 'The Rise and Decline of Gradualism in Slovenia' (2004) 16:4 *Post-Communist Economies* 459.

Rosenfeld, Michael, 'The Rule of Law and the Legitimacy of Constitutional Democracy' (2001) 74 *Southern California Law Review* 1307.

Rosenfeld, Michael, 'A Pluralist Theory of Political Rights in Times of Stress' in Wojciech Sadurski (ed), *Political Rights under Stress in 21st Century Europe* (Oxford, Oxford University Press, 2006).

Rosenfeld, Michel, Sadurski, Wojciech and Toniatti, Roberto, 'Central and Eastern European Constitutionalism a Quarter Century After the Fall of the Berlin Wall: Introduction to the Symposium' (2015) 13(1) *International Journal of Constitutional Law* 119.

Rost, Lisa Charlotte 'Equality, Before & After Taxes, The Gini Index, Explained' *Chartable* (8 April 2018) https://blog.datawrapper.de/weekly-chart-gini/ (accessed 24 April 2019).

RTV Slovenia, Financial Plan 2018, 25 January 2018, www.rtvslo.si/files/letno_porocilo/financni_nacrt_2018.pdf (accessed 23 April 2019).

Rülke, Steffen, *Venedig-Kommission und Verfassungsgerichtsbarkeit* (Köln, Heymanns, 2003).

Rupnik, Jacques and Zielonka, Jan, 'The State of Democracy 20 Years On: Domestic and External Factors' (2013) 27 *East European Politics and Societies* 3.

Sachs, Jeffrey D, 'Government, Geography, and Growth: The True Drivers of Economic Development', *Foreign Affairs* (September/October 2012).

Sadurski, Wojciech, 'Partnering with Strasbourg: Constitutionalisation of the European Court of Human Rights, the Accession of Central and East European States to the Council of Europe, and the Idea of Pilot Judgements' (2009) 9(3) *Human Rights Law Review* 397.

Sadurski, Wojciech, 'Postcommunist Constitutional Courts in Search of Political Legitimacy', EUI LAW Working Paper no 2001/11.

Sadurski, Wojciech, 'Constitutional Courts in the Process of Articulating Constitutional Rights in the Post-Communist States of Central and Eastern Europe, Part I: Social and Economic Rights', EUI LAW Working Paper no 2002/14.

Sadurski, Wojciech (ed), *Constitutional Justice, East and West: Democratic Legitimacy and Constitutional Courts in Post-Communist Europe in a Comparative Perspective* (The Hague, Kluwer Law International, 2003).

Sadurski, Wojciech, *Rights Before Courts: A Study of Constitutional Courts in Postcommunist States of Central and Eastern Europe*, 2th edn (Dordrecht, Springer, 2014).

Sadurski, Wojciech, 'A Response to Daniel Smilov and Michael Hein' (2015) 39(3) *Southeastern Europe* 431.

Sadurski, Wojciech, 'Transitional Constitutionalism Versus the Rule of Law?' (2016) 8(2) *Hague Journal on the Rule of Law* 337.

Sadurski, Wojciech, 'What Is Going on in Poland Is an Attack against Democracy' *Verfassungsblog* (15 July 2016) http://verfassungsblog.de/what-is-going-on-in-poland-is-an-attack-against-democracy/ (accessed 24 April 2019).

Sadurski, Wojciech, 'That Other Anniversary' (2017) 13(3) *European Constitutional Law Review* 417.

Sadurski, Wojciech, 'Judicial "Reform" in Poland: The President's Bills Are as Unconstitutional as the Ones He Vetoed' *Verfassungsblog* (28 November 2017) http://verfassungsblog.de/judicial-reform-in-poland-the-presidents-bills-are-as-unconstitutional-as-the-ones-he-vetoed/ (accessed 24 April 2019).

Sainati, Tatiana, 'Human Rights Class Actions: Rethinking the Pilot-Judgment Procedure at the European Court of Human Rights' (2015) 56 *Harvard International Law Journal* 147.

Sajó, András and Losonci, Vera, 'Rule by Law in the East Central Europe: Is the Emperor's New Suit a Straitjacket?' in Douglas Greenberg, Stanlet N Katz, Melanie Beth Oliviero and Steven C Wheatley (eds), *Constitutionalism and Democracy: Transitions in the Contemporary World* (Oxford, Oxford University Press, 1993).

Šalamun, Tomaž, *Four Questions of Melancholy: New & Selected Poems*, (New York, White Pine Press, 1996), http://romanianstudies.org/content/2013/04/22/poetry-in-translation-clxxxvii-tomaz-salamun-b-1941-slovenian-poet-thought-64-gand-64/ (accessed 24 April 2019).

Sanders, Anne and Danwitz, Luc von, 'The Polish Judiciary Reform: Problematic under European Standards and a Challenge for Germany' *Verfassungsblog* (28 March 2017) http://verfassungsblog.de/the-polish-judiciary-reform-problematic-under-european-standards-and-a-challenge-for-germany/ (accessed 24 April 2019).

Save the Children, 'End of Childhood 2018 Report: The Many Faces of Exclusion, https://resourcecentre.savethechildren.net/node/13429/pdf/endofchildhood_report_2018_english_0.pdf (accessed 24 April 2019).

Scharpf, Fritz W, 'Problem-Solving Effectiveness and Democratic Accountability in the EU' (2003) MPIfG working paper.

Schmahl, Stefanie and Breuer, Marten (eds), *The Council of Europe: Its Law and Policies* (Oxford, Oxford University Press, 2017).

Schmitter, Philippe C., 'Intermediaries in the Consolidation of Neodemocracies: The Role of Parties, Associations and Movements' (1997) Working Paper no 130 (Institut de Ciències Polítiques i Socials).

School of Advanced Social Studies (FUDŠ), 'Analiza medijskega prostora v Republiki Sloveniji', Final Report, 2015, www.mk.gov.si/fileadmin/mk.gov.si/pageuploads/Ministrstvo/raziskave-analize/mediji/2015_Analiza_medijskega_prostora_v_RS.pdf (accessed 23 April 2019).

Šelih, Ivan, 'Dolgotrajnost sodnih postopkov skozi letna poročila varuha' *Varuh človekovih pravic RS* (24 August 2018) www.varuh-rs.si/medijsko-sredisce/aktualni-primeri/novice/detajl/dolgotrajnost-sodnih-postopkov-skozi-letna-porocila-varuha-1/?cHash=fec54496b45dc0aea9299bdcd053fbd7 (accessed 24 April 2019).

Shapiro, Michael A and Chock, Tamara Makana, 'Media Dependency and Perceived Reality of Fiction and News' (2004) 48 *Journal of Broadcasting & Electronic Media* 675.

Shaun, Walter, 'Inteview: Svetlana Aleksijevich: "After Communism We Thought Everything Would Be Fine. But People Don't Understand Freedom"' *The Guardian* (21 July 2017) www.theguardian.com/books/2017/jul/21/svetlana-alexievich-interview (accessed 24 April 2019).

Silva-Jáuregui, Carlos, 'Macroeconomic Stabilization and Sustainable Growth' in Mojmir Mrak, Matija Rojec and Carlos Silva-Jáuregui (eds), *Slovenia: From Yugoslavia to the European Union* (Washington, DC, World Bank, 2004).

Simón, Janos, 'The Change of Function of Political Parties at the Turn of Millennium' *ICPS* (2003) 18, www.icps.cat/archivos/WorkingPapers/wp221.pdf?noga=1 (accessed 24 April 2019).

Simoneti, Marko, Rojec, Matija and Gregorič, Aleksandra, 'Privatisation, Restructuring, and Corporate Governance of the Enterprise Sector in Mojmir Mrak, Matija Rojec and Carlos Silva-Jáuregui (eds), *Slovenia: From Yugoslavia to the European Union* (Washington, DC, World Bank, 2004).

Skovsgaard, Morten, Albæk, Erik, Bro, Peter and de Vreese, Claes, 'A Reality Check: How Journalists' Role Perceptions Impact their Implementation of the Objectivity Norm' (2013) *14*(1) *Journalism* 22.

'Slovenia Top in ECHR Report by Human Rights Violation Rate' *Slovenia Times* (18 August 2015) www.sloveniatimes.com/slovenia-top-in-echr-report-by-human-rights-violation-rate (accessed 24 April 2019).

'Slovenia's Judges Appalled at Doukoff's Criticism' *STA* (2003) english.sta.si/779193/slovenias-judges-appalled-at-doukoffs-criticism (accessed 24 April 2019).

Smekal, Hubert, Šipulová, Katarína, Pospíšil, Ivo, Janovský, Jozef and Kilian, Petr, *Making Sense of Human Rights Commitments: A Study of Two Emerging European Democracies* (Brno, MUNI Press, 2016).

Smilov, Daniel and Toplak, Jurij (eds), *Political Finance and Corruption in Eastern Europe: The Transition Period* (Farnham, Ashgate, 2007).

Smith, Adam, *Inquiry into the Nature and Causes of the Wealth of Nations* (Oxford, Clarendon Press, 1976).

Snyder, Timothy, *Black Earth: The Holocaust as History and Warning* (New York, Tim Duggan Books, 2015).

Sokoloff, Kenneth L and Engerman, Stanley L, 'Institutions, Factor Endowments, and Paths of Development in the New World' (2000) 14(3) *Journal of Economic Perspectives* 217.

Šorli, Marko, 'Neučinkovit sodni sistem – uspešno vodenje?' [2013] *Pravna praksa* 3/2013 24.1.2013.

Šorli, Nevenka, 'Odstopna izjava članice Sodnega Sveta' [2003] *Odvetnik 31*.

Spac, Samuel, 'Judiciary Development after the Breakdown of Communism in the Czech Republic and Slovakia' (2014) 9(3–4) *CEU Political Science Journal* 234.

Special Eurobarometer 461: Designing Europe's Future, ec.europa.eu/commfrontoffice/publicopinion/index.cfm/ResultDoc/download/DocumentKy/78720 (accessed 24 April 2019).

Spruk, Rok, 'Primerjalna gospodarska uspešnost Slovenije po 20 letih' (2011) https://sites.google.com/site/rokspruk/research/primerjalna-gospodarska-uspesnost-slovenije.

Spruk, Rok, *The Failure of Economic Nationalism in Slovenia's Transition: Political Economy Behind the Calamity of Kleptocratic Institutions and Economic Performance* (Lambert Academic Publishing, 2012).

Stališče Ustavnega sodišča o Poročilu Vrhovnega sodišča o odločbah Ustavnega sodišča, s katerimi so bile razveljavljene odločbe Vrhovnega sodišča, www.us-rs.si/aktualno/novice/stalisce-ustavnega-sodisca-o-porocilu-vrhovnega-sodisca-o-odlocbah-ustavnega-sodisca-s-katerimi-so-b/ (accessed 24 April 2019).

Stane, Granda (president of Združenje za Slovensko Besedo), 'Je odziv enak pri Dumančičevi in Možini?', 12 August 2018.

Statistical Office of the Republic of Slovenia, 'Regions in Figures – Statistical Portrait of Slovene Regions 2018', www.stat.si/StatWeb/File/DocSysFile/9960/regions_in%20_Figures_2018.pdf (accessed 24 April 2019).

Statistical Office of the Republic of Slovenia, Milen Jankovič, 'In 2017 the GDP Growth was 6.5% in Slovenia; The Highest was in the Jugovzhodna Slovenija Region (by 10.4%)', www.stat.si/StatWeb/en/news/Index/7820 (accessed 24 April 2019).

Statistical Office of the Republic of Slovenia, Simona Krže, 'Actual Individual Consumption Per Capita in Slovenia in 2017 23% Lower than the EU-28 Average', www.stat.si/StatWeb/en/News/Index/7839 (accessed 24 April 2019).

Statistical Office of the Republic of Slovenia, Stanka Intihar, 'In 2017 at-Risk-of-Poverty Rate Slightly Lower (13.3%), at-Risk-of-Poverty Threshold Higher than in 2016', www.stat.si/StatWeb/en/News/Index/7464 (accessed 24 April 2019).

Statistical Office of the Republic of Slovenia, Stranka Intihar, 'Unchanged at-Risk-of-Poverty Rate in 2014 (14.5%); Household Income Slightly Higher', www.stat.si/StatWeb/en/News/Index/5426 (accessed 24 April 2019).

Statistični urad Republike Slovenije, *National Accounts on the Economic Crisis in Slovenia* (2016).

Statute of the Council of Europe, London, 5 May 1949.

Stefanone, Michael A, Lackaff, Derek and Rosen, Devan, 'The Relationship between Traditional Mass Media and "Social Media": Reality Television as a Model for Social Network Site Behavior' (2010) 54(3) *Journal of Broadcasting & Electronic Media* 508.

Sternad, Marjan, Cvahte Ojsteršek, Tina, Topolšek, Darja and Justinek, Gorazd, 'The Influence of Logistics Barriers on Lead Times and Service Levels in Slovenia' (2016) 23(4) *International Journal of Logistics Systems and Management* 519.

Število zaposlenih v javnem sektorju 2007–2011, www.ajpes.si/doc/Statistike/Place_javni_sektor/Porocila/Stevilo_zaposlenih_javni_sektor_2007-2011.pdf (accessed 24 April 2019).

Štih, Peter, Simoniti, Vasko and Vodopivec, Peter, *Slovenska zgodovina: družba, politika, kultura* (Ljubljana, Inštitut za novejšo zgodovino 2008) www.sistory.si/publikacije/pdf/zgodovina/Slovenska-zgodovina-SLO.pdf (accessed 24 April 2019).

Štih, Peter, Simoniti, Vasko and Vodopivec, Peter, *A Slovene History. Society, Politics, Culture* (Ljubljana, Inštitut za novejšo zgodovino, 2009).

Strahovnik, Vojko, 'Pomen moralne teorije za etično vzgojo' (2017) 28(1/2) *Šolsko polje* 45.

Strahovnik, Vojko and Škarja, Gašper, 'Upravljanje etike in integritete ter etični kodeksi v upravi' (2014) 14(4) *Hrvatska i komparativna javna uprava* 905.

Šturm, Lovro, 'O kratenju človekovih pravic in temeljnih svoboščin v Sloveniji v obdobju 1945–1950' in Drago Jančar (ed), *Temna stran meseca: kratka zgodovina totalitarizma v Sloveniji 1945–1990: Zbornik Člankov in dokumentov* (Ljubljana, Nova revija, 1998).

Šturm, Lovro, *Omejitev oblasti: ustavna izhodišča javnega prava* (Ljubljana, Nova Revija, 1998).

Šturm, Lovro (ed), *Brez milosti: ranjeni, invalidni in bolni povojni ujetniki na Slovenskem* (Ljubljana, Nova revija, 2000).

Šturm, Lovro, 'Ústavní souvislosti vyrovnávání se s totalitní minulostí ve Slovinsku' in Konference středoevropských ústavních soudů, *Vyrovnání se s komunistickou minulostí ve státech střední Evropy* (Brno, Linde Praha, 2003).

Šturm, Lovro, 'Pravna država' in Lovro Šturm (ed), *Komentar Ustave Republike Slovenie – Dopolnitev A* [*Commentary on the Constitution of the Republic of Slovenia, Supplement – A*] (Ljubljana, Fakulteta za državne in evropske študije, 2011).

Šturm, Lovro, 'Analiza kršitev človekovih pravic in temeljnih svoboščin. Vmesno poročilo. Prikaz raziskave za obdobje 2004–2013' *Zbor za republiko* (2015) zborzarepubliko.si/wp-content/uploads/2015/09/US.Up_.Analiza-krsitev-CP.doc (accessed 24 April 2019).

Šturm, Lovro, 'Revolucionarno kazensko pravo na Slovenskem po drugi svetovni vojni' in Mateja Čoh Kladnik (ed), *Brezpravje v imenu ljudstva: Zbirka Totalitarizmi- vprašanja in izzivi* 5 (Ljubljana, Študijski center za narodno spravo, 2016).

Šturm, Lovro, 'Slovenia. Law and Non–Law after 1941' (2016) on file with authors.

Šturm, Lovro, 'Začetek revolucionarnega kazenskega prava na Slovenskem in njegovi odmevi po drugi svetovni vojni in po demokratizaciji in osamosvojitvi Slovenije' (2017) 25(3) *Acta Histriae* 719.

Šturm, Lovro, 'Constitutional Court Review of Mass and Systematic Violations of Human Rights and Redress of Injustices', Ljubljana, November 2016, on file with authors.
Supreme Court of Slovenia, Annual Report (2017).
Šušteršič, Janez, 'Political Economy of Slovenia's Transition' in Mojmir Mrak, Matija Rojec and Carlos Silva-Jáuregui (eds) *Slovenia: From Yugoslavia to the European Union* (Washington, DC, World Bank, 2004) 399–412.
Svallfors, Stefan, 'Public Attitudes' in Francis G Castles, Stephan Leibfried, Jane Lewis, Herbert Obinger and Christopher Pierson (eds), *The Oxford Handbook of the Welfare State* (Oxford, Oxford University Press, 2010).
Teršek, Andraž, *Etika politike: Esejistični komentar ustave, z novo ustavo* (Ljubljana, UMco, 2018).
Teršek, Andraž, *Pravna ignoranca škodi: kritika pravne prakse 1, 2* (Univerzitetna založba Annales 2015).
Teršek, Andraž, 'Razumevanje svobode izražanja in svobode tiska: konceptualizacija ob sodnem primeru Grims proti Mladini (2016)' (2017) 3/4 *Javna uprava* 5.
Teršek, Andraž, *Socialna ustavna demokracija* (Koper, Zložba Univerze na Primorskem, 2017).
Teršek, Andraž, 'Commentary of Article 39 of the Slovenian Constitution' in Matej Avbelj (ed), *Commentary of the Constitution of the Republic of Slovenia* (Nova Gorica, Nova univerza, 2019).
Teršek, Andraž, Komentar 2. člena ustave (načelo socialne države), in Matej Avbelj (ed), *Komentar Ustave Republike Slovenija* (Nova Gorica, Nova Univerza–Evropska Pravna Fakulteta, 2019).
Teršek, Andraž and Toplak, Jurij, 'Kje v Sloveniji sodišča kršijo ustavne pravice – kršitve ustavnih pravic po območjih višjih sodišč' (2017) Pravna praksa.
Tismaneanu, Vladimir, *The Devil in History: Communism, Fascism and Some Lessons of the Twentieth Century* (Berkeley, University of California Press, 2012).
Tomaž, Šalamun, 'Thought' 64' (Duma' 64), Centre for Romanian Studies, 'Poetry in Translation (CLXXXVIII)', trans Michael Biggins in Tomaž Šalamun, *Four Questions of Melancholy: New & Selected Poems* (New York, White Pine Press, 1996) http://romanianstudies.org/content/2013/04/22/poetry-in-translation-clxxxvii-tomaz-salamun-b-1941-slovenian-poet-thought-64-gand-64/> (accessed 24 April 2019).
Tomšič, Matevž, 'Crisis and (Re)Structuring of the Slovenian Political Space' in Frane Adam (ed), *Slovenia: Social, Economic and Environmental Issues* (Nova Science Publishers 2017).
Tomšič, Matevž. 'Decline of elite consensus and destabilisation of political space in East-Central Europe' (2017) *Corvinus Journal of Sociology and Social Policy* 151, tabela, cjssp.uni-corvinus.hu/index.php/cjssp/article/view/24 (accessed 24 April 2019).
Tomšič, Matevž and Prijon, Lea, 'Elites, Ideologies and Crisis in Slovenia' (2003) 6(2) *Raziskave in Razprave* 71.
Tomšič, Matevž and Prijon, Lea, 'Person-Based Politics in Italy and Slovenia: Comparing Cases of Leadership's Individualisation' (2013) *International Social Science Journal Vol 64, Issue 213/214, 237–248*.
Tomšič, Matevž and Prijon, Lea, *Ideological Profile and Crisis Discourse of the Slovenian Elites*, www.eisa-net.org/be-bruga/eisa/files/events/warsaw2013/Tomsic%20Prijon_Ideological%20Profile%20and%20Crisis%20Discourse%20of%20Slovenian%20Elites.pdf (accessed 24 April 2019).
Toplak, Simona, 'Norost v vladi Mira Cerarja – generalni sekretar vlade Darko Krašovec zahteva: Vsi slovenski sodniki in sodišča, izločite se!' *Finance* (20 April 2016) www.finance.si/8844060 (accessed 24 April 2019).
Transparency International, 'Corruption Perception Index 2017', 21 February 2018, www.transparency.org/news/feature/corruption_perceptions_index_2017#table (accessed 24 April 2019).
Transparency International, 'Corruption Perception Index 2018', www.transparency.org/cpi2018 (accessed 24 April 2019).
Trochev, Alexei, 'Meddling with Justice: Competitive Politics, Impunity, and Distrusted Courts in Post-Orange Ukraine' (2010) 18(2) *Demokratizatsiya* 122.

Trpin, Gorazd, 'Komentar 159. člena ustave' in Lovro Šturm (ed), *Komentar Ustave Republike Slovenie* (Ljubljana, Fakulteta za podiplomske državne in evropske študije, 2002).

Tully, James, *Strange Multiplicity – Constitutionalism in an Age of Diversity* (Cambridge, Cambridge University Press, 1995).

Turk, Žiga, 'If Bulc Is Nominated, the Next Dan Brown Novel Should Be about the Brussels Bubble' *Euractiv* (14 October 2014) www.euractiv.com/section/eu-priorities-2020/opinion/if-bulc-is-nominated-the-next-dan-brown-novel-should-be-about-the-brussels-bubble (accessed 24 April 2019).

Uitz, Renata, 'Constitutional Courts and the Past in Democratic Transition' in Adam Czarnota, Martin Krygier and Wojciech Sadurdski (eds), *Rethinking the Rule of Law after Communism* (Budapest, Central European University Press, 2005).

Uitz, Renáta, 'The Return of the Sovereign: A Look at the Rule of Law in Hungary – and in Europe' *Verfassungsblog* (5 April 2017) https://verfassungsblog.de/the-return-of-the-sovereign-a-look-at-the-rule-of-law-in-hungary-and-in-europe/ (accessed 24 April 2019).

United Nations Development Programme, 'Human Development Indices and Indicators: 2018 Statistical Update', Briefing note for countries on the 2018 Statistical Update Slovenia, 2.

United Nations Development Programme, 'Human Development Reports', Germany, http://hdr.undp.org/en/countries/profiles/DEU (accessed 24 April 2019).

United Nations Development Programme, 'Human Development Reports', Slovenia, http://hdr.undp.org/en/countries/profiles/SVN (accessed 24 April 2019).

United Nations Development Programme, Human Development Reports, Human Development Indicators 2018, Slovenia, http://hdr.undp.org/en/countries/profiles/SVN (accessed 24 April 2019).

United Nations Principles relating to the Status of National Institutions (Paris Principles), General Assembly Resolution 48/134, 20 December 1993, www.ohchr.org/EN/ProfessionalInterest/Pages/StatusOfNationalInstitutions.aspx (accessed 24 April 2019).

United Nations, 'Consideration of Reports Submitted by States Parties Under Article 19 of the Convention: Slovenia', CAT/C/SVN/CO/3/Add.1, 29 August 2012.

United Nations, 'Concluding Observations on the Combined Third and Fourth Periodic Reports of Slovenia', CRC/C/SVN/CO/3-4, 8 July 2013.

United Nations, Human Rights Committee, 'Concluding observations on the third periodic report of Slovenia', CCPR/C/SVN/CO/3, 21 April 2016.

United Nations, Human Rights Committee, 'Concluding Observations on the Third Periodic Report of Slovenia', CCPR/C/SVN/CO/3, 21 April 2016.

United Nations, Human Rights Council, 'Report of the Working Group on the Universal Periodic Review: Slovenia', A/HRC/28/15, 10 December 2014.

United Nations, Human Rights Council, Working Group on the Universal Periodic Review, 'Compilation prepared by the Office of the United Nations, High Commissioner for Human Rights in accordance with paragraph 15 (b) of the annex to Human Rights Council resolution 5/1 and paragraph 5 of the annex to Council resolution 16/21: Slovenia', A/HRC/WG.6/20/SVN/2, 18 August 2014.

Uprimny, Rodrigo, 'The Constitutional Court and Control of Presidential Extraordinary Powers in Colombia' in Siri Gloppen, Roberto Gargarella and Elin Skaar, *Democratization and the Judiciary: The Accountability Function of Courts in New Democracies* (London, Frank Cass, 2004).

Uprimny, Rodrigo, 'Judicialization of Politics in Colombia: Cases, Merits and Risks' (2007) 49(6) *SUR International Journal on Human Rights* 56.

Uredništvo, '55 milijonov evrov, ki jih namenjate aktivistom za odstavitev Damirja Črnčeca' *Domovina.je* (22 September 2018) www.domovina.je/55-milijonov-evrov-ki-jih-namenjate-aktivistom-za-odstavitev-damirja-crnceca/ (accessed 24 April 2019).

'Ustavne razprave 2001–2003, Izbor gradiv Državnega zbora' [2004].

Uzelac, Alan, '(In)Surpassable Barriers to Lustration: Quis Custodiet Ipsos Custodes?' in Vladimira Dvořáková and Anđelko Milardović (ed), *Lustration and Consolidation of Democracy and the Rule of Law in Central and Eastern Europe* (Zagreb, Political Science Research Centre Zagreb, 2007).

Uzelac, Alan, 'Survival of the Third Legal Tradition?' (2010) 49 *Supreme Court Law Review* 377.

Valič Zver, Andreja, Hančič, Damjan, Kolarič, Boštjan, Letnar Černič, Jernej and Podbrešič Renato, 'National Report on the Crimes of Communism in Slovenia: Country Report', in David Svoboda, Cóílín O'Connor and Jiří Liška (eds), *Crimes of the Communist Regimes: International Conference: An Assessment by Historians and Legal Experts: Proceedings* (Prague, Institute for the Study of Totalitarian Regimes, 2011).

Van Cuilenburg, Jan, 'Media Diversity, Competition and Concentration: Concepts and Theoriess' in Els de Bens (ed) *Media between Culture and Commerce* (Bristol, Intellect Books, 2007).

Van Dijk, Pieter, 'The Venice Commission on Certain Aspects of the European Convention of Human Rights Ratione Personae' in Stephan Breitenmoser, Bernhard Ehrenzeller, Marco Sassòli, Walter Stoffel and Beatrice Wagner Pfeifer (eds), *Human Rights, Democracy and the Rule of Law: Liber Amicorum Luzius Wildhaber* (Zurich/Baden-Baden, Dike/Nomos, 2007).

Vasev Boris, Cerar Gregor and Banjanac Lubej, Saša, 'Bruseljske zahteve: "Gre za neke vrste kapitalistični fundamentalizem"' *RTVSLO* (30 May 2013) www.rtvslo.si/slovenija/bruseljske-zahteve-gre-za-neke-vrste-kapitalisticni-fundamentalizem/309959 (accessed 24 April 2019).

Vavken, Luka, 'Delovanje in upravljanje sistema rednega sodstva' (master's thesis, University of Ljubljana Faculty of Law, 2016).

Verfassungsblog, 'Hungary: Taking Action', https://verfassungsblog.de/hungary-taking-action/ (accessed 24 April 2019).

Vidovic, Hermine, 'Slovenia: Rapid Growth with accelerating inflation' [2008] *Current Analyses and Forecasts* 1, https://wiiw.ac.at/slovenia-rapid-gdp-growth-with-accelerating-inflation-dlp-51.pdf (accessed 24 April 2019).

Virant, Gregor, 'Sodstvo – močna veja oblasti in hkrati učinkovit servis' [2007] *Pravna praksa* 3/2007.

Vlada, RS, Vrhovno Sodišče, RS, 'Sodni zaostanki v Republiki Sloveniji (analiza vzrokov in predlogi za zmanjšanje in odpravo), http://vrs-3.vlada.si/MANDAT12/VLADNAGRADIVA.NSF/aa3872cadf1c8356c1256efb00603606/6323247e81bcfcecc1257a70004f7ad4/$FILE/VGPoro%C4%8DiloLukenda.DOC (accessed 24 April 2019).

Vodušek Starič, Jerca, 'Kako se čistila Jugoslavija?' (2004) 4/5 *Gordogan* 36.

Voh Boštic, Anže, 'Zakaj močnim, bogatim in vplivnim uspe prelisičiti pravno državo' *Pod črto* (7 December 2017) podcrto.si/zakaj-mocnim-bogatim-in-vplivnim-uspe-prelisiciti-pravno-drzavo (accessed 16 February 2019) (accessed 24 April 2019).

'Volilna udeležna na parlamentarnih volitvah pada' (*STA* 3 June 2018) www.sta.si/2520667/volilna-udelezba-na-parlamentarnih-volitvah-pada (accessed 24 April 2019).

Voßkuhle, Andreas, 'Quo Vadis, Europa?', speech at Constitutional Court, Ljubljana, 19 December 2013.

Vrhovno sodišče, 'Letno poročilo o učinkovitosti in uspešnosti sodišč' (Ljubljana, 2018).

Vrhovno sodišče, 'Odziv na raziskavo dr. Šturma o kršitvah človekovih pravic' (2014) www.sodisce.si/sodni_postopki/objave/2014072513084464/ (accessed 24 April 2019).

Vrhovno sodišče, Poročilo o odločbah Ustavnega sodišča, s katerimi so bile razveljavljene odločbe Vrhovnega sodišča, www.sodisce.si/mma_bin2.php?nid=2017091111092486&static_id=20170911090104 (accessed 24 April 2019).

Vukelić, Majda, 'Pred kolapsom sodnega sistema' *Delo* (23 February 2018).

Waldron, Jeremy, 'Is the Rule of Law an Essentially Contested Concept (in Florida?)' (2002) 21(2) *Law and Philosophy* 137.

Walker, Neil, 'Legal Theory and the European Union: A 25th Anniversary Essay' (2005) 25(4) *Oxford Journal of Legal Studies* 581.

Weber, Max, *The Protestant Ethic and the Spirit of Capitalism* (London, Unwin University Books 1930).

Wedel, Janine R, 'Dirty Togetherness: Institutional Nomads, Networks, and the State–Private Interface in Central and Eastern Europe and the Former Soviet Union' [2003] *Polish Sociological Review* No. 142 (2003), pp. 139.

Weiler, JHH, 'Transformation of Europe' [1991] *Yale Law Journal* Vol. 100, Issue 8.

Weimann, Gabriel, *Communicating Unreality: Modern Media and the Reconstruction of Reality* (London, Sage, 2000).
Weinstein, James, 'An Overview of American Free Speech Doctrine and its Application to Extreme Speech' in Ivan Hare and James Weinstein (eds), *Extreme Speech and Democracy* (Oxford, Oxford University Press, 2009).
Weinstein, James, 'Extreme Speech, Public order, and Democracy: Lessons from The Masses' in Ivan Hare and James Weinstein (eds), *Extreme Speech and Democracy* (Oxford, Oxford University Press, 2009).
'The Wheels of Justice Grind Slow' *The Economist* (18 February 2016) www.economist.com/europe/2016/02/18/the-wheels-of-justice-grind-slow (accessed 16 February 2019).
Wolla, Scott A, 'Why Are Some Countries Rich and Others Poor?' *Page One Economics* (September 2017).
'World Bank joins IMF in criticism of Ukraine's anti-corruption draft law' *Reuters* (Kiev, 16 January 2018) www.reuters.com/article/us-ukraine-corruption-worldbank/world-bank-joins-imf-in-criticism-of-ukraines-anti-corruption-draft-law-idUSKBN1F5236 (accessed 24 April 2019).
www.echr.coe.int/Documents/Annual_report_2018_ENG.pdf (accessed 24 April 2019).
www.echr.coe.int/Documents/Stats_violation_1959_2017_ENG.pdf (accessed 24 April 2019).
www.economist.com/blogs/graphicdetail/2014/05/daily-chart?fsrc=scn/fb/wl/dc/growingupfast (accessed 24 April 2019).
www.vlada.si/fileadmin/dokumenti/cns/doc/0811071528505_a185v2cc.doc (accessed 24 April 2019).
Zadeva Intervju/Dežman – Poročilo varuhinje z mnenjem in priporočili, 2 August 2018, http://img.rtvslo.si/_up/drown/files/2018/08/03/1570547_dezman-2018_8_3.pdf (accessed 23 April 2019).
Zajc, Drago (ed), 'Evropeizacija slovenske politike: zbornik referatov' [1998] *Politološki dnevi*, Ljubljana: Slovensko politološko društvo, 1998.
Zajc, Zajc, 'Independence of Judiciary in Slovenia: Economic and Historic Perspective' [2014] *Acta Histriae* 22(3), 741–764.
Zalar, Teo, *Značilnosti slovenskega gospodarstva v obdobju med prvo in drugo svetovno vojno-diplomsko delo* (Ljubljana, Ekonomska fakulteta, 2008).
Žerdin, Ali, *Ujetniki omrežij* (Ljubljana, UMco, 2018).
Zevnik, Krištof, 'Govor na javni tribuni ZZZS' (26 March 2019) www.youtube.com/watch?v=9E-JrPd0kDU&feature=youtu.be (accessed 24 April 2019).
Žnidaršič Skubic, Viktorija 'Evropeizacija družinskega prava' in Franjo Štiblar, Janez Kranjc (eds.), Pravni vidiki slovenske samobitnosti leto po vstopu v EU (Ljubljana, Pravna fakulteta 2005).
Zobec, Barbara, 'Ponižano Vrhovno sodišče' *Finance* (19 September 2016).
Zobec, Jan, 'Odziv Jana Zobca: Policistovo ukrepanje zoper mene sem ocenil kot napad', *Delo (Sobotna priloga)* (23 June 2018) www.delo.si/sobotna-priloga/odziv-jana-zobca-policistovo-ukrepanje-zoper-mene-sem-ocenil-kot-napad-62246.html (accessed 24 April 2019).
Zobec Jan, 'Slovenia: Just a Glass Bead Game?' in Iulia Motoc and Ineta Ziemele (eds), *The Impact of the ECHR on Democratic Change in Central and Eastern Europe: Judicial Perspectives* (Cambridge, Cambridge University Press, 2016).
Zobec Jan, 'Sodniški novi razred' *Finance* (25 August 2018) https://www.domovina.je/jan-zobec-finance-si-sodniski-novi-razred/ (accessed 24 April 2019).
Zobec Jan, 'Telefonska justica po slovensko' *IUS-info* (30 April 2018) www.iusinfo.si/medijsko-sredisce/kolumne/219023 (accessed 24 April 2019).
Zobec Jan, 'Kot smetana na torti' [2018] *Pravna praksa* 48/2018.
Zobec Jan, 'Odškodninska odgovornost sodnika in odgovornost države zanj' (2013) *Pravni letopis 2013* http://www.ipp-pf.si/uploads/File/Pravni%20letopis/Pravni%20letopis%202013_v%20tisk.pdf (accessed 14 September 2019).
Zobec, Jan and Letnar Černič, Jernej, 'The Remains of the Authoritarian Mentality within the Slovene Judiciary' in Michal Bobek (ed), *Central European Judges Under the European Influence: The Transformative Power of the EU Revisited* (Oxford, Hart Publishing, 2015).
Zoretić, Josip, *Goli otok: Hell in the Adriatic* (Virtualbookworm.com Publishing, 2011).

Zubek, Radoslaw and Staronova, Katarina, 'Organizing for EU Implementation: The Europeanization of Government Ministries in Estonia, Poland and Slovenia' [2012] *Public Administration* 90(4).
Zupančič, Boštjan, M, 'Prolegomena to Comparative Law' in G Harutyunyan (ed), *New Millennium Constitutionalism: Paradigms of Reality and Challengens* (Yerevan, NJHAR, 2013).
Žužek, Aleš, 'Urban Vehovar: V Sloveniji smo enaki v revščini' *Siol.net* (7 November 2013) https://siol.net/novice/siol/urban-vehovar-v-sloveniji-smo-enaki-v-revscini-211055 (accessed 24 April 2019).
Zver, Milan (ed), *Človekove pravice in svoboščine v tranziciji: primer Slovenije* (Ljubljana, National Council of the Republic of Slovenia, Office of the Ombudsman, 1998).
Zyberi, Gentian and Letnar Černič, Jernej, 'Transitional Justice Processes and Reconciliation in the Former Yugoslavia: Challenges and Prospects' (2015) 33(2) *Nordic Journal of Human Rights* 132.

Index